THE HIDDEN PLACES OF

YORKSHIRE

including the Yorkshire Dales, Moors and Coast

By Barbara Vesey

Regional Hidden Places

Cambs & Lincolnshire
Chilterns
Cornwall
Derbyshire
Devon
Dorset, Hants & Isle of Wight
East Anglia
Gloucs, Wiltshire & Somerset
Heart of England
Hereford, Worcs & Shropshire
Lake District & Cumbria
Lancashire & Cheshire
Lincolnshire & Nottinghamshire
Northumberland & Durham
Sussex
Thames Valley
Yorkshire

National Hidden Places

England
Ireland
Scotland
Wales

Hidden Inns

East Anglia
Heart of England
Lancashire & Cheshire
North of England
South
South East
South and Central Scotland
Wales
Welsh Borders
West Country
Yorkshire
Wales

Country Living Rural Guides

East Anglia
Heart of England
Ireland
North East of England
North West of England
Scotland
South
South East
Wales
West Country

Published by: Travel Publishing Ltd, 7a Apollo House, Calleva Park, Aldermaston, Berkshire RG7 8TN

ISBN 1-904-43420-7

First published 1990, second edition 1993, third edition 1995, fourth edition 1998, fifth edition 2000, sixth edition 2002, seventh edition 2004

Printing by: Scotprint, Haddington

Maps by: © Maps in Minutes ™ (2004)
© Crown Copyright, Ordnance Survey 2004

Editor: Barbara Vesey

Cover Design: Lines & Words, Aldermaston

Cover Photograph: Rural View, Haworth, West Yorkshire
© www.britainonview.com

Text Photographs: © www.britainonview.com

Foreword

The *Hidden Places* is a collection of easy to use travel guides taking you in this instance on a relaxed but informative tour of Yorkshire. The county of Yorkshire is full of scenic historical and cultural diversity. In the northwest are the picturesque Dales with its varied scenery of peat moorland, green pastureland and scattered woods intersected by the numerous brooks, streams and rivers. To the northeast are the imposing Yorkshire Moors, the rich agricultural Vale of York, the chalky hills of the Wolds and the dramatic storm-tossed coastline. In the south are the industrial and commercial cities and towns, which have made such a major contribution to our industrial and cultural heritage

The covers and pages of the *Hidden Places* series have been comprehensively redesigned and this edition of The Hidden Places of Yorkshire is the eighth title to be published in the new format. All *Hidden Places* titles will now be published in this new style which ensures that readers can properly appreciate the attractive scenery and impressive places of interest in Yorkshire and, of course, throughout the rest of the British Isles.

Our books contain a wealth of interesting information on the history, the countryside, the towns and villages and the more established places of interest. But they also promote the more secluded and little known visitor attractions and places to stay, eat and drink many of which are easy to miss unless you know exactly where you are going.

We include hotels, inns, restaurants, public houses, teashops, various types of accommodation, historic houses, museums, gardens, and many other attractions throughout the area, all of which are comprehensively indexed. Most places are accompanied by an attractive photograph and are easily located by using the map at the beginning of each chapter. We do not award merit marks or rankings but concentrate on describing the more interesting, unusual or unique features of each place with the aim of making the reader's stay in the local area an enjoyable and stimulating experience. In this respect we would like to thank the many Tourist Information Centres in Yorkshire for helping us update the editorial content.

Whether you are visiting the area for business or pleasure or in fact are living in the counties we do hope that you enjoy reading and using this book. We are always interested in what readers think of places covered (or not covered) in our guides so please do not hesitate to use the reader reaction forms provided to give us your considered comments. We also welcome any general comments which will help us improve the guides themselves. Finally if you are planning to visit any other corner of the British Isles we would like to refer you to the list of other Hidden Places titles to be found at the rear of the book and to the Travel Publishing website at www.travelpublishing.co.uk.

Travel Publishing

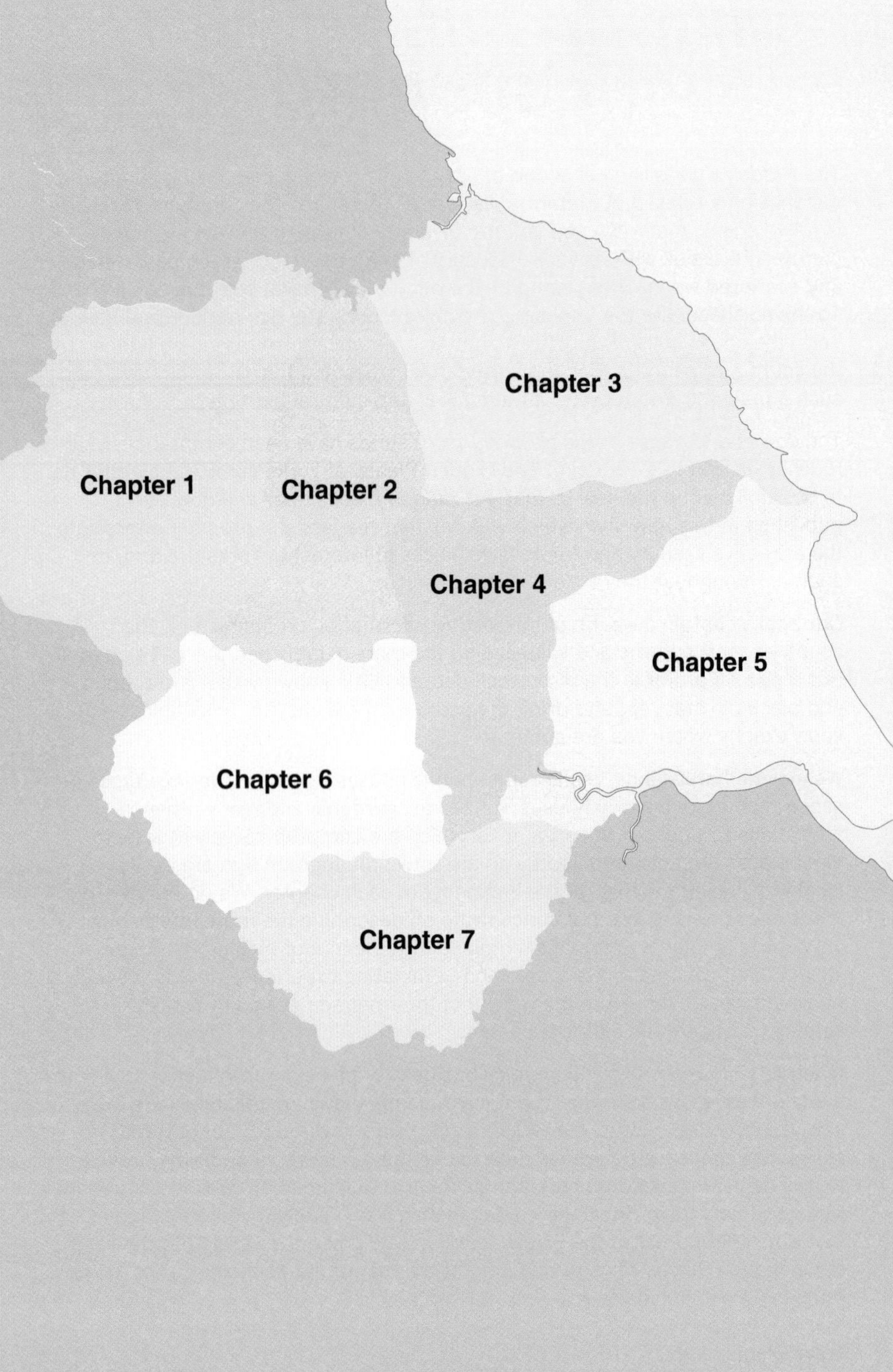
Chapter 3
Chapter 1
Chapter 2
Chapter 4
Chapter 5
Chapter 6
Chapter 7

Contents

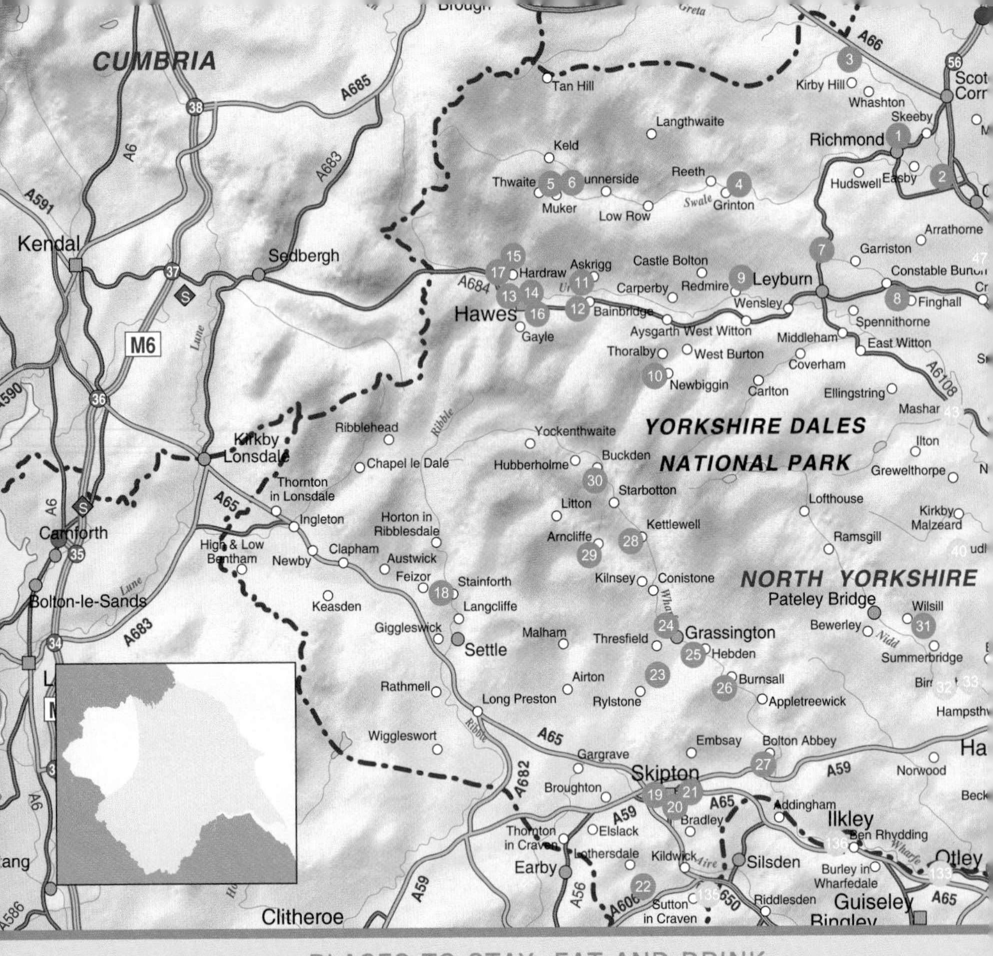

PLACES TO STAY, EAT AND DRINK

Richmondshire Museum, Richmond, North Yorkshire	1	Museum p7
Tudor Hotel, Brompton-on-Swale, North Yorkshire	2	Hotel p8
Bay Horse Inn, Ravensworth, North Yorkshire	3	Pub and Restaurant p10
The Bridge Inn, Grinton, North Yorkshire	4	Pub, Food and Accommodation p11
The Farmers Arms, Muker, North Yorkshire	5	Pub, Food and Accommodation p13
Swaledale Woollens, Strawbeck, North Yorkshire	6	Wools and Woollens p14
Cross Keys Inn, Bellerby, North Yorkshire	7	Pub with Food p19
The Queens Head, Finghall, North Yorkshire	8	Pub, Restaurant and Accommodation p20
The Bolton Arms, Redmire, North Yorkshire	9	Pub, Food and Accommodation p25
Street Head Inn, Newbiggin-in-Bishopdale, N Yorkshire	10	Pub, Restaurant and Accommodation p26
Thornsgill House & Cottage, Askrigg, N Yorkshire	11	Self Catering p28
Rose & Crown Hotel, Bainbridge, North Yorkshire	12	Pub, Restaurant and Accommodation p31
Dales Countryside Museum, Hawes, North Yorkshire	13	Museum p32
The White Hart Inn, Hawes, North Yorkshire	14	Pub, Food and Accommodation p33
The Green Dragon Inn, Hardraw, North Yorkshire	15	Pub, Food and Accommodation p34
Beckindales Continental Café, Hawes, N Yorkshire	16	Cafe p35

Denotes entries in other chapters

1 The Yorkshire Dales

The Yorkshire Dales, one of England and Wales' 11 National Parks, is an area rich in farmland, high moorland and deep valleys. The predominant limestone found here gives rise to many of the area's interesting geological features, such as those found around Malham, the waterfalls at Aysgarth and Hardraw, and White Scar Cave, while there is also an abundance of potholes and disappearing rivers that characterise the area. Considered by many to be the most appealing and beautiful region in the country, the Yorkshire Dales have been receiving increasing numbers of visitors since the arrival of the railways in the 19th century. Many of the settlements date

Yorkshire Dales

PLACES TO STAY, EAT AND DRINK

- House Tearoom & Crafts, Hardraw, N Yorkshire 17 Tea Rooms and Crafts p36
- Craven Heifer Hotel, Stainforth, North Yorkshire 18 Pub, Restaurant and Accommodation p38
- The Gallery Café Bar, Skipton, North Yorkshire 19 Cafe and Bar p47
- Rose & Crown, Skipton, North Yorkshire 20 Pub with Food p48
- The Craven Museum, Skipton, North Yorkshire 21 Museum p51
- The Dog & Gun Inn, Malsis, North Yorkshire 22 Pub and Restaurant p52
- Devonshire Arms, Cracoe, North Yorkshire 23 Pub, Food and Accommodation p56
- Scar Lodge, Hardy Grange, North Yorkshire 24 Bed and Breakfast p59
- The Clarendon Hotel, Hebden, North Yorkshire 25 Pub, Food and Accommodation p60
- Oatcroft Farm Barn, Burnsall, North Yorkshire 26 Self Catering p62
- Bolton Abbey, Bolton Abbey, North Yorkshire 27 Historic Building p64
- Racehorses Hotel, Kettlewell, North Yorkshire 28 Pub, Food and Accommodation p67
- The Falcon Inn, Arncliffe, North Yorkshire 29 Pub, Food and Accommodation p68
- The Buck Inn, Buckden, North Yorkshire 30 Pub, Restaurant and Accommodation p70
- Ye Olde Oak Inn, Low Laithe, North Yorkshire 31 Pub with Food p73

● Denotes entries in other chapters

back to the Bronze and Iron Ages. With the large industrial areas of Yorkshire and nearby Lancashire close to hand, the Dales are easily accessible but, with so much open countryside, visitors are able to avoid the more popular attractions and enjoy the beauty of the region in solitude.

Hardraw Force

Swaledale is the largest of the northern Dales, and also one of the grandest. It has a rugged beauty that is in contrast to the pretty and busier Wensleydale to the south. It is the Swaledale sheep, with their characteristic black faces, white muzzles and grey speckled legs, that have been adopted as the symbol for the National Park. The valley of the River Ure, Wensleydale, is perhaps the one that most people associate with the Yorkshire Dales. One of the longer dales, it is a place of green pastureland grazed by flocks of Wensleydale sheep, lines of drystone walls and, of course, the home of the famous cheese. Further south again is Wharfedale, a spectacular valley that is home to one of the National Park's most famous features, the Strid, where the River Wharfe charges through a narrow gorge just to the north of Bolton Abbey. To the east lies Nidderdale, a charming valley that was dubbed 'Little Switzerland' by the Victorians as its upper reaches are steep and wooded, with the River Nidd flowing through narrow gorges. To the west is Ribblesdale and the famous Three Peaks of Whernside, Ingleborough and Pen-y-ghent, home to a spectacular stretch of the famous Settle–Carlisle Railway. Finally there is Airedale, the valley of the River Aire, where near the river's source can be found the extraordinary limestone landscape around Malham Tarn. Further downstream lies Skipton, an ancient market town and 'Gateway to the Dales' – many people's first experience of this glorious region of Britain.

For all capabilities the Yorkshire Dales provide the perfect setting for walking, with some 1,000 miles of public footpaths and ancient trackways, along with miles of bridleways. The **Pennine Way**, Britain's first long-distance footpath, is some 270 miles in length and particularly inviting for ramblers. Meanwhile, the much shorter **Dales Way**, from Leeds to Lake Windermere in Cumbria, takes in old textile villages

River Swale from Richmond Castle

and the towns of West Yorkshire before heading through the western section of the Dales and on into Lancashire. There is also the **Trans Pennine Trail** which not only runs right across the country from east to west but also has a variety of extra diversions for those wishing to undertake shorter walks.

Richmond

The former county town of Richmondshire, which still survives as a parliamentary constituency today, Richmond has a long and distinguished history that dates back to 1071 when Alan Rufus, the 1st Earl of Richmond, built a castle here. The site of the fortification, 100 feet up on a rocky promontory with the River Swale flowing below, was not only imposing and well chosen but also gave rise to the name of the town that grew up around the castle – 'riche-mont' or 'strong hill'. **Richmond Castle** (English Heritage) was the first Norman castle in the country to be built, from the foundations upwards, in stone; the keep rises to over 100 feet high and has walls that are 11 feet thick; the cliff on the other side of the fortification makes this an impregnable defence. Additions were made over the subsequent years and the castle reached its final form in the 14th century but, since then, it has fallen into ruin, although a considerable amount of the original Norman stonework remains intact.

This inspiring setting has, not surprisingly, given rise to several legends over the centuries and, in particular, one that suggests that King Arthur lies buried in a cave beneath the castle. So the story goes, one day a simple potter, Thompson, stumbled across an underground passage that led to a chamber where, on further exploration, he discovered King Arthur and his knights lying in an enchanted sleep surrounded by priceless treasures. A voice warned him not to disturb the sleepers and he fled, then was later unable to relocate the passage. Another legend tells of a drummer boy who was sent down the passageway. Beating his drum as he walked, the boy's progress was followed on the surface by soldiers until, suddenly, the drumming stopped.

Richmond Castle

whose influence spread throughout Yorkshire and Lancashire, Richmond, like many other North Yorkshire towns and villages, developed a textile industry in the 18th century and, for some time, the town was famous for its knitted stockings.

Much of the town seen today dates from the Georgian period onwards and, in particular, there is the grand **Culloden Tower**, just off the town green, which was erected in 1747 by the Yorke family, one of whose members had fought at the Battle of Culloden the previous year. Unlike most follies, the interior of this three-storey tower is elaborately decorated in the rococo style and is now in the care of the Landmark Trust. The elder of the town's two bridges, Green Bridge, was erected in 1789 to the designs of John Carr after the existing bridge had been swept away by flood water. Richmond is also home to England's oldest theatre, the **Georgian Theatre Royal**, which was built in 1788 by the actor and manager Samual Butler; at that time it formed part of the theatre circuit that included Ripon, Harrogate, Beverley and Kendal. The connection with the theatrical Butler family ended in 1830; from then until 1848 it was used, infrequently, by travelling companies. However, in the mid-19th century the pit was floored over and from then until the

Though the passageway was extensively searched, the boy was never seen again – though it is said that his drumming can sometimes still be heard.

Today's visitors to Richmond Castle can take in the exceptional views from the top of the keep, which include the town, Swaledale and, on a clear day, the Hambledon Hills, and can follow the history of the castle through a series of interactive exhibits in the visitor centre. The castle is open throughout the year (limited opening in the winter). There is no access for wheelchairs.

At around the time that the castle was reaching its height, in 1315, Edward II granted Richmond the right to protect itself by a stone wall after Scottish raiders had caused considerable damage to the surrounding countryside. However, by the 16th century the walls were already in a state of disrepair and little survives today. A prosperous market centre during the Middle Ages,

1960s the theatre saw a variety of uses – as a wine cellar and a corn chandler's among others. After an extensive restoration programme, the theatre finally reopened in 1963 and, remarkably, with the majority of its original features still intact. The theatre is home to the **Georgian Theatre Museum**, which houses a unique collection of playbills as well as the oldest and largest complete set of painted Georgian scenery in the country.

For a complete insight into the history of this attractive and interesting town and the surrounding area, the **Richmondshire Museum** (see panel below), first opened in 1978, covers many aspects of Swaledale life. Along with the exhibits detailing the history of lead mining in the area, transport and domestic life, there is a Post Office from Grinton, Barker's Chemist's shop from Catterick Garrison and, most famously of all, the surgery set that was used in the filming of *All Creatures Great and Small*.

Found housed in the converted 12th century Church of the Trinity is the **Green Howards Museum**, which relates over 300 years of history of the North Riding's Infantry. Dating back to 1688, this regiment, one of the country's oldest and most famous, has fought in many campaigns. The exhibits here relate to the Crimean War, the Northwest Frontier of India and the Boer War, and there is archive film of the First World War. The museum is also home to the Collins' collection of uniforms and head-dresses, and there are more than 3,000 medals and decorations on display, including 18 Victoria Crosses and three George Crosses.

Westwards from this historic town lies **Swaledale**, which is for many the loveliest of the Yorkshire Dales. It runs through countryside that ranges from the dramatic lower dale with its steep-sided wooded hills to the austere upper reaches, where one's nearest neighbours may be several miles away. This rugged beauty makes quite a contrast to that of

Richmondshire Museum

Ryders Wynd, Richmond,
North Yorkshire DL10 4JA
Tel: 01748 825611

Tucked away down cobbled Ryders Wynd in Richmond is the **Richmondshire Museum**. Run by volunteers, it tells the story of the district from pre historic times. Attractions include the James Herriot vets surgery set from television's *All Creatures Great and Small*, a local chemist's shop and a Dales post office. There is a display about the former lead-mining industry in Swaledale, a transport section which includes a detailed model of Richmond railway station, a reconstruction of a cruck house containing domestic bygones and a gallery devoted to the history of Richmond and its people. Embroidery and a children's corner are among other features. The museum is open daily, 11am to 5pm, from Easter to the end of October.

The Tudor Hotel

Gatherley Road, Brompton-on-Swale,
Richmond, North Yorkshire DL10 7JF
Tel/Fax: 01748 818021
e-mail: info@thetudorhotel.net
website: www.thetudorhotel.net

Close to Catterick Racecourse in Brompton-on-Swale, **The Tudor Hotel** is a distinguished and distinctive inn offering great food, drink and accommodation.

The four ensuite guest bedrooms range in size; all are comfortable, handsome and welcoming, there is also a family room which sleeps 4. The Hotel is on route to the coast and the splendid coastal walks making it the perfect base from which to explore the region.

Sean and Maria Kenny arrived here early in 2004, at which time the inn had been closed for over a year. They have completely refurbished the inn with taste, style and an eye for careful conservation, and opened the doors in February of 2004. The interior is now classic and striking, a happy marriage of the traditional and modern such as the feature fireplace, oil paintings and traditional fixtures and furnishings. All is pristine and welcoming.

There is a good selection of real ales – including John Smiths and changing guest ales – lagers, cider, stout, wines, spirits and soft drinks, served all day every day.

Food is served seven days a week from 12 until 9 p.m. Both Sean and Maria cook, and the extensive menu features a range of expertly prepared starters, snacks and main courses together with a special children's menu. There are Theme nights and Karaoke, pool is also played. The inn's Monarch Room seats up to 70 people, and is available for functions – please ring for details.

Wensleydale just to the south – and there are other noticeable differences: the villages in Swaledale all have harsher, Nordic-sounding names, the dale is much less populated and the rivers and becks are more like fast-flowing mountain streams. At one time Swaledale was a hive of activity and enjoyed a prosperous period when the lead-mining industry flourished here – the valley still bears many of the scars left behind since mining declined. Today, key features of the dale are the **Swaledale Sheep**, easily recognised by their black faces, white muzzles and grey speckled legs. Introduced to the area as late as the 1920s, each flock of Swaledales knows its own territory and they are said to be 'heafed' to their own area of moorland. This means they can be safely left on unfenced terrain and will not wander off their traditional patch. Ewes teach this behaviour to their lambs. The sheep have to cope with extremely wild weather, and their hardiness is typified by the warmth and durability of their wool. Not surprisingly, the Swaledale ram has been adopted as the emblem of the Yorkshire Dales National Park.

There are several side-dales to Swaledale. The small, thriving market town of Reeth lies at the point where Arkengarthdale joins the valley of the River Swale; it was first settled by Norsemen who preferred the wild and remote countryside of the valley of Arkle Beck. Not considered important enough to warrant an entry in the *Domesday Book*, Arkengarthdale was also mined for lead but, today, the dale is chiefly populated by Swaledale sheep. At the head of this particularly rugged dale lies England's highest inn, Tan Hill.

Around Richmond

Easby

1½ miles SE of Richmond off the B6271

This small hamlet on the banks of the River Swale is home to the delightful and romantic remains of **Easby Abbey**, founded here in 1155 by Roald, Constable of Richmond Castle. The order of monks who resided here were of more modest leanings than the Cistercians and, as a result, the buildings possessed none of the grandeur of Rievaulx and Fountains, though the riverside setting is common to all. Easby Abbey's most notable feature is its replica of the Easby Cross, a Saxon cross dating from the 9th century. The extensive ruins can be reached by a pleasant riverside walk that is well signposted from Richmond.

Hudswell

2 miles SW of Richmond off the A6108

This ancient village was well established by the time that it was recorded in the *Domesday Book*. Standing high above the River Swale, it has, over the years, gravitated to a more sheltered position. The view of the churchyard of the late

BAY HORSE INN

Ravensworth, Richmond,
North Yorkshire DL11 7ET
Tel: 01325 718328

The **Bay Horse Inn** makes a very pretty picture with its mellow stone walls, cobbled front patio, colourful hanging baskets and tubs of flowers, all against a backdrop of mature trees. The interior is just as inviting. A stone door case, dating from the 1600s or even earlier, was almost certainly salvaged from Ravensworth Castle; the rest of the building dates back to 1725. The bar is traditional without losing any comfort, decorated with an eclectic mix of mementos that add to the homeliness and welcome ambience of the place, while the dining room/restaurant area is ornamented with a collection of memorabilia associated with the Grand National near-winner 'Crisp', whom Sue used to look after.

Your hosts Sue and Charlie bought the inn seven years ago when it had fallen on hard times, but have transformed the Bay Horse into a popular hostelry with a reputation for good ale and excellent food.

There are three real ales on tap here: Theakstons Best and two changing guest ales.

Charlie's very extensive menu caters for all palates, including those of vegetarians and children. There are cheese soufflé, Thai fishcakes and Yorkshire puddings among the starters; home-made beef crumble, duck breast in orange sauce and lamb hot pot are just three of the many main courses, together with delicious fresh fish dishes including salmon and dill lasagne and stuffed trout, curries, salads, sandwiches, and hearty favourites such as liver, bacon and onion casserole and shepherd's pie. The irresistible choice of desserts includes gold rush pie, baked Alaska, pecan toffee sponge and a range of ice creams. The restaurant seats 50; booking advised for Saturday evening and Sunday lunchtime. On the first Sunday of each month the inn hosts a quiz (everyone welcome). The inn is closed Tuesday lunchtime all year round, and also Wednesday lunchtime October to February. Children welcome.

19th century St Michael's Church is considered to be one of the finest in all of Richmondshire. From the village there is a walk down to the river that leads through pleasant woodland and also takes in some 365 steps. About halfway down, below a path leading off to an old lime kiln, lies **King Arthur's Oven**, a horizontal crack in the limestone which, it is claimed, has connections with Richmond Castle and the legend of King Arthur.

Reeth

8½ miles W of Richmond on the B6270

Considered the capital of Upper Swaledale, this small town featured in the *Domesday Book* while the surrounding villages, hamlets and moorland were written off as untaxable wasteland. The local lead-mining industry, which served the town well for many years until competition from abroad gradually caused its decline, was begun by the Romans. Today, Reeth is chiefly an agricultural centre. Until the late 19th century there were four fairs held here annually; today, the town holds one annual agricultural show in September, on the large town green. It remains a magnet for farmers the entire length of the dale and beyond. The long-established weekly market continues to be held every Friday.

Along the top of the green is High Row, with its inns, shops and outstanding Georgian architecture which reflects the affluence of the town in the 18th century when the trade in wool and lead was booming. Also here, housed in what was once the old Methodist Sunday School, is the **Swaledale Folk Museum**, which tells how the local mining, farming and craft industries have shaped the lives of those living in this beautiful dale. Other aspects of Swaledale life - such as the impact of Wesleyan Methodism and the exodus of the population to the industrial areas of the south Pennines, as well as local pastimes - are also revealed. The museum is open from Good Friday to the end of October.

The town is strategically sited at the point where the Arkle Beck joins the River Swale; from here, running northwards, is the small and remote valley – **Arkengarthdale.** First settled by Norsemen, their presence is still in evidence in the dale's place-names, such as Booze, Eskeleth and Whaw. The dale was completely overlooked during the Domesday survey, when it was considered of no value, but lead mining brought about a period of prosperity in the 18th and 19th centuries.

Just to the south of Reeth lies the quiet village of **Grinton**; its parish Church of St Andrew served the whole of Swaledale for centuries. For those people living in the upper reaches of the dale, when their days were ended their coffin would have to make a long journey down the track to Grinton on what was to become known as the **Corpse Way**.

Langthwaite

11 miles W of Richmond off the B6270

This is the main village of Arkengarthdale and it may seem familiar even to those who have never been here before, as its bridge featured in the title sequence of the popular television series *All Creatures Great and Small*. A pretty and isolated place, just outside Langthwaite lies the CB Hotel, named after Charles Bathurst, an 18th century Lord of the Manor who was responsible for the development of the dale's lead-mining industry. Bathurst's grandfather, Dr John Bathurst, was physician to Oliver Cromwell. John Bathurst purchased land here in 1659 with the exploitation of its mineral wealth very much in mind.

Low Row

12 miles W of Richmond on the B6270

During the Middle Ages the track along the hillside above this small village formed part of the Corpse Way, along which relays of bearers would carry the deceased in a large wicker basket to Grinton church for burial. The journey could take up to two days to complete; along the route are the large stone slabs where the bearers would rest their heavy burden.

Just on the edge of the village lies **Hazel Brow Organic Farm and Visitor Centre**, a family-run farm that provides all that is required for an interesting and entertaining day out. Down by the river there are the internationally-famous hay meadows, while higher up is the heather-clad moorland that is home to a flock of hardy Swaledale sheep. At lambing time children are offered the opportunity to bottle-feed lambs; there are also ponies to ride, calves to feed and different activities and demonstrations throughout the year, depending on the season.

Just to the southwest of Low Row is a signpost to the village of **Crackpot**. Despite its name this is a perfectly sensible-looking hamlet; its appellation simply means a place where crows "*crack*" congregate around a deep hole in the hills "*pot*".

Gunnerside

14 miles W of Richmond on the B6270

This charming Dales village was, until the late 19th century, a thriving lead-mining village. Gunnerside became known as the 'Klondyke of Swaledale' and, although the boom centred on lead rather than gold, the Old Gang Mines are the most famous in Yorkshire. The paths and trackways here are, in the main, those trod by the successions of miners travelling to work; the valley's sides still show the signs of the mine workings. In the village, tearooms offer such delights as Lead Miners' Bait and the delicious Gunnerside Cheese Cake, made from a recipe handed down from mining days.

After the closure of the mines, many families left the village to find work elsewhere in northern England, while still others emigrated to America and Australia. For many years afterwards one of the village's most important days was Midsummer Sunday, when those who had left would, if at all possible, return and catch up with their families and friends.

Muker

17 miles W of Richmond on the B6270

The road from Reeth passes over an old stone bridge across the River Swale before finally arriving in this engaging village of beige-coloured stone cottages overlooked by **St Mary's Church**, which dates back to the time of Elizabeth I and was one of the very few churches to be built in England during her reign. Most church-builders until that time spared no expense in glorifying the house of God, but at Muker they were more economical: the church roof was covered in thatch, its floor in rushes and no seating was provided. Despite such penny-pinching measures, the new church of 1580 was warmly welcomed, since it brought to an end the tedious journey along the

Corpse Way to the dale's mother church at Grinton.

The good people of Muker devised means of making further savings. For many years, the thrifty mourners of the parish shared a communal coffin: year after year, the same coffin would bear the departed to the churchyard, where the shrouded body would be removed, placed in the grave and the coffin reserved for use at the next funeral. It was not until 1735 that the vicar decreed that everyone buried in his parish deserved the dignity of a personal coffin.

On the gravestones in the churchyard, local family names such as Harker, Alderson and Fawcett feature prominently, as they do among the villagers still living here. Swaledale cuisine is equally durable, and the specialities on offer in the local tearooms include Swaledale Curd Tart, Yorkshire Rarebit and Deep Apple Pie with Wensleydale cheese.

The area's main crafts still revolve around the wool provided by the hardy Swaledale sheep, in great demand by carpet manufacturers and for impermeable jumpers favoured by fell-walkers, climbers and anyone else trying to defeat the British weather. The tradition of hand-knitting in Swaledale goes back at least 400 years when the lead miners and their families developed the craft to supplement their meagre wages. In the 16th century Elizabeth I set the fashion for stockings and, in a

Swaledale Woollens

Strawbeck, Muker in Swaledale, Richmond, North Yorkshire DL11 6QG
Tel/Fax: 01748 886251
e-mail: mail@swaledalewoollens.co.uk
website: www.swaledalewoollens.co.uk

Set in the village of Muker and reached via the B6270, **Swaledale Woollens** has been one of Yorkshire's premier attractions for 30 years.

Of the 50-odd recognised breeds of sheep in the UK, Swaledale sheep are among the hardiest, and their wool makes for durable, well-insulating clothing that is also lightweight and comfortable. Swaledale Woollens was established in 1974 to promote a wider use of this excellent wool, and the shop stocks a range of natural yarns for those who do their own hand- or machine-knitting, together with a large selection of beautiful and distinctive jumpers, cardigans, hats, scarves, gloves and other knitwear. All garments are made entirely from natural materials – most of the wools are undyed, with the patterns created by using the various shades of wool from different sheep – Swaledale, Welsh and Wensleydale wools, each with its own distinctive colour and particular characteristics. There are also dyed wools in a range of lovely colours. The shop also has a choice of ties, moccasins, sheepskins, rugs, wallhangings and much more.

short space of time, nearly everyone in the dale – including men and children – were involved in this cottage industry. Throughout the 17th and early 18th centuries the industry continued to keep the dalesfolk busy, but by the turn of the 19th century it had severely declined. In recent years the art of hand-knitting has been revived and, today, hand-knitted and machine-knitted sweaters, gloves and other woollens, made from the wool of the local sheep, can be purchased at **Swaledale Woollens** (see panel opposite). The company's shop in the village also has an interesting display on the history of knitting, wool and the Swaledale sheep.

Swaledale Cottages, nr Thwaite

Thwaite

18½ miles W of Richmond on the B6270

Surrounded by a dramatic landscape that includes Kisdon Hill, Great Shunnor, High Seat and Lovely Seat, this tiny village has ancient origins and, like so many places in Swaledale, its name is derived from the Nordic language, in this case the word *thveit*, meaning 'a clearing in the wood'. However, the woodlands that once provided both shelter and fuel for the Viking settlers have long since gone.

To the southwest of the village, on the road to Hawes in Wensleydale, lies **Buttertubs Pass**, one of the highest and most forbidding mountain passes in the country. The Buttertubs themselves are a curious natural feature of closely-packed vertical stone stacks rising from some unseen underground base to the level of the road. A local Victorian guide to the Buttertubs, perhaps aware that the view from above was not all that impressive, solemnly assured his client that 'some of the Buttertubs had no bottom, and some were deeper than that.' No one is quite sure where the Buttertubs name comes from, but the most plausible explanation is that farmers used its deep-chilled shelves as a convenient refrigerator for the butter they could not sell immediately. Unusually, these potholes are not linked by a series of passages as most are, but are free-standing.

The narrow road from Thwaite across the Buttertubs Pass is not for the faint-hearted driver as only a flimsy post and wire fence separates the road from a sheer drop of near Alpine proportions. It is, perhaps, more satisfying to cross the pass in the opposite direction, from Hawes, as when the summit of the pass is reached there are stupendous views of Swaledale.

Keld

18 miles W of Richmond on the B6270

The little cluster of stone buildings that make up this village stand beside the early stages of the River Swale. The place is alive with the sound of rushing water and it comes as no surprise that the word 'keld' is Nordic for spring. For lovers of green woodlands and breathtaking waterfalls, this village is definitely well worth a visit, and it has also managed to retain an impression of being untouched by modern life. Backed by rugged Cotterby Scar, **Wain Wath Force** can be found alongside the road towards Birkdale, while Catrake Force, with its stepped formation, can be reached from the village's main street. Though on private land, the falls - and, beside them, the entrance to an old lead mine - can still be seen. Kidson Force, the most impressive waterfall in Swaledale, can be reached most easily of all – by taking a gentle stroll of less than a mile from the village along a well-trodden footpath.

For serious walkers Keld is the most important crossroads in northern England, as here the south-to-north **Pennine Way** and the east-to-west **Coast to Coast Footpath** intersect.

Tan Hill

18 miles NW of Richmond off the B6270

Situated at the head of Arkengarthdale and on the border with County Durham, at 1,732 feet above sea level the **Tan Hill Inn** is England's highest pub and it is arguably one of the country's most remote public houses. Often cut off in winter, just over a hundred years ago the inn was a busy and bustling place as workers from the Tan Hill coal mines came here to quench their thirst while drivers also paused here while they waited for their horse-drawn carts to be filled with coal. Although the coal mines have long since closed, a coal fire burns brightly in the grate here every day of the year, and some 50,000 visitors still make the journey to this remote inn. Many visitors are walkers who stagger in from one of the most gruelling stretches of the Pennine Way, and who not only relish the warmth but also a sit-down and a pint of ale.

Despite its remote location, the inn comes alive on the last Thursday in May when the **Tan Hill Sheep Fair** takes place. Then, if only for a day, the Tan Hill Inn becomes the centre of agricultural Yorkshire.

Leyburn

The main market town and trading centre of mid-Wensleydale, Leyburn is an attractive town with a broad market place lined with handsome late-Georgian and Victorian stone buildings.

It was listed as 'Le Bourne' (meaning 'stream by the clearing') in the *Domesday Book*, and there are still three streams running through the town today. Despite its importance as a trading centre, the market only came to Leyburn as late as 1684 when Wensley, until then the dominant town in the dale, was decimated by the Plague. Leyburn remained part of the Wensley parish until its own church was built in 1868.

Just to the west of the town is a mile-long limestone scarp along which runs a footpath offering lovely panoramic views of the dale. Known as **The Shawl**, a popular local legend suggests that it gained its unusual name when Mary, Queen of Scots, dropped her shawl on the path during an unsuccessful attempt to escape from Bolton Castle. However, though Mary was kept prisoner at Bolton Castle for some time, a more likely explanation is that 'Shawl' is a corruption of the name given to the ancient settlement here. Archaeological finds in the fields around the scar suggest that the area has been inhabited for centuries. In the 19th century two adult prehistoric skeletons were found here along with other artefacts, including bits of charcoal and rubbing stones for grinding corn.

Back in the town itself there is the unusual **Violin Making Workshop** where visitors have the rare opportunity to see this ancient and fascinating craft, which has changed little over the centuries. The traditional tools and methods used by such master craftsmen as Stradivari are still employed here, and the workshop is open every day during the high season. Close by, other craftsmen are at work at **The Teapottery**, where a whole range of witty and unique teapots are created and then put on sale in the showroom. Not surprisingly, the workshop has a tea room and, naturally, the tea is served in their own astonishing teapots.

Both children and adults will enjoy the **Beech End Model Village**, a unique experience where visitors can 'drive' cars down the village streets and out into highly detailed countryside, press a button to see inside a perfect scale model of a house or shop and also hear the sounds of village life. Equally enchanting is the **Teddy Bear Workshop** where traditional Teddy Bears are designed and hand-crafted in small limited editions for collectors around the world. The workshop also stocks everything needed to create a Teddy Bear, from kits and patterns to mohair fabric and eyes, and there are also books and numerous other gifts to be found at Hartley Bear's Emporium.

Along with its links with Mary, Queen of Scots, Leyburn has several other interesting connections with famous people and, in particular, the town was the home of the 'Sweet Lass of Richmond Hill'. The girl featured in the song is Frances I'Anson who was born in Leyburn in 1766, the daughter of William I'Anson and Martha, and her birthplace, I'Anson House in the High Street, has 'WIA, 1746' inscribed over

Leyburn Market Square

Leyburn and, indeed, much of the filming for the successful television series took place in both Wensleydale and Swaledale.

To the east and west of Leyburn lies **Wensleydale**, perhaps above all the other dales the one that most people associate with this part of Yorkshire. At some 40 miles long it is certainly one of the longer of Yorkshire's dales; it is also greener and more gentle than most of its neighbours. The pasture land, grazed by flocks of Wensleydale sheep, is only broken by lines of drystone walls, and the dale is, of course, famous for its cheese - whose fortunes have recently been given an additional boost by association with the animated characters Wallace and Gromit, who have declared it to be their favourite.

Wensleydale is the only major dale not to be named after its river (the Ure), although until fairly recently most locals still referred to the valley as Yoredale or Uredale. The dale's name actually comes from the once-important town of Wensley where the lucrative trade in cheese began in the 13th century. The dale was also recorded in the 12th century as *Wandelesleydale* – 'Waendel's woodland clearing in the valley' – although Waendel himself has disappeared into the mists of time, his clearing is thought to have been somewhere near the attractive town of

the door. In 1787, Frances married Leonard MacNally, an Irish lawyer, who wrote the famous song some two years after they were wed. Frances died in Dublin in 1795 and lies buried in that city. Of the town's other famous connections: Peter Goldsmith, Admiral Lord Nelson's second surgeon, lived at Secret Garden House, Grove Square after his retirement and he lies buried in Wensley churchyard; on the town's war memorial is the name of John Alan Broadley, born in Leyburn in 1921. A true Second World War hero, Broadley received many honours and decorations in his short life, but he is perhaps best remembered as 'F for Freddie' of Dam Busters' fame. Finally, while it is well known that the real life James Herriot joined a veterinary practice in Thirsk, prior to this he spent the first ten years of his working life at the practice of Frank Bingham of Leyburn. The tales that have entertained several generations over the years often refer to incidents that occurred in and around

Wensley. Using the dale's other major settlement, Hawes, as a base, visitors can also follow the **Turner Trail**, which takes in the scenic sights that so impressed JMW Turner when he visited both here and neighbouring Swaledale in 1816.

As it flows down its valley, the River Ure is fed by a series of smaller rivers and becks, many of which have their own charming dales. Among these are **Coverdale**, the home of some of England's finest racecourse stables, peaceful Bishopdale, with its ancient farmhouses, and remote Cotterdale, with its striking waterfall. Most famously, Wensleydale, along with Swaledale and the area around Thirsk, are commonly referred to as Herriot Country since it was this region of fells and friendly villages that provided many of the locations for the television series *All Creatures Great and Small.* Based on the working life of vet, Alf Wight (1916-95), the stories recount the working life of dalesfolk between the 1930s and the 1960s with much humour and affection.

Around Leyburn

Garriston

3 miles NE of Leyburn off the A684

The rare Wensleydale longwool sheep, flocks of which can be seen grazing in the fields around this village, have a soft and luxurious fleece. The **Wensleydale**

Cross Keys Inn

Bellerby, Leyburn, North Yorkshire DL8 5QS
Tel/Fax: 01969 622256

At the heart of the lovely village of Bellerby, found on the A6108 north of Leyburn, **Cross Keys Inn** is a large and handsome inn dating back to the mid-1700s.

The inn is run by Rod and Tammy Marriott, who arrived here in May 2004 and proceeded to undertake a lot of hard work to refurbish and lovingly restore the inn to its former glory. Friendly and with a relaxed and welcoming atmosphere the inn is open every session Monday to Thursday and all day Friday to Sunday.

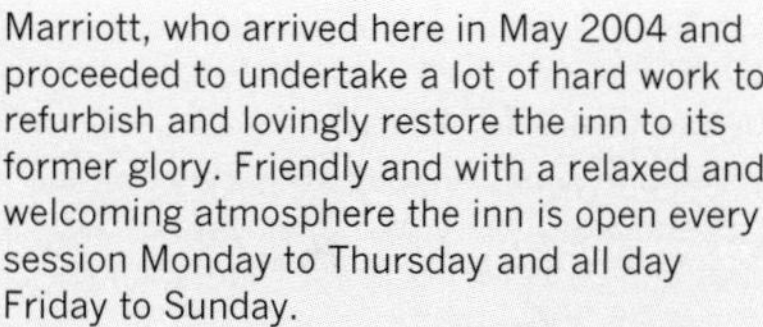

There are always at least four real ales including John Smiths, Copper Dragon (a Skipton brew) and changing guest ales, together with a good complement of lagers, cider, stout, wines, spirits and soft drinks. And to eat, there's a varied selection of hearty favourites using the freshest local produce.

Guests can enjoy their drink or meal indoors or in the attractive beer garden to the rear of the pub. Off-road parking. Children welcome.

The Queens Head

West Moor Lane, Finghall, Leyburn,
North Yorkshire DL8 5ND
Tel: 01677 450259

A superb country inn enjoying picturesque surroundings within the quiet village of Finghall, just off the A684 east of Leyburn, **The Queens Head** is owned and run by Sharon and Peter Farhall, who arrived in 2001 and who have over 25 years' experience in the trade.

This cosy pub is comfortable and welcoming, and retains much of its historic charm and character. Parts date back to the 14th century. From the rear of the premises visitors can see Wyvill Hall – reputedly the home of Toad of Toad Hall.

The pub opens on Mondays at 6 p.m. but is open all day every day other days of the week and on Bank Holidays. There are four

real ales on tap at this Free House: Theakstons Best, John Smiths, Black Sheep and Daleside. There is also a good range of lagers, cider, stout, wines, spirits and soft drinks.

Head chef Andrew Megson has built up a fine reputation for the menu, which offers a range of freshly prepared home-cooked dishes to suit all tastes and appetites. Favourites include the hot chicken salad and pork fillets, among many choices from the menu and specials board. Food is served Tuesday to Sunday at lunchtime (12 – 2.30) and every evening from 6 p.m. The no-smoking dining room is stylish and handsome, and seats 55. Booking is essential at weekends, though food can also be enjoyed in the bar areas. Children are welcome in the restaurant until around 9 p.m.

During the lifetime of this edition it is hoped that chalet-style accommodation will become available – please ring for details.

Longwool Sheepshop is a treat for anyone who appreciates good knitwear. Not only is there an extensive range of hand-knitting yarns and patterns to be found here, but customers can also purchase beautiful and unique hand-knitted garments along with fleeces and tops for spinners. The shop is open from April to October and occasionally out of season.

Constable Burton

3½ miles E of Leyburn on the A684

This village was recorded in the *Domesday Book* as 'Bortone'; later it was referred to as 'Roald-Burton', after a 12th century Constable of Richmond Castle. Just north of the village lies **Constable Burton Hall Gardens**, which are particularly famous for the fine terraced gardens designed and developed by Mrs Vida Burdon between 1932 and 1976. Featuring a collection of maples planted beneath ancient yew trees, the gardens also have a fabulous display of daffodils in early spring and extensive shrubbery and roses. The fine Georgian house, which provides an elegant backdrop to the gardens and surrounding 18th century parkland, was designed by John Carr and has remained in the same family, the Wyvills, since 1768. The house is not open to the public.

Spennithorne

2 miles SE of Leyburn off the A684

This pleasant little village dates back many years. The present Church of St Michael and All Angels stands on the site of a Saxon church, although the only remains of the ancient building are two ornamental stones set into the walls of the chancels, and a Saxon monument in the vestry.

Two of Spennithorne's earlier residents are worth mentioning: John Hutchinson was born here in 1675 and went on to become steward to the 6th Duke of Somerset as well as a rather controversial philosopher. Hutchinson vehemently disagreed with Sir Isaac Newton's Theory of Gravity and was equally ardent in asserting that the earth was neither flat, nor a sphere, but a cube. Though there are no records mentioning that Hutchinson was ever considered as of unsound mind, another resident of Spennithorne, Richard Hatfield, was officially declared insane after he fired a gun at George III.

Middleham

2 miles SE of Leyburn on the A6108

Famous for its castle, the childhood home of Richard III, and its thriving racehorse-training industry, Middleham is an enchanting little town with some handsome Georgian architecture. Despite its small population, the town boasts its own Mayor, Corporation and not one but two market places.

Rising high above the town are the magnificent remains of **Middleham Castle** (English Heritage), whose keep dates back to the 12th century and was the largest in the north of England. The glory days of this once mighty fortress came in the 15th century when most of the northern region of England was ruled from here by the Neville family. It was during this era that Richard III was sent here as a boy of 13 to be trained in the 'arts of nobilitie'. Richard was popular locally and he ensured the town's prosperity by granting it a fair and a twice yearly market – the people of Middleham had good reason to mourn his death at the Battle of Bosworth in 1485. Visitors to the castle today can take in the magnificent views of the keep from the oak viewing gallery, and also learn more of the castle's history and its influence on the surrounding area through the small exhibition here. Above the castle lies **William's Hill**, the site of Middleham's first castle, a Norman motte-and-bailey fortification.

Still a thriving community, Middleham is often referred to as the 'Newmarket of the North', as nearly 500 racehorses are stabled in and around the town. Strings of them can be seen walking through the town on their way to the training gallops on Low Moor. It was the monks of Jervaulx Abbey who founded this key industry and, by the late 18th century, races were being run across the moorland and the first stables were established here. Since then the stables have produced a succession of classic race winners, while one local trainer, Neville Crump, trained three Grand National winners in the space of just 12 years. On Good Friday each year the **Middleham Stables Open Day** takes place, when all the town's yards open their doors to visitors and various equine events held on Low Moor.

East Witton

3½ miles SE of Leyburn on the A6108

A quiet and attractive village, which was once an important market centre situated conveniently between the abbeys of Jervaulx and Middleham, East Witton sits beside the confluence of the Rivers Cover and Ure. Devastated by a fire in 1796, the village was rebuilt by the Earl of Ailesbury in 1809. Along with the new well-proportioned church, he laid the village out with pairs of houses facing each other across the large, tree-planted green. Just a short time after that conflagration, the village was struck by another tragedy when, in 1820, 20 miners perished in a coal-mining accident on Witton Fell. They all lie buried together in one grave in the churchyard.

To the west of the village lie the graceful ruins of **Jervaulx Abbey**, one of the very few privately-owned Cistercian abbeys and one of the great sister-houses to Fountains Abbey. The name *Jervaulx* is a French derivation of 'Yore' and 'Vale'. The Abbey was founded in 1156 by monks who came over from France following the Norman Conquest. These strictly disciplined monks, who followed a regime of silence, prayer, study, contemplation and manual labour, also saw the Abbey grow wealthy from sheep-rearing and horse-breeding and, before the Dissolution, Jervaulx owned vast areas of Wensleydale. The monks were forbidden to eat the soft cheese that they produced at the Abbey, so they sold it - thus the world-famous Wensleydale cheese was born. Despite its ruinous state, Jervaulx is among the most evocative of Yorkshire's many fine abbeys, and the grounds in which it stands have been transformed into beautiful gardens with the crumbling walls providing interesting backdrops for the sculptured trees and colourful plants and shrubs.

Close by, at High Jervaulx Farm, is **Brymor**, a real dairy ice-cream parlour founded in 1984. Made from double cream and from Guernsey milk from their own herds, which graze the lush pastures of Lower Wensleydale, this superb ice-cream is made with only the very best natural fruit flavours from that great ice-cream making nation – Italy. A real treat, a visit to the Moor family's parlour is a must for all ice-cream fans.

Coverham

3 miles S of Leyburn off the A6108

Situated beside the River Cover, in little-visited Coverdale, this village is perhaps best known for the ruins of Coverham Abbey (private), built in the late 1200s and of which only some decorated arches and a Norman gateway remain. Close by is **Braithwaite Hall** (National Trust), a remote 17th century stone farmhouse which, along with other surrounding buildings, has clearly been constructed using the Abbey's stones. In some of the walls, effigies from the old buildings can still be seen. The Hall is noted for its fine original features which include fireplaces, panelling and an oak staircase. The Hall can be visited by prior arrangement.

Also in the village is the delightful walled **Forbidden Garden**, which includes a grotto with an underground labyrinth of chambers and passages. There is a shop and refreshment room; admission is by pre-booked tickets only. The garden is open daily from April until October and on Sundays until Christmas.

Hard though it may be to believe, this quiet and unspoilt valley was once the main route between Richmond and Skipton and, as a result, teams of packhorses would travel the length of Coverdale on regular journeys. The village of Horsehouse is a reminder of those far-off days, while West Scrafton, further down the dale, was once inhabited by miners and quarrymen who worked in the nearby colliery until the early 20th century.

Wensley

1½ miles W of Leyburn on the A684

A peaceful little village beside the River Ure, surprisingly Wensley was once the dale's main settlement. Such was its importance that it gave its name to the valley. A great centre of trade for the whole of Wensleydale, it was the first village in the dale to be granted a market charter, in 1202. In the 1560s, however, Wensley was devastated by the Plague, and the market moved to Askrigg and Leyburn. However, the stately village Church of the Holy Trinity, rebuilt in 1719, still contains features from 1245 that are testament to the village's former wealth. Also inside can be seen the unusual Bolton family pews - actually a pair of opera boxes brought here from London during the 18th century. The Bolton family still live at nearby **Bolton Hall**, a massive 18th century mansion that is closed to the public, although its superb gardens are occasionally open during the summer months.

West Witton

3½ miles SW of Leyburn on the A684

Recorded in the *Domesday Book* as 'Witun', this village was then the largest settlement in Wensleydale. It was also unusual in that the houses here were of stone rather than the more common wood and thatch. West Witton is well known for its annual feast of St Bartholomew, the patron saint of the parish church, which takes place on the 24th August. In a unique ceremony, an effigy of a man, known as the Bartle, is carried through the village on this day. According to legend, the original Bartle was a breed of swine hunted over the surrounding fells before being captured and killed. The culmination of the three days of celebrations is the burning of the 'Owd Bartle' at Grassgill End.

Above the village to the west, on Capple Bank, is **Polly Peachum's Tower,** built by the Duke of Bolton for Lavinia Fenton, the original Polly Peachum of *The Beggars' Opera*.

Carlton-in-Coverdale

5 miles SW of Leyburn off the A684

Despite being the principal village of Coverdale, Carlton has a population of only around 100. Nevertheless, it has its own pub and is an excellent base from which to walk or tour the Yorkshire Dales National Park. During the 16th century a local man, Miles Coverdale, who took his name from this valley, published his own translation of the Bible – the first in English. Later revised, first in the Great Bible of 1539, which was placed in all the parish churches, and later in the Authorized Version of 1604, much of Coverdale's original prose has remained. The version of the Psalms used in the current Anglican Book of Common Prayer is also Coverdale's work.

Redmire

4½ miles W of Leyburn off the A684

Throughout its long history, this village is thought to have occupied several sites in the area, it has been in its present location for many years and on the village green stands an old oak tree, supported by props, which is estimated to be at least 300 years old. When John Wesley preached in the village during his two visits here, in 1744 and 1774, it

The Bolton Arms

Redmire, Leyburn, North Yorkshire DL8 4EA
Tel: 01969 624336
e-mail: pam@boltonredmire.fsnet.co.uk
website: www.bolton-arms.com

Redmire is found four miles west of Leyburn off the A684. This pretty village surrounded by hundreds of acres of open countryside is home to **The Bolton Arms**, an impressive and welcoming stonebuilt inn dating back some 300 years. Owned and personally run by John and Pam Berry, a charming couple whose hospitality is second to none. The inn is open Mondays from 7 p.m., every session Tuesday to Friday and all day at weekends and Bank Holiday Mondays, serving three real ales – John Smiths, Black Sheep and a guest ale – and quality home-cooked food.

Pam is a superb cook, creating a range of dishes – her specialities include home-made steak and kidney pie, curries, chilli and lasagne – with something for everyone on the menu and specials board. This fine inn also boasts three charming and supremely comfortable ensuite guest bedrooms, tastefully furnished and decorated to a high standard of quality, housed in the former stable block which has been lovingly converted to offer first-class accommodation which is available all year round.

is likely that he stood in the shade of this tree. On the hillside to the north of the village can still be seen the shafts, pits and other debris left by the lead and coal-mining industries that flourished here in the 19th century when Redmire was, chiefly, a village for miners.

Castle Bolton

5 miles W of Leyburn off the A684

Although Caslte Bolton, with its row of cottages on either side of the long village green, is dwarfed by the huge castle, the village - and its church (built in 1325) - pre-date the great fortification that is **Bolton Castle**. Dominating mid-Wensleydale for more than six centuries, the castle is one of the major tourist attractions in the area, as it is not only a magnificent example of a medieval castle but also provides stunning views over the dale. In 1379, the Lord of the Manor, Richard le Scrope, Lord Chancellor of England to Richard II, was granted permission to fortify his manor house. Using stone from a nearby quarry and oak from the Lake District, the building was finally completed some 20 years later. Down the decades the castle has played its part in the history of the area and the country and, along with connections with the Pilgrimage of Grace and Richard III, Mary, Queen of Scots was a reluctant visitor to the caslte when she was imprisoned here between 1568 and 1569. During the Civil War, Royalists were besieged here. Today, this luxurious

The Street Head Inn

Newbiggin-in-Bishopdale, Leyburn,
North Yorkshire DL8 3TE
Tel: 01969 663282 Fax: 01969 663745
e-mail: joanne.fawcett@virgin.net
website: www.streetheadinn.co.uk

A genuine gem, this – **The Street Head Inn** is a superb inn situated in the unspoilt valley of Bishopdale, some nine miles southwest of Leyburn on the B6160. This impressive inn dates back to around 1730. A former coaching inn, it is very large and spacious, with original features such as the oak and elm exposed beams, huge open fireplace and feature window created from the original coach entrance.

Superb food is served daily at lunch (12 – 2) and dinner (6 – 9). Booking is required at weekends. Guests choose off the varied and extensive menu from a range of delicious and hearty home-cooked dishes.

The inn also boasts five recently refurbished ensuite guest bedrooms. Each is decorated and furnished to the highest standards of comfort and quality, with a real home-from-home feel, enhanced by the lovely quilts and traditional features in each room. These rooms are available all year round. The accommodation has been given a 4 Diamond rating by the ETC.

Just a short walk from the inn, on the same road, Nigel has converted the old school house into wonderful self-catering accommodation that can sleep up to 20. Standing just over the road from Nigel's 250-acre farm, it is a picturesque and welcoming place to enjoy the scenic delights of the area.

Owners Nigel and Joanne Fawcett are very experienced in the trade, and bought this gracious premises in 2002. A farmer by occupation, Nigel's farm is within a short walk of the inn, and he has also run and owned different inns over the past 16 years in the nearby villages of Aysgarth, Reeth and Muker before arriving here. Ably assisted by manageress Joanne Harrington and Head Chef Trevor Bailey, the Fawcetts make this a place that is convivial and welcoming, and have a wealth of local knowledge they are happy to share with guests.

Open every session for ale, there are three real ales to choose from – Theakstons, John Smiths and Black Sheep – together with a good selection of lagers, wines, spirits, cider, stout and soft drinks.

fortified manor house is still occupied by a direct descendant of the 1st Lord Scrope and, following major conservation work in 1995, it remains one of the country's best-preserved castles. Visitors can tour the halls, galleries and state apartments, see the dungeons and explore the building that features in both *Elizabeth* and *Ivanhoe*. Meanwhile, along with the numerous tableaux that bring history to life and the breathtaking views from the battlements, the castle gardens are also well worth exploring, while the 14th century guest hall is now a tea room.

To the north of the River Ure, and reached by footpath from Castle Bolton, is the isolated dale – **Apedale** – that is named after its original owner, Api. Now a deserted valley with heather-clad moorland and wonderful views, Apedale still shows signs of former industry and activity when it was a busy lead-mining area.

West Burton

6½ miles SW of Leyburn off the A6160

One of the most picturesque villages in Wensleydale and situated at the junction of Bishopdale and Waldendale, West Burton developed around its large central green where a busy weekly market used to take place. A distinctive feature of the green is the market cross – actually a pyramid – erected in 1820, while most of the village consists of a collection of cottages that were originally built to house miners and quarrymen. Just to the east of the village a path leads across a small packhorse bridge to **Mill Force** - perhaps the most photogenic of the Wensleydale waterfalls and one that is particularly impressive when the river is in full spate.

Newbiggin-in-Bishopdale

8 miles SW of Leyburn off the B6160

As might be expected, the name of this Bishopdale village means 'new buildings' and it is indeed a relatively new settlement – it was first mentioned in 1230! **Bishopdale**, the valley of the Bishopdale Beck, is wide and was created by a glacial lake that has left it with rich, fertile soil. An unspoilt valley with hay meadows and stone barns, the dale is home to some of Wensleydale's oldest houses.

Carperby

7 miles W of Leyburn off the A684

This ancient village still shows a typical Danish layout with its long straggling street and a small green at one end. In some of the nearby fields, grassy terraces indicate the old ploughed strips left by both pre-Norman Conquest and medieval farming methods. One of the first villages to have a market (the charter was granted in 1305), Carperby's market cross dates from 1674 and it was from here that George Fox, the founder of the Quaker Movement, preached in the 17th century.

Thornsgill House & Askrigg Cottage Holidays

Moor Road, Askrigg, Leyburn,
North Yorkshire DL8 3HH
Tel Nos:
01969 650617 (Thornsgill House)
01969 650022 (Askrigg Cottage Holidays)
e-mails:
thornsgill.house@virgin.net
stay@askrigg.com
websites:
www.thornsgill.co.uk or www.askrigg.com

The wonderful **Thornsgill House** is situated in the lovely and historic village of Askrigg, in Upper Wensleydale within the boundaries of the Yorkshire Dales National Park. This handsome and welcoming Edwardian house is an ideal base from which to explore the many sights and attractions of the region.

Owned and run by Wendy Turner with able assistance from her mum Dorothy and dad Les, the house was built in 1907. Open every day except for Christmas Eve and Christmas Day, the house boasts three superb guest bedrooms – two ensuite and one with private bath – given a 4 Diamond rating by the ETC. This relaxed and peaceful house is the perfect place to unwind amid all the comforts of home. There are several excellent local pubs, and Wendy is happy to provide guests with packed lunches, snacks and light suppers in addition to the hearty and delicious breakfasts. No smoking throughout.

Nearby, Wendy's sister Sue and Sue's husband Ken own and run **Askrigg Cottage Holidays**, superb self-catering accommodation with four properties offering the very finest in comfort and quality. Each charming stonebuilt cottage dates back to the 17th century and has been lovingly restored to a high standard. They are spacious and welcoming. The Grade II listed Minnie's Cottage and Rook's Cottage sleep two and six respectively; Greystones sleeps five; Stockdale sleeps six. Surrounded by breathtaking scenery, each cottage boasts beautiful original features such as the exposed beams and open stonebuilt fireplaces, and is furnished with traditional pieces and the very best in modern amenities including fully-equipped kitchens. Guests return again and again to these delightful and idyllic cottages that are located in Askrigg and in the village of Thwaite. The cottages are available all year round and are close to local shops. Shorter breaks are available out of season.

Aysgarth

7½ miles W of Leyburn on the A684

This village is, of course, famous for the spectacular **Aysgarth Falls** where the River Ure thunders through a rocky gorge and drops some 200 feet over three huge slabs of limestone that divide the wonderful, natural feature into the Upper, Middle and Lower Falls. They provided a perfect location for the battle between Robin Hood and Little John in the film *Robin Hood, Prince of Thieves*, while Hardraw Force, further up Wensleydale, was also used as a location for the film.

Housed in a late 18th century mill that drew off water from the falls, the **Yorkshire Museum of Horse-Drawn Carriages** is home to a collection of nearly 60 Victorian coaches.

Aysgarth Falls

Also close to the falls is the **Church of St Andrew**, home of the Jervaulx Treasures – a vicar's stall that is made from the beautifully carved bench ends salvaged from the abbey. During the Middle Ages, Aysgarth was the largest parish in England, although it has long since been subdivided into more manageable areas. Aysgarth is home, too, of the Yorkshire Dales National Park Visitor Information Centre.

Askrigg

10½ miles W of Leyburn off the A684

Recorded in the *Domesday Book* as 'Ascric', this once-important market town lies on the edge of land that was designated by the Normans as a hunting forest and, although it has been a centre of trade for centuries, it did not receive its market charter until 1587. With the rise in importance of Hawes, further up the dale, the market here lapsed in the 19th century, but in the cobbles near the old market cross a bull-ring can still be seen, to which a bull would be attached by a long chain and set upon by dogs – a favourite Tudor spectator sport.

During the 18th century Askrigg was a thriving town with several prosperous industries. Cotton was spun in a nearby mill, dyeing and brewing took place here and it was also a centre for hand-knitting. However, the town is particularly famous for clock-making, introduced here by John Ogden in 1681. This now sleepy and quaint town was also one of the first places in the Dales to be supplied with electricity when, in 1908, the local miller harnessed the power of Mill Gill Beck.

Despite its long history, Askrigg is best known to today's visitors as 'Darrowby', the major location for the long-running television series *All Creatures Great and Small.* The 18th century Kings Arms Hotel often featured as 'The Drovers Arms', while Cringley House became known to viewers as 'Skeldale House', the home of the vets.

Askrigg's popularity as a tourist destination dates back to the days of Turner and Wordsworth, when the chief attractions here were the two waterfalls – **Whitfield Gill Force** and Mill Gill Force – which can be reached by taking one of the various footpaths that radiate from the village.

Although Askrigg is now linked with James Herriot and his colleagues, it was near here, at Carr End, that the Quaker Dr John Fothergill was born in 1712. An eminent medical practitioner who wrote the first clear account of diphtheria, Fothergill was also one of the foremost botanists of his day and, along with collecting plants from around the world, he was particularly interested in the introduction of plants to different countries, such as the growing of coffee, a native of Arabia, in the Americas.

Bainbridge

11½ miles W of Leyburn on the A684

At the time of the Norman Conquest, this area of Upper Wensleydale was a hunting forest, known as the Forest and Manor of Bainbridge, and the village was established around the 12th century as a home for 12 foresters. One of their duties was to show travellers the way through the forest and, should anyone still be out by nightfall, a horn would be blown to guide them home. This ancient custom continues today between the Feast of Holy Rood (27 September) and Shrove Tuesday, when a horn is blown every night at 9 pm.

Just to the east of Bainbridge is Brough Hill (private) where the Romans built a succession of forts known collectively as *Virosidum.* First excavated in the late 1920s, they now appear as overgrown, grassy hummocks. Much

Semer Water, Bainbridge

The Rose & Crown Hotel

Bainbridge, Wensleydale,
North Yorkshire DL8 3EE
Tel: 01969 650225 Fax: 01969 650735
e-mail: info@theprideofwensleydale.com
website: www.theprideofwensleydale.co.uk

Enjoying a superb location at Bainbridge in the heart of the Yorkshire Dales, **The Rose & Crown Hotel** lives up to its reputation as 'The Pride of Wensleydale'. Here guests will find a choice of bar areas ranging from a cosy snug to a relaxed lounge, and a superb 100-cover restaurant open every day for lunch and dinner.

Owners David and Sue Collinson take justified pride in serving up excellent food, with an award-winning head chef renowned for his seafood dishes. Everything is home-made in their own kitchens using local produce. Hearty snacks are served in all three bars and in the Dales Room Restaurant, which commands a view over the village green.

The inn dates back to the 15th century, and retains many original features alongside the very best in modern comforts. There are 12 attractive and welcoming ensuite guest bedrooms, some with four-poster beds, and the inn makes a perfect base from which to explore the many sights and attractions of the region.

more visible is the Roman road that strikes southwestwards from Bainbridge and was part of their trans-Pennine route to Lancaster. This ancient route passes close to the isolated lake of **Semer Water**, one of Yorkshire's only two natural lakes, which stretches for half a mile in length and teems with wildfowl. To the north the lake is drained by the River Bain. At little more than two miles long, it is the shortest named river in England. Also at the northern end of the lake lies the village of **Countersett**, whose name suggests that it may originally have been a Norse settlement. Relics found in the area date back to the Iron Age.

An enduring legend claims that a town lies beneath Semer Water, cast there by a curse. The story goes that one day a beggar came to what was then a thriving and prosperous city, standing where the lake now lies, and that he travelled from door to door asking for alms, food and drink. The self-satisfied citizens, however, refused to help him, shutting their doors in his face. As the beggar was leaving he passed the home of a poor crofter and, when he knocked on the door, the old couple invited him in and gave him food and drink. Suddenly, the beggar's meagre clothes vanished and an angel stood in his place, and declared, '*Semer Water rise, Semer Water sink, And cover all save this little house, That gave me food and drink.*' The story says that, at this, the waters did indeed rise, engulfing the gleaming spires of the city and leaving only the kindly couple's cottage safe and dry.

The intriguing postscript to this tale is that once, during a severe drought, the level of the lake fell - to reveal the remains of a Bronze-Age town.

Gayle

15½ miles W of Leyburn off the A684

An ancient village where archaeological finds indicate that there has been a settlement since prehistoric times, in the late 18th century a mill was built here, beside the Duerly Beck, which originally spun cotton but soon changed to wool, supplying local hand-knitters. In 1870 the old waterwheel was replaced by a turbine; this, in turn, gave the village electric street lighting as early as 1917.

Hawes

15½ miles W of Leyburn on the A684

Said to be the highest market town in England, there are no records of there being a settlement here before 1307. However, as trade developed, its position made it a crossing point for packhorses and drovers travelling between Lancashire and Yorkshire across the Pennines and, by 1700, it had received its market charter. However, it was the arrival of the

railway, in 1877, which connected the town with Leyburn and the Settle-Carlisle Railway, that ensured Hawes' future as a trading centre. Sheep and cattle are sold here in their thousands each year. Housed in the former railway station is the **Dales Countryside Museum** (see panel opposite), which tells the fascinating story of how man's activities have helped to shape the landscape of the Dales. Providing interesting historical details on domestic life, the lead-mining industry, hand-knitting and other trades as well as archaeological material, the museum covers many aspects of life in the Yorkshire Dales from as far back as 10,000 BC. The museum is open daily from 10:00am to 5:00pm except Christmas and incorporates a National Park and Tourist Information Centre.

Another local industry was rope-making. At **The Hawes Ropeworkers**, next door to the museum, visitors can still see rope being made into leads, clothes lines and much more. The gift shop here stocks a comprehensive range of rope-related items along with an extensive choice of other souvenirs of the dale.

Wensleydale's most famous product, after its sheep, is its soft, mild cheese, and at the **Wensleydale Creamery** not only can visitors sample this delicacy but also learn about its history through a series of interesting displays. With a museum, viewing gallery of the production area, cheese shop, gift shop

The White Hart Inn

Main Street, Hawes,
North Yorkshire DL8 3QL
Tel/Fax: 01969 667259
website: www.whiteharthawes.co.uk

In the heart of the historic market town of Hawes, **The White Hart Inn** has been refreshing tired and thirsty travellers since the 1600s. This gem of a pub and hostelry is run by Diane and Richard with able assistance from their daughters Carly and Sarah. All are locals born and bred and know how to offer genuine Dales hospitality.

Open all day every day for ale, the three real ales here are Theakstons, John Smiths and a guest ale, together with a good selection of draught keg ales, lagers, cider, stout, wines, spirits and soft drinks.

Excellent food is served daily at lunch (12 – 2.30) and dinner (7 – 9). Booking is advised at all times in summer, and essential all year round at weekends. This superb inn also has seven comfortable and welcoming guest bedrooms – and Hawes is the perfect place from which to explore the region or just relax and unwind.

The Green Dragon Inn

Hardraw, Hawes, North Yorkshire DL8 3LZ
Tel: 01969 667392
e-mail: mark@greendragonhardraw.com
website: www.greendragonhardraw.com
www.hardrawforce.com

Probably the most famous inn in Yorkshire, as it is the entry-point to the historic Hardraw Force waterfall, **The Green Dragon Inn** – and the waterfall itself – are owned by D. Mark Thompson. Mark has been here three years, after over 25 years' experience in the trade in the Yorkshire Dales.

Set in 15 acres that includes the falls, this superior inn offers great food, drink, accommodation and hospitality. Over the course of the inn's long history - it is said the inn's origins date back to the 13th century - it was certainly an outpost for the Cistercian monks from the great Abbey of Jervaulx up until the dissolution of the Monasteries in 1539, and some of England's greatest artists and writers including JMW Turner and Wordsworth, have trod the flagstone floors. Hardraw is Old English for 'shepherd's dwelling' – everywhere guests look they will see traditional features that add to the inn's comfort and ambience.

Open all day every day for liquid refreshment, there are up to six real ales available. Theakstons Best and Timothy Taylor Landlord are the regular ales, along with a selection of changing Yorkshire guest ales. Food is available all day in the summer months, and at lunch and dinner at other times. Guests choose off a printed menu and specials board from a good selection of dishes and home-made sweets.

The accommodation comprises 17 ensuite guest bedrooms and seven self-contained apartments. The rooms above the bar are reputedly haunted by a lady, possibly a former occupant of the Inn. One double room and also four of the seven apartments are on the ground floor. The tariff includes a hearty and delicious country breakfast. And Hardraw is, indeed, a place worth lingering in to explore further – set in rolling countryside and convenient for visiting sights and attractions of Wensleydale and the surrounding region. Children welcome.

and licensed restaurant, there's plenty here for cheese-lovers to enjoy.

Hardraw

15½ miles W of Leyburn off the A684

Located in a natural amphitheatre of limestone crags, **Hardraw Force** is the highest unbroken above-ground waterfall in England. Due to an undercut in the cliff, the breathtaking 98-feet cascade can be viewed from behind – as both JMW Turner and William Wordsworth so famously did. Best seen after heavy rain as, generally, the quantity of water tumbling over the rocks is not great, the falls have, on two separate occasions (in 1739 and 1881) frozen solid in a near 100-feet icicle. Like Aysgarth Falls, further down Wensleydale, Hardraw Force was used as a location for the film *Robin Hood, Prince of Thieves*.

The amphitheatre also provides superb acoustics, a feature that has been put to great effect in the annual brass-band competitions that began here in 1885 and have recently been revived.

Access to the falls is through the lovely old Green Dragon pub, where a small fee is payable. The inn itself is also interesting, as records indicate that there has been a hostelry on this site since at least the mid-13th century. At

Hardraw Force

The Cart House Tea Room & Craft Shop

Hardraw, Hawes, North Yorkshire DL8 3LZ
Tel: 01969 667691
website: www.hardrawforce.co.uk

Close to Hardraw Force waterfall, in the heart of Wensleydale and reached off the A684, east of junction 36 of the M6 or west of the A1, **The Cart House Tea Room & Craft Shop** is run by Clara and Mavis, sisters who were born on the nearby farm. Here visitors will find a cosy and welcoming place to enjoy wholesome home-made food, and to shop for high-quality country crafts.

Home-made scones are just one speciality on the menu, which includes home-baked breads, Fellman's lunch with Wensleydale cheese and home-made chutney, a range of tempting wholemeal sandwiches and a selection of mouthwatering cakes such as fruit cake, date and walnut, carrot and more. A takeaway service for light refreshments and basic provisions is available.

Of the vast range of crafts – including pottery, cards, jewellery and textiles – sold here, 75% are British made, and 25% locally made.

Open: 7 days a week March - November 10am – 5.30pm (closed Mondays in Spring and Autumn).

For anyone wishing to extend their stay in this delightful village, there's a quiet and secluded campsite nearby – please ask Clara or Mavis for details.

that time this land was a grange belonging to the monks of Fountains Abbey, who grazed their sheep on the nearby hills.

Cotterdale

18 miles W of Leyburn off the A684

This small valley of the Cotter Beck lies below the vast bulk of Great Shunner Fell, which separates the head of Wensleydale from the head of Swaledale. At one time only three families lived here, giving rise to the saying, 'Three halls, two kirks and a king, same road out as goes in,' although, later, the small community was expanded as miners came here when a small and, for a short time, profitable coal seam was worked on the hills above the dale. Although smaller than Hardraw, **Cotter Force** is an extremely attractive waterfall that is often neglected in favour of its more famous neighbour.

Settle

This small, delightful and unspoilt market town, which received its charter in 1249 from Henry III, still retains a lively weekly market (on Tuesdays) as well as some quaint old buildings. A busy stopping-place in the days of the stagecoach, when travellers journeying between York and Lancaster and Kendal would call here, Settle is most closely associated with the railways and, in particular, it is the home of the famous

Settle-Carlisle Railway, a proudly preserved memento of the glorious age of steam. The line is still flanked by charming little signal boxes that are a real tourist attraction. England's greatest historic scenic route, the railway passes through lowland valleys before climbing into the dramatic landscape of the Pennines on its route northwards to Carlisle. One of the last great mainline railways to be built, the 72 miles of track were first opened to passenger trains in 1876, but its construction took place in the midst of great controversy and even greater cost, in both money and lives. Dubbed 'the line that should never have been built,' there is a churchyard in Chapel-le-Dale where over 100 of the workers and miners who laboured under the most adverse conditions lie buried. Today, modern trains still thunder over the 21 viaducts, through the 14 tunnels and over the numerous bridges for which these workers gave their lives. Along with the scheduled regular services, there are also special excursions on certain days, along with charter trains organised by various operators throughout the country.

Preston's Folly, Settle

Settle is dominated by one of the railway's huge viaducts as well as by the towering limestone cliffs of **Castleberg Crag**. The town's architecture is equally striking – being mainly Victorian sandstone buildings, built at the height of the railway age. These include the arcaded Shambles (originally the butcher's slaughter houses), the French-style Town Hall and the Music Hall. Settle's oldest building, **Preston's Folly**, is an extravaganza of mullioned windows and Tudor masonry named after the man who created this anomalous fancy and impoverished himself in the process. Along with the grand buildings on the main streets, there are charming little side streets lined with Georgian and Jacobean dwellings and a maze of quirky little alleyways and ginnels that hide old courtyards and workshops.

In Chapel Street is the **Museum of North Craven Life**, which gives a historical, topographical and geological background to the area and tells the story of the local farming traditions through a series of imaginative displays. The museum also has an exhibition on the history of the building of the Settle-Carlisle Railway. Meanwhile, just

The Craven Heifer Hotel

Main Street, Stainforth, Settle,
North Yorkshire BD24 9PB
Tel: 01729 822599 Fax: 01729 823049
e-mail: info@cravenheiferhotel.co.uk
website: www.cravenheiferhotel.co.uk

Situated a couple of miles north of Settle towards Horton in Ribblesdate on the B6479, **The Craven Heifer Hotel** is at the heart of the village of Stainforth, adjacent to Stainforth Beck and next to the old packhorse bridge which spans the beck, a marvellously picturesque rural location.

Pat and Brian Williams took over as tenants in October of 2003, their first venture into this type of business (though Pat has been a qualified chef for some 30 years), and in a short time they have put the Craven Heifer back on the map. In such a stunning location, with scenic countryside in every direction, the famous Three Peaks (so popular with walkers) and the nearby famous Settle-Carlisle Railway, the area was crying out for an establishment providing quality food, well-kept ales, top-of-the-range accommoation and first-rate hospitality – and now there's all this and more at the Craven Heifer.

Open every session (apart from Monday lunchtime) Monday to Thursday and all day at weekends in winter, and all day every day in the summer months, there are always three real ales on tap from the Thwaites Brewery range. To complement these there is a very good range of lagers, cider, stout, wines, spirits and soft drinks.

Excellent food is available weekdays at lunch and dinner, and from 12 – 9 Saturdays, Sundays and Bank Holidays – booking advised at weekends. Pat's extensive menu includes specialities such as home-made steak and kidney pie and other traditional fare such as steaks, Cumberland sausage and fresh salmon fillet, along with a selection of curries. The daily specials board offers additional tempting dishes. All are expertly prepared and presented. The dining area is no-smoking; there's also a superb riverside beer garden.

The five beautiful guest bedrooms boast quality décor and furnishings, ensuring guests' comfort, and the tariff includes a hearty breakfast – the perfect start to a day's exploring the many sights of the region.

Children welcome.

outside the town and housed in an old cotton mill dating from the 1820s, Watershed Mill offers a superb choice of clothes, accessories and outerwear, while the Dalesmade Centre features a wide range of local crafts and gift ideas.

The features of the surrounding countryside are equally impressive. In particular there is the fascinating **Victorian Cave**, discovered in 1838 by Michael Horner. Although the instability of the rock in the area has caused the cave and the surrounding land to be closed to the public, the cave has yielded some interesting finds including Roman relics, Stone-Age artefacts and even 120,000-year-old mammoth bones.

Settle lies on the River Ribble, in **Ribblesdale**. The river's source can be found high up on the bleak moorland to the east of the county border with Lancashire, and flows through several ancient settlements along the way. At the Aire Gap, with Giggleswick opposite, Settle is overlooked not just by Castleberg Crag but also by Langcliffe Scar – both are parts of the mid-Craven Fault. Much is talked about **Craven Fault**, formed by a series of mighty earthquakes - but these took place over 30 million years ago, so today's visitors need not worry about visiting the area. The line of the fault, where the land to the northwest was lifted up and the land to the southeast slipped down, is still visible today. It was the action of water seeping into the limestone, which then froze (during the Ice Age) that has created the area's many caves and potholes, while erosion on the surface has formed the magnificent limestone pavements that are particularly impressive at Malham. These limestone areas support a varied range of plant life.

The area's greatest feature, the famous Three Peaks, have stood the test of time because they are capped by millstone grit. The high fells, composed of grits and sandstone, support heather moorland. Here too can be found the only bird unique to Britain, the red grouse, along with several birds of prey.

Around Settle

Langcliffe

1 mile N of Settle on the B6479

As its name suggests, this village lies in the shelter of the long cliff of the Craven Fault, where the millstone grit (sandstone) meets the silver-grey limestone. Although the majority of the houses and cottages that surround the village green are built from limestone, the addition of some sandstone buildings gives this pretty village a particular charm. The Victorian urn on top of the **Langcliffe Fountain** was replaced by a stone cross after the First World War in memory of those villagers who gave their lives for their country.

Stainforth

2 miles N of Settle on the B6479

This sheltered sheep-farming village was founded by the Cistercian monks, who first introduced the flocks to this area. It was also the monks who were responsible for building the 14th century stone packhorse bridge that carries the road over the local beck, a tributary of the River Ribble. Although the village is certainly old, there are few buildings that date beyond the days of the Civil War as, during those turbulent times, much of Stainforth was destroyed. **Catrigg Force**, found along a track known as Goat Scar Lane, is a fine waterfall that drops some 60 feet into a wooded pool. To the west is Stainforth Force, which flows over a series of rock shelves.

Horton in Ribblesdale

5 miles N of Settle on the B6479

The name of this village means 'the settlement on the muddy land' (or 'marsh'); it is believed to have been in existence long before the *Domesday Book*'s record of it in the 11th century. The oldest building here is the 12th century **St Oswald's Church**, which still shows signs of its Norman origins in the chevron designs over the south door. Inside, all the pillars lean peculiarly to the south, and in the west window there is an ancient piece of stained glass showing Thomas à Becket wearing his bishop's mitre.

This village is the ideal place from which to explore the limestone landscape and green hills of Upper Ribblesdale. To the east lies Pen-y-ghent (2,273 feet), one of the famous **Three Peaks.** For particularly energetic visitors to Horton there is the demanding Three Peaks Challenge, organised by the Pen-y-ghent Café. This 24-mile hike takes in not only Pen-y-ghent but also the other two peaks, Ingleborough and Whernside; those completing the trek within 12 hours qualify for membership of the 'Three Peaks of Yorkshire Club'. Less avid walkers will be glad to hear that the café not only supplies well-earned refreshments but also has a whole host of local information and runs a highly efficient rescue/safety service.

The whole of this area has been designated as being of Special Scientific Interest, mainly due to the need to conserve the swiftly eroding hillsides and paths. This is an ancient landscape with ash woodlands, primitive earthworks and rare birdlife such as peregrine falcon, ring ouzel and golden plover. There are also a great many caves in the area, along with several listed buildings including **Lodge Hall**, formerly known as Ingman Lodge. Before the 20th century, erring villagers would not travel to major towns to face trial; instead, judges would journey round the countryside on horseback, stopping to try cases. In the case of Horton, anyone then found guilty would be brought to Ingman Lodge to be hanged.

Long Preston

3½ miles SE of Settle on the A65

Although it is hard to imagine today, this pleasant little village which straddles the main road was once larger than Leeds! Close to the pretty St

Mary's Church, which dates back in part to the 12th century, the remains of a Roman encampment have been discovered. **Cromwell House**, so local legends say, once gave refuge to the Lord Protector himself.

Rathmell

2½ miles S of Settle off the A65

This old farming community - the oldest farm here dates from 1689 - lies beside the River Ribble. From Rathmell there are many footpaths along the riverbanks, through the nearby woods, and up to Whelpstone Crag. Also in the village is a row of late 17th century farm cottages known as Cottage Folk - the unusual name stems from the time they were built, when Richard Frankland founded a non-conformist college in Rathmell.

Giggleswick

½ mile W of Settle off the A65

This ancient village, which stands on the opposite bank of the River Ribble from Settle, is home to several interesting buildings including the 15th century Church of St Alkelda and the well-known Giggleswick School. Alkelda is thought to have been a Saxon saint who was strangled for her faith. Giggleswick School, founded by James Carr, was granted a Royal Charter by Edward VI in 1553. The school's fame dates back to 1927 when its observatory was used by the Astronomer Royal to observe the eclipse of the sun. Meanwhile, the school's chapel, the copper dome of which is a well-recognised local landmark, was built to commemorate the Diamond Jubilee of Queen Victoria by Walter Morrison, a school governor who lived at Malham Tarn House.

Just to the north of the village is the famous **Ebbing and Flowing Well**, one of many in the area that owe their unusual name to the porous nature of the limestone, which causes water to flow at some times but not at others. However, local legend suggests another explanation for the well's behaviour: one day a nymph who was being chased by a satyr prayed to the gods for help and was instantly turned into a well, which is said to ebb and flow with the nymph's panting breath. John Nevison, the 17th century highwayman and rival of Dick Turpin, is said to have evaded capture at the well when he paused here to let his horse quench its thirst. The well's water renewed the animal's strength and Nevison was able to escape by leaping from the top of a nearby cliff, now known as Nevison's Leap.

Feizor

3 miles NW of Settle off the A65

This village dates back to monastic times, when it lay on the well-trod route from Kilnsey to the Lake District used by the monks of Fountains Abbey. Although both Fountains Abbey and Sawley Abbey had possessions in this area, there are few reminders of those times today. However, the **Yorkshire Dales Falconry and Conservation Centre**, set in these dramatic limestone surroundings, does bring visitors to Feizor. The first privately-owned falconry centre in the north of England, its aim is to educate and make the public aware of the number of the world's birds of prey that are threatened with extinction and, through their successful captive-breeding programmes, to safeguard the birds' future for generations to come. Visitors here have the chance to see many of the Centre's birds in flight during the regular demonstrations and, along with the vultures, eagles, hawks, falcons and owls, there is also the chance to see 'Andy', an Andean Condor with a massive wingspan of 10 feet 6 inches!

Austwick

4½ miles NW of Settle off the A65

Originally a Norse settlement, the name 'Austwick' is derived from the Nordic for 'eastern settlement'. This charming place of stone cottages and crofts is surrounded by hills patchworked with drystone walls. The largely 17th century buildings, with their elaborately decorated stone lintels, flank what remains of the village green where the ancient cross stands as a reminder of the days when this was the head of a dozen neighbouring manors and the home of an annual cattle fair.

The most peculiar feature of the surrounding area has to be the **Norber Boulders**, a series of black rocks that stand on limestone pedestals and despite their contrived appearance, are completely natural. They are also known as the Norber Erratics because they are anomalous – the grey Silurian slate of which they are composed is usually found *beneath* limestone rather than above it - and they are thought to have been deposited by glacial action at the end of the last Ice Age.

Clapham

7 miles NW of Settle off the A65

By far the largest and most impressive building in this village is **Ingleborough Hall**, once the home of the Farrer family and now a centre for outdoor education. One member of the family, Reginald Farrer, was an internationally-renowned botanist responsible for introducing many new plant species into this country. Many examples of the plants he introduced can still be found in the older gardens of the village, while in the Hall's gardens there is a particularly pleasant walk, the **Reginald Farrer Nature Trail**, which leads from Clapham to nearby Ingleborough Cave.

Though the whereabouts of **Ingleborough Cave** has been known for centuries, it was not until the 19th century that its exploration was begun. One of these early explorers, geologist Adam Sedgwick, is quoted as saying, 'we were forced to use our abdominal muscles as sledges and our mouths as candlesticks,' which gives an excellent indication of the conditions the early potholers had to endure. However, their work proved very much worthwhile and the system of caves is extremely extensive. Today's visitors to the caves

Packhorse Bridge, Clapham

see only a small part of the five miles of caverns and tunnels but, fortunately, this section is easily accessible and particularly spectacular. As well as exotic cave formations and illuminated pools, there is **Eldon Hall Cavern**, home to a vast mushroom bed! There are regular guided tours and the caves are also accessible by pushchair. Just above the cave, on the southern slopes of Ingleborough, is **Gaping Ghyll Hole**, which is, at 365 feet deep, 450 feet long and 130 feet wide, the grandest and largest pothole in Britain and also part of the same underground limestone system as Ingleborough Cave. A favourite with potholers - who come to admire the main chamber, similar in size to York Minster - at both the Spring and August Bank Holiday weekends a winch is erected and it is possible to descend the hole on a bosun's chair.

This is an area that has a great abundance of natural waterfalls, but the waterfall near the village church is one of the very few that is man-made. In the 1830s the Farrer family created a large lake, covering some seven acres of land; the waterfall is the lake's overflow. As well as providing water for Clapham, a turbine was placed at the bottom of the waterfall and, with the help of the electric power it produced, the village was one of the first in the country to have electric street lighting. This is perhaps not so surprising as it might seem, as Michael Faraday, the distinguished 19th century scientist, was the son of the village blacksmith.

Keasden

6½ miles NW of Settle off the A65

A scattered farming community today, in the 17th century there were some 40 farms here (now dwindled to around 15) as well as many associated trades and craftsmen. The name *Keasden* comes from the Old English for 'cheese valley'; some of the farms still retain the vast stone weights of the cheese-presses, though unfortunately the recipe for the local cheese has long since been lost.

Newby

7 miles NW of Settle off the A65

This tiny hamlet was originally sited about a mile south of its present position. It moved here in the 17th century after the Plague had decimated the village's population. As a result, many of the buildings here date from that time. By the 19th century Newby had recovered from its tragic loss and had become a thriving weaving community, though this cottage industry was soon overtaken by the new factory systems. By 1871 the village had once again returned to peace and tranquillity.

Ingleton

10 miles NW of Settle on the A65

Mentioned in the *Domesday Book* – the name means 'beacon town' – Ingleton is certainly one of the most visited villages in the Yorkshire Dales and is particularly noted as being the gateway to the Three Peaks. From as long ago as the late 18th century, Ingleton has been popular with walkers as well as being famous for the numerous caves and other splendid scenery that lies close by, though some of these sights are more accessible than others. The coming of the railway, which gave those working in the towns easy and cheap access to the countryside, greatly increased the number of visitors who came here looking for clean country air and recreation. Though Ingleton is no longer served by the railway, the village is still dominated by the railway viaduct that spans the River Greta. The river, which is formed here by the meeting of the Rivers Twiss and Doe, is famous for its salmon leaps. Also of interest in the village is the parish **Church of St Mary**, which sits on a hill overlooking the river. Although the tower dates from the 13th century, the rest of the church was constructed in 1887. Its most prized possession is an elaborate font that dates back to around 1150. One story, dating from the time of the Commonwealth when the practice of baptism was illegal, suggests that this Norman font was thrown into the river by Cromwell's supporters and was not rescued until the beginning of the 19th century.

Discovered in 1865 by Joseph Carr, the **Ingleton Waterfalls**, which were not immediately made accessible to the public, have been delighting visitors since 1885. Considered by many to be

Ingleton Waterfalls

Ingleborough

on its summit. The most recent of these are the remains of a tower built by a local mill owner, Hornby Roughsedge. Although the intended use of the building is unknown, its short history is well documented. A grand opening was arranged on the summit; the celebrations got a little out of hand, probably helped by a supply of ale, and a group of men began to tear the structure down! At the highest point of the mountain is a triangulation point while, close by, a cross-shaped shelter provides protection from the elements independent of their direction. The shelter acts as a reminder that the weather can change quickly in this region and a walk to the summit, however nice the day at lower levels, should not be undertaken without careful thought as to suitable clothing. To the east of the summit plateau are the remains of several ancient hut circles and, beyond, the remains of a wall. The Romans are known to have used Ingleborough as a signal station, but the wall may have been built by the Brigantes, whose settlement on the mountain was called *Rigodunum*. The land encompassing the mountain is now the **Ingleborough National Nature Reserve**, known for its wildlife as well as its geology and, in particular, the

the most scenic waterfall walk in England, the footpath, which covers some four and a half miles, takes in **Pecca Falls** and Hollybush Spout along with Thornton Force, which tumbles 40 feet into a pool surrounded by a natural amphitheatre. Along with the waterfalls, there are also potholes in the area including **Alum Pot** (292 feet deep), down which Alum Pot Beck cascades. However, it is the nearby network of caverns known as **White Scar Cave** that are particularly popular. Discovered in 1923, the caves feature Britain's longest show-cave along with two waterfalls and superb stalactites. The cave remains at the same temperature throughout the year (8ºC) and there are guided tours all year round.

Of all the natural features to be seen from Ingleton, the most famous is **Ingleborough**, at 2,375 feet the middle of the Three Peaks, which shadows both the village and the surrounding area. As well as offering fine views on a clear day, there are also several interesting features limestone pavements and other features unique to this rockbed.

High and Low Bentham

11 miles NW of Settle on the B6480

Situated beside the River Wenning, a tributary of the River Ribble, these two villages have become linked over the centuries. Like many Pennine villages in the late 17th and early 18th centuries, Low Bentham was taken over by the textile industry and there was a linen mill established here. After a time the mill changed hands and also direction, when it was put to the specialised task of spinning silk before that, too, ceased in the 1960s. The growth in textiles in the area coincided with an increase in Quakerism within the local parish and, in 1680, a meeting house was founded in Low Bentham. Established as a place of non-conformist worship, by 1800 the village was also well known as a place of Wesleyan Methodism.

Thornton in Lonsdale

10½ miles NW of Settle off the A65

This small village of a few houses, an inn, and an interesting church dates back to at least the 12th century, though it is probably much older. The 13th century **Church of St Oswald** was unfortunately burnt almost to the ground in 1933; only the tower remains of the original building. The rest of the church was rebuilt to resemble the extensive restoration work that was undertaken here in 1870. On an outside wall of the tower is an unusual carving, of a rose, a thistle and a shamrock, believed to commemorate the union of England and Wales with Scotland and Ireland in 1801.

Chapel-le-Dale

10 miles NW of Settle on the B6255

To the north of this village lies **Whernside** (2,418 feet), the highest of the Three Peaks. There are only a few paths to the summit. Just below the top are a number of tarns; in 1917 it was noticed that they were frequented by black-headed gulls. Those walking to the top of the peak can still see the gulls today – a reminder that the northwest coast is fewer than 20 miles away.

Ribblehead

10½ miles NW of Settle on the B6255

Lying close to the source of the River

Ribblehead Viaduct

Ribble is an impressive structure, the **Ribblehead Viaduct**, built to carry the Settle-Carlisle Railway. Opened in 1876, after taking five years to construct, its 24 arches span the dark moorland and it is overlooked by Whernside. A bleak and exposed site, the viaduct is often battered by strong winds which, on occasion, can literally stop a train in its tracks.

Skipton

Often called the 'Gateway to the Dales', Skipton's origins can be traced to the 7th century when Anglian farmers christened it *Sheeptown*. Featuring in the *Domesday Book*, the Normans decided to build a castle here to guard the entrance to Airedale, and Skipton became a garrison town. One of the most complete and best-preserved medieval castles in England, **Skipton Castle** was begun in 1090. The powerful stone structure seen today was devised in 1310 by Robert de Clifford, the 1st Earl of Skipton. The Cliffords were a fighting breed and, throughout the Middle Ages, wherever there was trouble a member of the family was sure to be found. The 8th Lord Clifford, Thomas, and his son John were both killed while fighting for the House of Lancaster during the War of

Rose & Crown

10 Coach Street, Skipton,
North Yorkshire BD23 1LH
Tel: 01756 793884

The impressive **Rose & Crown** stands just off one of Skipton's main roads near the Canal Basin. Always known by this name, it dates back to 1736. The impressive exterior is festooned with hanging baskets and bodes well for what awaits guests inside: a warm welcome and comfortable surroundings. The interior boasts many original features and is welcoming and cosy throughout. Open fires and comfortable seating enhance the inn's warm ambience. Outside there's a patio area adjacent to the inn.

Dal and Rachel, after several years in the trade, came here in November of 2003 and have reclaimed the pub's proud heritage for quality and popularity. Locals and visitors alike proclaim the inn's hospitality and delicious food. Canal-boat owners make a point of stopping in whenever they pass through. It makes an excellent place to stop for lunch or a relaxing drink while exploring Skipton, 'Gateway to the Dales', and the surrounding area, rich in sights and attractions such as Malham, Broughton and the many delightful villages of the region.

Rachel does the cooking, creating hearty and tempting dishes such as home-made pies and a range of well-filled sandwiches, complemented by daily specials and the Sausage and Mash menu, which features various flavours of sausages accompanied by various types of mash.

Meals are served at lunchtime only, Monday to Saturday 12 – 2.30; the Sunday lunch (12 – 3) features a choice of two roasts or selections from the menu.

And to drink? A good range of draught ales including Tetleys and a changing guest ale, together with a collection of wines, spirits, cider, lager, stout and soft drinks.

Children welcome.

Evening entertainment at this fine inn includes a live DJ on Friday nights from 8 p.m., Sunday karaoke from 5.30 until 9 p.m., and occasional music quizzes. There's a small car park for guests.

Skipton Castle

walls are lined with shells collected by George Clifford in the 19th century while travelling in the South Seas. However, the most striking feature of the castle is the impressive 14th century gateway, which is visible from the High Street and carries the Clifford family motto *Desormais*, meaning 'Henceforth'.

Adjacent to the castle, at the top of the High Street, lies the parish **Church of the Holy Trinity**, originally built in the 12th century and replaced in the 14th. There is a wealth of interest inside the church, which has been topped by a beautiful oak roof since the 15th century. It is possible to spend much time discovering the centuries of artefacts in the church; the various tombs and memorials are just as interesting and include the many tombs of the Clifford family. The church, too, suffered damage during the Civil War and, again, Lady Anne Clifford came to the rescue, restoring the interior and rebuilding the steeple in 1655. Inside the church, among the many tombstones is that of the Longfellow family, which included the uncle of the American poet, Henry Wadsworth Longfellow. As well as the fine castle and church, the Normans also established Skipton as a market town and it received its first charter in 1204. The market thrives to this day and is very much an important

the Roses. Later, George Clifford, Champion to Queen Elizabeth I and a renowned sailor, fought against the Spanish Armada and, as well as participating in many voyages of his own, he also lent a ship to Sir Walter Ralegh.

However, it is thanks to Lady Anne Clifford that visitors to Skipton can marvel at the castle's buildings. Following the ravages of the Civil War, from which the castle did not escape, Lady Anne undertook a comprehensive restoration programme and, though little of the original Norman stonework remains, much of the work of the 1st Lord Clifford still stands. As well as an enormous banqueting hall, a series of kitchens still remain, with some of their original fittings. The beautiful Tudor courtyard is also extant. There is also a rather unusually decorated room whose part of daily life in the area.

With the development of the factory system in the 19th century, the nature of the town began to change. Textile mills were built and cottages and terraced houses were constructed for the influx of mill workers. However, not all were happy with the changes that the Industrial Revolution brought and, in 1842, a group of men, women and children set out from the Pennine cotton towns and villages to protest at the mechanisation taking place. By the time the group had reached nearby Broughton, their number had grown to 3,000 and the Skipton magistrates urged them to turn back home. The protesters continued on, however, surging on Skipton, and the worried magistrates sent for military help. Moving from mill to mill, the group stopped the looms. Special constables were quickly sworn in to help contain the situation and the Riot Act was read from the Town Hall steps. Though the protestors retreated to nearby Anne Hill, they refused to disperse and the soldiers were ordered to charge. During the ensuing violence, one soldier was killed and a magistrate blinded, while six of the group's leaders were arrested.

The **Leeds and Liverpool Canal**, which flows through Skipton, opened in 1816. The canal provided a cheap form of transport as well as linking the town with the major industrial centres of Yorkshire and Lancashire. The first of three trans-Pennine routes, the 127-mile canal has 91 locks along its length, as well as two tunnels, one of which is over a mile long. Though used well into the 20th century, the canal lost its freight trade and fell into disuse in the 1960s. Today the canal basin, behind the town centre, is busy with pleasure craft; boat journeys can be taken along a section in the direction of Gargrave. The towpath was also restored at the same time and there are a number of pleasant walks that include a stretch along the cul-de-sac Spring Branch beside the castle walls.

Before the days of the canal, travelling by road, particularly in winter, was often a hazardous business. One local tale tells how, on Christmas Eve, during a bad snow storm, a young waggoner set out from the town for Blubberhouses. Though an innkeeper tried to dissuade him, the young man carried on into the night – thinking only of his betrothed, Ruth. He soon lost his way in a snow drift and chilled by the fierce northerly winds, he fell to the ground in a comatose sleep. Safe in her cottage, Ruth suddenly awoke and ran out of the house crying that her John was lost. Two men hurried after her; by the time they had caught up with Ruth she was digging John out of the snow with her bare hands. He was none the worse for his misadventure and the couple married on New Year's Day.

A walk round the town is also well worth while and there are many interesting buildings to be found. One in particular is the Town Hall, now also home to the **Craven Museum**.

THE CRAVEN MUSEUM

Town Hall, High Street, Skipton,
North Yorkshire BD23 1AH
Tel: 01756 706407 Fax: 01756 706412
e-mail: museum@cravendc.gov.uk
website: www.cravendc.gov.uk

Crammed full of fascinating exhibits, **The Craven Museum** is a great place to explore the history of Skipton and the Craven Dales. The museum displays collections of local history, archaeology, natural history, art and geology in a small but very popular museum situated in the Town Hall at the top of Skipton's busy market place.

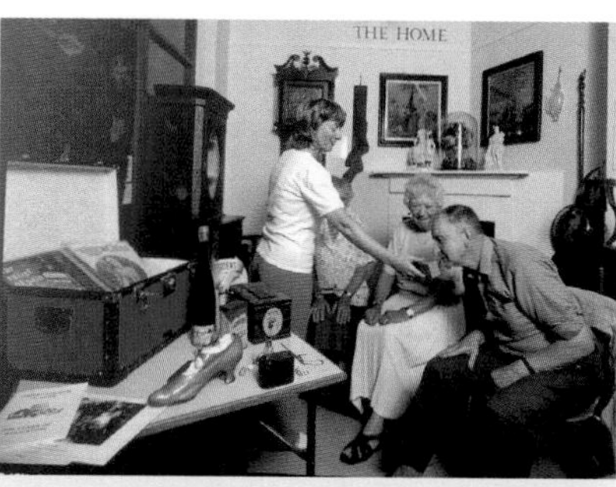

Family activity trails and interactive CD ROMs are available at all times. Admis-sion is free and the museum is open six days a week (closed Tuesday).

Dedicated to the surrounding area, there are many interesting displays relating to the geological and archaeological treasures that have been found locally, including a piece of Bronze-Age cloth that is considered the oldest textile fragment in the country. There are also displays of furniture illustrating the fine craftsmanship that went into even the most mundane household item and farming exhibits that reflect the changing lives of many of the people who lived off the surrounding land.

Almost opposite the Town Hall, on the High Street, are the premises of the *Craven Herald*, a newspaper established in 1874, although the publication had been produced for a short time in the 1850s. The building is fortunate in having retained its late-Victorian shopfront, as well as the passageway to one side, and it was first occupied by William Chippendale in the late 18th century. A trader in textiles, Chippendale made his money by buying, then selling on, the cloth woven by the farmers in their own homes. Close to the newspaper's offices is the Public Library, opened in 1910 and funded by Andrew Carnegie. A large, ornate building, it is in contrast to the town's older buildings and stands as a reminder of the change in character that Skipton underwent in the late Victorian age. It seems fitting that in a town which over many years has been dedicated to trade and commerce, Thomas Spencer, co-founder of Marks and Spencer, should have been born here in 1851. Skipton, too, was the home of Sir Winston Churchill's physician Lord Moran, who grew up here, the son of the local doctor.

As with many historic market towns, Skipton has a good many inns and public houses which have provided farmers with refreshment during the centuries of busy markets. The **Black Horse Inn** is one such pub and its date stone of 1676 is well worth a second look as it is carved with symbols of the butcher's trade: axes, animal heads and twisted fleeces. Originally called The

The Dog & Gun Inn

Colne Road, Malsis, Sutton-in-Craven,
Keighley, West Yorkshire BD20 8DS
Tel: 01535 633855

The Dog & Gun Inn is a superb public house situated in the hamlet of Malsis and found adjacent to the Colne-to-Keighley Road. Handsome inside and out, this welcoming inn's décor is traditional and comfortable, with original features such as the large brick- and oak-built fireplaces and beamed ceilings. Brass ornaments and other homely features add to the warm ambience.

Anita and Ross have been tenants here since April of 2002. Between them they have a wealth of experience: Ross has been a chef for more than 20 years, while Anita has worked in the brewing and licensing trade for over 25 years. This has been their first venture into running an inn, and their success is evident. Locals sing the inn's praises, while visitors return again and again to sample the great food, drink and hospitality.

Open every session and all day Saturdays, Sundays and Bank Holidays, there are always at least four real ales on tap, with Timothy Taylor Best, Landlord, Golden Best and Dark Mild the regular brews here. There is also a good range of lagers, wines and spirits, together with cider, stout and soft drinks. Superb quality food is served Monday to Friday from 12 – 2 and 5.30 –9.30, and Saturdays and Sundays from 12 – 9. Booking is advised on Fridays, Saturdays and Sundays. Ross oversees all the cooking, and diners can choose from the extensive menu or specials board from selection of expertly prepared and delicious dishes including specialities such as charcoal-grilled steaks, home-made steak pie, rack of lamb, poached chicken, curry of the day, pasta, salads and more. The puddings are well worth leaving room for, with tempting morsels including home-made bilberry pie, hot chocolate fudge cake and raspberry Pavlova, which can be complemented by a glass of dessert wine such as Muscat de Rivesaltes or Aleatico di Puglia. There are also ports, cognac and armagnac, for an after-dinner tipple.

The emphasis here is on home cooking, using local produce wherever possible. The no-smoking restaurant seats 60, while there is also seating outside in the handsome garden on fine days. Themed evenings are a regular event – please ring for details.

King's Head, the inn was built – unsurprisingly – by a butcher, Robert Goodgion. In the 19th century it served as headquarters for Lord Ribblesdale's cavalry when they would hold their annual training in the town.

As well as being situated on the banks of the Leeds-Liverpool Canal, Skipton also lies in the valley of the River Aire and it is still the main town in upper **Airedale** before the river flows into the more industrial region of West Yorkshire. While the construction of the navigable waterway linking the two great industrial areas of Lancashire and Yorkshire changed the lives of many living in the Dales, and certainly played a major part in establishing the local textile industry, farming has remained an important part of life in Airedale, and market day remains a key event in the daily lives of the dalesfolk.

Around Skipton

Embsay

1½ miles NE of Skipton off the A59

This village is home to the **Embsay Steam Railway**, based at the small country station that was built in 1888. As well as taking a scenic steam train journey to the end of the line at Bolton Abbey, a couple of miles away, there are over 20 locomotives, both steam and diesel, on display together with railway carriages. Special events are arranged throughout the year; opening times vary though the trains run every Sunday.

Embsay also played its part in the textile industry, and today one of its old mills has been converted into **Embsay Crafts**, where handiwork such as glass-painting, furniture-making, parchment craft and more can be seen; there are also regular demonstrations and classes.

Long before the days of railways, Embsay was home to an Augustinian priory, founded in 1130. However, for some reason the monks found life difficult here and, in 1145, they crossed Embsay Moor and moved to what is now Bolton Abbey. Those choosing to walk over the moor to the north of the village should take care, as the area is peppered with old coal pits and disused shafts. However, the view from **Embsay Crag** (1,217 feet high) is well worth the effort of climbing.

Kildwick

4 miles SE of Skipton off the A629

This picturesque village on the north bank of the River Aire is approached over a bridge that was built in the early 14th century by the canons of Bolton Priory. Kildwick also lies on the banks of the Leeds-Liverpool Canal and was once a hive of industry, with many spinning and weaving mills in the village and surrounding area producing wool and silk yarn and cloth. The decline of the textile industry has caused many of the mills to close, though some have now been converted to provide interesting accommodation or offices. The canal, which until the 1930s was still in commercial use, is now the preserve of pleasure craft, and Kildwick is a popular overnight mooring.

Lothersdale

4 miles SW of Skipton off the A629

A dramatic stretch of the **Pennine Way** passes through Lothersdale, which is set in a deep valley in the heart of the moors. Charlotte Brontë knew the village well; in *Jane Eyre* the house she calls 'Gateshead' is modelled on Lothersdale's Stonegappe, up on the hillside near the church.

Elslack

4 miles SW of Skipton off the A56

Overlooking this village is the **Pinhaw Beacon**, commanding some fine panoramic views over the heather-clad moorland. During the Napoleonic Wars, when there was great fear of an invasion from France, the beacon, one in a countrywide chain of communication signals, was manned 24 hours a day. Unfortunately, during a raging blizzard on a January night in 1805 the lookout, Robert Wilkinson, died of exposure. He was buried on the moor but his body was later exhumed – his grave can be seen in the parish churchyard to the northeast of the village.

Thornton-in-Craven

5½ miles SW of Skipton on the A56

An attractive village from where there are magnificent views of Airedale and on towards Pendle Forest in Lancashire. During the Civil War Thornton's manor house was ruined by Royalist soldiers shortly after Cromwell had attended a local wedding there; the present house is situated opposite the original site. Past parish records associated with the 12th century Church of St Mary were also lost as, unfortunately, they were accidentally burnt by the local rector.

Earby

6 miles SW of Skipton on the A56

Though the Yorkshire Dales are thought of as a once-thriving textile producer, for many centuries lead mining was also a key industry. The **Museum of Yorkshire Dales Lead Mining** is housed in an old grammar school founded in 1591 by Robert Windle. The museum opened in 1971, and features a large collection put together by several local-interest groups, who first began their work in 1945 when the Earby Mines Research Group was formed within the Earby Pothole Club. The museum, which has limited opening times, has many excellent displays including mine tubs, photographs, mine plans, small implements, mining machinery and miners' personal belongings.

Broughton

3½ miles W of Skipton off the A59

The Tempest family has been associated with this farming community for the past 800 years. Their family home, **Broughton Hall**, dates back to 1597. Enlarged in the 18th and 19th centuries, the Hall is open to the public on Bank

Holidays, when guided tours are conducted around this interesting building. The hall and the surrounding grounds may seem familiar to visitors, as they have been used frequently by film crews as an 'historic' location.

Gargrave

4 miles NW of Skipton on the A65

This picturesque little village in Upper Airedale was once a thriving market town and, after the Leeds-Liverpool Canal was built, also a busy transport centre. Lead from the nearby mines was loaded onto barges at the village's five wharves, while other goods were unloaded, ready for distribution to the surrounding area. The village, too, played a part in the textile boom and there were two cotton mills here.

The remains of Celtic crosses found within the village Church of St Andrew indicate that, although the present building is chiefly Victorian, there has been a church here for centuries – the original church was destroyed by the Scots during a raid in 1318. To the south of the village, at **Kirk Sink**, is the site of a Roman villa that was excavated in the 1970s. Relics recovered from the excavation work can be seen in Skipton and Cliffe Castle Museums, though the site itself has since been covered over.

Airton

7½ miles NW of Skipton off the A65

This charming Airedale village is well known to long-distance walkers, as it lies on the Pennine Way. Though small, there are a couple of buildings of interest including a corn mill (now converted into flats) that was first recorded in 1198. As sheep farming took over from corn, the mill, like so many in the southern dales, turned to cotton spinning though, with the advent of steam-powered machinery, the industry moved to nearby Skipton.

At the beginning of the 18th century Airton became a Quaker community, and the **Meeting House**, built on land donated by the well-known Quaker weavers William and Alice Ellis, can still be seen by the village green. Another legacy of the village's Quaker community is the absence of a public house as the drinking of alcohol was strictly forbidden by the Friends. Also found on the village green is a 17th century squatter's cottage, so called because, according to the law, any person building a house and having smoke rising from the chimney within 24 hours would be granted the freehold of the property including the land within a stone's throw of the front door.

Malham

9 miles NW of Skipton off the A65

Malham village was originally two settlements, Malham East and Malham West, which were separated by the beck. Each came under the influence of a different religious house: Bolton Priory and Fountains Abbey respectively. United after the Dissolution of the Monasteries, the focal point of Malham

Devonshire Arms

Grassington Road (B6265), Cracoe, Skipton, North Yorkshire BD23 6LA
Tel: 01756 730237 Fax: 01756 730142
website: www.devonshirearms-online.co.uk

Situated on the Skipton-to-Grassington Road in the handsome village of Cracoe, the **Devonshire Arms** is a traditional coaching inn dating back to very early in the 18th century. Its charm, cosiness and warmth are evident from when guests first step through

the door, as the décor, furnishings and ambience make you feel immediately welcome. Open every session weekdays (12 – 3; 7 – 11 p.m.), all day during the summer months and all day (11 – 11 and 11 – 10.30) Saturdays and Sundays all year round, this superb inn boasts a choice of five real ales including Cumberland Ale, Jennings Best Bitter, Snecklifter and a changing guest ale, together with a good selection of wines, spirits, lagers, cider, stout and soft drinks.

For dining, food is served Tuesday to Saturday at lunch (12 – 2) and dinner 6.30 – 8.30 Tuesday to Thursday; Fridays and Saturdays 6.30 – 9); the Sunday lunch is served from 12 – 4. Booking is advised for Friday and Saturday evening. The menu and specials board offer a superb range of delicious and expertly prepared meals.

Owners Tim and Sharon have been here since December of 2003. They have reclaimed the inn's longstanding reputation for service, quality and the warmest and most genuine Yorkshire hospitality, offering all their guests a comfortable and enjoyable ambience and a high standard of service. Anyone would be right to want to prolong their stay at this fine inn, in this lovely part of the world, and the inn offers four ensuite guest bedrooms, all of them very comfortably furnished and decorated. All are upstairs; one is a family room. The hearty, delicious breakfast is just what's needed to set you up for a day's sightseeing, walking or even just relaxing! Children welcome.

became the village green, where the annual sheep fairs were held. This pretty village of farms and cottages is one of the most visited places in the Yorkshire Dales, though it is not just the charming stone-built dwellings that visitors come to admire but also the spectacular limestone scenery that lies just to the north. The two ancient stone bridges in the village centre are worth a second glance, too. The New Bridge, also known as the Monks' Bridge, was built in the 17th century; the Wash-Dub Bridge dates from the 16th century and is of a 'clapper' design (limestone slabs placed on stone supports).

Malham Cove

To the north of the village lies the ancient glacial grandeur of **Malham Cove**, a 300-feet limestone amphitheatre that forms the most spectacular section of the mid-Craven Fault. As recently as the 1700s a massive waterfall, higher than Niagara Falls, cascaded over its edge! These days the water disappears through potholes at the top, called water sinks, and reappears through the cavern mouth at Aire Head near the village. A steep path leads to the limestone pavement at the top, with its characteristic clints and grykes, where water has carved a distinctive natural sculpture through the weaknesses in the limestone.

Just to the east lies the equally inspiring **Gordale Scar**, a huge gorge carved by glacial melt-water with an impressive waterfall leaping, in two stages, from a fissure in its face. Also nearby is another waterfall known as **Janet's Foss**, beside which is a cave where Janet, a friendly fairy, is said to have lived. To the north again is Malham Tarn, a glacial lake which, by way of an underground stream, is the source of the River Aire. The tarn, England's highest freshwater lake, lies at the centre of the **Malham Tarn Estate** (National Trust), some 7,200 acres of open limestone country that also includes Malham Tarn House, where such famous names as Ruskin, Darwin and Charles Kingsley (author of *The Water Babies*) found inspiration. Back in the village, at Townhead Barn, there is an interpretive centre along with an exhibition highlighting the history of farming in the Dales.

Grassington

One of the best-loved and most popular villages within the Yorkshire Dales National Park, Grassington in many ways is the epitome of a Dales' settlement, with its bustling market square and charming main street that reflects its role as a traditional working centre. Known as the capital of Upper Wharfedale, the historically important valley roads meet here, and the ancient monastic route from Malham to Fountains Abbey passes through the village.

Grassington's origins go back many centuries. There was certainly a Bronze-Age settlement here, while the remains of an Iron-Age village have been found, a Celtic field system lies on nearby **Lea Green**, and the village is mentioned in the *Domesday Book*. However, the settlement seen today, now part of the estate of the Duke of Devonshire, has narrow streets lined with attractive Georgian buildings and is a delight to wander around.

Housed in two 18th century lead-miners' cottages, in Grassington Square, the **Upper Wharfedale Folk Museum** contains many exhibits and displays relating to the lives of those who have lived in the dale. Along with items relating to the lead-mining industry, farming and crafts, there are displays of period costumes, folklore and the days of the railways.

Linton Falls, Nr Grassington

Throughout the year there were many festivals and holidays observed by the dales people and one, the **Feast Sports**, still takes place here on a Saturday in October. Among the many traditional events that are carried out there is the tea cake eating race, where children have to eat a tea cake then race to the other end of the field. The winner is the first child to whistle a tune.

Wharfedale, the valley of the River Wharfe, is, at 70 miles, the longest of the Yorkshire Dales and runs from the river's source on **Cam Fell** to Cawood where it joins the River Ouse. The Romans named a local Goddess, Verbeia, after the river and those who visit will understand why as the goddess was known for her treachery as well as her beauty. Wharfedale is one of the most spectacular and most varied of the Yorkshire Dales and no one who sees the river charging through the narrow gorge at The Strid, near Bolton Abbey, will deny that the power of the river is to be respected.

For many years, Wharfedale has been the place to which those working in the grim industrial towns of Yorkshire came for clean air and solitude. Today, it is probably the most popular of all Yorkshire's dales and there is certainly a lot on offer to those who visit here. The chief towns of the dale are little more than villages and they have retained much of their charm despite the various invasions of industry and tourism.

There is much to see in Wharfedale and, in keeping with much of the Yorkshire Dales National Park, there is a variety of landscape to discover. From the high moorland and fell to the deep, eroded limestone gorges, the valley varies almost, it seems, with every turn of the River Wharfe. It is not surprising, therefore, that Wharfedale has, over the years, inspired many of Britain's poets, writers, and painters and both Coleridge and Wordsworth were taken with its beauty while Ruskin enthused about its contrasts and Turner painted several scenes that also capture something of the dale's history and mystery.

Around Grassington

Hebden

1½ miles SE of Grassington on the B6265

Further east from this quiet hamlet are the wonderful **Stump Cross Caverns** that were discovered in 1858 by lead miners working nearby and have been open to the public ever since. Exploration since then has extended the network of caverns to over four miles in length and, along with revealing a fantastic collection of stalactites, stalagmites and unusual rock formations, animal bones dating back over 90,000

The Clarendon Hotel

Hebden, Grassington,
North Yorkshire BD23 5DE
Tel: 01756 752446
e-mail: rachel@theclarendon.fsnet.uk
website: www.theclarendon.fsnet.uk

John and Rachel Younger are a friendly and hospitable couple who offer all their guests a warm and genuine welcome to **The Clarendon Hotel**. This excellent inn is impressive inside and out, from the stonebuilt exterior, covered in creepers, to the cosy and intimate bar, lounge and dining areas inside, where the simple décor and comfortable furnishings add to the pleasant ambience.

The hotel began life as a farmhouse, then became an alehouse and, in the 1700s, a coaching inn on the Skipton-Harrogate road. Set in the heart of the Yorkshire Dales, the hotel is the perfect place to use as a base for exploring this particularly beautiful part of the county.

This Free House features three real ales – Tetleys, Timothy Taylor Best and a changing guest ale – as well as a range of draught lagers, wines, spirits, cider, stout and soft drinks.

Rachel has a wealth of experience in the catering trade, and her cooking is justly renowned in the area, creating freshly prepared and delicious dishes. A small sample from the specials board includes main courses such as steak, ale and mushroom pie, fresh haddock, roast joint of lamb, cassoulet of lamb, pork, sausage, haricot beans and duck, and goat's cheese and onion filo tart. The hotel is open for lunch (Tuesday to Sunday 12 – 2) and dinner (Tuesday to Thursday 6 – 8.30; Friday to Saturday 6 –9; Sunday 6 – 8).

In addition to fine food and drink, the hotel boasts three charming and supremely comfortable ensuite guest bedrooms. The area boasts scenic and historic delights such as Hebden itself, Harrogate, Skipton, Grassington, Appletreewick and Stump Cross Caverns, as well as some great walking, making this an excellent place to stay to have easy access to all of these sights and attractions.

years have also been found inside. Along with touring the caverns, which are open all year, visitors can take in the displays and exhibitions in the visitor centre where there is a gift shop and a tea room.

Thorpe

2 miles SE of Grassington off the B6160

This small hamlet, the full name of which is 'Thorpe-sub-Montem' (meaning 'below the hill'), lies in a secluded hollow between drumlins – long, low, alluvial mounds. As well as taking advantage of its hidden position, which proved ideal for secreting valuables and family members during Scots raids, the village was also known for its cobblers. Their fame was such that the monks of Fountains Abbey were among their regular customers. However, the influence of the monks did not prevent the high spirited cobblers from stealing nearby Burnsall's maypole and planting it on their own village green. The maypole did, eventually, return to its home village but not until the villagers of Burnsall had organised a rescue party.

According to local legend, Ralph Calvert, one of Thorpe's cobblers, stayed the night at Fountains Abbey while making his twice yearly visit to sell sandals to the monks. Travelling home the next day, Calvert reached Gill Ford, where the Grassington road crossed the river; he saw that it was swollen with recent rain and he removed his boots before wading across. Sitting to tie his laces on the other side, the devil appeared and, impressed by Ralph's lack of fear and, indeed, his boldness, Old Nick began to boast of his powers. Still unconcerned Ralph suggested that to display his power, the devil should build a bridge here across the river and, three days later, there was a bridge at Gill Ford that, ever since, has been known as Devil's Bridge.

Burnsall

2½ miles SE of Grassington on the B6160

Dramatically situated on a bend in the River Wharfe with the slopes of Burnsall Fell as a backdrop, Burnsall is thought to have been founded prior to the 8th century when Wilfrid, Bishop of York, built a wooden church here where now stands the village's 12th century place of

Burnsall, Wharfedale

Oatcroft Farm Barn

Oatcroft Farm, Burnsall, Skipton,
North Yorkshire BD23 6BN
Tel: 01756 720268

Here in Burnsall, situated on the River Wharfe and famed for its beauty, **Oatcroft Farm Barn** combines the best of old and new.This impressive traditional stonebuilt barn has been tastefully and sensitively converted so that the first floor offers spacious and very comfortable accommodation. There is a twin room and also a one-person bed settee in the lounge, where the French windows open onto a small patio. Facilities include the well-equipped kitchen/dining room. 3 Stars ETC.

worship. All that remains of Wilfrid's building is the font that can still be seen at the back of **St Wilfrid's Church**. The churchyard is entered via a unique lychgate and here can be seen two hogback tombstones and various other fragments that date back to the times of the Saxons and the Danes. The village school dates back to 1602.

However, it is not this sturdy Dales' church that draws visitors to Burnsall but its bridge. Today, this typical Dales' bridge of five stone arches is the start of the annual **Classic Fell Race** that takes place on a Saturday towards the end of August. Over the years, the flood waters of the River Wharfe have washed away the arches on several occasions but the villagers have always replaced them as this is the only crossing point for three miles in each direction.

Appletreewick

4 miles SE of Grassington off the B6160

This peaceful village, which is known locally as Aptrick, lies between the banks of the River Wharfe and bleak moorland and is overlooked by the craggy expanse of **Simon's Seat,** one of Wharfedale's best loved hilltops. Since monastic times, lead has been mined on the surrounding moorland and the northern slopes were the property of the monks of nearby Bolton Priory. The village was also the home of William Craven, a Lord Mayor of London, who returned to spend much of his amassed wealth on improvements and additions to Appletreewick's fine old buildings. The cottage where he was born was largely furnished by the similarly legendary Robert Thompson of Kilburn. Known as the Dick Whittington of the Dale, William Craven was born in 1548 and he moved to London when he became apprenticed to a mercer (a dealer in textiles and fine fabrics).

Just to the north of Appletreewick lie **Parcevall Hall Gardens**, a wonderful woodland garden that includes many varieties of unusual plants, shrubs and tress along with rock gardens, terraces, streams and reflective pools. Though the

16-acre gardens are high above sea level, (which provides the visitor with splendid views), many of the plants still flourish in these beautiful surroundings. The gardens, which are open between Easter and October, are particularly known for their special quality of peace and tranquillity.

The nearby gorge of **Trollers Gill** is said to be haunted by a fearsome ghost dog, with huge eyes and a shaggy coat, which drags a clanking chain. A local story, recorded in 1881, tells how a man, somewhat foolishly, went to the gorge in the middle of the night. He failed to return and his body, on which there were marks not made by human hand, was later found by shepherds.

Bolton Abbey

7½ miles SE of Grassington on the B6160

The village is actually a collection of small hamlets that have all been part of the estate of the Dukes of Devonshire since 1748. Bolton Abbey itself lies on the banks of the River Wharfe while the hamlets of Storiths, Hazelwood, Deerstones, and Halton East lie higher up.

The main attraction here is undoubtedly the substantial ruin of **Bolton Priory** (see panel on page 64), an Augustinian house that was founded in 1155 by monks from Embsay. The house had originally been founded at Embsay in 1120 by Cecily de Romille but, just 35 years later, she and her daughter, Alice, allowed the monks to move to this idyllic location on the banks of the River Wharfe. According to local legend, Alice donated the land to the Augustinians in memory of her son, the boy of Egremont. One day, her son, accompanied by a forester, was on his way home from hunting in Barden Forest when, in a burst of high spirits, he jumped the notorious Strid but his hunting dog, which he held on a leash, checked the boy's leap and he fell into the raging torrent. However, this tale is easily disproved as the boy was alive when the priory was founded and his signature appears on the foundation document.

After the Dissolution of the Monasteries the priory was sold to the 2nd Earl of Cumberland, Henry Clifford and it has since passed into the hands of the Dukes of Devonshire, the Cavendish family. The 14th century priory gatehouse, **Bolton Hall**, is the present Duke's shooting lodge. Visitors walking to the priory ruins from the village pass through a hole in the wall that frames one of the most splendid views of the romantic ruins.

In and around this beautiful village there are some 75 miles of footpaths and nature trails, skirting the riverbanks and climbing up on to the high moorland. Upstream from the priory ruins, however, lies one of the most visited natural features in Wharfedale, a point where the wide river suddenly narrows into a confined channel of black rock through which the water thunders. This spectacular gorge is known as the **Strid**

Bolton Abbey

Bolton Abbey Estate Estate Office,
Bolton Abbey, Skipton,
North Yorkshire BD23 6EX
Tel: 01756 718009
website: www.boltonabbey.com

Bolton Abbey near Skipton is the Yorkshire Estate of the Duke and Duchess of Devonshire. Situated in Wharfedale, in the Yorkshire Dales National Park this historic estate is a magnet for visitors drawn to its breathtaking landscapes and excellent facilities.

Visitors have flocked to Bolton Abbey for over one hundred years. On an August Bank Holiday in the 1890's the railway brought 40,000 people to Bolton Abbey; nearly as many people as now visit York in a week. After the First World War visitors arrived by train in their "Sunday Best" with the children carrying buckets, spades and fishing nets. Some fathers never got much further than the Devonshire Arms' Refreshment Room, but many removed their boots and rolled up their trousers to paddle with their children by the sandy river bank. Little has changed over the years; visitors still come to see the landscape that inspired artists like Turner and Landseer, and poets such as Wordsworth.

As the name suggests Bolton Abbey was originally a large monastic Estate, based around the 12th century priory. Legend has it that the Priory was established in 1120 by Cecily de Romille as an expression of her grief following the drowning of her son in the nearby Strid. Today, the ruins of the Priory set in an incomparable position overlooking the river Wharfe will evoke the past glories of the Estate whilst the restored and thriving parish church shows that the Estate is still very much a living community.

With 80 miles of moorland, woodland and riverside footpaths, the Estate offers something for all ages and abilities. One of the most popular is the nature trail leading to the Strid. Opened in 1810 by Rev. William Carr, Agent for the 66th Duke of Devonshire, the green trail follows the river Wharfe through Strid Wood, a Site of Special Scientific Interest, to the Strid. The famous Strid is where the river comes rushing through a narrow gorge cut into the rocks. It looks so tempting to jump over but beware, for people have underestimated the width with fatal results.

because, over the centuries, many heroic (or foolhardy) types have attempted to leap across it as a test of bravery.

Further upstream again lies **Barden Tower**, once the principal hunting lodge in the Forest of Barden that was rebuilt in the 15th century as a fortified dwelling by the 'Shepherd Lord', Henry Clifford. The tower was restored in the 1650s by Lady Anne Clifford but, despite still being lived in during the early 20th century, it is now in ruins though these are impressive.

Linton

1 mile SW of Grassington off the B6160

More correctly called 'Linton-in-Craven', this delightful and unspoilt village has grown up around its village green through which runs a small beck. This flat area of land was once a lake and around its edge was grown flax that the villagers spun into linen. The village is also the home of the **Church of St Michael and All Angels**, a wonderful building that is a fine example of rural medieval architecture.

Probably built on the site of a pagan shrine, the church lies some way from the village centre though its handsome bell-cote is a suitable landmark. Among the 14th century roof bosses can be seen the Green Man, an ancient fertility symbol of a man's head protruding through foliage, which was adopted by the Christian church. Spanning Linton Beck is a graceful packhorse bridge that was repaired by Dame Elizabeth Redmayne in the late 17th century. During the repair work, Dame Elizabeth had a narrow parapet added to the bridge to prevent carts from crossing because, so it is said, the local farmers refused to contribute to the cost of the repairs.

Rylstone

4 miles SW of Grassington on the B6265

Above this Pennine village, on Rylstone Fell, stands **Rylstone Cross** that was, originally, a large stone that looked rather like a man. In 1885, a wooden cross was erected on top of the stone to commemorate peace with France and the initials DD and TB, carved on the back of the cross, refer to the Duke of Devonshire and his land agent, Mr T Broughton.

At the beginning of the 19th century, when Wordsworth was touring the area, he heard a local legend that became the basis for his poem *The White Doe of Rylstone*, published in 1815. The story, set in the 16th century, concerns the local Norton family and, in particular, Francis who gave his sister Emily a white doe before he went off to battle. Francis survived the conflict but he was murdered in Norton Tower on his return. Emily was struck down with grief and she was comforted by the same white doe that returned from the wild following her brother's death. The doe remained with Emily and, long after her death, a white doe could be seen lying on Francis' grave.

Thresfield

1 mile W of Grassington on the B6160

Situated on the opposite bank of the River Wharfe from Grassington, Thresfield has at its centre a small village green called the Park, complete with the original village stocks. Perhaps the most striking building here is the Free Grammar School built in 1674 and, according to local people, its porch is haunted by a fairy known as 'Old Pam the Fiddler'. Thresfield was once famous for the production of besoms (birch brooms) but the last family to make them, the Ibbotsons, died out in the 1920s.

Conistone

2½ miles NW of Grassington off the B6160

This ancient settlement, whose name suggests that it once belonged to a king, is clustered around its maypole and village green and is home to an ancient bridge. However, the village Church of St Mary is thought to be even older and is believed to have been founded in Saxon times. The land surrounding Conistone is unusually flat and it was once the bottom of a lake formed by the melt water from the glacier that carved out Kilnsey Crag.

Kilnsey Crag

Kilnsey

3 miles NW of Grassington on the B6160

This small and ancient hamlet, which lies on the opposite bank of the River Wharfe from Conistone, is overlooked by **Kilnsey Crag**, the outline of which is particularly striking as one side of this limestone hill was gouged out by a passing glacier during the Ice Age. One of the most spectacular natural features in the Dales, the crag has a huge 'lip' or overhang that presents an irresistible challenge to adventurous climbers.

One of the local springs, which bursts from the limestone hillside above the village, has been put to various uses over the generations but, today, it is part of **Kilnsey Park and Trout Farm** where not only are delicious rainbow trout produced but there are also various water-based activities on offer.

Kettlewell, Upper Wharfedale

Kettlewell

5½ miles NW of Grassington on the B6160

Surrounded by the beautiful countryside of Upper Wharfedale, Kettlewell is a popular centre for tourists and walkers. At the meeting point of several old packhorse routes, which now serve as footpaths and bridleways, the village was a busy market centre and, at one time, home to 13 public houses that catered to the needs of the crowds. The market charter, which was granted in the 13th century, is evidence that Kettlewell was once a more important place than it is today and the various local religious houses of Bolton Priory, Coverham Abbey and

Racehorses Hotel

Kettlewell, North Yorkshire BD23 5QZ
Tel: 01756 760233 Fax: 01756 761036
e-mail: info@racehorseshotel.co.uk
website: www.racehorseshotel.co.uk

Set in the heart of Upper Wharfedale, **Racehorses Hotel** is a very welcoming inn and public house. Parts of this fine hostelry date back to the mid-17th century, when it was the stables for another inn – here extra horses would be put on to help with the hard pull in either direction.

Open for ale and other libations every session and all day Friday, Saturday and Sunday, the three real ales here are Black Sheep, Timothy Taylor and a changing guest ale. Excellent meals – chosen from the menu or specials board – are served daily at lunch (Monday to Friday 12 – 2; Saturday and Sunday 12 – 3) and dinner (6.30 – 9.30). There are no-smoking areas and a wonderful riverside beer garden. The convivial ambience throughout draws loyal locals and makes every visitor feel at home.

There are 13 superior ensuite guest bedrooms for anyone wishing to linger in this lovely part of the county. Off-peak special breaks are available weekdays.

Off-road car park. Children welcome.

Fountains Abbey all owned land in the area. After the Dissolution, the land became the property of the Crown until the 17th century when Charles I granted Kettlewell to a group of London merchants who, in turn, sold it to the locals. Today, Kettlewell is still governed by Trust Lords that are elected from the freeholders of the village. Today, Kettlewell is a conservation area, a charming place of chiefly 17th and 18th century houses and cottages while its original 13th century waterfall, later converted into a textile mill, has gone though evidence of a local lead mining industry remains.

Arncliffe Village

To the east of Kettlewell lies **Great Whernside** on which is **Tor Dyke**, an earthwork built by the Brigantes along this natural limestone outcrop to defend the route into Coverdale from the advancing Romans. Above the dyke is Hunter's Stone, a cross that was used by monks to guide them on the route between Kettlewell and Coverham Abbey.

Arncliffe

6½ miles NW of Grassington off the B6160

Situated in Littondale, this village's name dates back to Saxon times when the valley was referred to as 'Amerdale'.

The Falcon Inn

Arncliffe, Near Skipton,
North Yorkshire BD23 5QE
Tel: 01756 770205
website: www.thefalconinn.com

The Falcon Inn is one of that rare breed: a genuine traditional village inn. Tucked away in this picturesque village in the heart of the dales, a visit here is a step back in time to gentler, friendlier times. Real ale is served from the jug, there's pie and peas for lunch, and day tickets available (except Sundays) for fly fishing on the River Skirfare. The five guest bedrooms (available April to November) are comfortable and cosy.

A quiet and unspoilt place, many of the buildings around the central village green are listed and, in its early years, the long running television series *Emmerdale* was filmed here.

Near the village bridge stands **Bridge End** that was once the home of the Hammond family. While staying with the Hammonds, author Charles Kingsley was so taken with the village and the dale that he incorporated the house and his hostess in his famous work *The Water Babies*.

Litton

9 miles NW of Grassington off the B6160

This pretty village lends its name to this tranquil and peaceful dale, **Littondale,** which is actually the valley of the River Skirfare. Once part of a Norman hunting forest, the dale was originally called 'Amerdale' (meaning 'deep fork') and this ancient name is preserved in Amerdale Dub, where the River Skirfare joins the River Wharfe near Kilnsey.

Starbotton

7½ miles NW of Grassington on the B6160

This quiet little Wharfedale village, whose name comes from 'staurr' (a stake) and 'botn' (a valley bottom) was the scene, in 1686, of a disastrous flood when a huge head of water descended from the surrounding fells and swept away many of the houses and cottages. The damage was such that a national appeal was started and aid, in the form of money, was sent from as far afield as Cambridgeshire.

Buckden

9½ miles NW of Grassington on the B6160

Marking the beginning of Wharfedale proper, Buckden is the first full sized village of the dale and proudly boasts that it is also home to Wharfedale's first shop – its post office. Unusually for this area, the village was not settled by the Saxons but, later, by the Normans and it was the headquarters of the officers hunting in the forest of Langstrothdale. As the forest was cleared to make way for agriculture, Buckden became an important market town serving a large part of the surrounding area. Wool was one of the important sources of income for the dalesfolk and the local inn here still has some of the old weighing equipment from the days when the trade was conducted on the premises. The village is an excellent starting point for those wanting to climb **Buckden Pike** (2,302 feet), which lies to the east, and the route to the summit takes in not only superb views but also several waterfalls.

Designated in Norman times as one of the feudal hunting forests, **Langstrothdale Chase** was governed by the strict forest laws. Just to the south of the village, which lies on the eastern edge of the Chase, can be seen an old stone cross which was used to mark the forest boundary. Buckden's name means the 'valley of the bucks' but its last deer

The Buck Inn

Buckden, Upper Wharfedale, Skipton,
North Yorkshire BD23 5JA
Tel: 01756 760228 Fax: 01756 760227
e-mail: info@thebuckinn.com
website: www.thebuckinn.com

The very impressive **Buck Inn** is in the heart of the Yorkshire Dales, surrounded by the breathtaking beauty of this national park. The picturesque villages, fells and other natural beauties are easily reached on foot or by car, and the area also boasts a wide selection of museums, galleries and historic homes and buildings that speak of the region's proud heritage.

But it's certainly not just the scenery that has made this inn internationally renowned. A traditional Georgian coaching inn with every modern comfort, its Courtyard Restaurant has been awarded 2 Rosettes by the AA for its food, and its menu and specials board offer up a tempting range of dishes every day at lunch and dinner (Monday to Saturday 12 – 2 and 6.30 –9; Sundays 12 – 2.30 and 6.30 – 8.30) as well as afternoon tea. Booking is required for the restaurant.

Open every day from 11 – 11 Monday to Saturday and 11 – 10.30 on Sundays for ale, there are always at least three, and usually six real ales available depending on the season, including regulars such as Black Sheep, Copper Dragon and Timothy Taylor Landlord, complemented by changing guest ales. Together with these is a good range of spirits, wines, cider, stout, lagers and soft drinks. The wine list merits particular mention, with vintages from every wine region of the world.

The inn also boasts superb accommodation in 14 ensuite guest bedrooms (7 doubles, 4 twin, 1 single and the Wharfedale suite), all excellently furnished and decorated. Many feature magnificent views. Each room is individually designed and furnished to meet the inn's classic style and flair for matching comfort and luxury.

All accommodation is available all year round, and there are special mid-week breaks. Breakfast features home-baked breads, cakes, biscuits and preserves. Packed lunches also available on request.

was hunted and killed here in the 17th century.

Hubberholme

10 miles NW of Grassington off the B6160

This small village was originally two places: Hubberholme proper and Kirkgill, which takes its name from the nearby Church of St Michael and All Angels that was, at one time, a forest chapel. In the days when this church shared a curate with the church at Halton Gill, in Littondale, he would have to travel over Horsehead Pass to take the service here. A difficult journey in winter, the church's sexton would keep a look out from the top of the tower and would only ring the bell to summon the congregation after first sighting the priest on his horse. Each year, on New Year's Day, the villagers gather at the local pub for the **Hubberholme Parliament**. For that night, the public bar becomes the House of Commons, where the farmers congregate, while the room where the vicar and churchwardens meet is the House of Lords. Bidding then takes place between the farmers for the rent of a field behind the church and, encouraged by the vicar, the highest bidder gains the lease for the coming year.

Yockenthwaite

11½ miles NW of Grassington off the B6160

The unusual name of this small village is Viking in origin and, though once a prosperous place, Yockenthwaite is now a collection of old stone farms. On the surrounding fells lies a well-preserved Bronze Age stone circle and **Giant's Grave**, the remains of an Iron Age settlement. Owned by the National Trust, as is the nearby hamlet of Cray, this area of **Upper Wharfedale** is classic Yorkshire Dales countryside with grey limestone crags, rich pastures, wooded valleysides and drystone walls. The remains of prehistoric field patterns and of old lead mines can also still be seen.

Pateley Bridge

Considered by many to be one of the prettiest towns in the Dales, Pateley Bridge is perfectly situated as a base from which to explore Upper Nidderdale. Despite its compact size, the town is remarkably well connected by roads that have been here since the monastic orders established trade routes through Pateley Bridge for transporting their goods. A street market, whose charter was granted in the 14th century, has, however, been abandoned for some time although sheep fairs and agricultural shows still take place here.

However, Pateley Bridge is more than just a market centre – the nearby lead mines and spinning and handloom weaving provided employment for the local community. The construction of the turnpike road to Ripon in 1751, followed by the opening of a road to Knaresborough in 1756, gave the town a further economic boost. In the early 19th century, the brothers George and

John Metcalfe moved their flax spinning business to nearby Glasshouses and they expanded rapidly. The lead mines, too, were expanding, due to the introduction of new machinery and the town saw a real boom. The arrival of the railway in 1862 maintained this flourishing economy, making the transportation of heavy goods cheaper and the carriage of perishable foods quicker.

Much of the Pateley Bridge seen today was built in those prosperous years. A town of quaint and pretty buildings, the oldest is St Mary's Church, a lovely ruin dating from 1320 and from where there are some fine panoramic views. Another excellent vista can be viewed from the aptly named **Panorama Walk**, part of the main medieval route from Ripon to Skipton.

The **Nidderdale Museum**, a winner of the National Heritage Museum of the Year, is housed in one of the town's original Victorian workhouses and presents a fascinating record of local folk history. The imaginatively displayed exhibits include a complete cobbler's shop, a general store, a Victorian parlour, kitchen and schoolroom, a chemist's, a haberdasher's and joiner's shop, as well as agricultural, transport and industrial equipment and memorabilia. The museum is open daily from Easter to November and at weekends through the winter. The crossing of the River Nidd here was used by the monks of Fountains Abbey and the original ford was replaced by a wooden bridge in the 16th century. However, the present bridge, a stone construction, dates from the 18th century.

The valley of the River Nidd, **Nidderdale**, is a typical Yorkshire dale with drystone walls, green fields and pretty stone villages and it was christened 'Little Switzerland' by the Victorians as the upper reaches are steep and wooded, with the river running through gorges. It is this natural beauty that draws many people to the dale and there are several remarkable features that are well worth exploring. The source of the river lies up on the slopes of Great Whernside and, running for just 20 miles, it is smaller than its neighbours Wensleydale and Wharfedale and it has been designated an Area of Outstanding Natural Beauty.

The history of the dale is similar to that of its neighbours: the Romans and Norsemen both settled here and there are also reminders that the dale was populated in prehistoric times. It was the all powerful Cistercian monks of Fountains and Byland Abbeys who began the business-like cultivation of the countryside to provide grazing for cattle and sheep and the space to grow food. This great farming tradition has survived and, though prosperity came and went with lead mining, a few of the textile mills established in the golden age of the Industrial Revolution can still be found.

Best explored from Pateley Bridge, keen walkers will delight in the dale's wide variety of landscape that can be covered within a reasonable amount of time. High up on the moorland, famed for its brilliant colour in late summer, there are several reservoirs, built to provide water for the growing population and industry in Bradford. This area is a must for bird watchers as there are excellent opportunities for spotting a number of species of duck as well as Brent geese and whooper swans. Further down the valley, in the rich woodland, wildlife again abounds and the well-signposted footpaths help visitors reach the most spectacular sights.

Around Pateley Bridge

Wilsill

2 miles SE of Pateley Bridge on the B6165

Just to the east of the village are the extraordinary **Brimham Rocks** (National Trust), a series of strange and fascinating rock formations situated on rugged heather moorland. Formed into these remarkable shapes by years of erosion, some of these great millstone grit boulders have been given names such as 'Dancing Bear' and 'Idol Rock' – a huge boulder that rests on a base just a foot in diameter. The late 18th century Brimham House, originally a shooting lodge, is now home to an exhibition on the area.

Summerbridge

3½ miles SE of Pateley Bridge on the B6165

In 1825 Summerbridge was just a small settlement with a bridge and a corn mill but, in that year, New York Mill, a large flax mill, was built here and by the mid-19th century the village was flourishing, with five mills in operation, a rope works and a foundry.

Bewerley

½ mile S of Pateley Bridge off the B6265

Recorded as 'Bevrelie' (meaning 'a clearing inhabited by badgers') in the *Domesday Book*, this is Nidderdale's oldest settlement and it was also the site of the earliest and most important of Fountains Abbey's many granges. The recently restored Chapel, built here by one of the last abbots, Marmaduke Huby, acted for many years as the village school.

In the 17th century the Yorke family moved to the embellished hall at Bewerley following their purchase of the former lands of Byland Abbey in Nidderdale. During the subsequent years, the family laid out the parkland as well as rebuilding some of the village and, though the estate was sold in the 1920s and the hall demolished, the park remains and plays host to the annual Nidderdale Show. The name of the village's most influential family, however, is not lost as **Yorke's Folly**, two stone pillars built in around 1809, still stand on the hillside overlooking Bewerley. Close by is a curious rock, known as **Crocodile Rock** due to its shape, that is particularly popular with children.

Ramsgill

4 miles NW of Pateley Bridge off the A6265

This pleasant village, clustered around its well-kept green, was the birthplace of Eugene Aram in 1704. The son of a gardener at Newby Hall, Aram was arrested in 1758 in Kings Lynn for the murder of Daniel Clark in Knaresborough 13 years before. The trial took place in York and Aram caused a stir by conducting his own defence. However, he was convicted and later executed before his body was taken to Knaresborough where it was hung from a gibbet. The gruesome story has been the centre of many tales and songs including a very romantic version by Sir Bulwer Lytton.

Ramsgill is situated at the head of **Gouthwaite Reservoir**, built in the early 20th century by Bradford Corporation to satisfy the demand from the rapidly expanding town. Gouthwaite is now a popular and important site for wildfowl as are the dale's two other reservoirs, Scar House and Angram, which lie in a lonely yet beautiful setting at the head of Nidderdale.

Lofthouse

6 miles NW of Pateley Bridge off the A6265

This is a small Dales' village lying in the upper valley of the River Nidd and, unlike neighbouring Wharfedale, the stone walls and rocky outcrops are of millstone grit though the valley bottom consists of limestone. As a result, only in excessive weather is there water under the bridge here as, in normal conditions, the river drops down two sumps: Manchester Hole and Goydon Pot. The monks of Fountains Abbey certainly had a grange here but it is also probable that the village was first settled by Norsemen.

Nearby, in the heart of Nidderdale, lies **How Stean Gorge**, a spectacular limestone gorge that is up to 80 feet deep in places, through which the Stean Beck flows. Narrow paths, with footbridges cut into the steep-sided ravine, guide visitors along the gorge where the waters rush over the large boulders below. However, there are also many sheltered areas of calm water where fish hide under the rocks. As well as taking a stroll up this fascinating path, visitors can also step inside Tom Taylor's Cave and, along the walk, marvel at the wide variety of plant life that grows in this steep ravine.

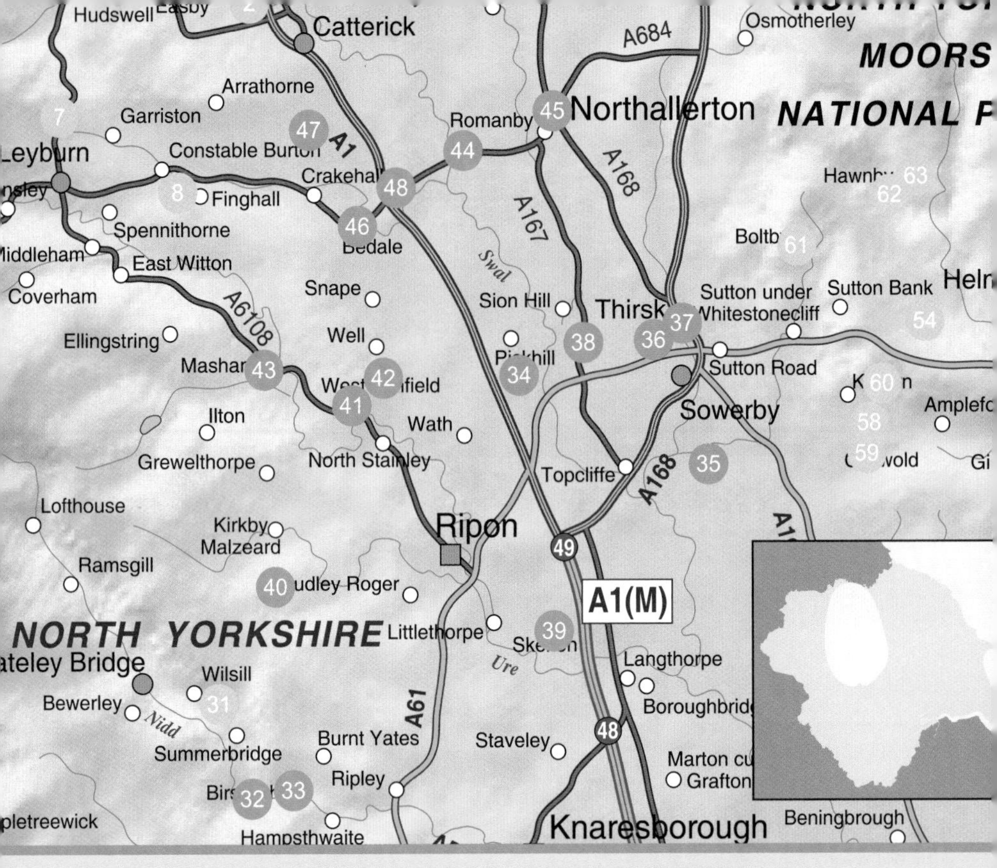

PLACES TO STAY, EAT AND DRINK

Brimham Guest House, Darley, North Yorkshire 32 Guest House p86

The Old Station Inn, Birstwith, North Yorkshire 33 Pub, Food and Accommodation p87

Black Horse, Ainderby Quernhow, N Yorkshire 34 Pub with Food p90

Ye Jolly Farmers Inn, Dalton, North Yorkshire 35 Pub, Food and Accommodation p91

The Three Tuns Hotel, Thirsk, North Yorkshire 36 Hotel and Restaurant p92

World of James Herriot, Thirsk, North Yorkshire 37 Museum p93

The Kings Arms, Sandhutton, North Yorkshire 38 Pub, Restaurant and Accommodation p94

The Black Lion, Skelton-on-Ure, North Yorkshire 39 Pub, Restaurant and Accommodation p96

Grantley Arms, High Grantley, North Yorkshire 40 Pub and Restaurant p99

The Bruce Arms, West Tanfield, North Yorkshire 41 Pub, Restaurant and Accommodation p100

Freemasons Arms, Nosterfield, North Yorkshire 42 Pub, Food and Accommodation p101

Theakston Brewery, Masham, North Yorkshire 43 Visitor Attraction p102

Wellington Heifer, Ainderby Steeple, N Yorkshire 44 Pub, Restaurant and Accommodation p104

The Black Bull, Northallerton, North Yorkshire 45 Pub, Food and Accommodation p106

The Waggon & Horses, Bedale, North Yorkshire 46 Pub, Food and Accommodation p107

The Greyhound Inn, Hackforth, North Yorkshire 47 Pub, Restaurant and Accommodation p108

Little Holtby, Leeming Bar, North Yorkshire 48 Bed and Breakfast p109

Denotes entries in other chapters

2 Yorkshire Spa Towns

Pump Room Museum, Harrogate

The two towns of Harrogate and Knaresborough dominate the lower section of Nidderdale and, though today Harrogate is the larger, for centuries Knaresborough was the more important of the two. Older than its neighbour, Knaresborough was inhabited long before the days of the Romans and, along with its Norman castle, it is now best known as being the home of England's most famous prophetess, Mother Shipton, and the Petrifying Well that stands beside her birthplace.

A small village until the 17th century, Harrogate developed into one of the country's foremost spa towns following the discovery of a chalybeate well in the late 16th century. As the fame of its healing waters spread, along with the fashion for seeking cures for any number of ailments increased, so Harrogate grew into the elegant and genteel town that it remains to this day. The key features here are the Georgian and Victorian architecture along with the wide tree-lined boulevards and the numerous gardens.

Further north lies Ripon, a cathedral city since Victorian times which also has a peaceful and gracious air. However, though the city endeavoured to cash in on the fashion for 'taking the waters', it did not have its own healing springs and so water had to be pumped in from Aldfield, near Fountains Abbey; many Edwardian spa buildings remain, along with some fine art-nouveau features and their surrounding gardens. Ripon is also home to one of the country's most beautiful racecourses and throughout the summer season there are race meetings here on what is known as Yorkshire's Garden Racecourse. Nearby, at Thirsk, is another of the county's delightful

Druids Circle, Masham

racecourses, although the town is best known as having been the home of the real-life James Herriot, Alf Wight.

Although ancient monuments litter this area such as the Devil's Arrows near Boroughbridge, and many of the settlements have Roman roots, it is the magnificent ruin of Fountains Abbey for which this region is best known. Set beside the River Skell, this was one of the wealthiest Cistercian houses in the country in medieval times and, today, the remains are Yorkshire's only World Heritage Site. However, there are other places of interest to see close by, including the fine stately home of Newby Hall, the Northern Horticultural Society's Harlow Carr Botanical Gardens and the breweries at Masham.

Harrogate

Well-recognised as one of England's most attractive towns and a frequent winner of 'Britain in Bloom', Harrogate features acres of gardens that offer a vast array of colour throughout the year, open spaces and broad tree-lined boulevards. However, until the 17th century Harrogate – or 'Haregate' as it was then called – was nothing more than a collection of cottages close to the thriving market town of Knaresborough. One day while out walking his dog, William Slingsby, of Bilton Hall near Knaresborough, discovered a spring bubbling up out of the rock and, having tasted the water, found it to be similar to that he had drunk at the fashionable wells of Spa, in Belgium. Expert opinion was sought and, in 1596, Dr Timothy Bright confirmed the spring to be a chalybeate well and the waters to have medicinal powers – curing a wide variety of illnesses and ailments, from gout to vertigo. Slingsby's well became known as **Tewit Well**, after the local name for pewits, and it can still be seen today covered by a dome on pillars. Other wells were soon found in the area: St John's Well in 1631 and the **Old Sulphur Well** that went on to become the most famous of Harrogate's springs. Though this particular spring had been known locally for years it was not until 1656 that this sulphurous smelling well, nicknamed the 'Stinking Spaw', began to attract attention.

During the mid-17th century bathing in the heated sulphurous waters became fashionable as well as a cure for various

Turkish Baths, Harrogate

ailments and lodging houses were built around the sulphur well in Low Harrogate. Bathing took place in the evening and, each morning, the patients would drink a glass of the water with their breakfasts. The cupola seen over the well was erected in 1804. In order to serve the growing number of people arriving at Harrogate seeking a cure for a wide variety of complaints the Queen's Head Hotel was built and it is probably the oldest inn here as it dates from before 1687. When stagecoaches began to arrive in the 18th century the inn moved with the times and it became the first at the spa to serve the needs of the coaches. By the late 1700s it was one of the largest hotels in this fast growing town and, though the hotel changed its name to the Queen's Hotel in 1828 and underwent extensive renovation and remodelling in the mid-19th century, it did not survive the decline of the spa and, in 1951, it became the offices for the Regional Hospital Board. Many other hotels were built including the Crown Inn, next to the Old Sulphur Well, which too became a coaching inn in 1772 and hosted a visit by Lord Byron in 1806. However, one of the town's most famous hotels, The Majestic, an early 20th century red brick building, does survive and it was the place where Sir Edward Elgar stayed while visiting Harrogate.

In 1842 the Old Sulphur Well was enclosed in the splendid Royal Pump Room. This major water place for spa visitors has been painstakingly restored to illustrate all aspects of Harrogate's history. Now the **Royal Pump Room Museum**, there are a number of interesting displays and exhibitions here that include stories of watery miracles, Russian royalty and even disappearing crime writers. The sulphur water, the strongest in Europe, still rises beneath the building and can still be sampled. The museum is open daily throughout the year.

There will be few Harrogate residents who have not heard of Betty Lupton, the almost legendary 'Queen of the Wells' who, for over 50 years, dispensed the spa waters, dishing out cupfuls to paying visitors, who were then encouraged to walk off the dubious effects of the medicine by taking a trip around the Bogs Fields, known today as the Valley Gardens. She conducted her business in the ostentatiously named **Royal Baths**

Market Square, Harrogate

visited the town and described it as *'the queerest place, with the strangest people in it leading the oddest lives of dancing, newspaper reading and table d'hôte'*. Though its status as a spa town has declined, it is still a fashionable place, a sought-after conference location, home of the annual Northern Antiques Fair and a town with much to offer the visitor. Along with developing as a spa, Harrogate also became a centre for shopping for the well-to-do and the many old fashioned shops are typified by Montpellier Parade, a crescent of shops surrounded by trees and flowerbeds.

Another attractive aspect of the town is **The Stray** that is unique to Harrogate and virtually encircles the town centre. These 200 acres of open space are protected by ancient laws to ensure that the residents of, and visitors to, the town always have access for sports, events and walking. The spacious lawns are at their most picturesque during the spring when they are edged with crocus and daffodils. Originally part of the Forest of Knaresborough the land was, fortunately, not enclosed under the 1770 Act of Parliament. The large grit stone pillar, beside The Stray, marks the boundary of the Leeds and Ripon turnpike. On The Stray stands the

Assembly Rooms which, in their heyday, were full of rich visitors sampling the waters. Today, the buildings have been restored to house the Turkish Baths where visitors can enjoy a sauna and solarium, and they are open to the public daily. Housed in the oldest of the town's surviving spa buildings and originally built in 1806, the **Mercer Art Gallery** is home to a superb collection of fine art along with the Kent Bequest – an archaeological collection that includes finds from both ancient Greece and Egypt.

By the late 18th century Harrogate had become one of Europe's most fashionable spa towns and it was not only serving the needs of those with acute and chronic ailments but also members of 'good society'. Fuelled by competition from spa towns abroad, Harrogate sought to provide not only medical care for the sick but also to appeal to the needs of the rich and fashionable. In 1858, Charles Dickens

Commemorative Oak Tree that was planted in 1902 by Samson Fox to commemorate the ox roasting that took place here as part of the celebrations for Queen Victoria's Jubilee in 1887 and the end of the Boer War in 1902.

Perhaps the most well-known tale associated with Harrogate surrounds the disappearance of Agatha Christie in 1926. In a set of circumstances reminiscent of one of her novels, Agatha went missing in December of that year, possibly as a result of marital difficulties. Her crashed car was discovered near a chalk pit close to her home but the novelist was nowhere to be found and one of the largest police manhunts was put into operation. Agatha had, in fact, travelled to Harrogate after abandoning her car, and booked into the Old Swan Hotel under the name of her husband's mistress, Theresa Neele. After 10 days she was spotted and her husband came to collect her, putting her disappearance down to loss of memory. However, this did not dispel rumours that the marriage was in trouble or that the surprising event was nothing more than a publicity stunt. Whatever the truth, two years later the couple divorced and Colonel Christie married his long-time mistress Theresa. Today, Harrogate is perhaps better known as 'Brawton' in the long running television series *All Creatures Great and Small* – the place to which James and Helen Herriot came when the vet took a well-earned half-day off.

Just to the west of the town lie **Harlow Carr Botanical Gardens** that were established in 1948 by the Northern Horticultural Society and now cover some 68 acres. The gardens feature all manner of plants in a wide variety of landscapes, including herb, scented, rock, bulk and woodland gardens, which allow members of the public to see how they perform in the unsympathetic conditions of northern England. The society, as well as having their study centre here, has also opened a fascinating **Museum of Gardening**.

Around Harrogate

Ripley

4 miles N of Harrogate on the A6165

Still very much an estate village, Ripley is a quiet and pretty place with cobbled streets, a castle, a wonderful hotel and an interesting history. This title was granted to Thomas Ingilby in the 1300s, for killing a wild boar in Knaresborough Forest that was charging at Edward III, and it remains with the family today. The magnificent **Ripley Castle** has been home to the family since 1325 and, open to the public, it is set in an outstanding Capability Brown landscape with lakes, a deer park and an avenue of tall beeches over which the attractive towers can only just be seen. However, its tranquillity belies the events that have taken place here over the centuries and particularly after the battle at Marston Moor when Cromwell, exhausted after his day's slaughter, camped his troops here and chose to rest in the castle.

The Ingilbys, however, were Royalists and his intrusion was met with as much ill-will as possible; they offered him neither food nor a bed. Jane Ingilby, aptly named 'Trooper Jane' due to her fighting skills, was the house's occupant and, having forced the self-styled Lord Protector of England to sleep on a sofa with two pistols pointing at his head, declared the next morning, 'It was well that he behaved in so peaceable a manner; had it been otherwise, he would not have left the house alive.' Cromwell, his pride severely damaged by a woman, ordered the immediate execution of his Royalist prisoners and left Trooper Jane regretting using her pistols during the previous night. Visitors to the castle today, which is open all year round (though with limited opening times in winter), will receive an altogether warmer welcome. Along with the fine Georgian and Tudor rooms, there is the Civil War armour in the Knight's Chamber and a secret priest's hole that was discovered by accident in 1964. Outside, the walled garden contains the National Hyacinth Collection as well as rare fruits and vegetables while the recently restored hothouses are home to a tropical plant collection.

Ripley Castle

The village church, built in around 1400, also bears scars from the Civil War when Cromwell's firing squads used it as a place of execution for their Royalist prisoners. Also of interest here is the Town Hall that is rather curiously named the Hotel de Ville. It was built in 1827 by Sir William Amcotts Ingilby when he was remodelling the village on one that he had seen during a recent visit to Alsace Lorraine.

Knaresborough

3½ mile NE of Harrogate on the A59

This ancient town of pantiled cottages and Georgian houses is precariously balanced on a hillside by the River Nidd while a stately railway viaduct, 90 feet high and 338 feet long and completed in 1851, spans the gorge. There are many unusual and attractive features in the town, amongst them a maze of steep-stepped narrow streets leading down to the river and numerous alleyways. In addition to boating on the river, there are many enjoyable riverside walks.

The town is dominated by the ruins of

River Nidd, Knaresborough

Knaresborough Castle that was built high on a crag overlooking the River Nidd by Serlo de Burgh, who had fought alongside William the Conqueror at Hastings. Throughout the Middle Ages, the castle was a favourite with royalty and the court and it was to Knaresborough that the murderers of Thomas à Becket fled in 1170, while Queen Philippa, wife of Edward III, also enjoyed staying at Knaresborough and she and her family spent many summers here. However, following the Civil War, when the town and its castle had remained loyal to the king, Cromwell ordered its destruction. Along with touring this once royal fortification, with its dungeon and mysterious underground sallyport, visitors to Knaresborough can find out more about the town's history at the **Old Courthouse Museum**. Not only is the museum home to a rare and an original Tudor courtroom, but also the Pike and Plumes Gallery that illustrates what life was like during the Civil War and, among the displays, is the linen shirt worn by the Royalist Sir Henry Slingsby when he went to the gallows.

The nearby Bebra Gardens are named after Knaresborough's twin town in Germany and its attractive flower beds are complemented by luxurious lawns and a paddling pool. In the High Street, visitors should keep an eye out for **Ye Oldest Chymists' Shoppe** in England that dates back to 1720. For the last century and more, it has been owned by the Pickles family who manufacture some 40 lotions, ointments and creams. Amongst their potions are Fiery Jack, a rubbing ointment, Snowfire for chapped hands, and the self-explanatory Snufflebabe Vapour Rub.

However, Knaresborough is probably best known for **Mother Shipton's Cave**, the birthplace of the famous prophetess, and for its **Petrifying Well** that provides a constant source of curiosity to the visitor. The effects that the well's lime-rich water has on objects are truly amazing and an array of paraphernalia, from old boots to bunches of grapes, are on view – seemingly turned to stone. It is little wonder that these were considered magical properties by the superstitious over the centuries or that the well was associated with witchcraft and various other interesting tales. The foremost tale concerns Mother Shipton, who was said to have been born in the cavern situated by the well on 6th July 1488 and who has the reputation of being England's most famous fortune-teller. The story goes that she was born in the midst of a terrible storm and was soon found to have a strange ability to see the future. As she grew older her prophetic visions became more widely known and also feared throughout England. However, the most singular feature about Mother Shipton has to be that she died peacefully in her bed, as opposed to being burnt at the stake as most witches were at that time although she had been threatened with burning by, amongst others, Cardinal Wolsey, after she had warned him on a visit to York that he might see the city again but never enter. True to her prediction Wolsey never did enter York, for he was arrested on a charge of treason at Cawood. She is also reputed to have foretold the invasion and defeat of the Spanish Armada in 1588 and Samuel Pepys recorded that it was Mother Shipton who prophesied the disastrous Great Fire of London in 1666. Both the cave and the well can be found in the Mother Shipton Estate, part of the Ancient Forest of Knaresborough, which offers visitors beautiful walks beside the River Nidd in grounds that were classically landscaped in the 18th century.

Also on the banks of the River Nidd is the famous **St Robert's Cave** that is, in fact, an ancient hermitage. Robert was the son of a mayor of York who, at the time of his death in 1218, was so beloved by the people of Knaresborough that they would not allow the monks of Fountains Abbey to bury him and, instead, they kept his bones and he was finally interred beneath the altar in the Chapel of Our Lady of the Crag. His final resting place is guarded by the statue of a larger than life-size figure of a knight in the act of drawing a sword. Close by is the **House in the Rock** (closed to the public) that was hewn out of the solid rockface by Thomas Hill, an eccentric weaver, between 1770 and 1786. It was Hill's son who renamed the house Fort Montagu and flew a flag and fired a gun salute on special occasions. Another of Knaresborough's attractive amenities is **Conyngham Hall**, a majestic old house enclosed within a loop of the River Nidd. Once the home of Lord Macintosh, the Halifax toffee magnate, the hall itself is not open to the public but its landscaped grounds, stretching down to the river, are and provide tennis, putting and other activities.

Knaresborough certainly seems to have a reputation for being home to both exceptional and odd characters and, following in this tradition, there is 'Blind Jack of Knaresborough'. Jack Metcalfe was born in 1717 and, although he lost his sight at the age of six, he went on to achieve fame as a roadmaker. A remarkable person who never allowed his blindness to bar him from any normal activities, Jack rode, climbed trees, swam and was often employed to guide travellers through the wild Forest of Knaresborough. He was also a talented fiddle player and one of his more roguish exploits was his elopement with Dolly Benson, the daughter of the innkeeper of the Royal Oak in Harrogate, on the night before she was due to marry another man. However, Jack's most memorable achievement, and for what he is best remembered, was the laying of roads over the surrounding bogs and marshes that he achieved by laying a foundation of bundles of heather, a feat that had never been done before.

Just south of Knaresborough lie **Plumpton Rocks**, a series of dramatic millstone grit rocks set beside an idyllic lake with woodland paths that were laid out in the 18th century. Declared a garden of special historic interest by English Heritage, the garden is open every weekend and daily during July and August.

Goldsborough

5 miles E of Harrogate off the A59

An estate village since the time of the Norman Conquest, this rather special village was sold by the Earl of Harewood in the 1950s to pay enormous death duties. The charming 12th century **Church of St Mary** has some interesting features including a Norman doorhead and an effigy of a knight and it is also has the image of the 'Green Man', the Celtic god of fertility, which is well hidden on one of the many Goldsborough family tombs. In 1859, while the church was being restored, a lead casket was discovered containing Viking jewellery and coins. In the 1920s, Mary, the daughter of George V and Queen Mary, lived here after her marriage and her eldest son, George, was christened in the church.

Spofforth

4½ miles SE of Harrogate on the A661

Situated on the tiny River Crimple, this ancient village is home to the stirring ruins of **Spofforth Castle** (English Heritage) that was originally built in the 16th century by the powerful Percy family. Replacing a manor house that had repeatedly been laid to waste, the castle was destroyed during the Civil War. Among the many events that took place here it is said to have been the birthplace of Harry Hotspur.

Just southeast of the village is the splendid Palladian mansion, **Stockeld Park**, which was built between 1758 and 1763 by Paine. Containing some excellent furniture and a fine picture collection, the house is surrounded by extensive parkland that offers garden walks. The house is privately owned and is open only by appointment.

Beckwithshaw

2½ miles SW of Harrogate on the B6161

This village, as its name suggests, was once bounded by a stream and woodland though, sadly, most of the trees have now gone. Once part of the great Forest of Knaresborough, a local legend tells how John O'Gaunt promised John Haverah, a cripple, as much land as he could hop around between sunrise and sunset. By throwing his crutch the last few yards, just as the sun was setting, John Haverah managed to secure himself seven square miles, the remainder of which is, today, called **Haverah Park**.

Hampsthwaite

4 miles NW of Harrogate off the A59

This picturesque Nidderdale village lies on an ancient Roman route between Ilkley and Aldborough and traces of Roman tin mining have been found in the area. The village Church of St Thomas has remnants of a Saxon building in the tower and, in the churchyard, is buried Peter Barker. Known as 'Blind Peter', Barker was a local character very much in the tradition of Jack Metcalfe and he, too, did not let his disability hinder him: he was a skilled cabinet-maker, glazier and musician. The mysterious portrait of the bearded man hanging in the church, painted by the local vicar's daughter, may well be that of Peter Barker.

Birstwith

5 miles NW of Harrogate off the B6165

Evidence in the form of a Neolithic axe head suggests that this one-time estate village in the valley of the River Nidd was a Stone Age settlement in what was to become known as the Forest of

The Old Station Inn

Station Road, Birstwith, Harrogate, North Yorkshire HG3 3AG
Tel/Fax: 01423 770254
e-mail: riccaven@freeuk.com

Back in the great days of the railways, the lovely village of Birstwith was a stop on the line that ran between Skipton and Harrogate – and today the venerable station house, which dates back to 1857, is the disinguished **Old Station Inn**. Run by brothers Richard and Michael, with able assistance from bar-manager Wendy, the inn has been tastefully refurbished since they took over in 2003 and is now strikingly handsome and always welcoming.

Open for both sessions Tuesday to Friday and Bank Holiday Mondays, all day Saturday and all day in summer on Sundays, there are three real ales on tap, including a changing guest ale, together with a good range of lagers, cider, stout, wines, spirits and soft drinks.

Delicious food is served Tuesday – Saturday at lunch and dinner, and Sunday lunchtime, with a range of favourites such as mixed grills, steaks, fisherman pie, home-made soups and much more. Michael has been a chef for over 25 years, and guests can be assured of expertly prepared and presented dishes. Booking is required for Thursdays and Sundays.

During the lifetime of this edition bed and breakfast accommodation will be available – please ring for details.Children welcome.

Knaresborough. Along with both quarrying and coal mining, Birstwith also had a cotton mill beside the river but all that remains is the weir that was created to ensure a good head of water for the mill-race. A notable visitor to the village was Charlotte Brontë, who stayed with the Greenwood family at Swarcliffe Hall for around six months in 1840s while she was governess to the children. Unfortunately the Swarcliffe estate is no more and the Hall is now a private boys' school.

Burnt Yates

5½ miles NW of Harrogate on the B6165

Located at one of the highest points in the Nidderdale, Burnt Yates enjoys some fine views of the surrounding hills and moors. The tiny village school of 1750 still stands and it was originally endowed to provide education in the three 'Rs' for 30 poor boys and for an equivalent number of poor girls to learn the skills of needlework and spinning.

Ripon

This attractive cathedral city, on the banks of the Rivers Ure, Skell, and Laver, dates from the 7th century when Alfrich, King of Northumbria granted an area of land here, surrounding a new monastery, to the Church. Later that century, in AD672, St Wilfrid built one of England's first stone churches on the high ground between the three rivers and brought in plasterers, stonemasons

Ripon Cathedral

and glaziers from France and Italy to undertake the work. At the time of the demise of the Northern Kingdom in the mid-10th century, the monastery and church were destroyed, though the Saxon crypt survives to this day. By the time of the Norman Conquest, Ripon was a prosperous agricultural settlement under ecclesiastical rule and it was at this time that a second St Wilfrid's Church, instigated by the first Norman Archbishop of York, Thomas of Bayeux, was erected on the site of the Saxon building. On Christmas Day 1132, monks from York worshipped here while they were making a journey to found Fountains Abbey and, traditionally, the people of Ripon follow this ancient route on Boxing Day. The 1,300-year-old Crypt is all that remains of the original Saxon church and, at its northeastern corner, is a narrow passage known as The Needle. According to the 17th century antiquary, Thomas Fuller, women whose chastity was suspect were made to pass through this passageway and if they were unable to do so their reputations were irretrievably tarnished.

The magnificent **Cathedral of St Peter and St Wilfrid** now stands on this site and it was begun in the mid-12th century by Archbishop Roger of York and was originally a simple cruciform building although the west front was added in the 1250s and the east choir in 1286. Rebuilding work was begun in the 16th century but the disruption of the Dissolution of the Monasteries caused the work to be abandoned and it was only the intervention of James I in the early 1600s, which saved the building from ruin. Then established as a collegiate church, the diocese of Ripon was formed in 1836 and the church became a cathedral. Often referred to as the 'Cathedral of the Dales', the building, though one of the tallest cathedrals in England, is also the smallest. Discovered in 1976 close to the cathedral, the **Ripon Jewel** is the only surviving trace of the magnificence that was characteristic of the cathedral's early history. A small gold roundel inlaid with gemstones, the jewel's design suggests that it was made to embellish a relic casket or cross ordered by St Wilfrid.

Throughout the Middle Ages, the town prospered: its market charter had been granted by King Alfred in the 9th century and, at one time, Ripon produced more woollen cloth than Halifax and Leeds. The collapse of the woollen industry saw a rise in spur manufacture in the 16th century and their fame was such that Ripon spurs were referred to in the old proverb 'As true steel as a Ripon rowel.'

As well as having three rivers, Ripon also has a canal and it was the most northerly point of England's canal system. Built between 1767 and 1773 to improve the navigation of the River Ure, the waterway was designed by John Smeaton, builder of the Eddystone Lighthouse. However, by 1820 the company running the canal had fallen into debt and it was little used after that time. The final stretch of the **Ripon Canal** and its Canal Basin have recently been reopened and, along with providing a mooring for pleasure crafts, the basin also provides an insight into the history of the waterway and local crafts.

Fortunately for today's visitor, the Industrial Revolution, and all its associated implications, by-passed Ripon and it was not until the early 20th century that the town flourished, though briefly, as a spa. However, many ancient customs and festivals have survived down the centuries and perhaps the most famous is the sounding of the Wakeman's Horn each night at 9 p.m. in the market place. Dating back to the 9th century, the Wakeman was originally appointed to patrol the town after the nightly curfew had been blown and, in many ways, this was the first form of security patrol. The Wakeman was selected each year from the town's 12 aldermen and those choosing not to take office were fined heavily. Today, this old custom is revived in the Mayor-making Ceremony when the elected mayor shows great reluctance to take office and hides from his colleagues.

As might be expected any walk around this ancient town reveals, in its buildings, its interesting and varied past. At the heart of the town is the **Market Place** and here stands a tall obelisk that was erected in 1702 to replace the ancient market cross. Restored in 1781, at its summit are a horn and a rowel spur, symbolising Ripon's crafts and customs. Situated at the edge of the square are the 14th century Wakeman's House and the attractive Georgian Town Hall.

Although the town had no spring of its own, it did make a bid to become a fashionable spa resort and the sulphur mineral water was pumped from Aldfield near Fountains Abbey. However, the scheme failed but the **Spa Baths** building, opened in 1905 by the Princess of Battenberg, is a reminder of those times and now houses the city's swimming pool. It is a fine example of art nouveau architecture, and the surrounding Spa Gardens are still a pleasant place for a walk.

Near to the cathedral is Ripon's old Courthouse that was built in 1830 on the site of an earlier 17th century Common Hall and it was used for both the Quarter Sessions and the Court Military. Adjacent to this fine Georgian courthouse is a Tudor building that was part of the Archbishop of York's summer palace. Also not far away is the House of Correction, built in 1686, which served as the local prison between 1816 and 1878 and then became the police station until the late 1950s.

This austere building is now home to the **Ripon Prison and Police Museum**, established in 1984, which depicts the history of the police force and gives visitors a real insight into the life of a prisoner in Victorian times as well as displays on early punishments such as confinement in stocks, pillory and public whipping. Almost as unfortunate as those prisoners were the inmates of the local workhouse and **Ripon Workhouse Museum** is one of the city's newer attractions. The restored vagrants' wards of 1877 provide a chilling insight into the treatment of paupers in Yorkshire workhouses and the displays include a 'Victorian Hard Times Gallery'. These museums are open daily from Easter to October.

Finally, there is **Ripon Racecourse** that dates back to 1713 although racing has been held in the town since 1664 and the present course was opened in 1900. Meetings are held here between April and August and the course, known as Yorkshire's Garden Racecourse, is widely regarded as one of the most beautiful in the country.

Around Ripon

Wath

4 miles N of Ripon off the A1

Just to the south of the village lies the stately home of **Norton Conyers** that has been owned by the Graham family since 1624 though, undoubtedly, the house's main claim to fame is the visit made here by Charlotte Brontë. During her stay the novelist heard the story of Mad Mary, supposedly a Lady Graham. Apparently Lady Graham had been locked up in an attic room, now tantalisingly inaccessible to the public, and Charlotte eventually based the character of Mrs Rochester in her novel *Jane Eyre* on the unfortunate woman. The house also features in the same novel as 'Thornfield Hall'. Visitors to the hall will also see the famous painting of Sir Bellingham Graham on his bay horse, as Master of the Quorn hunt and it is rumoured that ownership of the painting was once decided on the throwing of a pair of dice. Other family pictures, furniture and costumes are on display and there is a lovely 18th century walled garden within the grounds. The hall and grounds are open on a limited basis.

Sion Hill

9 miles NE of Ripon off the A167

Celebrated as the 'last of the great country houses', **Sion Hill Hall,** with its light, airy and well-proportioned rooms, all facing south, is typical of the work of the celebrated Yorkshire architect, Walter Brierley. Dubbed the 'Lutyens of the North', Brierley completed the building in 1913 for Percy Stancliffe and his wife Ethel, the wealthy daughter of a whisky distiller. Although the rooms have remained unaltered since they were built their contents certainly have changed. In 1962, the Sion Hill Hall was bought by Herbert Mawer, a compulsive but highly discerning collector of antiques and during the 20 years he lived here, Herbert continued to add to what was already, probably the best collection of Georgian, Victorian and Edwardian artefacts in the north of England. Furniture, paintings, porcelain, clocks (all working) and ephemera crowd the richly furnished rooms and make Sion Hill a delight to visit. A recent addition to the many sumptuous displays is a charming exhibition of dolls from the early 1900s.

In the hall's Victorian walled garden is another major visitor attraction – the **Birds of Prey and Conservation Centre** where, in this beautiful English garden, visitors can see eagles, hawks, kites, falcons and owls fly freely during the regularly held demonstrations. There are

The Three Tuns Hotel

Market Place, Thirsk,
North Yorkshire YO7 1LH
Tel: 01845 523124 Fax: 01845 526126
e-mail: Threetuns@talk21.com
website: www.the-three-tuns-thirsk.co.uk

A magnificent, historic premises that dates back to 1698, **The Three Tuns Hotel** stands proudly overlooking the market square at Thirsk, just a short walk from the James Herriot Centre. Originally the family home of the Bells, who played an important role in the development of the town, in 1740 the house was adapted to become a coaching inn. The coaching stables can still be seen in the carpark. The London, Edinburgh, Newcastle, Leeds and Darlington coaches all would stop here to enjoy the hospitality on offer. Today this legacy continues, with owners Mary and Philip Nelson providing excellent food, drink and accommodation to all visitors.

The décor and furnishings boast many original features, and exemplify the grace and style of a bygone age. All 12 guest bedrooms are ensuite, and each individually designed – one has a four-poster – with guests' comfort in mind. All rooms have a simple elegance that make them supremely comfortable. Special offers available out of season.

Within easy reach of the stunning countryside made famous in Herriot's work, and also of York, Harrogate, Whitby and many other of North Yorkshire's premiere attractions, this superb hotel makes the perfect touring base.

Quality cuisine is served daily from midday until 8 p.m. The menu's accent is distinctly Yorkshire, with a range of traditional dishes expertly prepared and presented. The menu includes roast beef with home-made Yorkshire puddings, lamb shank with minted gravy, poached cod and vegetable lasagne, along with a selection of sandwiches, a range of sausages (their country herb variety was voted Yorkshire Sausage of the Year in 1999) and other delicious and hearty favourites.

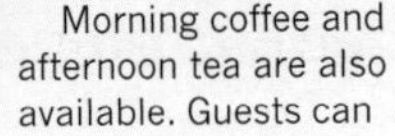

Morning coffee and afternoon tea are also available. Guests can dine in the no-smoking restaurant, the cocktail bar or a smaller dining room. All are convivial and welcoming, with handsome décor and comfortable furnishings.

Real ales on tap include John Smiths Cask and changing guest ales.

over 80 birds here from 34 different species and the centre brings to life the skill and art of falconry. Visitors also have the chance to learn about the breeding and training programmes that take place here to ensure that these birds, and their skills, are retained for future generations. The centre is open daily from March to October.

Thirsk

10 miles NE of Ripon off the A19

Thirsk has become famous as the home of veterinary surgeon Alf Wight, author of *All Creatures Great and Small*, who is perhaps better known as James Herriot. In his immensely popular books, Thirsk is clearly recognisable as 'Darrowby' and, in 1999, **The World of James Herriot** (see panel below), housed in the actual 'Skeldale House' of the television series was opened. Visitors can take a trip back in time to the 1940s, explore the life and times of the world's most famous country vet and learn more about Alf Wight. There is the chance to see the old Austin car used in the series and also the opportunity to take part in a TV production. The attraction is open daily, all year round.

The World of James Herriot

23 Kirkgate, Thirsk, N. Yorkshire YO7 1PL
Tel: 01845 524234 Fax: 01845 525333
e-mail: jamesherriot@hambleton.co.uk
website: www.worldofjamesherriot.org

Celebrating the world's most famous veterinary surgeon, **The World of James Herriot** opened in the spring of 1999 and since then has welcomed more than 200,000 visitors. The attraction occupies the original house, now a Grade II listed building, in which James Herriot lived and worked. The house has been lovingly restored to how it was in the 1940s and '50s with many original pieces of furniture donated by the author's family. After passing through the famous red door, visitors enter the dining room which doubled as the practice office. Then on to the cosy family room where you'll hear James' favourite music – Bing Crosby – playing. Further down the corridor is the practice dispensary where he would make up his prescriptions. Next door is the small surgery where James would treat domestic animals. At the heart of the house is the large kitchen, the hub of family life.

The garden has also been taken back to the 1950s, re-creating a typical English cottage garden complete with a small vegetable plot. A further exhibit concentrates on the film and TV adaptations of James Herriot's bestselling books – here you'll find the original Austin 7 tourer car, three studio sets from *All Creatures Great and Small*, and some original 1970s cameras and equipment.

Just across the road from this famous surgery is the birthplace of another son of Thirsk. The building is now the town's **Museum** and tourist office and a plaque outside records that Thomas Lord was born here in 1755 and, some 30 years later, he was to create the famous cricket ground in Marylebone that still bears his name. A more recent celebrity whose home is in Thirsk is Bill Foggitt, renowned for his weather forecasts based on his precise observations of nature.

Thirsk appeared in the *Domesday Book* not long after William the Conqueror had granted the Manor of Thirsk to one of his barons, Robert de Mowbray. The Mowbrays became a powerful family in the area, a fact reflected in the naming of the area to the north and west of Thirsk as the Vale of Mowbray. In the early 1100s the family received permission to hold a market at Thirsk but then blotted their copybook by rebelling against Henry II in 1173. The rebellion failed and their castle at Thirsk was burnt to the ground and no trace of it remains today. The market, however, is still thriving and is held twice weekly on Mondays and Saturdays. An old market by-law used to stipulate that no butcher was allowed to kill a bull for sale in the market until the beast had been baited by the town dogs. This by-law was abandoned in the early 1800s and the bull-ring to which the animal was tethered has also disappeared.

This pleasant small town of mellow

The Kings Arms

Sandhutton, Thirsk,
North Yorkshire YO7 4RW
Tel: 01845 587263 Mobile: 07903 312971
e-mail: juliewhitlam@aol.com

A superb early 18th-century former coaching inn, **The Kings Arms** stands in the picturesque village of Sandhutton, on the A167 and approximately three miles west of Thirsk and south of Northallerton.

Andy and Julie Whitlam took over here as owners in March of 2004. It is their first venture into the licensing trade, though Andy has 18 years' experience as a professional chef.

The interior is a picture, cosy and stylish, with a wealth of charming original features.

Closed Mondays from October to Easter and open every other session, there are three real ales here – Black Sheep, Timothy Taylor Landlord and John Smiths – together with a good selection of lagers, cider, stout, wines, spirits and soft drinks.

Really excellent food is served every day at lunch 12 – 2) and dinner (Monday to Saturday 5.30 – 9, Sundays 7 – 9). Guests choose from the menu and specials board – specialities include steak and ale pie and giant filled Yorkshire pudding. Booking required Friday and Saturday evening. The restaurant seats 20 and there's a no-smoking lounge that can seat 16 additional diners.

This fine inn also boasts two quality ensuite guest bedrooms.

Thirsk Church

brick houses has a sprawling Market Place and a magnificent 15th century St Mary's Church that is generally regarded as the finest parish church in North Yorkshire. It was here that the real life 'James Herriot' married his wife, Helen. Cod Beck, a tributary of the River Swale, wanders through the town, providing some delightful and well-signposted riverside walks.

On the edge of town, the **Trees to Treske Visitor Centre** is an imaginative exhibition exploring how trees grow, the character of different woods and examples of the cabinet maker's craft. Nearby is **Thirsk Racecourse**, known to devotees of the turf as the 'Country Racecourse'. There are around 12 race meetings each year, all well attended by visitors keen to experience this intrinsic feature of Yorkshire life. Travelling through the areas between the Yorkshire Dales and the North York Moors, visitors are constantly reminded of the great tradition of horse breeding and training for which the county is famous. The tradition runs deep: even the long flat straight stretch of main railway line between York and Darlington is known as the 'racecourse'.

Skelton-on-ure

3 miles SE of Ripon off the B6265

This charming little village has some surviving cottages, dating from 1540, which are built from small handmade bricks with pantiled roofs. A ferry used to cross the River Ure, at this point, to Bishop Monkton and, in 1869, it was the scene of a notorious hunting accident. Members of the York and Ainsty Hunt boarded the ferry in order to follow a fox that had swum across the river. Half way across the horses panicked, capsizing the boat, and the boatman, along with five hunt members, were drowned.

Hidden away just to the south of the village is one of the area's finest stately homes, **Newby Hall**. Designed and built by Robert Adam in the 18th century, much of this superb Georgian house is open to the public and, along with fine classical statuary, Bogelins tapestries and fine Chippendale furniture, visitors can see the splendid Billiard Room with its fine portrait of Frederick Grantham Vyner. An ancestor of the family that had lived here from the mid-19th century, Frederick was murdered by Greek bandits after being kidnapped.

The Black Lion

Skelton-on-Ure, Ripon,
North Yorkshire HG4 5AJ
Tel/Fax: 01423 322516

Situated just a short drive from Ripon, **The Black Lion** is a distinctive, quality public house dating back to 1830. The décor looks a picture – pristine and handsome, with a wealth of original features – and the ambience is always warm and welcoming.

Open every session except Tuesday lunchtime and all day Saturdays and Sundays, Cumberland Ale is the regular here, along with two rotating guest ales. The pub hosts a beer festival held in June and July every year – please ring for details.

Food is served Wednesday – Monday 12 – 2 and 6.30 – 9; booking is required Friday to Sunday. Home-cooking and local produce are the order of the day, with tempting dishes such as honey minted lamb steak, brie and broccoli bake, lemon sole, beef in red wine and local seafood. The no-smoking restaurant seats 45 comfortably. Children welcome.

Nearby there's a lovely caravan site with 10 electric hook-ups, available all year round.

The house is perhaps most famous for its superb tapestries and there is also a fine collection of Chippendale furniture.

It is, though, the award-winning **Newby Hall Gardens** that draw most people to the house: extensive and well-designed, it was the present owner's father who transformed a 9-hole golf course into the 25 acres of gardens that offer something for everyone whatever the time of year. The gardens' famous double herbaceous borders form the main point of attraction here and from which there are formal compartmental gardens. Also found here are a wonderful Woodland Discovery Walk, a miniature railway, plenty of other attractions specially designed for children, a shop and a restaurant.

Newby Hall

Boroughbridge

5½ miles SE of Ripon on the B6265

This attractive and historic town dates from the reign of William the Conqueror though it was once on a main thoroughfare used by both the Celts of Brigantia and, later, the Romans. The bridge over the River Ure, from which the village takes its name, was built in 1562 and formed part of an important road link between Edinburgh and London. Busy throughout the coaching days with traffic passing from the West Riding of Yorkshire to the North, Boroughbridge has now returned to its former unassuming role of a small wayside town now bypassed by the A1(M) that takes most of the 21st-century traffic from its streets.

The great **Devil's Arrows**, three massive Bronze Age monoliths, stand like guardians close to the new road and form Yorkshire's most famous ancient monument, which is thought to date from about 2000 BC. The monoliths, the tallest of which is 30 feet high, stand in a line running north to south and are fashioned from millstone grit that has been seriously fluted by weathering. A local legend, however, attributes the great stones to the Devil suggesting that they were, actually, crossbow bolts that he fired at nearby **Aldborough** that was, at the time, a Christian settlement. A quiet little backwater today, at the time of the Romans, Aldborough was a thriving town known as 'Isurium Brigantum', the capital of the Celtic tribe of the Brigantes.

Studley Roger

2 miles SW of Ripon off the B6265

This small hamlet, in the valley of the River Skell, is home to **Fountains Abbey** (National Trust), the only World Heritage Site in Yorkshire and certainly its greatest ecclesiastical ruin. The abbey was one of the wealthiest Cistercian houses in the country and its remains are the most complete of any Cistercian

Fountains Abbey

abbey in Britain. Founded in 1132, with the help of Archbishop Thurstan of York, the first buildings housed just 13 monks of the order and, over the centuries its size increased, even spreading across the River Skell itself. The abbey reached its peak in the 15th century with the grandiose designs of Abbot Marmaduke Huby, whose beautiful tower still stands as a reminder of just how rich and powerful Fountains became. In fact, the abbey was run on such businesslike lines that, at its height, as well as owning extensive lands throughout Yorkshire, it had an income of about a thousand pounds a year, then a very substantial sum indeed.

It is commonly thought that one of the abbey's friars, renowned for his strength and skill as an archer, challenged Robin Hood to a sword fight. Forced to concede, the friar joined the Merry Men of Sherwood and became known as 'Friar Tuck'. The Dissolution hit the abbey as it did all the powerful religious houses. The abbot was hanged, the monks scattered, and its treasures taken off or destroyed. The stonework, however, was left largely intact, possibly due to its remote location. In 1579, Sir Stephen Proctor pulled down some outbuildings, in order to construct **Fountains Hall**, a magnificent Elizabethan mansion that still stands in the abbey's grounds and part of which is open to the public. Along with the guided tours that reveal the abbey's turbulent history there are various other activities and trails here for all the family along with exhibitions, a restaurant and a shop.

Close to the abbey are the magnificent **Studley Royal Gardens** (National Trust) that were created in the early 18th century before they were merged with nearby ruins in 1768. Started by John Aislabie, the disgraced Chancellor of the Exchequer and founder of the South Sea Company that spectacularly burst its bubble in 1720, the landscaping took some 14 years. It then took a further 10 years to complete the construction of the buildings and follies found within the gardens. With a network of paths and the River Skell flowing through the grounds, it is well worth exploring these superb gardens.

North Stainley

4½ miles NW of Ripon on the A6108

Just over 100 years ago, in 1895, excavations in a field just outside the village revealed the site of a Roman villa called 'Castle Dykes' though all that can be seen now are the grassed outlines of the foundations and the moat. However, the discovery does prove that there has been a settlement here for many centuries. The monks of Fountains Abbey also knew North Stainley and **Slenningford Grange** is thought to have been one of their many properties and a fishpond, dating from medieval times, can still be seen here.

Just to the south of the village lies the **Lightwater Valley Theme Park** set in 175 acres of scenic grounds that provides

The Grantley Arms

High Grantley, Ripon,
North Yorkshire HG4 3PJ
Tel: 01765 620227 Fax: 01765 620504
website: www.grantleyarms.com

The Grantley Arms is a fine old inn dating back to the late 1600s and set in the picturesque village of High Grantley. Popular with locals and visitors alike, the pub's handsome décor and comfort are just two of its many attractions adding to its warm ambience. The bar areas are spacious; the restaurant is air-conditioned and can seat 30 people. The food comes highly recommended. Head chef Paul appointed in 2002, prepares an excellent range of dishes, such as slow-roasted lamb, pheasant, venison sausages, halibut steak and red pepper and goat's cheese parcels - just a sampling of the 20 or more main courses to choose from.

To complement your meal there's a good range of draught ales and an excellent selection of wines.

Food is served Tuesday to Saturday: lunch (12 – 2); dinner (5.30 – 9); Sundays (12 to 3.30). Guests select from the à la carte menu or special's board. Special two or three course lunches are also available, and there's an evening 'early bird' menu between 5.30 and 7 Tuesday to Friday. Booking is advisable.

thrills and spills for all the family. The park boasts 'Ultimate', the biggest roller coaster in the world (as authenticated by the *Guinness Book of Records*), the Rat Ride, Falls of Terror and the Viper to name just a few and there are plenty of more appropriate activities and rides for younger children as well. Also within the grounds is Lightwater Village that offers a wide variety of retail and factory shops, a garden centre, restaurant and coffee shop.

Kirkby Malzeard

6 miles NW of Ripon off the A6108

Dating back to the 11th century, the village's **Church of St Andrew** is noted for its associations with witchcraft and, in particular, the northeastern corner of the churchyard that was favoured by practitioners of the black arts as a venue for conducting their strange rituals and charms. Black magic aside, the church has been pealing its bells for over 400 years and records show that in 1591 one of the bells was recast, a process that took place inside the church building!

This traditional Yorkshire village is also one of the few places in the country that can boast its own Sword Dance. Certainly a pagan ritual, thought to date back to prehistoric times, the performance of the dance is supposed to make the grass grow tall and to wake the earth from her winter's sleep.

Many of the farms around the village are dairy farms and at **Kirkby Malzeard Dairy** they still produce the traditionally made Coverdale cheese. Very much a local speciality, it is one of the few remaining Dales' cheeses still made though, at one time, each dale had its own particular variety.

West Tanfield

6 miles NW of Ripon on the A6108

This attractive village on the banks of the River Ure is home to a remarkable Tudor gatehouse known as the **Marmion Tower** which overlooks the river and has a beautiful oriel window. The tower is open to the public. For many years, West Tanfield was associated with the powerful Marmion family and the 14th century Church of St Nicholas contains many effigies belonging to the family.

Just outside the village lie the **Thornborough Circles**, interesting late Neolithic or early Bronze Age oval earthworks whose purpose still remains a mystery.

Grewelthorpe

6½ miles NW of Ripon off the A6108

It has long been thought that the Romans had a camp to the north of this leafy village and the discovery early in the 20th century of the complete skeleton of a Roman soldier confirmed

The Freemasons Arms

Nosterfield, North Yorkshire DL8 2QP
Tel/Fax: 01677 470548

Adjacent to the B6267 at Nosterfield, south of Bedale and west of Thirsk, **The Freemasons Arms** is a superb inn housed in buildings that began life in the 17th century as cottages. Before these were knocked together, it is believed that the pub occupied the building to the left of its present site. A Free House, it is owned by Kristian Stephenson, who has been here since 2002 and who has made the inn a great success.

Open every session, there are up to four real ales available – Theakstons, Black Sheep and changing guest ales – together with a good complement of lagers, cider, stout, wines, spirits and soft drinks.

Food is served every day at lunch (12 – 2) and dinner (6 – 9). Kristian is a qualified chef, and employs another chef to help him create the many delicious dishes on the menu and specials board. Specialities include steaks from a local Nosterfield herd and local lamb.

Accommodation is available here in a charming cottage nearby, let on a self-catering basis and available all year round.

the story. The remains were reburied in the churchyard at Kirkby Malzeard but the soldier's sandals are on view in the York Museum.

Just north of the village are the beautiful **Hackfall Woods** through which the River Ure flows. During the 19th century the Victorians developed the woodland, creating waterfalls and transforming the 18th century follies that had been built here into splendid vantage points. Following a period of neglect that began with the sale of the woodland in the 1930s, Hackfall Woods are now in the care of the Woodland Trust and the area is being gradually restored to its 19th century condition.

Ilton

9½ miles NW of Ripon off the A6108

Close to this village is one of the area's most interesting and unusual features, the **Druid's Temple** and, although the name suggests that this was an ancient meeting place for pagan worshippers, it is, in fact, a charming folly. Resembling a miniature Stonehenge, the folly was built in the 1820s by William Danby of the nearby Swinton Estate and it was inspired by a similar temple Danby saw on his travels in Europe. His building project was intended to provide work for local unemployed people and the resultant construction is considered one of the best Druidic follies in the country. The footpath to the folly from the village follows part of the long distance footpath known as the **Ripon Rowel Walk**.

Masham

9 miles NW of Ripon on the A6108

Set beside the River Ure, Masham (pronounced Massam) is a very picturesque place whose location, within easy reach of the abbeys of Fountains and Jervaulx and between the corn-growing lowlands and the wool-producing hills, caused it to become an important market centre with a charter that dates back to 1250. The town's wealth was built on sheep and it has also given its name to a particular breed. In fact, such was the animal's importance in creating Masham's buoyant economy that the prebend's stall in York Minster occupied by the canon of Masham was known as the 'Golden Stall'. The sheep fairs held in the town in the 18th and 19th centuries were among the largest in the country and in September the

Theakston Brewery & Visitor Centre

Masham, Ripon, North Yorkshire HG4 4YD
Tel: 01765 684333
website: www.theakstons.co.uk

For beer drinkers, the first place to visit in the Yorkshire Dales is the home of the legendary 'Old Peculier', the **Theakston Brewery**.

Trained guides take visitors on an informative tour of the entire brewing process. Robert Theakston began brewing 170 years ago at the Black Bull Inn in 1827. Forty eight years later, his son Thomas built the famous brewery on Masham's Paradise Fields, where it stands today.

Visitors are given the opportunity to meet the people involved in the creation of real Theakston ales. Most of the original equipment is still in use today, and with a trained tour guide, visitors can follow the entire brewing process, from selecting the ingredients to filling the casks.

Meet the people behind the beer, ask questions or simply soak up the atmosphere of the brewer's art. Watch one of only seven brewery coopers in England crafting the wooden casks that Theakston's still use for supplying local pubs.

After the tour, visitors are invited to the Visitor Centre Bar, where they can enjoy real British beer by a roaring log fire. The admission price includes a complimentary half pint of beer, from a comprehensive selection of Theakston ales, including Old Peculier and Theakston Cool Cask - you'll be spoilt for choice.

Masham Sheep Fair revives those heady days, giving visitors the chance of seeing many rare breeds of sheep and goats as well as witnessing events such as dog agility and sheep racing!

However, today, the town is famed for its beer and it boasts two celebrated breweries – Theakston's and Black Sheep. **Theakston's Brewery and Visitor Centre** (see panel on page 102), noted for its Old Peculier brew, was founded in 1827 by two Theakston brothers, Thomas and Robert. Adjoining the brewery today is a modern visitor centre that illustrates the process of brewing and the art of cooperage. Those taking the tour (which must be pre-booked) should be aware that there are two flights of steep steps along the route and the tour is not suitable for children under 10. Interestingly, the name of the famous brew derives from the fact that Masham, in medieval times, had its own Peculier Court (meaning special rather than odd), an ecclesiastical body with wide-ranging powers.

Established in the early 1990s, the **Black Sheep Brewery** was founded by Paul Theakston, the 5th generation of Masham's famous brewing family after the take over of the family firm. Housed in part of the former Lightfoot Brewery, which Paul's grandfather took over in 1919; along with the guided tour visitors also get the chance to sample the traditionally made ale. Meanwhile, the old Maltings building is home to a shop selling all manner of 'sheepy' items and a popular bistro.

Away from the breweries there are several other buildings of note in Masham including the 15th century Church of St Mary, whose spire dominates the town. First mentioned in the *Domesday Book*, all that remains of this earlier church is a Saxon cross in the churchyard, while there is a stained glass window that celebrates the new millennium. The meeting place of the Peculier Court, **College House**, is now home to the Women's Institute and it was this court, whose origins date back to the 12th century, that exercised a great deal of local power and was able to prosecute the townsfolk for non-attendance at church, swearing, drunkenness and harbouring a Catholic priest.

Well

8 miles NW of Ripon off the B6267

This pretty village takes its name from **St Michael's Well** that was already being venerated long before the Romans settled in the area and, close to the well, the remains of a spacious Roman villa were discovered. Part of the villa's tessellated pavement is now on display in the parish church that is, itself, a venerable old building with foundations that date back to Norman times. The church's greatest treasure, however, is a font cover dating from 1325 and this is one of the oldest in the country. It was a gift to the church from Ralph Neville, Lord of Middleham, who also founded the line of almshouses nearby that were rebuilt by his descendants in 1758.

The Wellington Heifer

Ainderby Steeple, Northallerton,
North Yorkshire DL7 9PU
Tel: 01609 775542 Fax: 01609 761683
e-mail: catelou@fsmail.net
website: www.wellingtonheifer.co.uk

The Wellington Heifer is a charming and welcoming inn reached via the A684 east of Northallerton. Located near the church in the lovely village of Ainderby Steeple, this picture-postcard inn enjoys scenic views over open countryside. A former coaching inn dating back to the early 18th century and full of atmosphere and character, the interior comprises a bar, no-smoking lounge and no-smoking restaurant, and is handsomely decorated and furnished throughout, with exposed brickwork, open fires and other attractive features that enhance the inn's convivial and homely ambience.

After a career in the RAF, leaseholder Bob Hedley retired in 2002 and he and his wife Cath took over the lease of the pub. They keep three real ales on tap – Tetleys, Black Sheep and a changing guest ale – complemented by a good choice of lagers, cider, stout, wines, spirits and soft drinks.

Head chef Damien has been working here for five years and, with the assistance of second chef Penfold, prepares excellent menus at lunch and dinner seven days a week. Featuring a good selection of home-made dishes, the specialities of the house include honey and mint lamb rump steak, steak and ale pie, Wensleydale chicken, leek, mushroom and onion pancake. The latest addition to the menu – the Wellington Heifer burger made from the finest locally-reared beef, onion and seasonings – has proved justly popular. Such is the inn's popularity and its great reputation for food, bookings are required at weekends, particularly for Sunday lunch. Weekday specials are available at lunchtimes, featuring two courses for a special price. Other deals include the Senior Citizens' special two-course lunches on Monday, Tuesday and Wednesday. Party menus – for groups of more than six – are available all year round.

Accommodation is also available here in two delightful and supremely comfortable ensuite guest bedrooms, and this quiet, relaxing village makes a perfect base from which to explore the many sights and attractions of the region.

All proceeds from the regular quiz nights – held once a fortnight on Sunday evenings – go to the Great North Air Ambulance Charity.

Major credit cards accepted. Children welcome. If you are travelling by car, there is parking at the rear.

Snape

9½ miles NW of Ripon off the B6268

This quiet and unspoilt village, where the original timber-framed cottages stand side by side with their more modern neighbours, is still dominated by its castle as it has been for centuries. Reached via an avenue of lime trees, **Snape Castle** has a famous, if somewhat complicated, royal connection in that it was the home of Lord Latimer of Snape (a member of the Neville family), the first husband of Catherine Parr, Henry VIII's last wife. The Nevilles owned the castle for over 700 years and its beautiful chapel, still used by the villagers, saw the marriages of many Latimers and Nevilles.

To the north of the village and set in over 1000 acres of parkland lies **Thorp Perrow Arboretum**, a place that is unique to Britain, if not Europe, in that it was the creation of one man, Col Sir Leonard Ropner (1895-1977). Sir Leonard travelled all over the world collecting rare and unusual species for Thorp Perrow and today the hundreds of trees he enthusiastically collected are in their prime. The arboretum was initially Sir Leonard's private hobby but after his death, his son, Sir John Ropner, decided to open the 85-acre garden to the public and the arboretum is now one of the area's prime attractions. A treasure trove of specimen trees and shrubs, woodland walks, nature trail, tree trails, a large lake, picnic area and children's play area, the arboretum also embraces the Milbank Pinetum, planted by Lady Augusta Milbank in the mid-19th century, and the medieval Spring Wood dating back to the 16th century. Thorp Perrow provides interest all year round but perhaps the most popular time is the spring when visitors can see one of the finest and most extensive plantings of daffodils in the north of England, amongst which are some old and unusual varieties. In addition to the fascinating collection of trees, visitors will also find an information centre, a tea room and a plant sales area.

An additional attraction at Thorp Perrow are the Falcons of Thorp Perrow, a bird of prey, captive breeding and conservation centre that has been created within a large, formerly derelict walled garden and that opened in 2000. As well as learning about these magnificent birds, visitors can watch them fly during the daily demonstrations and also gain **hands-on experience**.

Northallerton

The county town of North Yorkshire, Northallerton has a broad High Street of almost half a mile long that is typical of the county's market towns. In the stagecoach era, the town was an important stop on the route from Newcastle to London and several old coaching inns still stand along the High Street. The most ancient is **The Old Fleece**, a favoured drinking haunt of Charles Dickens during his several visits to Northallerton and it remains a truly

The Black Bull

101 High Street, Northallerton,
North Yorkshire DL7 8PP
Tel: 01609 773565

Dating back to the late 17th century, **The Black Bull** is an excellent inn open all day every day for ale, serves great food at lunch and teatime, and boasts seven charming and comfortable ensuite guest bedrooms. This family-run pub run by the Widdowson family, who have been here since 2002, employs the culinary talents of cook Joan, who has been serving up tempting dishes for more than 22 years. This convivial and welcoming inn in the heart of Northallerton is well worth seeking out.

Dickensian place with great oak beams and a charming olde worlde atmosphere. The Old Fleece recalls the great days of the stagecoach that came to an abrupt end with the arrival of the railway. One day in 1847, a coach called the Wellington made the whole of the 290-mile journey from Newcastle to London, via Northallerton, completely empty. The era of this romantic – if uncomfortable and extremely expensive – mode of transport was over.

Northallerton has many old buildings of interest, including an ancient **Grammar School** whose history goes back to at least 1322. The school was rebuilt in 1776 at the northern end of the High Street but, by the end of the 19th century it had a 'no-good reputation' and, by 1902, there were only 13 pupils on the register. Things then went from bad to worse as, in 1903, the headmaster was convicted of being drunk and disorderly. Fortunately the school, now Northallerton College, has recovered its reputation and its academic excellence and has also moved to new buildings while the 18th century school is now offices.

The town also boasts a grand medieval church, a 15th century almshouse and, of more recent provenance, a majestic County Hall built in 1906 and designed by the famous Yorkshire architect Walter Brierley. The oldest private house in Northallerton is Porch House that bears a carved inscription with the date '1584'. According to tradition, Charles I came here as a guest in 1640 and returned seven years later as a prisoner.

Around Northallerton

Bedale

7½ miles SW of Northallerton on the A684

This pleasant little market town developed around the point where the Saxon track from Ripon joined the route from Northallerton to Wensleydale and it featured in the *Domesday Book* where it was described as having 500 acres of ploughed land, six acres of meadow, a church and a mill. A meeting place for traders for centuries, in 1251 Henry III granted a charter for a weekly market that still flourishes today and the 14th century market cross still stands at the top of Elmgate, a narrow street leading from the river to the market place. As commercial activity increased, water power was harnessed from the **Bedale Beck** for the processing of wool; skinners and tanners worked down by the ford and the town was a lively hub of cottage industry.

The curving main street leads to the beautiful parish Church of St Gregory that incorporates architectural styles from the 11th to the 16th centuries and the building also has a fine fortified tower. Just inside the churchyard is an old building dating from the mid-1200s that served as a school in the 18th century.

Opposite the church stands **Bedale Hall** that houses the library and a local Museum. The north front of the building is a particularly fine example of the Georgian architecture which gives Bedale its special character. Meanwhile, another building of interest is the 18th century **Leech House** that is so called because it was once used by the local chemist to store his leeches!

Crakehall

8½ miles SW of Northallerton on the A684

Sometime around 1090 the Domesday

The Greyhound Inn

Hackforth, Bedale, North Yorkshire DL8 1PB
Tel/Fax: 01748 811415

The Greyhound Inn is a charming country coaching inn occupying a scenic location in a quiet village a couple of miles north of the A684 (Bedale to Leyburn Road) and a mile and a half west of the A1 just south of Catterick. Once a farmhouse, built between 1710 and 1720, it was later an alehouse and then a coaching inn, and has always been known throughout its long history as The Greyhound. There was once a smithy and stabling to the rear.

Superior inside and out, this hidden jewel is large and impressive. Whitewashed and attractive outside, with a patio area with picnic tables to the front and a lovely, well-kept beer garden to one side, the interior is traditional and welcoming, with a wealth of bygone memorabilia and other homely touches.

New owner David Hill took over in December of 2003. Chefs Nicola and Andrea have been here for several years, and are responsible for the inn's reputation for outstanding food. They create an impressive range of delicious home-cooked meals at lunch and dinner. Guests choose from the menu or specials board from a selection of original dishes. The no-smoking restaurant seats 42. Children welcome. Booking required at weekends.

Three ales are on tap – John Smiths, Black Sheep and Theakstons Best and these are complemented by a good choice of lagers, cider, stout, spirits and soft drinks. The wine list deserves special mention. In a room to the rear of the courtyard David is creating a Courtyard Lounge – one side will house comfy Chesterfield-style seating, whilst the other will be a no-smoking intimate dining area seating 12.

Four en suite guest bedrooms – a double, twin and two family rooms – are available all year round, providing superb accommodation in tasteful and welcoming surroundings.

Sights and attractions in the area include walking in the Yorkshire Dales, game and course-fishing, the East Coast, Lake District and urban centres of York, Durham, Catterick, Ripon, Thirsk, Sedgefield, Wetherby, Richmond and Northallerton.

For atmosphere, food, drink, accommodation and hospitality, look no further · this superb inn is peerless.

Little Holtby

Leeming Bar, Northallerton,
North Yorkshire DL7 9LH
Tel: 01609 748762 Fax: 01609 748822
e-mail: littleholtby@yahoo.co.uk
website: www.littleholtby.co.uk

Elegance and style are everywhere to be seen at **Little Holtby**, a charming and classic country house set in nine acres with outstanding views across the Dales. This excellent place is the home of gracious and charming owner Dorothy, a marvellous hostess who has been providing bed and breakfast accommodation since 1992. Situated just two miles north of the junction of the A1 and the A684, 10 minutes from Bedale and 20 minutes from Northallerton, and close to the start of the Wensleydale private railway, it's open all year round. Rated 4 Diamonds/Silver Award by the ETC, there are three superb guest bedrooms – two ensuite, one with private bath. One room has a four-poster bed.

The dining room and sitting room are equally elegant, and contribute to the relaxed and peaceful atmosphere of the house. Discounts for stays of longer than two nights. With the many sights and attractions of the region within easy reach, and facilities for golf, tennis, riding, fishing and walking nearby, it makes an excellent touring base.

Book commissioners arrived in Crakehall and noted details of a mill on the beck that runs through this picturesque village and, more than 900 years later, there is still a mill on the very same spot. The present **Crakehall Water Mill** building dates from the 1600s while its mighty machinery was installed in the 18th and 19th centuries. Still a working mill today visitors can watch the whole process in operation and then, if they wish, purchase a bag or two of the top quality flour it produces.

Catterick Village

9 miles NW of Northallerton on the A1

Ever since the time of the Romans, when the settlement was known as 'Cataractonium', Catterick has been associated with the armed forces and, located on the Roman highway between London and Hadrian's Wall, is the garrison that also stands close to the place where Paulinus, Bishop of York baptised 10,000 Christians in the River Swale. Today, the large army camp is some way from the village to the west but there are many reminders of Catterick's military connections here. However, the village's connections with Nelson are not immediately obvious but it was Alexander Scott, vicar of Catterick in 1816, who was at Nelson's side when he died at the Battle of Trafalgar. Also, the Admiral's sister-in-law, Lady Tyrconnel, lived at nearby **Kiplin Hall**, a beautiful Jacobean country home famed for its wonderful interior plasterwork and medieval fishponds. The hall also contains many mementoes of Nelson and Lady Hamilton and, on display in the Blue Room, is a folding library chair from the Admiral's cabin on *HMS Victory*.

Moulton

10 miles NW of Northallerton off the A1

This small village is home to two fine manor houses that were both built by members of the same family – the Smithsons. The Manor House, in the village centre, was originally built in the late 16th century and was improved greatly in the mid-17th century. Meanwhile, just to the south of the village lies **Moulton Hall** (National Trust) that was built by George Smithson following his marriage to Eleanor Fairfax in 1654.

Similar in size to the original Smithson family home and somewhat resembling it, Moulton Hall has a fine stone exterior with Dutch gables and an excellent example of a carved staircase inside. The Hall is open by appointment only.

Middleton Tyas

12 miles NW of Northallerton off the A1

Situated in a sheltered location but also close to the Great North Road, the position of the Middleton Tyas' church, away from the village centre and at the end of a long avenue of trees, seems strange. However, when the Church of St Michael was built it served not only Middleton Tyas but also Moulton and Kneeton (the latter no longer exists), between which Middleton lay. During the 18th century the village saw a period of prosperity when copper was found and mined from the fields near the church and several grand houses were built including **East Hall**, which belonged to Leonard Hartley, who founded the industry, though his son, George, had a grander house on the outskirts of Middleton that was designed by John Carr of York.

Aldbrough

15 miles NW of Northallerton off the B6275

To the west of the village, lie the enormous complex of earthworks known as **Stanwick Camp** (English Heritage), a series of banks and ditches that were excavated in the 1950s. Their discovery also revealed that the constructions had been carried out in the 1st century.

Piercebridge

17 miles NW of Northallerton on the A67

This picturesque village, in upper Teesdale, was once an important Roman fort and was one of a chain of forts linking the northern headquarters at York with Hadrian's Wall; another fort in the chain can be found to the south at Catterick. The Romans are thought to have originally chosen Piercebridge as a suitable river crossing back in AD 70, when Cerialis attacked the British camp at Stanwick. The remains of the fort, which are visible today, can be dated from coin evidence to around AD 270. The site is always open though the finds from the excavations are housed in the Bowes Museum at Barnard Castle.

The attractive River Tees forms part of the northern boundary of North Yorkshire and though Teesdale is not, strictly, a Yorkshire Dale it is well worth visiting. In its upper reaches, the river is noted for its waterfalls though the narrow valley soon widens to give attractive meadow land.

PLACES TO STAY, EAT AND DRINK

The Downe Arms, Castleton, North Yorkshire	49	Pub, Food and Accommodation	p117
Hollins Farm, Glaisdale, North Yorkshire	50	Bed and Breakfast	p119
The Arncliffe Arms, Glaisdale, North Yorkshire	51	Pub, Food and Accommodation	p119
The Dog & Gun Country Inn, Potto, North Yorkshire	52	Pub, Restaurant and Accommodation	p122
Duncombe Park, Helmsley, North Yorkshire	53	Historic Building	p124
The Hare Inn, Scawton, North Yorkshire	54	Pub with Food	p125
The Feversham Arms Inn, Farndale, North Yorkshire	55	Pub, Food and Accommodation	p126
Valley View Lodges, Nawton, North Yorkshire	56	Self Catering	p128
The Golden Lion Inn, Great Barugh, North Yorkshire	57	Pub and Restaurant	p130
Newburgh House, Coxwold, North Yorkshire	58	Bed and Breakfast	p131
The Fauconberg Arms, Coxwold, North Yorkshire	59	Pub, Restaurant and Accommodation	p132
Black Swan Country Inn, Oldstead, North Yorkshire	60	Pub, Food and Accommodation	p133
High Paradise Cottages, Boltby, North Yorkshire	61	Self Catering	p135
Laskill Grange, Hawnby, North Yorkshire	62	Self Catering	p136
The Hawnby Hotel, Hawnby, North Yorkshire	63	Hotel and Restaurant	p137
Moorlands Country House, Levisham, N Yorkshire	64	Country House Hotel	p140

Denotes entries in other chapters

3 The North York Moors

North Yorkshire Moors

Some 40 miles across and about 20 miles deep, the North York Moors National Park encompasses a remarkable diversity of scenery: moorland, woodland and dales. There are great rolling swathes of moorland rising to 1,400 feet above sea level that are stark and inhospitable in winter; still, wild and romantic in summer; and, in the autumn, they are softened by a purple haze of flowering heather.

Almost one fifth of the area is woodland and most of it is managed by Forest

PLACES TO STAY, EAT AND DRINK

● Denotes entries in other chapters

Whitby Harbour

Enterprise, which has established many picnic sites and forest drives. Just as the Yorkshire Dales have large areas of moorland, so the North York Moors have many dales, including Eskdale, Ryedale and Farndale but there are more than a hundred in all. Cut deep into the great upland tracts, the dales are as picturesque, soft and pastoral as anywhere in Yorkshire. To the west lies the mighty bulk of the Cleveland Hills while to the east are the rugged cliffs of the Heritage Coast.

Settlements are few and far between in the North York Moors: indeed, there may have been more people living here in the Bronze Age (1500-500 BC) than there are now, judging by the 3,000 or so 'howes' (burial mounds) that have been discovered. Also scattered across these uplands is a remarkable collection of medieval stone crosses. There are more than 30 of them and one, the **Lilla Cross,** is reckoned to be the oldest Christian monument in northern England. It commemorates the warrior Lilla who, in AD626, died protecting his king, Edwin, from an assassin's dagger. Most of them have names, such as Fat Betty that has a stumpy base surmounted by the top of a wheelhead cross, but perhaps the finest of these monuments is **Ralph Cross**, found high on Westerdale Moor. It stands nine feet tall, lies at almost precisely the geographical centre of the moors and has been adopted by the North York Moors National Park as its emblem.

Two spectacularly scenic railways wind their way through this enchanting landscape and both provide a satisfying and environmentally friendly way of exploring this comparatively undiscovered area. The Middlesbrough to Whitby route, called the **Esk Valley Line,** runs from west to east following the course of the River Esk and passing through a succession of delightful villages. Meanwhile, the vintage steam locomotives of the **North York Moors Railway** start at Pickering and run northwards for 18 miles through Newton Dale to join the Esk Valley Line at Grosmont. The dramatic route through this glacial channel was originally engineered by George Stephenson himself.

A considerable stretch of the Heritage Coast, which was so designated in 1979, is encompassed within the National Park boundary and along this coastline, from Staithes to Filey, is some of the most striking coastal scenery in the country. There are high cliffs, rocky coves, miles of sandy beaches and a scattering of picture postcard fishing villages. From these small harbours fishermen have, for centuries, sailed out in their distinctive cobles to harvest the sea and, from Whitby, the sturdy whaling ships set off on their dangerous missions in what is now an abandoned trade. This coastline is, however, most famous for its connections with Captain James Cook, one of the country's greatest navigators and seafarers. The family moved to Great Ayton when James was eight years old but by the age of 16 he had left home and moved to Staithes before finally becoming a naval apprentice in Whitby where he learnt his seafaring skills. It was also from this ancient fishing town, with is associations with Count Dracula, that Cook set out on many of his voyages of discovery in his famous, but surprisingly small, boat *Endeavour*.

Great Ayton

This appealing village, set around the River Leven, is an essential stopping point for anyone following the **Captain Cook Country Tour**, a 70-mile circular trip taking in all the major locations associated with the great seafarer. Cook's family moved to Great Ayton when he was eight years old and he attended the little school that is now the **Captain Cook Schoolroom Museum.** The building dates back to 1785 and was built as a school and poorhouse on the site of the original charity school that was built in 1704 by Michael Postgate, a wealthy, local landowner. It was at the Postgate School that James received his early education that was paid for by Thomas Skottowe, his father's employer. The museum first opened in the 1920s and the exhibits here relate to Cook's life and to the 18th century village in which he lived. The family had moved to Great Ayton in 1736 but in 1745 James moved to Staithes before finally becoming an apprentice seaman in Whitby. James Cook joined the Royal Navy in 1755 and first surveyed the coast of Canada before being appointed 1st Lieutenant in 1768 and given command of his most famous ship, *Endeavour*. After locating Tahiti and New Zealand in 1769, Cook went on to discover Australia in 1770 and, following further voyages in the Pacific Ocean, he was killed by natives of Hawaii in 1779. The museum is open daily from April to October.

The Great Ayton of today is very different from the village that James Cook would have known. Now a pleasant place with the two spacious greens of High and Low Green, with the River Leven flowing through it, this now conservation area was, in the 18th and 19th centuries, home to much industrial activity, including weaving, tanning, brewing and tile making. Situated in a secluded position on Low Green is the 12th century **Church of All Saints**, where James, along with his family, came to worship. Still medieval in structure, the original tower and western portion of the nave were demolished in the late 19th century to make more room for burials. Inside the church is a memorial tablet to Thomas Skottowe while James' mother, Grace, who died in 1765, lies buried in the churchyard.

The Cook family's first home in Great Ayton was **Aireyholme Farm**, on the outskirts of the village, and they moved here in 1736 when James' father was appointed as bailiff by Thomas Skottowe, then the Lord of the Manor. The farm can still be seen from a footpath that leads from the village and also takes in Roseberry Topping and Captain Cook's Monument. After James left the village and moved to Staithes, the family continued to live here and, in 1775, his father built his own cottage in Bridge Street after beginning work as a stonemason. The Cook Family Cottage remained James' father's home until 1772, when he went to live with a married daughter in Redcar and the dwelling was sold. In 1934 the cottage was dismantled, brick by brick, and shipped to Australia and it was faithfully reconstructed in Fitzroy Gardens in Melbourne where it stands to this day. The site of the cottage in Great Ayton is marked by a granite obelisk.

Standing proudly on High Green is the **James Cook Sculpture**, which depicts the great man at the age of just 16, looking towards Staithes. Unveiled in 1997, it was created by the internationally renowned sculptor Nicholas Dimbleby and it commemorates the life of James Cook along with the contribution that the village made to his development.

An altogether more impressive monument can be found to the southeast of Great Ayton on Easby Moor. At 60 feet high the giant obelisk of local sandstone that is the Captain Cook Monument is visible for miles around and it was erected by Robert Campion, a Whitby banker, in 1827. The monument can only be reached by a steepish climb on foot but it is well worth making the effort as from the base there are stupendous views over the Moors, the Vale of Mowbray and across to the oddly shaped hill called **Roseberry Topping**. The loftiest of the Cleveland Hills and sometimes called the Matterhorn of Yorkshire, Roseberry's summit towers 1,000 feet above Great Ayton.

Around Great Ayton

Castleton

8 miles SE of Great Ayton off the A171

Spread across the hillside above the River Esk, Castleton is a charming village that at one time was the largest settlement in Eskdale and it still has a weekly market and a station on the scenic **Esk Valley Railway** that runs between Whitby and Middlesbrough. Its amber-coloured **Church of St Michael and St George** was built in memory of

The Downe Arms

3 High Street, Castleton, Whitby,
North Yorkshire YO21 2EE
Tel: 01287 660223
e-mail: thedownearms@yahoo.co.uk

Dating back to the early 18th century, **The Downe Arms** is a fine inn situated in the heart of the North Yorkshire moors, south of the A171. The inn began life as three cottages, which were later converted into a coaching inn on the York-to-Stockton route. Picture-postcard inside and out, the inn commands fine views all round and the interior features exposed stone walls, flagstone flooring, handsome beamwork and other original features.

Open all day every day, there are always at least three real ales on tap at this warm and welcoming inn, together with a good range of lagers, cider, stout, wines, spirits and soft drinks. Food is served 6 – 9 Monday, 12.30 – 9 Tuesday to Saturday and 12.30 – 2 on Sundays. Owner Jeremy Thorpe is also a fine chef, with a daily-changing menu of tempting dishes that make the most of local produce. Jeremy and his wife Trish have many years' experience in the trade and offer all their guests the best in hospitality. The inn also boasts five quality ensuite guest bedrooms.

the men who fell in the First World War, and inside there is some fine work by Robert Thompson, the famous 'Mouseman of Kilburn': the benches, organ screen and panelling at each side of the altar all bear his distinctive 'signature' of a crouching mouse.

Danby

9 miles E of Great Ayton off the A171

This village is home to **The Moors Centre** that provides an excellent introduction to the North York Moors National Park and is housed in Danby Lodge, a former shooting lodge that is set in 13 acres of riverside, meadow, woodland, formal gardens and picnic areas. Visitors can either wander on their own along the waymarked, woodland walks and nature trails or join one of the frequent guided walks. Inside the lodge various exhibits interpret the natural and local history of the moors, there is a bookshop stocked with a wide range of books, maps and guides, and a tea room serving refreshments. The centre is open all year round expect for January.

Downstream from The Moors Centre is a narrow, medieval, packhorse bridge, one of three to be found in Eskdale. This particular one is known as **Duck Bridge** but the name has nothing to do with aquatic birds and it was originally called Castle Bridge but was renamed after an 18th century benefactor, George Duck, who paid for the bridge to be repaired.

To the south of the bridge are the remains of **Danby Castle** that was built in the 14th century and, originally much larger, was once the home of Catherine Parr, the last wife of Henry VIII. In Elizabethan times, the justices met here and the Danby Court Leet and Baron, which administers the common land and rights of way over the 11,000 acres of the Danby Estate, still meets here every year in the throne room. One of the court's responsibilities is issuing licences for the gathering of sphagnum moss, a material once used for stuffing mattresses but now more commonly required for flower arranging. The castle is now a private farmhouse and is not open to the public.

Lealholm

12½ miles SE of Great Ayton off the A171

An attractive village situated in the Esk Valley, the houses at Lealholm are clustered around a 250-year-old bridge that spans the river and a short walk from here leads to some picturesque stepping stones that also form a river crossing. A much-travelled foreign journalist remarked, "*Elsewhere, you have to go in search of beautiful views; here, they come and offer themselves to be looked at.*" On one of the stone houses, now a tea room and restaurant, a carved inscription reads "Loyal Order of Ancient Shepherds" together with the date 1873 in Roman numerals. The Loyal Order ran their lodge on the lines of a men-only London club but their annual procession through the village, and the subsequent festivities, were one of the highlights of the autumn. In recent years, Lealholm has become very popular with naturalists who come to study the wealth of trees, ferns, flowers and rare plants in the deep, dramatic ravine known as Crunkley Gill. Sadly, the ravine is privately owned and not open to the public.

Eskdale is the largest, and one of the loveliest, of the dales within the National Park and it is also unusual in that it runs west to east – the Esk being the only moorland river that does not find its way to the River Humber. Instead, the river winds tortuously through the dale to join the sea beneath the picturesque cliffs at Whitby. Along the way, many smaller dales branch off to the north and south – Fryup, Danby, Glaisdale – while even narrower ones can only be explored on foot. The Esk is famed for its salmon fishing but permits are required and these can be obtained from the local branches of the National Rivers Authority. Walkers will appreciate the Esk Valley Walk, a group of ten linking walks that traverse the length of the valley.

Glaisdale

13½ miles SE of Great Ayton off the A171

This picturesque village lies at the foot of a narrow dale beside the River Esk and **Arncliffe Woods** are just a short walk away. The ancient stone bridge here was built in around 1620 by

HOLLINS FARM

Glaisdale, Whitby, North Yorkshire YO21 2PZ
Tel: 01947 897516

Set in the Esk Valley just nine miles from Whitby and surrounded by acres and acres of picturesque countryside, **Hollins Farm** offers relaxing and comfortable accommodation in a superb 16th-century traditional farmhouse.

There are two large and handsome ensuite guest bedrooms decorated and furnished to a high standard. A sitting room is available to guests, and the conservatory is just the place to relax after a day's walking or sightseeing. 3 Diamond rating by the ETC. Camping facilities are also available.

Thomas Ferris, Mayor of Hull who, as an impoverished young man, had lived in Glaisdale and had fallen in love with Agnes Richardson, the squire's daughter. To see Agnes, Ferris had to wade or swim across the river and he swore that if he prospered in life he would build a bridge here. Fortunately, he joined a ship that sailed against the Spanish Armada and captured a galleon laden with gold. Tom returned to Glaisdale a rich man, married Agnes and later honoured his promise by building what has always been called the **Beggar's Bridge** or Lovers' Bridge.

Egton Bridge

15½ miles SE of Great Ayton off the A171

This little village, which lies tucked around a bend in the River Esk, plays host each year to the famous **Gooseberry Show**, which was established in 1800 and is held on the first Tuesday in August. The show attracts entrants from all over the world who bring prize specimens along in an attempt to beat the current record of 2.18oz for a single berry.

Meanwhile, the village, itself, is

THE ARNCLIFFE ARMS

Glaisdale, Whitby, North Yorkshire YO21 2QL
Tel: 01947 897555
website: www.arncliffearms.co.uk

Set in a very scenic location popular with walkers and all those who enjoy the delights of the North Yorkshire Moors, **The Arncliffe Arms** is a superb place with excellent food, drink and accommodation. Open every session for ale, Black Sheep, Timothy Taylor Landlord and a changing guest ale are complemented by lagers, cider, stout, wines, spirits and soft drinks. Delicious food is served daily at lunch and dinner. Making an ideal base from which to explore the many sights and attractions of the region, the inn offers six attractive and comfortable ensuite guest bedrooms.

dominated by the massive **Church of St Hedda** that was built in 1866 and has a dazzling roof painted blue with gold stars while the altar incorporates some distinguished Belgian terracotta work. Appropriately, St Hedda's is a Roman Catholic Church since it was at Egton Bridge that the martyr Nicholas Postgate was born in 1596. He was ordained as a priest in France and returned to the moors to minister to those still loyal to the outlawed Catholic faith. He travelled disguised as a jobbing gardener and eluded capture for many years but was finally betrayed for a reward of £20. He was 81 years old when he was hung, drawn and quartered at York: a sad story to be associated with such a delightful village.

Grosmont

16½ miles SE of Great Ayton off the A169

This quiet village's name is derived from 'gros mont' – the French for big hill – and it was here that the Normans built a castle. Although the castle is no longer in existence, **Grosmont Station**, the terminus of the North Yorkshire Moors Railway, is very much in evidence and has been restored to the British Railway's style of the 1960s. For those finishing their journey here (or starting) there are also locomotive sheds at the station.

Beck Hole

17 miles SE of Great Ayton off the A169

This pretty little hamlet lies on the route of the **North Yorkshire Moors Railway** that was constructed in the 1830s and was designed by the great engineer George Stephenson. Initially, the trains were made up of stage coaches placed on top of simple bogies that were pulled by horses. At Beck Hole, however, there was a 1 in 15 incline up the line to Goathland so the carriages had to be hauled by a complicated system of ropes and water-filled tanks. Charles Dickens was an early passenger on this route and wrote a hair-raising description of his journey. The precipitous incline caused many accidents so, in 1865, a 'Deviation Line' was blasted through solid rock and although the gradient is still one of the steepest in the country, at 1 in 49, it did open up this route to steam trains. The original 1 in 15 incline is now a footpath, so modern walkers will understand the effort needed to get themselves to the summit, let alone a fully laden carriage.

Every year, Beck Hole plays host to the **World Quoits Championship**, a game that appears to have originated in Eskdale and involves throwing a small iron hoop over an iron pin set about 25 feet away. Appropriately enough, one of the houses on the village green has a quoit serving as a door knocker. On the hillside, a mile or so to the west of Beck Hole, is the curiously-named **Randy Mere**, the last place in England where leeches were gathered commercially. An elderly resident of Goathland in 1945 recalled how as a young man he had waded into the lake and emerged in minutes with the slug-like creatures firmly attached to his skin. For those who are interested, the leeches are still there.

Goathland

17½ miles SE of Great Ayton off the A169

This attractive village, some 500 feet high up on the moors, is, today, perhaps best known as 'Aidensfield', the main location for the television series *Heartbeat*. However, this village, with its old stone houses scattered randomly around the spacious sheep-cropped green, was popular long before the long running television series made it famous. Earlier visitors mostly came in order to see **Mallyan Spout**, a 70-feet high waterfall locked into a crescent of rocks and trees. These early visitors were also interested in Goathland's rugged church and the odd memorial in its graveyard to William Jefferson and his wife. The couple died in 1923 within a few days of each other, at the ages of 80 and 79, and chose to have their final resting place marked by an enormous anchor.

In the award-winning **Goathland Exhibition Centre** is the full explanation of the curious tradition of the **Plough Stots Service** that is performed in the village every January. It is said to be an ancient ritual for greeting the new year that originated with the Norsemen who settled here more than a thousand years ago. 'Stots' is the Scandinavian word for the

North Yorkshire Moors Railway

bullocks that dragged a plough through the village, followed by dancers brandishing 30-inch swords. This pagan rite is still faithfully observed but with the difference that nowadays Goathland's young men have replaced the stots in the plough harness. The Exhibition Centre can also provide information on the many walks in the area including one of the oldest thoroughfares in the country, **Wade's Way.** If legend is to be believed, the ancient route was built by a giant of that name but it is actually a remarkably well-preserved stretch of Roman road.

The village, too, lies on the route of the **North Yorkshire Moors Railway** and **Goathland Station** has a newly

The Dog & Gun Country Inn

Potto, Hutton Rudby,
North Yorkshire DL6 3HQ
Tel/Fax: 01642 700232

The picturesque village of Potto, east of the A19 and west of the A172 not far from Northallerton and Darlington, is home to the superb **Dog & Gun Country Inn**. Joanne and John Proud live up to their name as owners here; they arrived in 1998 and have in that time overseen a programme of conscientious refurbishment, so that the pub retains its original charm and elegance while gaining modern comforts and convenience. Parts of the building date back to between 1710 and 1720; it has been listed as an inn since the mid-18th century. Impressive and welcoming, the décor throughout retains the character of this traditional inn.

There is also a very pleasant beer garden. Sunday night there's a fun quiz held from 9.30 p.m.

Open every session, the real ales available are Black Sheep and a rotating guest ale.

Quality food is available at lunch (12 – 2.30) seven days a week, and at dinner Monday to Saturday 6.30 – 9.30, 7 – 9.30 on Sundays. Diners choose off the menu or daily specials board from a range of delicious home-cooked dishes such as rack of English lamb, mixed grills, lemon sole roulade and vegetarian stroganoff. The selection of tempting desserts is worth leaving room for.

Thursday night is Steak Night, when the steaks are bigger and the prices smaller; booking is advised on this night and for Friday and Saturday evenings and Sunday lunch, to avoid disappointment. The newly refurbished restaurant will seat 60.

Joanne and John are a local couple with good knowledge of the sights and attractions of the region, including the scenic countryside surrounding the inn itself.

There are five handsome and welcoming ensuite guest bedrooms that, in common with the rest of the inn, are gracious, elegant and supremely comfortable. The tariff includes a hearty breakfast and does not fluctuate throughout the year. There are discounts for longer stays.

Off-road car park. Children welcome. No-smoking areas throughout the inn.

refurbished tea room, with authentic furniture and artefacts that take visitors back to the age of steam, while recent additions include a cattle dock and coal drops.

Ingleby Greenhow

3 miles S of Great Ayton off the B1257

Located on the very edge of the National Park, Ingleby Greenhow enjoys a favoured position, protected from east winds by the great mass of Ingleby Moor. The beckside church looks small and unimposing from the outside but, inside, there is a wealth of rugged Norman arches and pillars, the stonework carved with fanciful figures of grotesque men and animals.

Stokesley

3 miles SW of Great Ayton on the B1365

This pleasing market town lies beneath the northern edge of the North York Moors and its peace is only troubled on market day that has taken place here every Friday since its charter was granted in 1223. There are rows of elegant Georgian and Regency houses reached by little bridges over the River Leven that flows through the town and an old water wheel marks the entrance to the town. In the Middle Ages, Stokesley was owned by the Balliol family, one of whose descendants is remembered as the founder of the Oxford college of that name.

Osmotherley

11 miles SW of Great Ayton off the A19

Long distance walkers will be familiar with this attractive moorland village since it is the western starting point for the **Lyke Wake Walk**, which winds for more than 40 miles over the North York Moors to Ravenscar on the coast. At the centre of the village is a heavily carved cross and, next to it, a low stone table that was probably once a market stall and also served John Wesley as a pulpit.

About a mile northeast of the village lies **Mount Grace Priory** (English Heritage) that is quite unique amongst Yorkshire's ecclesiastical treasures as the 14th century building, set in these tranquil surroundings, was bought in 1904 by Sir Lothian Bell who decided to rebuild one of the well-preserved cells. Such a violation of the building's integrity would provoke howls of outrage from purists if it were proposed today, however, when English Heritage inherited the Carthusian Priory, it decided to go still further by reconstructing other outbuildings and filling them with replica furniture and artefacts to create a vivid impression of what life was like in a medieval monastic house. The Carthusians were an upper class order whose members dedicated themselves to solitude – even their meals were served through an angled hatch so they would not see the servant who brought them. Most visitors find themselves fascinated by Mount

Grace's sanitary arrangements that were ingeniously designed to take full advantage of a nearby spring and the sloping site on which the priory is built. Along with discovering what life was like for a monk in this almost hermit-like order, visitors can also wander around the remains of the Great Cloister and outer court and see the new monks' herb garden that was specifically designed to aid contemplation and spiritual renewal. Mount Grace Priory is open all year though times are limited in the winter.

Helmsley

Situated on the banks of the River Rye, at the edge of the North York Moors National Park, Helmsley is one of North Yorkshire's most popular and attractive towns. Its spacious market square is typical of the area but the striking Gothic memorial to the 2nd Earl of Feversham, which stands in the square, is not. An astonishingly ornate construction, it was designed by Sir Giles Gilbert Scott and looks like a smaller version of his famous memorial to Sir Walter Scott that stands in Edinburgh.

The Earls of Feversham lived at **Duncombe Park** (see panel below), whose extensive grounds sweep up to within a few yards of the Market Place. Most of the original mansion, designed by Vanbrugh and built in 1713, was gutted by a disastrous fire in 1879 and only the north wing remained habitable and that, in its turn, was ruined by a second fire in 1895. The Fevershams lavished a fortune on rebuilding the grand old house, largely to the original design, but the financial burden eventually forced them to lease the house and grounds as a preparatory school for girls. Happily, the Fevershams were able to return to their ancestral home in 1986 and the beautifully

Duncombe Park

Helmsley, York YO62 5EB
Tel: 01439 770213
Fax: 01439 771114

A girls' school for 60 years, this Baroque mansion built in 1713 is now the family home of Lord & Lady Feversham. Visit the restored principal rooms, typical of a late 19th century "grand interior", and the landscaped "green garden" with its temples and terraces, set in dramatic parkland and has been described as 'the supreme masterpiece of the art of the landscape gardener'; or explore the National Nature Reserve within over 400 acres of rolling Parkland. End a perfect day visit the Parkland Centre Tearoom & Shop, taste the delights of homemade food and browse at your leisure the unusual hand made crafts made in Yorkshire. Interpretation area, toilet facilities and free parking.

Rievaulx Abbey

restored house and lovely grounds are now open to the public between April and October, Sundays to Thursdays. Visitors can tour the principal rooms that remain fine examples of the 'grand interior' of the early 20th century, while there is glorious parkland that includes a National Nature Reserve, ancient trees and waymarked walks.

Before they were ennobled, the Feversham's family name was Duncombe and it was Sir Thomas Duncombe, a wealthy London goldsmith, who established the family seat here when he bought **Helmsley Castle** (English Heritage) and its estate in 1687. Founded in the early 1100s and severely damaged during the Civil War, the castle was in a dilapidated state but its previous owner, the Duke of Buckingham, had continued to live there in some squalor and discomfort. Sir Thomas quickly decided to build his more suitable residence nearby, abandoning the ruins to lovers of the romantic and picturesque. Visitors to the castle can see a special exhibition detailing its history while, at the boundary of the castle, is the Helmsley Walled Garden, a glorious Victorian garden that originally dates back to 1756 and incorporates an organic kitchen garden, bold borders, glass houses and

The Feversham Arms Inn

Church Houses, Farndale, Kirkbymoorside,
York, North Yorkshire YO62 7LF
Tel: 01751 433206
e-mail: fevershamfarndale@hotmail.com
website: www.fevershamarmsinn.co.uk

The excellent **Feversham Arms Inn** is located within Farndale, in the heart of the famous North Yorkshire Moors' Daffodil Valley. Always attractive, when the wild daffodils are in bloom during April it takes on a magical feel. This rural country inn is surrounded by some of the most picturesque and unspoilt countryside in Northern England, and would make a delightful stopping-place for anyone exploring the area.

Owner Frances Debenham has been here for nearly 20 years, and has made this fine inn into one of the most popular in the area. The premises date back over 200 years, and are cosy, full of character and offer a spacious interior and a large beer garden. The warm and friendly bar, recently refurbished by in keeping with traditional style, stocks a good range, with two real ales available – Tetleys and Black Sheep – together with a selection of lagers, cider, stout, wines, spirits and soft drinks. Award-winning home-cooked bar meals, daily specials and an à la carte selection are served each lunch-time and evening, and there's a traditional lunch every Sunday. The house specialities include steak-and-ale pie and game pie in winter. Frances is happy to provide catering for weddings, family celebrations and meetings.

Anyone wanting to escape the hustle and bustle and stop at this rural retreat should note that there are three ensuite family-sized guest bedrooms, all of which enjoy superb countryside views, as well as a self-catering holiday cottage that sleeps up to four people and has a fully-equipped kitchen and every amenity.

Packed lunches are supplied for guests off on a day's exploration of York, Pickering, Malton, Whitby and the coast, and the many castles, museums and natural delights – walking, bird-watching, biking, fishing – available in the region.

over 150 varieties of clematis climbing up the imposing walls. The garden is open throughout the year, and at weekends in the winter.

Just to the west of Helmsley and standing amongst wooded hills beside the River Rye, rise the indescribably beautiful remains of **Rievaulx Abbey** (English Heritage), which has been described as the most exquisite monastic site in Europe: JMW Turner was enchanted by this idyllic landscape and Dorothy Wordsworth spellbound. Founded in 1131, Rievaulx was the first Cistercian abbey in Yorkshire and, with some 700 people – monks, lay brothers, servants – eventually living within its walls, it also became one of the largest. Like Kirkham Abbey a few years earlier, Rievaulx was endowed by Walter l'Espec, Lord of Helmsley, who was still mourning the loss of his only son in a riding accident. The abbey was soon a major landowner in the county, earning a healthy income from farming and, at one time, it owned more than 14,000 sheep as well as having its own fishery at Teesmouth and iron-ore mines at Bilsdale and near Wakefield.

Looking down on the extensive remains of the abbey is **Rievaulx Terrace** (National Trust), a breathtaking example of landscape gardening completed in 1758. The cunningly contrived avenues draw the eye to incomparable views of the abbey itself, to vistas along the Rye Valley and to the rolling contours of the hills beyond. Another feature of the terrace are the two mid-18th century temples, one of which has an elaborate ceiling painting and fine period furniture.

Around Helmsley

Church Houses

9½ miles NE of Helmsley off the A170

Set beside the River Dove in one of the North York Moors' most famous beauty spots, Farndale, this village, in the spring, is surrounded by riverbanks full of thousands of wild daffodils – a short-stemmed variety whose colours shade from a pale buttercup yellow to a rich orange-gold. According to local tradition, the bulbs were cultivated by monks who used the petals in their medical concoctions and Yorkshire folk often refer to daffodils as Lenten Lilies because of the time of year in which they bloom. The flowers, once mercilessly plundered by visitors, are now protected by law and 2,000 acres of Farndale are designated as a local nature reserve.

Gillamoor

6½ miles NE of Helmsley off the A170

This pleasant little village is well worth a visit to see its very rare, and very elegant, four-faced sundial that was erected in 1800 and also to enjoy the famous **Surprise View**. This is a ravishing panoramic vista of Farndale, with the River Dove flowing through the valley far below and white dusty roads climbing the hillside to the heather-covered moors beyond.

Also of interest is the village church that was once the church at Bransdale about six miles away! In the late 1700s, Bransdale's Church was in good repair but little used: Gillamoor's was dilapidated but the villagers wanted a place of worship. A solution was reached by appointing a single stonemason, James Smith, to remove Bransdale church stone by stone and re-erect it at Gillamoor.

Kirkbymoorside

5½ miles NE of Helmsley on the A170

This charming and ancient market town of fine Georgian houses, narrow twisting lanes and cobbled market place, straggles up the hillside and, where the town ends, the moors begin – it is appropriate then that its name means 'church by the moorside'. It was here that one of the 17th century's most reviled politicians ended his life in what is now Buckingham House but was then part of the adjoining King Head's Hotel. George Villiers, 2nd Duke of Buckingham, was a favourite of Charles II and had come to the town to hunt in the nearby Forest of Pickering. While out for a day's sport he was thrown from his horse and badly injured and, having been taken back to the King's Head, he died later that day. An entry in the parish register notes the date, 1687, and reads: 'April 17th George Viluas: Lord Dooke of Bookingham.'

Nunnington

4 miles SE of Helmsley off the B1257

This delightful old agricultural village is home to **Nunnington Hall** (National Trust), which lies just to the east beside the banks of the River Rye and has a picturesque packhorse bridge within its grounds. A manor house dating back to the late 17th century, the house has a magnificent panelled hall, fine tapestries and china and the famous Carlisle collection of miniature rooms that are exquisitely furnished in different period styles – all to one eighth scale. Nunnington Hall is also famous for its haunted room. Meanwhile, outside in the grounds is a walled garden with delightful mixed borders, spring flowering meadows and orchards of traditional Ryedale fruit varieties. The hall is open from March to October.

Back in the village church there is an ancient tomb, surmounted by the stone effigy of Sir Walter de Teyes, who died in 1325. However, local legend suggests that this is actually the final resting place of Peter Loschy, who is said to have killed a dragon in the nearby woods. Loschy and his dog battled with the magic beast for several hours but each time the monster sustained a wound it would roll on the ground and the injury would heal. Loschy finally defeated the dragon after his dog carried away the pieces that he had hacked off the creature.

Hovingham

8 miles NW of Malton on the B1257

This charming village, which boasts now fewer than three village greens, has remained unspoilt down the years and, today, the idyllic scene is just as it was when Arthur Mee noted, '*Hall, church and village gather round like a happy family.*' Overlooking one of the village greens is an elegant Victorian school that is still in use and boasts a lovely oriel window.

The village is also home to **Hovingham Hall**, an imposing Georgian mansion, which was built in 1760 for Sir Thomas Worsley, the Surveyor General to George III. Almost exactly 200 years later, on June 8th 1961, his descendant, Katherine Worsley returned here for a royal reception following her marriage to the Duke of Kent. There is an unusual entrance to the estate that leads directly off the village green but the huge archway opens, not as one would expect, on to a drive leading to the hall but to a vast riding school and stables. The Worsley family still live at the hall and, therefore, it is only open to visitors by arrangement.

Ampleforth

4 miles SW of Helmsley off the B1257

Set on the southern slopes of the Hambleton Hills, Ampleforth is perhaps best known for its Roman Catholic

The Golden Lion Inn

Great Barugh, Malton,
North Yorkshire YO17 6UZ
Tel: 01653 668242
e-mail: quaff@goldenlioninn.com
website: www.goldenlioninn.com

The Golden Lion Inn is an excellent establishment situated in the picturesque village of Great Barugh, in the heart of the North Yorkshire countryside. It can be found by driving west out of Malton on the B1257 – pass through the village of Swinton and then turn right at the signpost for Kirbymoorside, follow this road for about 3 miles. The Inn is on the right after you turn left into the village.

This Free House is run by Chris and Sam, who bought it in February 2004 after fleeing the hustle and bustle of London. Parts of this distinguished Inn date back to the early 1600s. They have extended the dining area by knocking through into what was living accommodation, creating an increased and beautiful dining area. During the renovations – which were sensitively and carefully done – original stonework (circa 1600) was exposed. Traditional features such as flagstone floors and brickbuilt fires are married happily to fresh modern elements that add to the Inn's charming and welcoming ambience.

Three to four real ales are available, with Black Sheep and Worthington the permanent ales, complemented by two changing guest ales. Together with these there's a good range of lagers, cider, stout, wines, spirits and soft drinks.

In their short time here the owners have built up a growing reputation for the quality of the food. Meals are served at lunch (12 – 2pm) and dinner (5 – 8.30 Mon-Thurs) (5 – 9pm Fri & Sat) (12noon – 7.30pm Sun) booking is advised for Friday and Saturday evenings and Sunday lunch. Opening times are seasonal and it is advised to check with The Golden Lion Inn after late September and prior to mid July. All dishes are home cooked and make use of the freshest local ingredients. One staple of the menu is an excellent choice of steaks – fillet, T-bone, sirloin and rump. Their menu is varied and caters for most tastes and you'd be hard pressed to find something that doesn't suit! Outside there's a pleasant beer garden to the rear with stunning views to the Moors and off-road parking.

public school, Ampleforth College, which lies to the east of the village. Established by the Benedictine community that came here in 1809, who were fleeing from persecution in post-revolutionary France, the monks built an austere-looking abbey in the Romanesque style amongst whose treasures are an altar stone rescued from Byland Abbey and finely crafted woodwork by the 'Mouseman of Kilburn', Robert Thompson.

Coxwold

6½ miles SW of Helmsley off the A19

One of the area's most picturesque villages, Coxwold is set in a narrow valley on the edge of the Hambledon Hills and its main street is lined with well-tended grassy banks and attractive stone cottages. At the western end of the village stands the 500-year-old **Shandy Hall,** the home of Laurence Sterne, Coxwold's vicar in the 1760s and the author of *Tristram Shandy*, a wonderfully bizarre novel that opened a vein of English surreal comedy leading directly to The Goons and the Monty Python team. The architecture of the hall, which is Tudor in origin, includes some appropriately eccentric features – strangely-shaped balustrades on the wooden staircases, a Heath Robinson type of contraption in the bedroom powder-closet by which Sterne could draw up pails of water for his ablutions and a tiny, eye-shaped window in the

THE FAUCONBERG ARMS

Coxwold, York, North Yorkshire YO61 4AD
Tel: 01347 868214 Fax: 01347 868054
e-mail: Fauconbergarms@aol.com
website: www.fauconbergarms.co.uk

A truly outstanding inn set in a scenic location in the picturesque village of Coxwold, **The Fauconberg Arms** is a historic place dating back more than 400 years. Many, many years ago it was known as the Belle Assez Arms – that name, as its current one, coming from the crest of arms of the one-time Lord of the Manor.

This welcoming family-run inn is managed by Julie and Stefan, with able assistance from their sons John (who is head chef) and Will (who runs the bar). Together they have many years' experience in catering and the licensing trade.

The classic interior is tasteful and traditional, combining the best of old-world features with modern comfort. Exposed beamwork and stonework, the enormous open fireplace and other traditional elements and decorative touches add to the cosy and relaxed ambience.

Open every session, the inn serves up real ales from Theakstons and John Smiths, together with an occasional guest ale.

It's the inn's food that brings visitors from all over the country. Food is available at every session, and the fine restaurant is open Wednesday to Saturday evening and for Sunday lunch (other times by arrangement). Booking is essential Saturday evening and Sunday lunchtime. There is also a private dining room that can accommodate up to 14 people – please ring or visit the inn's website for details. The menu includes expertly prepared roast rump of lamb, whole baked trout, duck breast, baked camembert and salmon fillet. The menu is complemented by daily specials that can include dishes such as whole Whitby lobster, steaks and more. All dishes use the freshest ingredients to create the most tempting and enjoyable dining experience.

This excellent inn also boasts four quality ensuite guest bedrooms – a twin and three doubles – available all year round. The tariff includes a hearty breakfast.

huge chimney stack opening from the study to the right of the entrance. A more conventional attraction here is the priceless collection of Sterne's books and manuscripts.

The Rev Sterne much preferred the cosmopolitan diversions of London to the rustic pleasures of his North Yorkshire parish and rarely officiated at the imposing village church, with its striking octagonal tower, three-decker pulpit and Fauconberg family tombs. A curiosity inside the church is a floor brass in the nave recording the death of Sir John Manston in 1464. A space was left for his wife Elizabeth's name to be added at a later date but the space remains blank to this day. Meanwhile, outside, against the wall of the nave, is Sterne's original tombstone, moved here from London's Bayswater when the churchyard there was deconsecrated in 1969.

Just to the south of Coxwold is **Newburgh Priory,** which was founded in 1145 as an Augustinian monastery but, since 1538 after the Dissolution, it has been the home of the Fauconberg family. Now a chiefly Georgian country house, the priory is noted for its fine interiors and its beautiful water garden. An old tradition asserts that Oliver Cromwell's body is interred here. Cromwell's daughter, Mary, was married to Lord Fauconberg and when Charles II had her father's corpse hanged at Tyburn and his head struck off, Lady Fauconberg claimed the decapitated body, brought it to Newburgh and, it is said, buried the remains under the floorboards of an attic room. The supposed tomb has never been opened and the Fauconbergs even resisted a royal appeal from Edward VII when, as Prince of Wales, he was a guest at their home. The house, which is still the home of the Earls of Fauconberg, and its extensive grounds are open to the public during the spring and summer months.

Another ancient ecclesiastical building, **Byland Abbey** (English Heritage), now in ruins set in tranquil green meadows, can be found just to the northeast of Coxwold. The Cistercians began building their vast compound in 1177 and Byland Abbey grew to become the largest Cistercian church in Britain. However, much of the damage to its fabric was caused by Scottish soldiers after the Battle of Byland in 1322 and the English king, Edward II, who had been staying at the abbey, fled after his defeat, abandoning vital stores and priceless treasures. In a frenzy of looting, the Scots made off with everything the king had left and ransacked the abbey buildings for good measure. The ruined west front of the abbey, with only the lower arch of its great rose window still in place, gives a vivid impression of how glorious this building once was and visitors can also see the largest collection of medieval floor tiles, still in the their original settings, here. The abbey is open daily from April to October.

Kilburn

7 miles SW of Helmsley off the A170

Kilburn is actually two villages, known locally as 'high town' and 'low town' that are set just under half a mile apart. The view from the green in High Kilburn takes in large vistas of the Vales of York and Mowbray while the beck that flows through Low Kilburn becomes, as it reaches Easingwold, the River Kyle. During the Middle Ages, the village was the home of the King's Forester and all the land to the west was one of the Royal hunting grounds.

However, Kilburn is best remembered as being the home of one of the most famous of modern Yorkshire craftsmen, Robert Thompson – the Mouseman of Kilburn. Robert's father was a carpenter and he apprenticed his son to an engineer; however, at the age of 20, inspired by seeing the medieval wood carvings in Ripon Cathedral, Robert returned to Kilburn and begged his father to train him as a carpenter. An early commission from Ampleforth Abbey to carve a cross settled his destiny and from then, until his death in 1955, Robert's beautifully crafted ecclesiastical and domestic furniture was in constant demand. His work can be seen in more than 700 churches, including Westminster Abbey and York Minster. Each piece bears his 'signature' – a tiny carved mouse placed in some inconspicuous corner of the work. According to a family story, Robert adopted this symbol when one of his assistants happened to use the phrase "as poor as a church mouse." (Signing one's work was not a new tradition: the 17th century woodcarver Grinling Gibbons' personal stamp was a pod of peas.) Robert Thompson's two grandsons have continued his work and their grandfather's former home is now both a memorial to his genius and a showroom for their own creations.

Just north of the village is one of the area's most famous features the **White Horse** that was inspired by the prehistoric White Horse hill-carving at Uffingham in Berkshire. John Hodgson,

Kilburn's village schoolmaster, enthused his pupils and villagers into creating this splendid folly in 1857. At some 314 feet long and 228 feet high, the figure is visible from as far away as Harrogate and Otley. However, unlike its prehistoric predecessor in Berkshire, where the chalk hillside keeps it naturally white, Kilburn's 'White' horse is scraped from grey limestone that needs to be regularly groomed with lime-washing and a liberal spreading of chalk chippings.

Boltby

8 miles NW of Helmsley off the A170

Boltby is an engaging village tucked away at the foot of the Hambleton Hills, close to where the oddly-named Gurt of Beck tumbles down the hillside and, depending on how much rain has fallen on the moors, passes either under or over a little humpback bridge. On the plain below is **Nevison House**, which is reputed to be the home of the 17th century highwayman, William Nevison or 'Swift Nick' as Charles II dubbed him. Some historians claim that it was Swift Nick, not Dick Turpin, who made the legendary ride on Black Bess from London to York to establish an alibi.

Sutton-under-Whitestonecliff

8 miles W of Helmsley on the A170

Boasting the longest place name in England, Sutton is more famous for the

Laskill Grange

Hawnby, Helmsley,
North Yorkshire YO62 5NB
Tel: 01439 798268
e-mail: suesmith@laskillfarm.fsnet.co.uk
website: www.laskhillgrange.co.uk

Laskill Grange comprises Laskhill Farm, Barn Conversions and Keldholme Cottages – offering superb and idyllic holiday accommodation to suit every guest. At the gracious and elegant farmhouse, bed and breakfast accommodation is offered, with three double, two twin and one single ensuite guest bedrooms. Each room boasts many fine traditional features, complemented by the tasteful and stylish décor and furnishings to ensure guests' every comfort. The lounge has an open fire, while the grounds include a lovely garden with lake, stream and summer-house.

The Grange also offers excellent self-catering accommodation in five superb barn conversions reached just across a courtyard from the main farmhouse. The Forge sleeps six, The Granary sleeps four to six, The Smithy and The Coach House sleep four and Bridge Cottage sleeps two. The Coach House is suitable for guests with disabilities. All boast traditional features such as exposed oak beams and stone fireplaces, complemented by modern conveniences such as the well-fitted kitchens fully equipped with cooker, microwave, dishwasher and washing machine. Outside there is a barbecue area, patio and a shared garden activity area. Guests are welcome to enjoy free fishing on the nearby River Seph. All fuel, power, linen and towels are included in the tariff. Pets are allowed in some of the cottages.

The three cottages at Keldholme are charming 300-year-old buildings set in the quiet village from which they take their name. Orchard Cottage, Cedar Cottage and Robin's Nest all sleep four, and are tasteful renovations that ensure guests' comfort. The décor and furnishings are first-class and very tasteful, and each has access to its own garden.

This peaceful rural retreat is reached by taking the B1257 out of Helmsley to reach the village of Hawnby, or the A170 east from Thirsk to reach Keldholme. Rievaulx Abbey, Nunnington Hall, Castle Howard, Mount Grace Priory, Byland Abbey, Ryedale Folk Museum, York, Beverley and the delights of the Heritage Coast are all within easy reach.

THE HAWNBY HOTEL

Hilltop, Hawnby, Helmsley, York,
North Yorkshire YO62 5QS
Tel: 01439 798202 Fax: 01439 798344
e-mail: info@hawnbyhotel.co.uk
website: www.hawnbyhotel.co.uk

Built in the early 19th century, **The Hawnby Hotel** is a cosy and very appealing hotel in a peaceful rural setting. Reached via the B1257 out of Helmsley, this fine hotel has nine ensuite guest bedrooms and one self-catering cottage. Six of the nine guest bedrooms are located in the main building, while the other three are within the refurbished stables opposite. All rooms are decorated and furnished to a very high standard of comfort and quality. Rated 4 Diamonds by the ETC,

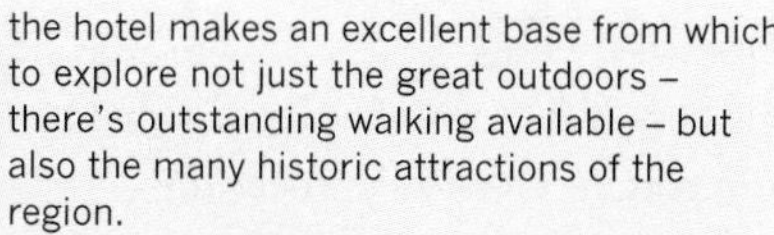

the hotel makes an excellent base from which to explore not just the great outdoors – there's outstanding walking available – but also the many historic attractions of the region.

The hotel is open every session Monday to Thursday and all day Friday to Sunday for a range of ales, lagers, wines, spirits and soft drinks. The hotel's menu boasts a selection of delicious dishes served at lunch and dinner.

precipitous cliff that towers above it from the east – **Sutton Bank**. From the top of the bank there is one of the grandest landscape views in England, which looks out across the vast expanse of the Vale of York to the Pennine Hills far away to the west. The real life James Herriot called it the *"finest view in England,"* and he certainly knew this area well since his large veterinary practice covered the farms from here right over to the Yorkshire Dales.

There is a National Park Information Centre at the summit of Sutton Bank and a well-marked Nature Trail leads steeply down to, and around, **Lake Gormire,** an Ice Age lake trapped here by a landslip. Gormire is set in a large basin with no river running from it: any overflow disappears down a 'swallow hole' and emerges beneath White Mare Cliffs. The lake is one of Yorkshire's only two natural lakes, the other being Semer Water in Wensleydale

Sutton Bank used to be a graveyard for caravans because of its steep (1 in 3) climb and sharp bends. On one July Saturday in 1977, some 30 vehicles broke down on the ascent and five breakdown vehicles spent all day retrieving them. Caravans are now, not surprisingly, banned from this route. Though the bank may be a challenge to cars, its sheer-sided cliffs create powerful thermals making this a favoured spot for gliders and bright-winged hang-gliders.

Pickering

This busy little town developed around an important crossroads where the Malton to Whitby and the Thirsk to Scarborough roads intersect. It is also the largest of the four market towns in Ryedale and is, quite possibly, the oldest as it claims to date from 270 BC when the market is said to have been founded by a King of the Brigantes called Peredurus. In fact, it is a legend concerning Peredurus that gives the town its name. One day, the king was swimming in a pond at the source of the nearby Costa Beck and, while in the water, unbeknown to him, the young king lost a ring – a valuable family heirloom. On returning to his castle, Peredurus discovered his loss but after an extensive and fruitless search it seemed lost forever. Many years later, the king was back at Costa Beck, fishing, and there he caught a huge pike. That evening, as he cut open the cooked fish to serve his wife and sons, the ring fell out of the fish's belly! The story lives on in the name of the town 'Pike-a-Ring' and can also be seen on the town's coat of arms.

As an attempt to dominate the local area, William the Conqueror ordered the construction of a motte and, later, in the 12th century, the once splendid **Pickering Castle** (English Heritage) and a royal hunting lodge were erected on the site. Though now ruined the castle and lodge still offer visitors, through the exhibitions, an insight into lives at both the castle and within the royal forest some 800 years ago. There are also some wonderful views from here out across the North York Moors.

Another building worthy of the visit is the parish **Church of St Peter and St Paul** as it contains some remarkable 15th century murals. During the glum days of Puritanism, these lively paintings were denounced as idolatrous and plastered over and they stayed forgotten for some 200 years before being rediscovered when the church was being restored in 1851. Unfortunately, the vicar at that time shared the Puritans' sentiments and, despite opposition from his parishioners and even from his bishop, had them smothered again under whitewash. A more liberal successor to the vicar had the murals restored once again in 1878 and they now give a vivid idea of how cheerful, colourful and entertaining many English churches were before the unforgivable vandalism of the Puritan years. These superb paintings, sharp, vigorous and well-observed, happily embrace scenes from the Bible, old legends and actual history: a real insight into the medieval mind that had no difficulty in accepting both the story of St George slaying the dragon and the martyrdom of St Thomas à Becket as equally real, and inspiring, events.

Due to the town being situated at the heart of the fertile Vale of Pickering, it is not surprising that its early reputation was based on farming and, in the case of Pickering, it was the breeding and rearing of pigs and horses. Vast quantities of pork were transported across the moors to Whitby, salted and used as shipboard rations while the famous Cleveland Bay horses, with their jet-black manes and tails, were extensively bred in the area and in Eskdale, a little further north, they still are. These sweet-natured, sturdy and tireless animals have always been in great demand and during the 19th century their equable temperament made them ideal for pulling Hansom cabs and street-cars while, today, they are often seen in more dignified circumstances, such as taking part in State Processions.

Hole of Horcum, nr Lockton

Housed in a gracious Regency mansion is the **Beck Isle Museum**, whose numerous display areas are crammed full of a wonderful assortment of curious, mysterious and commonplace items from the last 200 years or so. There are intriguing re-creations of typical Victorian domestic rooms, shops, workshops and even a pub while the museum is also home to the comprehensive collection of photographs by Sydney Smith. The exhibition presents a remarkable picture of the Ryedale area as it was more than half a century ago and it is made even more interesting by displaying the very cameras and other photographic equipment used by Sydney Smith.

Pickering is the southern terminus of the North York Moors Railway, the most popular heritage railway in Britain and from here visitors can take a nostalgic steam journey through 18 miles of stunning scenery to the northern terminus at Grosmont. **Pickering Station** itself has recently been restored to its 1937 condition, with the help of a Heritage Lottery Fund, and, of particular interest, are the original fixtures and fittings that have been installed in the Booking and Parcel Office. There is also a tea room here and the railway is open daily from March to November.

Around Pickering

Low Dalby

4½ miles NE of Pickering off the A169

This village is the starting point for the **Dalby Forest Drive**, a 9-mile circular route that runs through what was once the Royal Hunting Forest of Pickering. After the demise of the ancient forest, the heath became an enormous rabbit warren that provided fur for felt hats but today, now owned by the Forestry Commission, the forest has become a

The Moorlands Country House

Levisham, Pickering,
North Yorkshire YO18 7NL
Tel: 01751 460229 Fax: 01751 460470
e-mail: ronaldoleonardo@aol.com
website: www.moorlandslevisham.co.uk

Set amid some truly spectacular countryside, **The Moorlands Country House** is an outstanding country house inn and hotel. Rated 5 Diamonds (Gold Award) by the English Tourism Council, it can be found off the main A169 (Pickering–Whitby road) via Lockton. Winner of the Yorkshire Guest Accommodation of the Year in 2003, and a close runner-up for overall whole-country winner of this prize in that year, this elegant residence is set in acres of beautiful well-tended gardens with unmatchable views in every direction.

This licensed premises offers a range of thirst-quenchers and a menu of home-made appetizers, entrees and desserts to tempt every palate.

The seven guest bedrooms within the main house are of the highest quality. All ensuite, they are spacious, attractive and supremely comfortable. One room boasts a four-poster bed.

Behind the main house there is Moorlands Cottage, a cosy and charming self-catering cottage, purpose-built for two people that has been awarded a 5-Star rating by the ETC. Furnished and equipped to a high standard, the cottage has full facilities and guests can enjoy access to the surrounding woodland, pond and mature gardens. Non-smokers only. No pets.

Built in 1895, The Moorlands is handy for many of the interesting attractions in and around Ryedale, including Duncumbe Park, Nunnington Hall, Rievaulx Abbey, Castle Howard. The North Yorkshire Moors steam railway is also nearby, along, of course, with all of the natural beauties of North Yorkshire. Scarborough and Whitby are just half an hour away, York some 40 minutes' drive. Golf days and horse-riding can be arranged by the owners for guests' enjoyment.

Closed November to March.

popular place for those wishing to see a wide variety of wildlife in the various habitats the area has to offer. The Visitor Centre in Low Dalby has plenty of information about the forest and the various facilities available, including the waymarked trails, picnic sites, children's play areas and the orienteering course. The centre is open from Easter to October.

Lockton

5 miles NE of Pickering off the A169

To the north of the village is the **Hole of Horcum**, a huge natural amphitheatre that, so the story goes, was scooped out of Levisham Moor by the giant Wade and is now a popular centre for hang gliders.

Levisham

5 miles NE of Pickering off the A169

Just to the west of the village, in the scenic valley of Newton Dale lies Levisham Station, one of several that lies on the route of the North Yorkshire Moors Railway. This stop is the ideal location for walking with a wide variety of wildlife and flowers within short distance of the station.

Thornton-le-Dale

2½ miles E of Pickering on the A170

As long ago as 1907, a *Yorkshire Post* poll of its readers acclaimed Thornton-le-Dale as the most beautiful village in Yorkshire

The Horseshoe Inn

Main Street, Levisham, Pickering,
North Yorkshire YO18 7NL
Tel: 01751 460240 Fax: 01751 460347
e-mail: info@horseshoeinn-levisham.co.uk
website: www.horseshoeinn-levisham.co.uk

With its quite outstanding setting, **The Horseshoe Inn** is well worth seeking out. This superb family-run inn is joint-owned by Jules and Paul Tatham and Betty and Stuart Elsworth. Set in the heart of the North Yorkshire moors in the picturesque village of Levisham, found west off the A169 Pickering-Whitby road, the inn dates back to the 16th century and has plenty of character and style.

Open every session, real ales on tap are Theakstons Best and Theakstons Olde Peculiar, together with a changing guest ale; there's also lager, cider, stout, wines, spirits and soft drinks to quench every thirst. Hearty and delicious food is served at lunch (12 – 2) and dinner (6.30 – 9) every day. The inn's chefs conjure up a range of delights such as Ryedale lamb, local pork, wild duck, pan-flashed calves' liver and a choice of four vegetarian dishes.

The inn also boasts six superior ensuite guest bedrooms, two on the ground floor, offering comfortable and attractive accommodation in an ideal location.

Crumbs of Comfort

Maltongate, Thornton-le-Dale, Pickering, North Yorkshire YO18 7RF
Tel: 01751 477996
website: www.crumbs-of-comfort.com

Owned and personally run by Alison and Gail, charming and welcoming hosts, **Crumbs of Comfort** is a cosy and welcoming tea room and gift shop. Gail is queen of the kitchen while Alison looks after front of house and the gift shop. Quality is the byword here, where home-cooking and baking are among the finest to be found in the region.

Open 10 a.m. to 4.30 p.m. Thursday to Tuesday in summer and Thursday to Sunday from November to late April, the mouthwatering dishes served up include hot snacks such as bacon or sausage sandwiches, light lunches of omelettes or home made quiche and freshly prepared sandwiches filled with local homecooked beef or ham and a wide selection of homemade cakes and puddings, chosen from the menu and daily specials board. Gail's scones are a particular treat – they positively melt in your mouth.

The gift shop stocks a good selection of hand-crafted ceramics, distinctive clothing, picture frames, home-made jams and preserves, and more.

and, despite very stiff competition for this title, most visitors find themselves in agreement. Such is the village's charms that the North York Moors National Park actually creates a special loop in its boundary to include this picture postcard village that, somewhat confusingly, is also frequently shown on maps as 'Thornton Dale'. Meanwhile, near the parish church of All Saints is one of the most photographed houses in Britain and it may seem familiar as it regularly appears on chocolate boxes, jigsaws and calendars.

Ebberston

6½ miles E of Pickering off the A170

About a mile to the west of Ebberston, in the early 18th century Mr William Thompson, MP for Scarborough, built himself what is possibly the smallest stately home in England, **Ebberston Hall**. From the front the house appears to be just one-storey high, with a pillared doorway approached by a grand flight of stone steps flanked by a moderately sized room on each side. In fact, behind this modest front, there is an extensive basement. The hall is open to visitors by appointment only.

Brompton-by-Sawdon

9 miles E of Pickering on the A170

This ancient village has long associations with the Cayley family and, although it is not known when they first arrived here, a Cayley was the Lord of the Manor in Brompton in 1572.

The Coachman Inn

Pickering Road West, Snainton, Scarborough, North Yorkshire YO13 9PL
Tel: 01723 859231 Fax: 01723 850008
e-mail: enquiries@coachmaninn.co.uk
website: www.coachmaninn.co.uk

Located on the edge of the village of Snainton just off the B1258, reached via the A170, **The Coachman Inn** carries on a proud tradition dating back over 240 years of providing great food, drink and accommodation. This Grade II listed inn is owned by Helen and Roger, with able assistance from Helen's mum, Pat. Extensive and tasteful renovations have been underway since they bought the inn in May of 2004, ensuring that this inn offers the very best in comfort and quality.

Roger is a professional chef of over 20 years' standing – his daily-changing menus boast a range of hearty traditional dishes such as steak, Whitby whiting, Brompton lamb's liver and escalopes of chicken. At lunch, delicious sandwiches are added to the menu. Meals are served every day at lunch (12 –2 Mon-Fri; 12 – 2.30 Sat; 12 – 2.30 Sun) and Mon-Thurs 7 – 9, Fri-Sat 7 – 9.30 for dinner. The inn also boasts five ensuite guest bedrooms – please ring for details. Children welcome.

However, it is the 6th Baronet who is the best-known member of the family. Sir George Cayley (1773-1857) was a pioneer aviator who achieved successful flights with small gliders in Brompton Dale although it was his coachman, in 1853, who, under duress, made the first true glider flight in history. Not surprisingly, the coachman quickly handed in his notice after what must have been a hair-raising voyage.

It was in the medieval church of this small village, on an autumn day in 1802, that William Wordsworth was married to Mary Hutchinson whose family lived at nearby Gallows Hill Farm. Mary's home, now the **Wordsworth Gallery**, plays host to an exhibition on both the poets Wordsworth and Coleridge while the medieval barn is now filled with designer gifts, ladies clothes and a licensed tea rooms. The gallery is open all year round but closed on Sundays and Mondays.

Kirby Misperton

3½ miles S of Pickering off the A169

The 375 acres of wooded parkland surrounding Kirby Misperton Hall provide an attractive setting for **Flamingo Land Theme Park and Zoo** where not only are there a variety of white-knuckle rides that are sure to thrill children and adults alike but also there are over 1,000 animals, birds and reptiles. Along with the tigers, zebras, camels and penguins, beyond doubt, the most spectacular sight here is that of the flock of pink flamingos gathered around the lake fringed with willow trees.

Appleton-le-Moors

5 miles NW of Pickering off the A170

Located just inside the southern boundary of the North York Moors National Park, Appleton-le-Moors is noted for its fine church whose tower and spire provide a landmark for miles around. It was built in Victorian times to a design by JL Pearson, the architect of Truro Cathedral, and it has the same Gothic style as the Cornish cathedral.

Cropton

4 miles NW of Pickering off the A170

This tiny village, so records indicate, has been brewing ales from as far back as 1613 even though home-brewing was illegal in the 17th century. Despite a lapse in the intervening decades, brewing returned to the village when, in

Ryedale Folk Museum

Hutton le Hole, York YO626UA
Tel: 01751 417367
e-mail: info@ryedalefolkmuseum.co.uk

Ryedale Folk Museum is a wonderful working museum insight into bygone eras. Here you will find the finest collection of thatched buildings in Yorkshire - the rescued and restored houses chart the changes in rural life, from the simplicity of the early Tudor crofter's cottage to the cosy Victorian clutter of the White Cottage.

There were mines and railways in nearby Rosedale, bringing a completely different way of life to the moors - explore the story behind these and the Elizabethan glass furnace and other moorland industries. Rural workers such as tinsmith, wheelwright, blacksmith, saddler, shoemaker and joiner each have a workshop with the tools of their trade on display and regular demonstrations take place including weaving, spinning, woodwork and cane and rushwork. An outstanding collection of tools also records the extraordinary changes in agriculture over the last 300 years, from wooden pitchforks onwards.

In the growing gardens, there are the medicinal herbs of the crofter's garth and the more recent cottage garden flowers, whilst the Victorian vegetable garden contains old varieties of vegetables as they used to be. The working landscape explores the way it was once used and how the way of life has altered it over the years. Farm animals, rare wild flowers and historic crops are sights to be seen here and a project is underway to help conserve the vanishing cornfield flowers. Over 40 varieties are growing here.

A gift shop sells a selection of books, maps and souvenirs. Open March to November - ring for details.

1984, the cellars of the village pub were converted to accommodate a micro-brewery – **Cropton Brewery**. From the brewery's visitor centre there are guided tours of the brewery and from the inn visitors can not only sample its highly regarded and distinctive ales but also enjoy some regional food.

Hutton-le-Hole

7 miles NW of Pickering off the A170

Long regarded as one of Yorkshire's prettiest villages, Hutton-le-Hole has a character all of its own. Facing the village green and standing on one of Hutton's oldest sites, is the **Ryedale Folk Museum** (see panel opposite), an imaginative celebration of 4,000 years of life in North Yorkshire from prehistoric times to the 20th century. Among the historic buildings to be seen at this large open-air museum is a complete Elizabethan Manor House rescued from nearby Harome and reconstructed here; a medieval crofter's cottage with a thatched, hipped roof, peat fire and garth; and an old village Shop and Post Office fitted out as it would have looked just after Elizabeth II's Coronation in 1953. Other exhibits include workshops of traditional crafts, such as tinsmiths, coopers and wheelwrights, and an Edwardian photographic studio. The National Park also has an Information Centre here and throughout the year there are special events such as a Rare Breeds Day and re-enactments of Civil War battles by the Sealed Knot.

Anyone interested in unusual churches should make the short trip from Hutton-le-Hole to **St Mary's Church, Lastingham**, about three miles to the east. The building of a monastery here in the 7th century was recorded by no less an authority than the Venerable Bede who visited Lastingham not long after it was completed. That monastery was rebuilt in 1078 with a massively impressive crypt that is still in place – a claustrophobic space with heavy Norman arches rising from squat round pillars. The church above is equally atmospheric, lit only by a small window at one end.

Rosedale Abbey

9 miles NW of Pickering off the A170

This is the largest settlement in Rosedale, the charming, steep-sided valley of the River Severn, and it takes its name from the small nunnery that was founded here in 1158. Nothing of the old abbey has survived although some of its stones were recycled to build the village's houses. A peaceful village now, Rosedale was once crowded with workers employed in iron-ore mines on the moors in an industry that reached its peak here between 1860 and 1880. It was said that, such was the shortage of lodgings during the 1870s, "the beds were never cold," as workers from different shifts took turns to sleep in them. The great chimney of the smelting furnace was once a striking landmark on the summit of the moor

The Europa Hotel

20 Hudson Street, Whitby,
North Yorkshire YO21 3EP
Tel/Fax: 01947 602251
email: europahotel-whitby@btconnect.com
website: www.europahotel-whitby.com

An elegant Victorian residence built in 1881, **Europa Hotel** is located in the heart of Whitby, positioned on the West Cliff and with three miles of golden beach, shopping and most of the town's famous attractions all within easy walking distance. This unassuming hotel has a charm all its own – intimate and family-run, it has every amenity and comfort to ensure that guests enjoy a relaxing and pleasant stay. Owners Anne and Michael have been here since 1997, earning the hotel its 4-Diamond AA rating and building up the hotel's reputation for quality and first-class service.

This lovely hotel offers nine attractive and comfortable ensuite guest bedrooms – one twin, one family and seven double rooms – covering three floors. Each room is attractively decorated and furnished, and equipped with every amenity guests have come to expect. The gracious lounge/bar is a welcome retreat where guests can relax and enjoy a quiet drink. In the restaurant, hearty breakfasts are served using locally-sourced produce whenever available. Vegetarians and special dietary requirements are happily catered for.

Whether visitors are seeking a relaxing retreat or are keen to explore the many sights, historic houses, castles, coastline and all that this region has to offer, this hotel makes a perfect base – a real home from home, with a friendly ambience and a high standard of hospitality. Places of interest in and around the town include Whitby Abbey and St Mary's Church, routes tracing the steps of both Captain Cook and Dracula, Whitby ghost walks, Victorian Jet Works, North Yorkshire Moors steam railway and more traditional seaside locations such as Robin Hood's Bay and Scarborough.

Children welcome. No smoking. No evening meals.

but, in 1972, it was found to be unsafe and demolished. A reconstruction of Rosedale's drift mine can be seen in the Ryedale Folk Museum at Hutton-le-Hole.

Whitby Abbey

High on the moorland above Rosedale Abbey stands **Ralph Cross**, one of more than 30 such stone crosses dotted across the moors. It was erected in medieval times as a waymark for travellers and when the North York Moors National Park was established in 1952, the Park authorities adopted Ralph Cross as its emblem.

Whitby

Whitby has several claims to fame – it was Captain James Cook's home port and it was, according to Bram Stoker's famous novel, the place where Count Dracula, in the form of a wolf, loped ashore from a crewless ship that had drifted into the harbour – but its greatest claim is as being one of the earliest and most important centres of Christianity in England. High on the cliff that towers above the picturesque old fishing town stand the imposing and romantic ruins of **Whitby Abbey** (English Heritage) and it was here, in AD 664, that many of the most eminent prelates of the Christian Church were summoned to attend the Synod of Whitby. They were charged with settling once and for all a festering dispute that had riven Christendom for generations: the precise date on which Easter should be celebrated. The complicated formula they devised to solve this problem is still in use. Today's visitors can climb the 199 steps up to the haunting abbey ruins and, from here, there are commanding views over the town and beyond. Not surprisingly, the beauty of the dramatic ruins has also inspired many writers, painters and engravers.

Just a short walk from the abbey is **St Mary's Church**, a unique building 'not unlike a house outside and very much like a ship inside'. Indeed, the fascinating interior, with its clutter of box-pews, iron pillars and long galleries, was reputedly fashioned by Whitby seamen during the course of the 18th century. The three-decker pulpit is from the same period and the huge ear trumpets for a rector's deaf wife were put in place about 50 years later. St Mary's stands on top of the cliff with the old town clustering around the harbour mouth far below.

Bram Stoker began writing his famous novel, *Dracula*, in 1895 while staying on the coast of Scotland but he had previously visited Whitby and it is his detailed, happy descriptions of the abbey ruins, St Mary's churchyard and other places in the town that make his story all the more sinister. Another author, Mrs Gaskell, used Whitby in her novel *Sylvia's Lovers*, where the town becomes 'Monkshaven' and St Mary's 'St Nicholas parish church'.

The old port of Whitby developed on the slim shelf of land that runs along the east bank of the River Esk, an intricate muddle of narrow, cobbled streets and shoulder-width alleys. Grape Lane is typical, a cramped little street where ancient houses lean wearily against each other. Young James Cook lived here during his apprenticeship and he lodged at the handsome house in the lane that was owned by his master, the Quaker shipowner, Captain John Walker. The house where Cook and the other apprentices studied and slept when not aboard Walker's coal ships sailing between Newcastle and London is now the **Captain Cook Memorial Museum**. As well as celebrating the years that Cook spent in Whitby, along with his later achievements, the museum also features other displays on life in the navy during the 18th century. The museum is open daily during the season and during the weekend in March. The **Whitby Museum** (see panel below) was founded in 1823 and it remains an independent establishment to this day. Found in Pannett Park and open daily from May to September and closed on Mondays throughout the rest of the year,

Whitby Museum

Pannett Park, Whitby,
North Yorkshire YO21 1RE
Tel: 01947 602908
website: www.whitby-museum.org.uk

In **Whitby Museum** there are worlds to explore from geology to jet carving, from birdlife to bygones, costumes to clocks and from Whitby Abbey to a pirate's pigtail. Ships and men from Whitby travelled the globe, fishing for whales in the Arctic, fighting the African slave trade, exploring the south seas with Capt. Cook. In the Museum are many of the treasures they brought back. Whitby jet jewellery was especially popular under Queen Victoria. Jet was also used for all sorts of miniature carvings.

Founded in 1823 to display local Jurassic fossils, this amazing 'Cabinet of Curiosities' still retains its Victorian atmosphere. The Museum is run by Whitby Literary and Philosophical Society. Visitors are welcome to use the Society's Library and Archives on weekday mornings.

The White House Hotel

Upgang Lane, Whitby,
North Yorkshire YO21 3JJ
Tel: 01947 600469 Fax: 01947 821600
e-mail: white.househotel@btconnect.com

A top-of-the-range establishment, **The White House Hotel** is a charming and welcoming establishment located on the edge of Whitby looking towards the beaches and adjacent to a golf course. This friendly and popular place serves up great food and drink every day at lunch and dinner – booking is advised for non-residents at all times. There are 16 comfortable and handsome ensuite guest bedrooms, 11 in the main buildings and five in converted farm buildings. Guests can stay on B&B or dinner and B&B rates.

the museum, though small, is a true treasure trove of Whitby's past. Also in the park is the **Pennett Art Gallery**, which holds a permanent collection of over 500 paintings including the largest collection of George Weatherill watercolours in the country.

By the early 19th century, old Whitby was full to bursting and a new town began to burgeon on the west bank of the River Esk. The new Whitby, or 'West Cliff', was carefully planned with the recent industry of tourism in mind and there was a quayside walk or promenade, a bandstand, luxury hotels and a Royal Crescent of upmarket dwellings reminiscent of Buxton or Cheltenham but with the added advantage of enjoying a sea air universally acknowledged as 'invariably beneficial to the health of the most injured constitution'.

In a dominating position on West Cliff, a bronze statue of Captain Cook gazes out over the harbour he knew so well and nearby the huge jawbone of a whale, raised as an arch, recalls those other great Whitby seafarers, the whalers. Between 1753 and 1833, Whitby was the capital of the whaling industry, bringing home 2,761 whales in 80 years. Much of that success was due to the skills of the great whaling captains William Scoresby and his son, also named William. The elder William was celebrated for his great daring and navigational skills, as well as for the invention of the crow's nest, or masthead lookout. His son was driven by a restless, enquiring mind and occupied himself with various experiments during the long days at sea in the icy Arctic waters. He is most noted for his discoveries of the forms of snow crystals and the invention of the Greenland Magnet that made ships' compasses more reliable. The whaling industry is now, thankfully, long dead, but fortunately the town's fishing industry is not, as many of Whitby's restaurants bear witness – they are famous for their seafood menus. The **Whitby Archives Heritage Centre**, which is open all year, holds an exhibition of local photographs

Long Leas Farm & Swallow Holiday Cottages

Hawsker, Whitby, North Yorkshire YO22 4LA
Tel: 01947 603790 Fax: 08707 052362
e-mail: jillian@swallowcottages.co.uk
website: www.swallowcottages.co.uk

Long Leas Farm & Swallow Holiday Cottages occupy a scenic and peaceful rural location just a few minutes' drive from Whitby. Near-derelict when owners Jill and Brian McNeil arrived in 1996, the farm and cottages have been carefully and tastefully renovated to create an outstanding holiday destination. An ideal base from which to explore the Heritage Coastline, 'Heartbeat Country' and the many waymarked coastal and country walks, horse-riding, fishing, golf and many other diversions, Jill and Brian are always happy to supply information, as they have a wealth of local knowledge and experience.

Reached from the north via the A171, from the south on the A169 to the A171, this fine establishment is set in its own extensive grounds. The main farmhouse is a Grade II listed building featuring two ensuite family-sized guest bedrooms that are attractive, comfortable and welcoming. The tariff includes a hearty breakfast. Children welcome.

Located two miles south of Whitby on the A171 and set in their own extensive grounds, four charming and welcoming cottages have been converted from traditional farm buildings – rated 4 Stars by the ETC – available all year round. *Cobweb* and *Far View* cottages feature a master bedroom with ensuite facilities and another twin bedroom. There's also a second bedroom, open-plan kitchen and spacious dining room and lounge. *John's Cottage* has a double bedroom and, upstairs, a twin bedroom in the galleried area. *Bumbleby Cottage* is fully equipped for wheelchair disabled, with two double and one triple bedroom. All enjoy panoramic views of the surrounding countryside. All linen and towels are provided, and all boast a fully-equipped kitchen, central heating, cooker, microwave, fridge, television and electric fire. Well-behaved pets are welcome. Cycle hire available.

and along with its local history research facilities also has a shop and heritage gallery. Meanwhile, the **Museum of Victorian Whitby** has a re-creation of a 19th century lane in the town complete with interiors and shop windows along with miniature rooms and settings.

One of Whitby's unique attractions is **The Sutcliffe Gallery,** in Flowergate, which celebrates the great photographer Frank Meadow Sutcliffe who was born in Whitby in 1853. His studies of local people, places and events powerfully evoke the Whitby of late-Victorian and Edwardian times in photographs that are both beautifully composed and technically immaculate. Few visitors to the gallery can resist the temptation to purchase at least one of the nostalgic prints on sale.

Another popular souvenir of the town is jet, a lustrous black stone that enjoyed an enormous vogue in Victorian times as, after the death of Prince Albert, jewellery in jet was the only ornament the Queen would allow herself to wear. The Court and the middle classes naturally followed her example and for several decades Whitby prospered greatly from the trade in jet. By 1914, workable deposits of the stone were virtually exhausted and a new generation shunned its gloomy association with death. Recent years have seen a revival of interest in the glossy stone and several shops have extensive displays of jet ornaments and jewellery. The original **Victorian Jet Works,**

established in 1867, are open daily and visitors can see the craftsmen at work as well as purchase jet from a wide range of interesting and contemporary jewellery designs.

Robin Hoods Bay

Around Whitby

Robin Hood's Bay

5 miles SE of Whitby off the A171

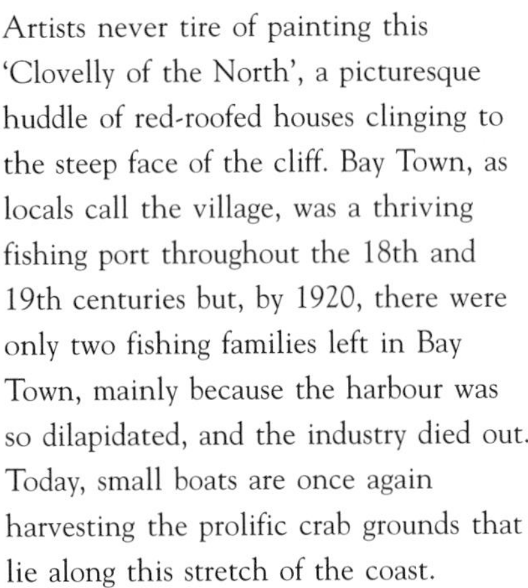

Artists never tire of painting this 'Clovelly of the North', a picturesque huddle of red-roofed houses clinging to the steep face of the cliff. Bay Town, as locals call the village, was a thriving fishing port throughout the 18th and 19th centuries but, by 1920, there were only two fishing families left in Bay Town, mainly because the harbour was so dilapidated, and the industry died out. Today, small boats are once again harvesting the prolific crab grounds that lie along this stretch of the coast.

Because of the natural isolation of the village, smuggling was almost as important as fishing to the local economy and the houses and inns in Bay Town were said to have connecting cellars and cupboards. It was claimed that "a bale of silk could pass from the bottom of the village to the top without seeing daylight". Those were the days, too, when press gangs from the Royal Navy were active in the area since recruits with a knowledge of the sea were highly prized. Apparently, these mariners were also highly prized by local women and they smartly despatched the press gangs by means of pans and rolling pins.

Shipwrecks off the shore of Bay Town were frequent, with many a mighty vessel tossed onto its reefs by North Sea storms. On one memorable occasion in the winter of 1881, a large brig, *The Visitor*, was driven onto the rocks. The seas were too rough for the lifeboat at Whitby to be launched there so it was dragged eight miles through the snow and let down the cliffside by ropes and six men were rescued. The same wild seas threatened the village itself, every storm eroding a little more of the chalk cliff to which it clings but, fortunately, Robin Hood's Bay is now protected by a sturdy sea wall. **The Old Coastguard Station**, which dates from the 19th century, is being restored by the National Trust in partnership with the North York Moors National Park Authority.

The most extraordinary building in Robin Hood's Bay is undoubtedly **Fyling Hall Pigsty**, which was built in the 1880s by Squire Barry of Fyling Hall in the classical style although the pillars supporting the portico are of wood rather than marble. Here the Squire's two favourite pigs could enjoy plenty of space and a superb view over the bay. The building is now managed by the Landmark Trust who rent it out to holidaymakers. Also in the village is the **Robin Hoods Bay and Flyingdales Museum**, a small, volunteer run museum that concentrates on local history, farming, maritime history and the seashore. The museum is open during the afternoons, from May to September.

Ravenscar

7½ miles SE of Whitby off the A171

The coastline around Ravenscar is particularly dramatic and, fortunately, most of it is under the protection of the National Trust. There are some splendid cliff-top walks and outstanding views across Robin Hood's Bay. During the late 19th century there was an unsuccessful

attempt to turn the scattered village, which was then known as Peak, into a small town and, though the roads were built, little of the land made available to potential buyers was ever developed. Along with the small church and a couple of village shops, the only building of any size here is the Raven Hall Hotel that, so local legend has it, was visited by George III, when it was a private house, while he was recovering from one of his recurring bouts of insanity.

Staintondale

10 miles SE of Whitby off the A171

This small coastal village is home to two very different animal centres. At the **Staintondale Shire Horse Farm** (see panel on page 153) visitors can enjoy a 'hands-on' experience with these noble creatures, watch a video of the horses working and follow a scenic route around the area. Cart rides are also usually available and there is also a café, souvenir shop, picnic area and a play area with a variety of small farm animals to entertain the children including eight Shetland ponies. At nearby **Wellington Lodge Llamas** a variety of treks on llama-back are on offer, ranging from a three or four hour journey to a whole day's outing. The llamas have many years of trekking experience and are sure-footed and friendly and they carry heavy loads of food, drink, stools and extra clothing leaving the rider free to admire the splendid surroundings.

Cloughton

12½ miles SE of Whitby on the A171

This village lies less than a mile from the coast and the rocky inlet of **Cloughton Wyke**, where, in 1932, a huge whale was cast, or threw itself, ashore. Press photographers and postcard publishers rushed to the scene and paid the smallest local children they could find to pose beside the stranded Leviathan and, for a while, Cloughton village was busy with a steady stream of sightseers. Their numbers quickly diminished as the six tons of blubber began to rot and, in Cloughton itself, residents came to dread an east wind: it reached them only after washing over the vast, decaying hulk lying on the rocks.

Cloughton also lies on the edge of the North York Moors National Park and, high above the village, is an old sandstone quarry from which the building stones of Scarborough Castle were extracted.

Scarborough

17 miles SE of Whitby on the A165

With its two splendid bays and dramatic clifftop castle, Scarborough was targeted by the early railway tycoons as the natural candidate for Yorkshire's first seaside resort. The railway arrived in 1846, followed by the construction of luxury hotels, elegant promenades and spacious gardens, all of which confirmed the town's claim to the title 'Queen of

Watering Places'. High society and people like the eccentric Earls of Londesborough, established palatial summer residences here and an excellent train service brought countless thousands of 'excursionists' from the industrial cities of Yorkshire's West Riding.

Scarborough Castle and Harbour

Even before the advent of the railway, Scarborough had been well known to a select few. They travelled to what was then a remote little town to sample the spring water discovered by Mrs Tomyzin Farrer in 1626 and popularised in a book published by Dr Wittie who named the site Scarborough Spaw. Anne Brontë came here in the hope that the spa town's invigorating air would improve her health, a hope that was not fulfilled. She died at the age of 29 and her grave lies in St Mary's churchyard at the foot of the castle.

Scarborough Castle (English Heritage) can be precisely dated to the decade between 1158 and 1168 and surviving records show that the construction costs totalled £650. The castle was built on the site of a 4th century Roman fort and signal station and its gaunt remains stand high on Castle Rock Headland, which lies between and dominates the town's two sweeping bays. The spectacular ruins of the great rectangular stone keep still stand over three storeys high and often provide a splendid backdrop for staged battles commemorating the invasions of the Danes, Saxons and the later incursions of Napoleon's troops. Over the centuries, the castle has played host to many historical figures including, in 1155, William le Gros who was deprived of the castle by Henry II, and Richard III who stayed here, with his wife, while he made the port his supply base for his warships. The surrounding cliffs are also well worth exploring and they lie on the final part of the famous Cleveland Way. The castle is open all year round, with limited opening in the winter.

As befits an old settlement, Scarborough does maintain several ancient traditions and, on Shrove Tuesday, the respectable citizens of Scarborough exercise their right to skip along the highways, although, today, this is mostly confined to the area around

The Everley Hotel

Hackness, Scarborough,
North Yorkshire YO13 0BT
Tel: 01723 882202 Fax: 01723 882461

The Everley Hotel is a large impressive traditional stonework structure dating from 1754. Situated in the Vale of Derwent, in the National Park, about four miles from Scarborough it is an ideal location for walkers, cyclists and tourists who will appreciate the local scenery and wildlife. The view from the garden at the rear of the building is spectacular and is appreciated by diners and visitors alike. The interior is both comfortable and welcoming, with many traditional features including carved panels and furniture by a local craftsman - look out for the "gnome".

Barbara and Bill Tinsley have operated The Everley since 2001 and have specialised in offering good quality restaurant and bar meals using, where possible, fresh local ingredients. The bar offers four hand-pulled ales including Ruddles County and Webster's Yorkshire Bitter as well as lagers and cider. An extensive wine list is available with wines from around the world.

Meals are available at lunchtime (12 – 2pm) Wednesday to Sunday, and for evenings (7 – 9pm) Tuesday to Saturday. Guests are able to select from the printed menu or from the specials board. As well as traditional favourites such as griddled local lamb chops, deep-fried fish in crispy beer batter and home-made steak and Ruddles ale pie, daily specials may include such dishes as monkfish and salmon skewers with saffron sauce or medallions of beef fillet topped with a blue cheese fritter. Vegetarian dishes are always available. Traditional Sunday Lunch is available (12-2.00pm) offering Roast Beef and Yorkshire pudding, and a selection of other dishes. All dishes are freshly cooked to order and the home-made sweets are a speciality of the house.

Accommodation is available all year round except at Christmas and New Year. All rooms are double, en-suite with every amenity to ensure a pleasant and relaxing stay.

Foreshore Road. Meanwhile, at this same time of year the local people also maintain the tradition of sounding the Pancake Bell, a custom that was started by the wives of the town to alert their menfolk in the fields and down by the harbour that they were about to begin cooking the pancakes at the beginning of Lent.

Sunset at Scarborough

Along with its two sandy beaches, this long-established resort, naturally, offers a vast variety of entertainment for all tastes and all members of the family. There is **Peasholm Park**, with its glorious gardens and events, including the unique sea battle in miniature on the lake, while there are the intellectual attractions of the town's theatre and museums. **The Stephen Joseph Theatre** is well-known for staging the premiere performances of comedies written by its resident director, Alan Ayckbourn, the world's most performed living playwright. On Vernon Road is the country's finest Georgian museum, the **Rotunda Museum**, which includes amongst its exhibits a genuine ducking stool for witches as well as numerous displays on the history and local history of the area. Also worth visiting is the **Wood End Museum** on The Crescent, which was once the home of the eccentric Sitwell family. Here, in the birthplace of the poet Edith Sitwell, there are permanent displays of the family books and photographs, as well as changing exhibitions of local wildlife. The double-storied conservatory and the aquarium here are particularly interesting. The museum is open throughout the season from Tuesday to Sunday and on Wednesdays and weekends for the rest of the year. Meanwhile, there is always something new to see at the **Scarborough Art Gallery** whose exhibitions feature paintings of the town and also works by local artists. The gallery is open every day except Mondays during the season and, in its basement, is Crescent Arts, the only contemporary gallery in the town that provides a lively and

Wykeham Tea Rooms

Hill Yard, Wykeham, Scarborough,
North Yorkshire YO13 9QD
Tel: 01723 865212
website: www.wykehamtearooms.co.uk

Standing adjacent to the main Pickering-to-Scarborough road (A170) at Wykeham, **Wykeham Tea Rooms** and gift shop are set in traditional farm buildings – a truly lovely setting for a truly lovely establishment. Owners Stuart and Carol Norman have been here since 1998, creating a destination for anyone interested in tempting baked goods or quality hand-made crafts, all in a **smoke-free atmosphere**. Open seven days a week in summer, 10 a.m. to 5 p.m., and 5 or 6 days 10 – 4 in winter. The tea rooms seat 28, with room for another 12 to 16 people outside on the patio when the weather is fine.

Carol does all the cooking, creating a range of delicious and tempting home-made dishes and puddings such as soups, freshly prepared sandwiches filled with smoked salmon, coronation chicken, Wykeham rarebit or home-cooked ham, to name but a few, together with other mouth-watering favourites including jumbo scones, cakes and more. Her deep egg custards are justly popular. She uses local produce wherever possible to create the very freshest and most tasty treats. The range of teas include Lady Grey, Yorkshire Blend, Lapsang Suchong and a selection of herbal, fruit and organic teas. Her proper cream teas are well worth making a special visit here to sample. The coffees served include Taylors Imperial Blended and rich Italian roasts. Bookings can be taken for small parties in the tea rooms.

Gifts and crafts line the shelves around the tea room, gift shop and gallery, home to a wealth of the finest products from all over the world – candles, glass ware, table linen, handbags,soft toys, decorative pieces for the home, collectibles, pictures by local artists, a large range of specially prepared jams and chutneys, souvenirs of the region and much more are here to choose from. There's also an outstanding selection of cards and giftwrap.

stimulating programme of exhibitions.

There are here, too, a full range of 'fun' attractions and amusements including the **Scarborough Sea Life Centre** whose famous three pyramids are home to thousands of fascinating sea creatures including orphaned, sickly or injured seal pups; **Atlantis**, a heated outdoor waterpark with two of the world's largest waterslides; Kinderland, a unique landscaped park full of traditional play structures and activities for children; and Millennium, which takes visitors on an adventure through the last 1,000 turbulent years of the country's history.

East Ayton

17½ miles SE of Whitby on the A170

Victorian visitors to Scarborough, occasionally tiring of its urban attractions, welcomed excursions to beauty spots such as the **Forge Valley** near East Ayton. Thousands of years ago, a sharp-edged glacier excavated the valley and there then followed centuries of natural growth that has softened its hills with overarching trees and, quite by chance, created one of the loveliest woodland walks in England. A short diversion from the circular route, which leads from the village to the old forge, from which the valley takes its name, leads to the ruins of **Ayton Castle**. Dating from around 1400, this is one of the most southerly of the hundreds of pele towers built in those turbulent times as a protection against invading Scottish marauders. In more peaceful days, many of these towers had a more comfortable mansion added but their defensive origins are still clearly recognisable.

Cayton

20 miles SE of Whitby on the B1261

Cayton is one of only 31 'Thankful Villages' in England that were so named after the First World War because all of their men came back safely from trenches of Flanders. Cayton had all the more reason to be grateful since 43 of its men returned – more than to any other of the Thankful Villages. The village is home to the **Stained Glass Centre**, which hosts an exhibition illustrating the history of Stained Glass as well as explaining how a stained glass window is made. The centre is owned and personally run by Valerie Green, whose great grandfather, William Lazenby, opened a stained glass works in Bradford in 1884 and then proceeded to pass his skills down through his family. A tour around the centre's showroom shows the versatility of stained glass and there are many interesting, hand-made items for sale.

Filey

23 miles SE of Whitby on the A1039

With its six mile crescent of safe, sandy beach, Filey was one of the first Yorkshire resorts to benefit from the early 19th century craze for sea bathing and its popularity continued throughout Victorian times and this little town has

The Downcliffe House Hotel

The Beach, Filey, North Yorkshire YO14 9LA
Tel: 01723 513310 Fax: 01723 512659
e-mail: info@downcliffehouse.co.uk
website: www.downcliffehouse.co.uk

The Downcliffe House Hotel is a top-quality establishment overlooking Filey Bay and has been described in the press as one of the best 10 seaside hotels in Europe. Tremendous views greet guests at this gracious Victorian hotel, which began life as a private house and remained so until the mid-1990s. Refurbished to recapture its original glory, the hotel is a happy mix of traditional features and every modern comfort.

There are 12 ensuite guest bedrooms (all no-smoking) on three floors. The accommodation includes four-poster rooms, mini-suite rooms – a good mixture of sizes. Families are welcome. The tariff includes a hearty breakfast, served from 8.30 to 9.30 every morning – just the thing to set guests up for a day's sightseeing or walking in the region, which offers many scenic delights and diversions. One of the few unspoilt resorts on the North Yorkshire Coast, walking, sailing, birdwatching and golf are all popular pastimes at this quiet location. Tariffs are static throughout the year, though out of season offers include three nights for the price of two, and there are two- and three-night packages available in the autumn.

Food is served to residents and non-residents alike. Everything from morning coffee and light refreshments – available from 10 a.m. – to lunches (12 – 2.30) and dinner (from 6 p.m.) is served in the charming restaurant. All food is freshly prepared to order. Booking is advised for non-residents for evening meals. Meals can be taken in the restaurant, bar or out on the lovely verandah that overlooks Filey Bay and its six miles of golden sand.

Licensed for residents and diners only, the hotel serves a good selection of draught beers, lagers, cider, stout, wines (the wine list boasts more than 30 varieties), spirits and soft drinks.

Guests are sure to enjoy a relaxing and memorable stay at this elegant and supremely comfortable hotel. Closed in January.

always prided itself on being rather more select than its brasher neighbour just up the coast, Scarborough. Included in the list of distinguished visitors to the resort there is Charlotte Brontë, Jenny Lind (the Swedish Nightingale), the composer Frederic Delius and the actress Dame Madge Kendall while, before the First World War, the Mountbatten family enjoyed holidays here. Inevitably, modern times have brought the usual scattering of amusement arcades, fast food outlets and, from 1939 to 1983, a Butlin's Holiday Camp capable of accommodating 10,000 visitors. But Filey has suffered less than most seaside towns and with its many public parks and gardens still retains a winning, and rather genteel, atmosphere. The town's famous sands were used, in 1910, for the now famous Blackburn flying school and it was here that the first fatal aviation crash involving a passenger took place. However, Filey's greatest claim to fame is the naval battle that took place off its shores in 1779 between the American privateer, John Paul Jones, and the Royal Navy. Though a stronger force, the Navy was defeated by the American who went on to become known as the Father of the American Navy.

Until the Local Government reforms of 1974, the boundary between the East and North Ridings ran right through Filey: the town lay in the East Riding while the parish church and graveyard in the North. This curious arrangement gave rise to some typically dry Yorkshire humour. If a resident of Filey town admitted that they were feeling poorly, the response might well be "Aye, then tha'll straightly be off t'North Riding" – in other words, the graveyard.

Despite the fact that there is no harbour at Filey, it was once quite a busy fishing port and occasionally a few cobles – direct descendants of the Viking longships that arrived here more than a thousand years ago – can still be seen beached on the slipways. Filey's parish church, the oldest parts of which date back to the 12th century, is appropriately dedicated to St Oswald, the patron saint of fishermen, and the

Estbek House

East Row, Sandsend, nr Whitby,
North Yorkshire YO21 3SU
Tel: 01947 893424 Fax: 01947 893625
e-mail: reservations@estbekhouse.co.uk
website: www.estbekhouse.co.uk

Estbek House is a fine Georgian property dating from about 1750, overlooking the East Beck of Sandsend, which flows into the sea 20 yards away. The house now functions as a splendid restaurant with rooms, and since February 2004 has been owned and run by David Cross and Tim Lawrence. Tim and his chef James use local produce as much as possible in their superb dishes, many of

which feature vegetables, salads and herbs from their own garden. The menu changes daily to reflect what's best and freshest in the markets, fish and seafood are usually prominent: locally caught sole, haddock, cod and lobster, seared crayfish served hot with samphire and a herb salad; Whitby crab; kipper marinated in coriander, cracked pepper and lemon served with potato salad. Other typical dishes might include tomato and rosemary tart, orange & passion fruit chicken, coconut-based curry with monkfish, chicken or vegetables. This fine food deserves fine wine, and Estbek House has an extensive main list and a connoisseur cellar list. There are two dining areas – one in bistro style, the other more traditional, just right for a romantic candlelit dinner. There are seats for 36, with another 18 in the flower-bordered courtyard, and booking is recommended at the weekend and during the summer holiday period.

The house is also an excellent, relaxed base for discovering the delights of coast and countryside, and the five tastefully appointed non-smoking bedrooms are warm and comfortable, with central heating, television, telephone, tea tray and hairdryer; four are en suite, while the fifth has private facilities. The house was built for the use of the manager of the alum works that once dominated this coastline, producing a substance that was more valuable than gold; its main purpose was to help fix colours in fabrics, particularly red. Sandsend is a picturesque village on the A174 a short drive or a pleasant walk along the long sandy beach to Whitby. Sections of the long-closed coast railway now form part of the Sandsend Trail that runs round the village.

Fishermen's Window here commemorates men from the town who died at sea. It was around this church that the old town grew and it has long been the focal point of Filey. However, the town's history goes back to well beyond medieval times and traces of a Roman settlement, dating back to the 4th century, have been found along with a signal station, built on Carr Naze, that was abandoned in around AD 400.

Housed in a lovely old building that dates back to 1696, the **Filey Museum** has numerous displays on the history of the town as well as items on the seashore, fishing and the town's lifeboat. The museum is open from Good Friday to October, Sunday to Friday and on Saturdays in July and August.

Just to the north of the town, the rocky promontory known as **Filey Brigg** strikes out into the sea and this massive mile-long breakwater of calcareous gritstone protects the town from the worst of the North Sea's winter storms. The word Brigg comes from the Old Norse for jetty or landing place and, over the centuries, the promontory has been the graveyard for many boats. From the Brigg, there are grand views southwards along the six-mile-long bay to the cliffs that rise up to Flamborough Head and Scarborough Castle.

Hunmanby

24½ miles SE Whitby off the A165

It was at this village that, in 1907, the grave of a 1st-century British charioteer was uncovered and, along with his skeleton and that of his horses, were found fragments of the chariot wheels. Also in the grave was a rectangular strip of shiny metal that archaeologists believe was fixed to the side of the chariot as a mirror so that the driver could see the competitors behind him – the world's first wing mirror! Another curiosity in Hunmanby is the village lock-up with two cells and tiny windows designed for human miscreants and next to it is a circular stone pinfold intended for straying cattle.

Sleights

3 miles SW of Whitby on the A169

This village is home to the **River Gardens and Perry's Plants**, an historic Victorian tea garden on the banks of the River Esk that also has an international reputation for the hardy plants that are for sale in its nursery. The gardens are open daily from March to October.

Sandsend

2½ miles NW of Whitby on the A174

This pretty village grew up alongside Mulgrave Beck as it flows into the sea at 'sands end' – the northern tip of the long sandy beach that stretches some two and a half miles from here to Whitby. The Romans had a cement works nearby and later generations mined the surrounding hills for the elusive jet stone and for alum. The Victorians built a scenic railway along the coast and, although the railway track was dismantled in the 1950s, sections of the route now form part of the **Sandsend Trail**, a pleasant and leisurely walk around the village.

Goldsborough

4½ miles NW of Whitby off the A174

Just outside this small village are the remains of one of the five signal stations built by the Romans in the 4th century when Saxon pirates were continually raiding the North Yorkshire coastal towns. The stations were all built to a similar design with a timber or stone watchtower surrounded by a wide ditch.

Lythe

3½ miles NW of Whitby on the A174

Perched on a hilltop, Lythe is a small cluster of houses with a sturdy little church that is well worth a visit while, just to the south, lies **Mulgrave Castle**, the hereditary home of the Marquis of Normanby. The castle grounds, which are open to the public, contain the ruins of Foss Castle that was built shortly after the Norman Conquest. Charles Dickens once spent a holiday at Mulgrave Castle and, although he found it a beautiful place, it is not known whether the great author witnessed the ancient custom of 'Firing the Stiddy'. This celebrates notable events in the Normanby family and begins with dragging the anvil from the blacksmith's shop, upturning it and placing a charge of gunpowder on its base. A fearless villager then approaches with a 20 feet long metal bar, its tip red hot, and detonates the powder.

In the 1850s, Mulgrave Castle was leased by an exiled Indian Maharajah, Duleep Singh, who enjoyed going hawking on the moors in full oriental dress. One story told of this colourful gentleman is that he had the first road between Sandsend and Whitby constructed because his elephants disliked walking along the beach. Charming though its sounds this story has never been proven.

Runswick

6½ miles NW of Whitby off the A174

This is a picturesque fishing village whose attractive cottages cling to the steep sides of the cliff and whose perilous position proved to be disastrous in 1682 when the cliff face collapsed and the whole of Runswick, with the exception of a single cottage, tumbled into the sea. Following the setting up of a disaster fund, the village was completely rebuilt.

Like many remote communities, superstition was once widespread in Runswick and, even at the beginning of the 20th century, many still believed in witches and almost everyone would avert their gaze or cross the road to avoid someone afflicted with the 'Evil Eye'. The Rev Cooper, Vicar of Filey, visited the village at the turn of the century and came across a particularly horrible superstition. Apparently, it was considered unlucky to save a drowning man and the vicar was told of men who were nearly dragged ashore and then, by the advice of elders, abandoned in the waves to their fate lest ill-fortune should result from saving them.

Staithes

8½ miles NW of Whitby on the A174

Visitors to this much-photographed fishing port leave their cars at the park in the modern village at the top of the cliff and then walk down the steep road to the old wharf and the old stone chapels and rather austere houses testify to the days when Staithes was a stronghold of Methodism. The little port is proud of its associations with Captain James Cook, who came here, not as a famous mariner, but as a 17-year-old assistant in Mr William Sanderson's haberdashery shop. However, James did not stay here long and he left in 1746 to begin his naval apprenticeship in Whitby. The **Captain Cook and Staithes Heritage Centre**, which includes a life size street scene from 1745 along with Sanderson's shop, has over 200 books dating from 1773 of Cook's life and his famous voyages. Also here are 62 of Webber's original engravings, which were made during the great seafarer's third voyage of discovery, and a scale model of his ship *Endeavour*. Meanwhile, there are other displays that concentrate on life in Staithes through the centuries. The centre is open daily all year and at the weekends in January.

Staithes is still a working port with one of the few fleets in England still catching crabs and lobsters and, moored in the harbour and along the river, are the fishermen's distinctive boats. Known as cobles, they have an ancestry that goes back to Viking times. Nearby is a small sandy beach, popular with families (and artists), and a rocky shoreline extending north and south pitted with thousands of rock pools hiding starfish and anemones. The rocks here are rich in fossils and also ingots of 'fools gold', which is actually iron pyrites and virtually worthless.

Staithes

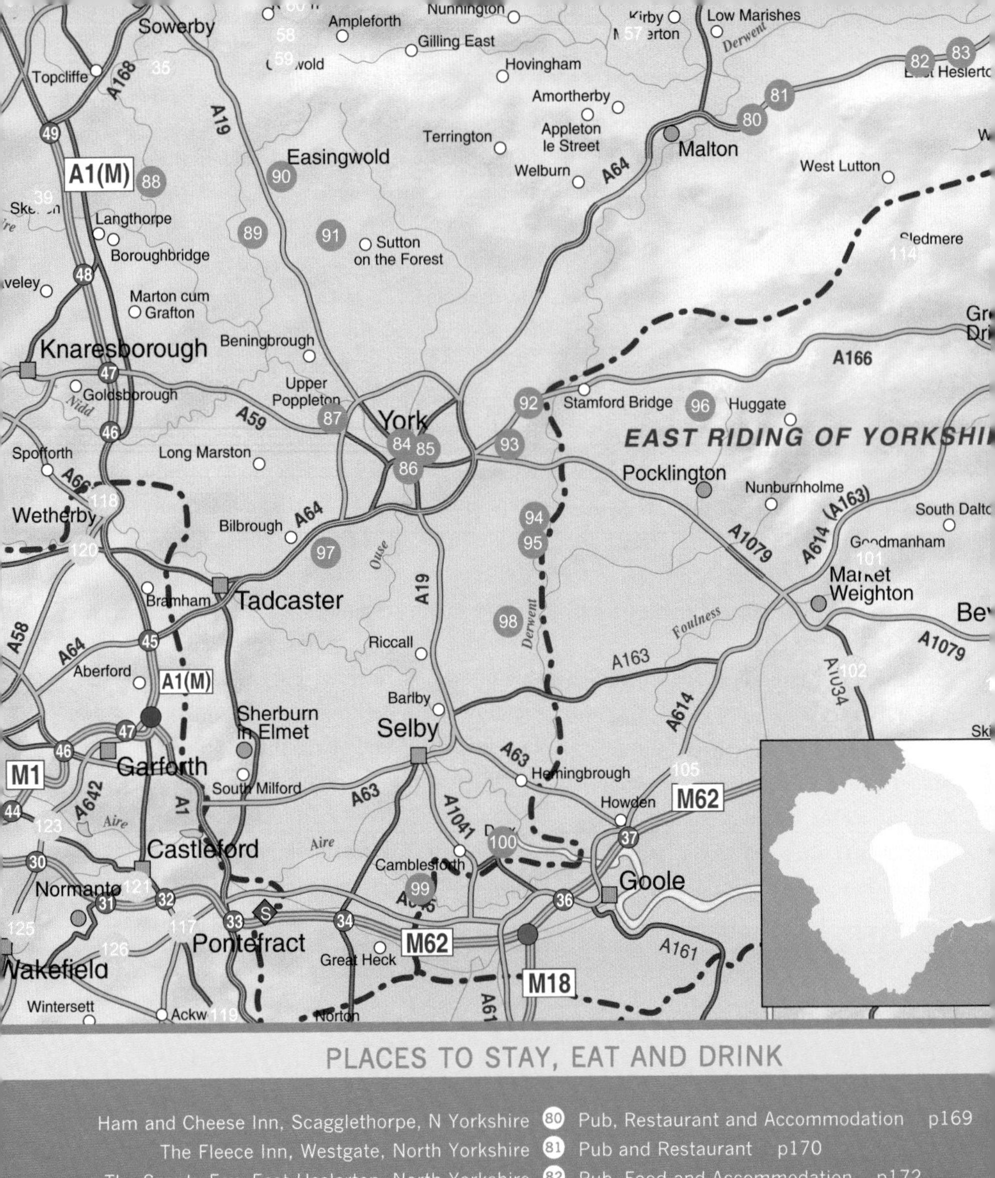

PLACES TO STAY, EAT AND DRINK

Ham and Cheese Inn, Scagglethorpe, N Yorkshire	80	Pub, Restaurant and Accommodation	p169
The Fleece Inn, Westgate, North Yorkshire	81	Pub and Restaurant	p170
The Snooty Fox, East Heslerton, North Yorkshire	82	Pub, Food and Accommodation	p172
East Riding, Sherburn, North Yorkshire	83	Pub with Food	p173
Castle Howard, York, North Yorkshire	84	Historic Building	p174
Jorvik Viking Centre, York, North Yorkshire	85	Visitor Attraction	p177
Archaeological Resource Centre, York, N Yorkshire	86	Visitor Attraction	p181
Red Lion Motel & Inn, Upper Poppleton, N Yorkshire	87	Pub, Food and Accommodation	p182
The Oak Tree Inn, Helperby, North Yorkshire	88	Pub with Food	p183
The Blue Bell Country Inn, Alne, North Yorkshire	89	Pub, Restaurant and Accommodation	p184
The Commercial, Easingwold, North Yorkshire	90	Pub with Food	p185

Denotes entries in other chapters

4 York & The Yorkshire Wolds

Allerton Park

This region of North Yorkshire, between the North York Moors and the East Riding, between West Yorkshire and the Heritage Coast, is dominated by the city of York. The first settlement of any note here was created by the Romans, who named their garrison town 'Eboracum', and, from then on, York has been an important and influential force not only in Yorkshire but also in the rest of the country. Known to the Saxons as 'Eoferwic' and the Vikings as 'Jorvik', it was the creation of the magnificent Minster, started in the early 13th century that saw the city truly

PLACES TO STAY, EAT AND DRINK

● Denotes entries in other chapters

begin to develop. A major trading centre and, at one time, the second largest city in the country, York is also remembered as the heart of the railway network in the north of England. Not surprisingly, there is plenty to see here and, along with the numerous imaginative museums and galleries, visitors will want to walk around its medieval streets and soak up the atmosphere that encompasses architectural styles from at least the last 700 years.

York Minster

Many of the towns in this area were founded by the Romans and, indeed, both Tadcaster and Malton date back to the days of the Imperial rule. Both, too, have a history of brewing and, although many of the breweries have long since gone, the tradition still continues to this day. Although this area has a long history there are two museums that focus on more recent events and, more specifically, those of the Second World War. Eden Camp, near Malton, is a modern history theme museum housed in a genuine prisoner of war camp that is dedicated to illustrating the lives of ordinary people during the war. Meanwhile, situated on an old RAF airfield at Elvington that was once home to Bomber Command, the Yorkshire Air Museum concentrates on telling the story of the airmen who flew on daring raids from Yorkshire's numerous wartime airbases.

The land in this region is key agricultural land and the vast open expanses have been cultivated for centuries. The economy of much of the area has been reliant on farming and, although now not as labour intensive as it once was, this remains a major industry. Throughout this area the skyline is dotted with the spires and towers of churches that were built in those relatively prosperous times but there are two other features of the landscape that are of particular interest. Firstly there are the giant cooling towers of Drax Power Station, the largest coal-fire electricity generating plant in

Europe while, to the southwest of Malton, there is the grandeur of Castle Howard. Vanbrugh's first commission as an architect, and a resounding success, this glorious palace is filled with equally superb collections of furniture, paintings and china but most people will remember it as Brideshead in the 1980s television adaptation of the Evelyn Waugh novel, *Brideshead Revisited.*

Malton

Malton has been the historic centre of Ryedale ever since the Romans came and, in fact, there are three Maltons, the Roman, the old and the new, which can all be found in separate places. The Romans built a large fort and called it 'Derventio' after the river Derwent beside which it stood and, for many years, archaeologists were puzzled by the large scale of the fort. However, the mystery was solved in 1970 when a building dedication was uncovered that revealed that the fort housed a cavalry regiment, the Ala Picentiana, and the extra space was needed to accommodate their horses.

Old Malton, which is located just to the north of the Roman fort, is an interesting and historic area on the edge of open countryside and to the south of New Malton. Nearby villages such as Settrington and their secluded country lanes are home to many famous racehorse stables: for those up and about early enough the horses can be seen out on their daily exercises. In the centre of

The Ham and Cheese Country Inn & Restaurant

Scagglethorpe, Malton,
North Yorkshire YO17 8DY
Tel/Fax: 01944 758249
e-mail: enq@thehamandcheese.co.uk
website: www.thehamandcheese.co.uk

Excellent food, real ales and a warm welcome await guests at **The Ham and Cheese Country Inn & Restaurant.** Impressive inside and out, the inn can be found just off the main A64 in the picturesque village of Scagglethorpe, east of Malton. Dating back (as an inn) to 1907, before that time it was the setting for one of the first farm shops in the country, with local farmers bringing their produce here to sell – one of the shop's best sellers was home-cured bacon, and it is believed that the inn takes its unique name from this time. Closed Mondays except Bank Holidays, the inn serves a minimum of two real ales together with a range of lagers, cider, stout, wines, spirits and soft drinks. Food is served Tuesday to Sunday at lunchtime and Tuesday to Saturday evening. The food is a big draw here, and rightly so: everything from the home-made chips to main courses and truly mouthwatering puddings is home-made. During the lifetime of this edition a new no-smoking restaurant will be added to the building and bed-and-breakfast accommodation will become available – please ring or see the website for details.

THE FLEECE INN

Westgate, Rillington,
North Yorkshire YO17 8LN
Tel: 01944 758464 Fax: 01944 758097

Found five miles east of Malton on the A64 Scarborough road, **The Fleece Inn** is an impressive place built in the 18th century and sympathetically upgraded over the years. Its smart exterior bodes well for what's inside, and indeed the interior is spacious, bright and modern while remaining warm and welcoming. The furnishings are comfortable and elegant, and there's a wealth of exposed wood and tasteful adornments on the walls.

This family-run pub, owned and run by Jennie, Lynn and Trevor Hodgson since 1999, is open every session Monday to Thursday and all day Friday to Sunday. Tetleys is the regular real ale here; there's also a changing guest ale, together with a good selection of lagers and cider, stout, wines, spirits and soft drinks.

Next to the lounge bar is the restaurant, The Rillington Grill, also kept in apple-pie order. This is where diners from the locality and further afield head to relax in comfort and enjoy top-quality meat, poultry, fish and vegetarian dishes, simply prepared and served in generous portions. Food is served from 12 – 9 Mon-Sat and 12 - 8 on Sundays in the Summer and from 3 – 9 Mon-Thu, 12-9 Fri and Sat and 12-8 on Sundays in winter. Guests choose from printed menus or the specials board from a range of tempting dishes such as char-grilled steaks, home-made steak and ale pie and lasagne, Whitby scampi, chilli con carne and more. There's also a special children's menu. Friday night is curry night, with three home-made curries to choose from between 6 and 9 p.m.

Once a fortnight on a Saturday the pub hosts live music from 9 p.m., showcasing a range of different musical styles and artists. In winter there's a quiz night every Wednesday evening from 9.

The pub has a large beer garden and plenty of off-road parking.

Old Malton stands a beautiful fragment of **St Mary's Priory** that incorporates a particularly fine Norman doorway. The priory was built in around 1155 by the only monastic order in Christendom to have originated entirely in England – the Gilbertines. The order was founded in 1148 by a Lincolnshire parish priest, St Gilbert of Sempringham. Parts of the parish church are almost as old as the priory but one of its most interesting features is relatively modern, the work of the 'Mouseman of Kilburn', Robert Thompson. A gifted woodcarver and furniture maker, Thompson signed all his pieces with a discreetly placed carving of a mouse. There is one on the stout oak door of the church and, inside, the stalls are carved elaborately with all manner of wondrous beasts and historical and mythical scenes.

The River Derwent has always been vitally important to the town and it rises in the moors near Scarborough and then runs inland through the Vale of Pickering, bringing with it an essential element for what was once a major industry in Malton – brewing. In the 19th century, there were nine breweries here but, now, only the Malton Brewery Company survives and it operates in a converted stable block behind the Crown Hotel in Wheelgate. The company welcomes visitors but request that they pre-book a visit.

The Malton of today is a traditional agricultural town that is renowned for its livestock, street and farmers' markets. Many relics from the Roman excavation site, showing the sophisticated life-style of the Roman centurions and civilians, can be seen in the **Malton Museum** where there are also items from the Iron Age settlement that preceded the Roman garrison. Here, too, can be seen the work of the potteries at Norton and Crambeck and the museum, Ryedale's major archaeological museum, is open from Easter to October from Monday to Saturday. Meanwhile, at Orchard Fields, the site of Malton's and Norton's Roman fort and vicus can be explored.

A mile or so north of Old Malton is **Eden Camp**, a modern history theme museum that is dedicated to re-creating the dramatic experiences of ordinary people living through the Second World War. This unique museum is housed in the huts of a genuine prisoner-of-war camp, built in 1942, and here visitors are transported back to wartime Britain through the sounds, lighting effects and smells that are used to create as true an image of the era as possible. Here one can experience what it was like to live through an air raid, to be a prisoner of war, or a sailor in a U-boat under attack. Amongst the many other exhibits are displays on Fashion in the 40s, Children at War and even one on Rationing. Right next door to Eden Camp is **Eden Farm Insight,** a working farm with a fascinating collection of old farm machinery and implements, (including a very old horse wheel), lots of animals, a blacksmith's and a wheelwright's shop, as well as a choice of farm walks, all clearly signposted and with useful information

The Snooty Fox

Scarborough Road, East Heslerton,
North Yorkshire YO17 8EN
Tel: 01944 710554

Set back off the A64 Malton-Scarborough road, seven miles northeast of Malton, **The Snooty Fox** is a charming and welcoming Free House offering great food, drink and accommodation. Surrounded by five acres of well-tended grounds, with views across the Yorkshire Wolds, the inn is open for every session Tuesday to Sunday. Brand-new owners Stephen and Jean Butterworth offer all their guests a warm welcome and genuine hospitality. Combining the best of traditional features and modern comforts, this fine inn makes the perfect place to stop for a drink, meal or longer stay.

There are two real ales available, one 'resident', one a guest ale. Chef Alan prepares a range of delicious meals at lunch and dinner (Tuesday to Friday 12 – 3 and 5 – 8; Saturday 12 – 8; Sunday 12 – 7). Guests choose from the menu or daily specials board from the range of hearty and expertly prepared dishes. The inn also boasts a coffee room for morning drinks and breakfast. The interior is warm and welcoming, with traditional features such as the exposed beamwork and open fireplaces. Indoor activities include the games room; outside there's a fully-equipped children's play area.

The excellent accommodation comprises five ensuite chalet-style guest bedrooms – three doubles and two family rooms – detached from the main inn. Handsome and comfortable, they are decorated and furnished to a very high standard. Excellent camping facilities are also available in five acres with shower/toilet block, washing up amenities and more. Ideally situated within easy reach of the coast, countryside and heritage sites, the inn is equidistant from Scarborough and York - just 25 minutes' drive from both – and makes an excellent base from which to explore the many sights and attractions of the region. Ganton Golf Club's championship course is just five minutes away.

boards. The farm also offers a café, gift shop and a picnic and play area.

Around Malton

East Heslerton

9½ miles NE of Malton on the A64

This little village is distinguished by one of the many churches gifted by Sir Tatton Sykes of Sledmere House in the mid-1800s and, designed in the style of the 13th century, the church has a fine west portico, a vaulted chancel and an iron screen of very fine workmanship. The north tower has an octagonal belfry and spire and statues of the four Latin Doctors (Ambrose, Augustine, Gregory and Jerome) originally sculpted for Bristol Cathedral.

Welburn

5 miles SW of Malton off the A64

This typical Ryedale stone village has an ancient history and, nearby, various Roman remains have been unearthed over the centuries. Found in the delightful and peaceful setting beside the River Derwent, just a couple of miles south of the village, are the remains of **Kirkham Priory**. According to legend, the priory was founded in 1125 by Walter l'Espec after his only son was thrown from his horse and killed at this very spot. (A few years later, Walter was to found another great abbey at Rievaulx.) Visitors to Kirkham pass through a noble, exquisitely decorated gatehouse but one of the most memorable sights at the priory, perhaps so as it is unexpected, is the sumptuous lavatorium in the ruined cloister. Here the monks washed their hands at two bays, with lavishly moulded arches supported by slender pillars, and each bay is adorned with fine tracery.

Meanwhile, just to the north of

Castle Howard

York, North Yorkshire YO60 7DA
Tel: 01653 648333
e-mail: house@castlehoward.co.uk
website: www.castlehoward.co.uk

Castle Howard, winner of York Tourism Bureau's 'Out of Town Attraction of the Year' award, is now so much more than a magnificent 18th century house with extensive collections and breathtaking grounds featuring temples, lakes and fountains.

Historical characters, such as the original architect, Sir John Vanbrugh and the 6th Countess, Lady Georgina provide a first person observation of what life was like at Castle Howard. Other characters include Widow Etty, whose husband was killed in an accident during the construction of Castle Howard; the 18th century Governess awaiting the next generation, busying herself with the tutorage of the young visitors; the 5th Earl's Butler, who is a fountain of knowledge and good sense - just what is needed to curb the rash spending of the Earl; the School Mistress, helping to run the school relocated to Castle Howard during the Second World War, who can be spotted covering 'indecent' statues and ensuring the girls do not run down the corridors.

The range of tours around the house and gardens are very popular and include restoration and renovation; the great fire of 1940; the haunts of *Brideshead Revisited*; the history of the Roses and many more. There are various places to stop and enjoy refreshments and a plant centre and tree nursery, both open for sales to the public. A varied programme of events takes places throughout the year, including the Proms Spectacular and Archaeology Weekends.

Open daily between February and November, a land-train is available to transport visitors from the car park to the house and there is disabled access to many parts.

Welburn and lying in the folds of the Howardian Hills, is one of the most glorious stately homes in Britain – **Castle Howard** (see panel opposite). Well known to television viewers as the Brideshead of *Brideshead Revisited*, Castle Howard has been amazing visitors ever since it was completed in the early 1700s but, perhaps the most astonishing fact about the magnificent palace concerns its architect, Sir John Vanbrugh. A solider and a successful playwright, this was Vanbrugh's first commission as an architect and before beginning to create this sublime house he had never overseen the placing of one block of masonry on another! However, Vanbrugh's design was a triumph and his success lead him to, later, create Blenheim Palace for the Duke of Marlborough and Stowe (now a school). The great house's connections with *Brideshead Revisited* go back to before the days of the television adaptation of Evelyn Waugh's novel (which was published in 1945) as the author visited here in 1937. The fantastic baroque surroundings are an ideal match for Waugh's image of England's aristocratic past although he actually based his black comedy about the 'bright young things' on the Lygon family who lived at Madresfield in Worcestershire.

The home of the Howard family for 300 years, the palace now houses a series of unique collections of statuary, furniture, ceramics and paintings while, outside, it is surrounded by spectacular gardens and sweeping parkland. Even that world-weary 18th century socialite, Horace Walpole, was stirred to enthusiasm on arriving at Castle Howard: *'Nobody had informed me that at one view I should see a palace, a town, a fortified city, temples on high places, the noblest lawn in the world fenced by half the horizon and a mausoleum that would tempt one to be buried alive: in short, I have seen gigantic places before, but never a sublime one.'*

Today's visitors can not only tour the palace and wander the gardens but there are also boat trips on the great lake, an adventure playground, a woodland garden with a notable botanical collection, craft studios and demonstrations and cafeterias. Finally, housed in the handsome 18th century stableyard is **Jorvik Glass**, which was established in 1995, and offers a beautifully crafted range of functional and decorative glassware that is all manufactured on the premises. In the adjoining hot glass studio visitors can watch at close quarters the traditional techniques of glass-blowing, a difficult skill whose history has been traced back to Syria in the 1st century BC. The individually hand-made glassware pieces created at Jorvik Glass are supplied to numerous gift shops, galleries and department stores and a mail order catalogue is also available.

West Lutton

9 miles SE of Malton off the B1253

West Lutton church is yet another of the many repaired or restored by Sir Tatton Sykes in this corner of Yorkshire and it stands overlooking the village green and pond, its lych gate reached by a tiny bridge. A few miles to the southwest of West Lutton, a minor road leads to one of the most haunting sights in the county – the deserted medieval village of **Wharram Percy.** There had been a settlement here for over 5,000 years but by the late 1400s the village stood abandoned although, for a while, the church continued to serve the surrounding hamlets but, in time, that too became a ruin. The manor house of the Percy family, who gave the village its name, the peasant houses dating back to the 13th century, a corn mill and a cemetery complete with exposed skeletons are all that remains of this once thriving community. Until fairly recently it was assumed that the villagers had been driven from their homes by the Plague but scholars are now certain that the cause was simple economics: the lords of the manor, the Percys, turned their lands from labour-intensive crop cultivation to sheep farming that needed only a handful of shepherds and, unable to find work, the villagers slowly drifted elsewhere.

River Ouse, York

York

As Duke of York, George VI once said, '*The history of York is the history of England,*' and though this is a bold claim it is also well justified. For almost 2,000 years the city has been at the centre of great events and, better than any other city in England, it has preserved the evidence of its glorious past. With one of the grandest cityscapes in the country, York is dominated by the largest medieval gothic cathedral north of the Alps and **York Minster** can be seen from just about anywhere in the city (it is illegal to build a higher structure). A sublime expression of medieval faith, the cathedral was begun in 1220 and the work was on such a scale that it was not completed until two and a half centuries later. Its stained glass windows – there are more than a hundred of them – cast a celestial light over the many treasures within. A guided tour of the Great Tower gives fantastic views across the city while a visit to the crypt reveals some of the relics from the Roman fortress that stood here nearly 2,000 years ago.

This superb building has survived, seemingly unscathed, from three major fires. The first occurred in 1829 and was started by a madman, Jonathan Martin, who believed that God wanted him to destroy the church and so he started a fire using prayer and hymn books. The fire was not discovered until the following morning by which time the east end of the Minster had been severely damaged. The second blaze, in 1840, was caused by a workman leaving a candle burning and, as a result of his carelessness, the central part of the nave was destroyed. The most recent conflagration was in July 1984, shortly after a controversial Bishop of Durham had been installed. Some attributed the fire to God's wrath at the Bishop's appointment; the more prosaic view was that it had been caused by lightning. The subsequent restoration has allowed modern masons and craftsmen to demonstrate that they possess skills just as impressive as those of their medieval forebears.

The Minster actually stands on the site of an even older building, the headquarters of the Roman legions and the Imperial troops arrived here in AD 71 when the governor, Quintus Petilius Cerealis, chose this strategic

Jorvik Viking Centre

16 Coppergate Walk, York,
North Yorkshire YO1 9NT
Tel: 01904 643211

The world famous **JORVIK** centre in York transports visitors back in time to experience the sights, sounds and · perhaps most famously · the smells of 10th century York. Over 20 years of archaeological research led to the new re-creation of Viking Age York in JORVIK, which re-opened to wide acclaim in April 2001. The new JORVIK now presents a far broader view and more detailed depiction of life in the Viking Age. Visitors to the centre are shown that, in AD975, York was a bustling commercial centre where 10,000 people lived and worked. Travelling in state-of-the-art time capsules, visitors are carried past and through two storey dwellings, enjoying views over backyards and rooftops, and even glimpsing the Viking Age equivalent of today's Minster.

February 2002 saw the launch of the new 'Viking Voyagers' exhibition. Visitors can get the low-down on all aspects of sea-faring from trading in the Far East and raiding in the North East, to life on board and the technicalities of mastering the ocean waves.

The year-long exhibition features hands-on activities, artefacts and new academic research around the theme of Viking ships and is not to be missed.

18 years after it first opened, JORVIK still retains its status as one of the world's icon attractions and its many superb qualities make it an enduring favourite with children and adults alike.

position, beside the Rivers Ouse and Foss, as his base for a campaign against the tribe of the Brigantes. The settlement was named 'Eboracum' and it was from this garrison that Hadrian directed the construction of his great wall and, later, General Constantine was proclaimed Emperor here. The legions finally left the city around AD 410 but the evidence of their three and a half centuries of occupation is manifest all around York in buildings like the **Multangular Tower,** in rich artefacts treasured in the city's museums and even in a pub: at the **Roman Bath Inn** are the remains of steam baths used by the garrison residents. The Multangular Tower is all that is left of the city's defensive walls that were erected by the Romans in around AD 300. Situated in the pretty Museum Gardens, the tower is a neighbour of the **Yorkshire Museum** where visitors can take a journey back through time and discover the history and treasures of York and Yorkshire from Roman times, through the Saxon and Viking eras, to the days of the Middle Ages. Here, too, are the majestic ruins of **St Mary's Abbey**, a monastic house that was once one of the most powerful and influential in the north of England.

Little is known of York during the Dark Ages but by the 8th century the city had been colonised by the Anglo-Saxons, who named it 'Eoferwic', and it was already an important Christian and academic centre. The Vikings put an end to this settled period in the city's history when they invaded in the 9th century and changed the name once again, this time to 'Jorvik'. The story of York during those years of Danish rule is imaginatively told in the many displays at the **Jorvik Centre** (see panel on page 177). Using technology from the 21st century, the centre transports visitors back to the Viking age when Jorvik was the trading hub of the Viking world. There is a bustling market thronged with Danes bartering for chickens, corn and other provisions and wares, dark smoky houses and a busy wharf where goods transported along the city's two rivers are off-loaded. These experiences all come complete with the authentic sights, sounds and even smells that make this both fun and educational for all the family. Artefacts excavated from the numerous archaeological digs that have taken place in York over the years are on show in a futuristic gallery that uses the very latest technology to display the items as they would have appeared in the Viking age. The centre has its own gift shop and café.

After the Norman Conquest, the city suffered badly during the Harrowing of the North when William the Conqueror mounted a brutal campaign against his rebellious northern subjects. Vast tracts of Yorkshire and Northumberland were laid waste and some historians reckon that it took over a hundred years for the area to recover from this wholesale devastation. The only remaining part of York Castle, which was built by William the Conqueror, is **Clifford's Tower** (English Heritage) and, erected in the

13th century by Henry III, it remains a proud symbol of the might of the medieval kings. However, the present tower owes its existence to a particularly shameful episode in York's history when, in 1190, the city's Jewish community were offered sanctuary in the former wooden structure and were then brutally massacred as the tower was destroyed.

Gate House and York Minster

Opposite the tower is the **York Castle Museum**, a marvellous place that details the everyday life of the people of Britain over the past 400 years. Visitors can see the prison cell where the notorious highwayman, Dick Turpin, was held, wander down re-created Victorian and Edwardian streets complete with a bank and a police station and be amazed by the collections of costume, textiles and militaria that are on display here. The museum is open daily, all year round. The City Walls, some of the best preserved medieval fortifications in the world, were constructed in the 14th century and a walk around them is a superb way to see the city. Also during this era, the city was one of the country's three main centres of memorial brass manufacture along with London and Norwich and, close to the Minster, brasses were engraved by hand in medieval workshops ready for distribution to the north of England and the Midlands. For an insight into this craft a visit to the **Jorvik Brass Rubbing Centre** is a must and it houses one of the largest private collections of brasses in the country – there are over 45 to choose from. Visitors here can also try their hand at brass rubbing.

York Castle Museum

The network of medieval streets around the Minster is another of the city's major delights and the narrow lanes are criss-crossed by even narrower footpaths – ginnels,

The Shambles, York

snickets or snickelways – that have survived as public rights of way despite being built over, above and around. Narrowest of all the snickelways is Pope's Head Alley, which is more than 100 feet long but only 31 inches wide, while, Whip-ma-Whop-ma-Gate, allegedly, is where felons used to be "whipped and whopped". However, probably the most famous of these ancient streets is **The Shambles**, whose name comes from 'Fleshammels', the street of butchers and slaughterhouses. The houses here were deliberately built close together to keep the street out of direct sunlight and thus protect the carcasses that were hung outside the buildings on hooks. Many of the hooks can still be seen in place.

During these years, York was the second largest city in England and it was then that the town walls and their 'bars', or gates, were built. The trade guilds were also at their most powerful and, in Fossgate, one of them built the lovely black and white timbered **Merchant Adventurers Hall**, Europe's finest medieval guild hall that dates from 1357-62. The Merchant Adventurers controlled the lucrative trade in all "goods bought and sold foreign" and they spared no expense in building their Great Hall where they conducted their affairs beneath a complex timbered roof displaying many colourful banners of York's medieval guilds. Found in the very heart of the city is the elegant **Treasurer's House** (National Trust), which was originally the home of the Treasurers of York Minster. Restored to its former splendour by Yorkshire industrialist Frank Green in the late 19th and early 20th centuries, this glorious house, with its 17th century façade, is home to furniture, glass and china from the 16th to the 20th centuries, an impressive medieval hall and a delightful garden in the shadow of the Minster. To this period, too, belong the **York Mystery Plays**, first performed in 1397 and subsequently every four years.

During Tudor times, York's importance steadily declined but it re-emerged in the 18th century as a fashionable social centre. Many elegant Georgian houses, of which **Fairfax House** in Castlegate is perhaps the most splendid, were built at this time and they add another attractive architectural dimension to the city. Designed by John Carr, this architectural masterpiece is York's premier historic house museum and Fairfax House is also home to the famous Noel Terry Collection of English 18th century furniture and clocks.

The following century saw York take on a completely different rôle as the hub of the railway system in the north. At the heart of this transformation was the charismatic entrepreneur George Hudson, founder of what became the Great Northern Railway and part visionary, part crook. His wheeler-dealing eventually led to his disgrace but even then the citizens of York twice elected him as Lord Mayor and he still has a pub named after him. It was thanks to Hudson that York's magnificent railway station, with its great curving roof of glass, was built, and it remains a tourist attraction in its own right. Nearby, in Leeman Street, is the **National Railway Museum,** the largest of its kind in the world. This fascinating museum covers some 200 years of railway history, from Stephenson's *Rocket* to the Channel Tunnel. Amongst the thousands of exhibits demonstrating the technical and social impact of the 'Iron Horse' are Gresley's record-breaking locomotive, *Mallard*, Queen Victoria's royal carriage and displays demonstrating the workings of the railway system. There is also an

Archaeological Resource Centre

St Saviourgate, York,
North Yorkshire YO1 8NN
Tel: 01904 654324

Become an archaeological detective at The ARC. What was it really like living in Viking times? The **Archaeological Resource Centre** (ARC) is the educational resource centre associated with the renowned attraction, JORVIK. The ARC welcomes all visitors who are curious about York's Viking past, encouraging them to come and find out more about archaeology and what the city was like when our Viking ancestors inhabited it over a thousand years ago.

Visitors are guided by an archaeologist and can actively participate in a range of activities. They can even explore a Viking's rubbish pit, handling 1,000-year-old bones, pottery, bits of leather shoe and beautifully carved antler hair combs.Also at The ARC, the 'Sensory Detective Garden' helps everyone - including those with disabilities - interpret buildings of the past using interactive clues. The site also presents fragments of lost buildings

excavated by the York Archaeological Trust.

Visitors can also see the ARC's special exhibition, based on the BBC TV series, *"Blood of the Vikings"*, which explores some of the secrets of skeletons found at an archaeological dig in Riccall outside York, and seeks to answer whether these were the defeated Viking armies of 1066.

extensive library and reading room (booking advised) and the 'Brief Encounter' restaurant is themed on the classic movie. The museum is open daily all year round.

Another aspect of railway history is on view at the **York Model Railway**, next door to the station, which has almost one third of a mile of track and up to 14 trains, from modern Intercity to freight trains and even the Orient Express, running at any one time. Machinery of a very different kind is on display at the **Museum of Automata**, which explores the world of man-made objects that imitate the movement of both humans and other living creatures. The museum traces the history of automata, from the simple articulated figurines of ancient civilisations, through to displays of modern robotics; the Automata Shop sells contemporary pieces, music boxes, mechanical toys and craft kits suitable for all ages.

In a beautifully restored church close to the Shambles is the **Archaeological Resource Centre** (see panel on page 181), an award-winning hands-on exploration of archaeology for visitors of all ages. Along with meeting practising archaeologists, who are happy to demonstrate how to sort and identify genuine finds or to try out ancient crafts, visitors also have the chance, through a series of interactive computer displays, to learn how modern technology helps to provide an interpretation of the past.

Along with the numerous museums, galleries and places of interest that this city has to offer visitors there is one, very popular, attraction that is well worth seeking out. The **Original Ghostwalk of York**, which starts from the King's Arms pub on Ouse Bridge each evening, provides an entertaining and unusual insight into the more macabre aspects of York's long history. At the last count, York was reckoned to have some 140 resident ghosts within its walls and on this guided walk visitors take in some of their haunts and hear dark tales and grim accounts of murder, torture and intrigue.

The Red Lion Motel and Country Inn

Boroughbridge Road, Upper Poppleton, York, North Yorkshire YO26 6PR
Tel: 01904 781141 Fax: 01904 785143
website: www.red-lion-motel.co.uk

Extensively and tastefully modernised within the last two years, **The Red Lion Motel and Country Inn** is an outstanding early 18th-century inn located just a couple of miles from the centre of York and offering great food, drink and accommodation. Open every session and for meals at lunch seven days a week and dinner Monday to Saturday, the inn also boasts 18 chalet-style ground-floor ensuite letting rooms providing a high standard of quality and comfort, with every amenity including facilities for guests with disabilities.

Finally, for anyone who has not had their blood chilled enough with a ghost walk there is **York Dungeon**, a spine tingling place where visitors are taken on a tour of York during the 14th century. In the company of grisly guides the Plague ravaged streets of the city are walked before visitors learn about the labyrinth of haunted tunnels, pits and passageways that lie far beneath the city's streets. The horror of the 16th century Witch trials is graphically illustrated, while visitors can also see Dick Turpin, the world's most famous highwayman, languishing in his cell on the eve of his execution.

Around York

Beningbrough

6 miles NW of York off the A19

This ancient settlement lies on the banks of the River Ouse, at the edge of the great Forest of Galtres, and it is home to the fine **Beningbrough Hall** (National Trust). In the early 18th century John Bouchier decided to replace the manor house in which his family had lived for around 150 years with a much grander property and the hall was completed in 1716. With one of the most impressive baroque interiors in the country, the hall is the perfect backdrop for the collection of portraits on display here from the National Portrait Gallery while there is also a Victorian laundry and potting shed to explore. The Gardens, too, are fascinating and they contain one of the largest collections of top fruit in the north of England. An ideal place for all the family, there is also a wilderness play area for children and a restaurant and shop. The house and gardens are open from Saturday to Wednesday during the season and also on Fridays during July and August.

Easingwold

12½ miles NW of York off the A19

This agreeable market town was once surrounded by the Forest of Galtres, a vast hunting ground that was the preserve of the Norman kings, and it lies

The Blue Bell Country Inn

Main Street, Alne, York,
North Yorkshire YO61 1RR
Tel: 01347 838331
website: www.bluebellalne.co.uk

Just 11 miles northwest of York off the A19, in the quiet and secluded village of Alne set alongside the River Kyle, **The Blue Bell Country Inn** is a fine place to enjoy great food, drink and hospitality. Run by Michael and Annette Anson with help from their son David, who runs the bar, this one-time country farmhouse is a hostelry upholding the best traditions of English country pubs. Cheerful and welcoming inside and out, there are well-kept gardens to the front and rear, and an air of warm hospitality throughout. Lots of style and class are in evidence in the handsome lounge, bar and restaurant.

Here guests will find a choice of at least three real ales (John Smiths, Black Sheep and Timothy Taylor Landlord) and a good selection of wines together with lagers, cider, stout, spirits and soft drinks – something, in fact, to quench every thirst.

Food is available at lunchtime Saturday and Sunday and Bank Holiday Mondays, and at dinner Monday to Saturday. Both Michael and Annette cook – Michael does the superb main courses such as beef stroganoff, roast duckling, vegetable and cheese Wellington, seared venison and pheasant and the justly popular fish and seafood dishes, which include sea bass, salmon, lemon sole, lobster, king prawn and monk fish, while Annette creates the starters and the tempting range of sweets. Together they have earned the inn a fine reputation for fresh, delicious food, and have made this a destination pub for great meals. The outstanding Stables Restaurant has original features such as the low-beamed ceiling. Guests can also dine in the cosy lounge. Booking is advised at weekends. Children welcome.

During the lifetime of this edition, bed and breakfast accommodation will become available at the inn. Please telephone or visit the inn's website for more details.

The Commercial

Market Place, Easingwold, York,
North Yorkshire YO61 3AN
Tel/Fax: 01347 821252

Set in historic Market Place in the charming town of Easingwold, **The Commercial** is a friendly and welcoming pub built in the 1850s. Historically a centre for market traders and their clients, today this traditional pub attracts locals and visitors alike. Open all day, every day for real ales plus a selection of draught keg ales, lagers, cider, stout, wines, spirits and soft drinks, great food is served at lunchtime Tuesday to Sunday and Bank Holidays, and at dinner Tuesday to Saturday and Bank Holidays. The home-made steak pie is very popular, as is the Sunday carvery and vegetarian option. Children welcome.

at the foot of the Howardian Hills. However, Easingwold's prosperity dates back to the 18th century when it flourished as a major stage coach post and, at that time, the town could offer a choice of some 26 public houses and inns. Until the recent construction of a bypass the old town was clogged with traffic but it is now a pleasure again to wander around the market place with its impressive **Market Cross** and, nearby, the outline of the old bull-baiting ring, set in the cobbles, can still be seen. Easingwold used to enjoy the distinction of having its own private railway, a two and a half mile stretch of track along which it took just 10 minutes to reach the main east coast line at Alne. Older residents fondly remember the ancient, tall-chimneyed steam locomotive that plied this route until its deeply regretted closure to passenger traffic in 1948.

Sutton-on-the-Forest

8 miles N of York on the B1363

This village is home to **Sutton Park,** a noble early 18th century mansion built in 1730 by Thomas Atkinson and

The New Inn Motel

Main Street, Huby, York,
North Yorkshire YO61 1HQ
Tel/Fax: 01347 810219
e-mail: enquiries@newinnmotel.freeserve.co.uk
website: www.newinnmotel.co.uk

The welcoming and modern **New Inn Motel** offers purpose-built accommodation in eight charming and comfortable chalet-style dwellings located just nine miles north of York in the village of Huby and to the rear of the New Inn public house. Rated 3 Diamonds by the AA, accommodation is available Easter to the end of October and during some winter months – please ring for details. Special midweek breaks Monday to Thursday, and the tariff includes a hearty breakfast. Local amenities include golf, bowling, squash, fishing, riding, river trips and more.

The Duke of York

Gate Helmsley, York,
North Yorkshire YO41 1JS
Tel: 01759 373698

Standing adjacent to the York–Stamford Bridge Road in the village of Gate Helmsley, **The Duke of York** is a fine pub with great food, drink and hospitality.

The inn began life as three country cottages, and dates back to the late 18th century. This very attractive premises is adorned at the front with hanging baskets and other floral displays. The interior is just as welcoming and friendly, a striking mix of traditional and modern decoration and furnishings with a wealth of exposed woodwork and brickwork, polished oak bar and plenty of comfortable seating.

Leaseholders Chris and Joanne arrived in October of 2003, joining Joanne's mum, Dee, who has been here since November of 2001. They have worked hard to build the inn's reputation, so that it is now justly popular and renowned among locals and visitors alike.

Open from midday until 11 p.m. Monday to Saturday, and from midday until 10.30 p.m. Sundays, there are four real ales served – John Smiths, Timothy Taylor Landlord, Black Sheep and Tetleys – together with a good range of lagers, wines, spirits, cider, stout and soft drinks.

The food draws guests from far and near, who come to sample dishes such as home-made specialities – pies, roasts, vegetarian meals and more – served at lunch (12 – 2.30) and dinner (5.30 – 9) Monday to Friday, and weekends from midday until 9 p.m. Booking is required Friday and Saturday evenings. No-smoking restaurant. Children welcome. Off-road parking.

This fine inn can be reached via the A166 and is handy for a relaxing stop while visiting the many sights and attractions of York, Malton, Stamford Bridge and the many lovely villages of the Yorkshire Wolds.

containing some fine examples of Sheraton and Chippendale furniture and paintings from Buckingham House (now Buckingham Palace) and some much-admired decorative plasterwork by the Italian maestro in this craft, Cortese. Capability Brown designed the lovely gardens and parkland in which can be found a Georgian ice-house, herbaceous and rose borders full of rare and interesting plants, an Edwardian Fernery, well-signposted woodland walks and a nature trail. The house is open from April to September, Wednesdays, Sundays and Bank Holiday Mondays while the gardens are open daily.

Stillington

10 miles N of York on the B1363

Mentioned in the *Domesday Book*, this ancient village is home to Stillington Hall, once owned by the Croft family and it is believed that Croft Original Sherry originated from here. In 1758, one of the great works of English literature almost perished in the fireplace of Stillington Hall. The parson of Coxwold had been invited to dinner by the family and, when the meal ended, he was asked to read from the book he had just completed. The guests had all wined and dined well and were soon dozing off and, so incensed was he by their inattention, that the parson threw the pages of his manuscript onto the fire. Fortunately his host, the Squire of Stillington, rescued them from the flames and Laurence Sterne's immortal *Tristram Shandy* was saved for posterity.

Murton

3 miles E of York off the A64

Although a small village, Murton is an important, modern livestock centre and it is also home to the **Yorkshire Museum of Farming**, which can be found at Murton Park. As well as wandering around the fields and pens, visitors can also see reconstructions of a Roman fort, a Danelaw village from the Dark Ages and Celtic Roundhouses along with bumping into Romans, Vikings and Saxons. Other attractions at the park include the Derwent Valley

The Grey Horse Inn

Main Street, Elvington, York,
North Yorkshire YO41 4AG
Tel: 01904 608335 Fax: 01904 607576
Reservations: 01904 607999
e-mail: greyhorse@elvington.net
website: www.greyhorse.elvington.net

The Grey Horse Inn is a picture-postcard village inn standing opposite the village green in Elvington, some six miles southeast of York on the B1228. Reached from junction 47 of the M1 via the A59 and A64, this whitewashed and pristine inn dates back to the late 1700s. Picnic tables, hanging baskets and window boxes adorn the frontage, while the interior is equally charming, with its wealth of wood, subtle lighting and cosy seating enhancing the welcoming ambience. The lounge area has plush leather sofas, while upstairs is the bright and stylish Hayloft Function Room with its warm yellow walls decorated with watercolours, pale wood furniture and an intimate atmosphere. There is lots of bygone memorabilia on display including old photographs of village life.

Run by David Forster and Jason Butler, the inn was voted CAMRA (York Branch) Country Pub of the Year in 2000. Open Monday and Tuesday 5.00 to 11, Wednesday and Thursday 12.00 to 2.30 and 5.00 to 11, Fridays and Saturdays midday to 11 and Sundays midday to 10.30, this excellent Free House serves up five real ales, including regulars John Smiths, Timothy Taylor Landlord and Black Sheep. Guests can also choose from a good range of lagers, cider, stout, wines, spirits and soft drinks.

Delicious food is served at all opening times until 9 p.m. (except Monday night). Guests choose from the printed menu and specials board from a range of tempting dishes such as beef lasagne, wholetail scampi, rump or gammon steaks and more, all expertly prepared and presented. Home cooking is the order of the day. Tea-time specials are available between 6 and 7.30 p.m. Booking advised.

This fine inn also boasts two ensuite guest bedrooms – a double and a family room – available all year round and providing superb accommodation with full facilities.

Light Railway, a children's play area and a café fashioned on a farmhouse kitchen.

Elvington

6½ miles SE of York on the B1228

During the Second World War, RAF Elvington was the largest Bomber Command station and it was from here that British, Canadian and French crews flew on missions to Europe. Today, the former airfield is now the **Yorkshire Air Museum** (see panel below), a living museum to the allied air forces who served in Yorkshire throughout the war. Housed in authentic buildings, there are numerous exhibits that trace the history of aviation while visitors can also gain a unique insight into just what life was like for a lone air gunner in his turret or hear the sounds of a wartime bomber station. There are various flying displays and exhibitions throughout the year, a historic military vehicle collection to explore and homecooked food is served

The Yorkshire Air Museum

Halifax Way, Elvington, York,
North Yorkshire YO41 4AU
Tel: 01904 608595 Fax: 01904 608246

Over the past few years **The Yorkshire Air Museum** has become one of the most fascinating and dynamic Museums of its type in the country. With its unique collection of over 40 internationally recognised aircraft and displays all combined into this historic site, make the Museum a very special place for aviation enthusiasts young and not so young. The aircraft collection covers aviation history from the pioneering 1849 work of the Yorkshire born Sir George Cayley, recognised internationally as the true "Father of Aeronautics", to WWII aircraft and modern military jets. The Museum has one of the largest special events calendars in the North.

RAF Elvington was established in 1942 as the home for 77 Squadron and from 1944 until the end of the war the only two French bomber squadrons were based here. The French link has remained ever since the two Halifax squadrons left England to become the start of the new French Air Force in 1945, and by courtesy of the French Government, the Museum now displays the only Mirage Mk. III jet fighter in the UK. The Museum is the largest of only a few original wartime bomber bases left open to the public.

The excellent displays house internationally recognised artefacts and in the many original buildings you can explore histories on a varied list of related topics. These include Barnes Wallis; Air Gunners; Airborne Forces and Home Guard as well as observing aircraft restoration workshops and seeing how wartime life was like in the French Officers' Mess or the Airmen's Billet.

The famous NAAFI restaurant is well known for its excellent fare and the Museum shop is well stocked for that extra special gift or keepsake. The site is ideal for private functions, corporate events and conferences.

in the museum's famous NAAFI restaurant. The museum is open daily all year round.

Bishop wilton

8½ miles E of York off the A166

A small and unspoilt village off the A166 east of York, between Stamford Bridge to the west and Pocklington to the south, in Saxon times a country retreat of the bishops of York. The Saxons – whose bishops gave the village its name – began the lovely village church, which has a fine Norman chancel arch and doorway. The remarkable black-and-white marble flooring is copied from the Vatican. A good centre for walking and touring, within easy reach of both York and the coast.

Tadcaster

9½ miles SW of York off the A64

The lovely magnesian limestone used in so many of Yorkshire's fine churches came from the quarries established here in Roman times and their name for Tadcaster was simply 'Calcaria', meaning limestone. By 1341, however brewing had become the town's major industry, using water from River Wharfe, and three major breweries are still based in Tadcaster: John Smiths, whose bitter is the best selling ale in Britain, Samuel Smiths, established in 1758 and the

oldest in Yorkshire, and the Tower Brewery, owned by Bass Charringtons. The distinctive brewery buildings dominate the town's skyline and provide the basis of its prosperity. Guided tours of the breweries are available by prior booking.

Also worth visiting is **The Ark**, the oldest building in Tadcaster that dates back to the 1490s. During its long history, The Ark has served as a meeting place, a post office, an inn, a butcher's shop and a museum and it now houses the Town Council offices and is open to the public during office hours. This appealing half-timbered building takes its name from the two carved heads on the first floor beams and they are thought to represent Noah and his wife, hence the building's name. Tadcaster also offers some attractive riverside walks, one of which takes walkers across the **Virgin Viaduct** over the River Wharfe. Built in 1849 by the great railway entrepreneur George Hudson, the viaduct was intended to be part of a direct line from Leeds to York but, before the tracks were laid, Hudson was convicted of fraud on a stupendous scale and this route was never completed.

A few miles southwest of Tadcaster lies **Hazelwood Castle,** which since 1996 is an exceptional country house hotel. However, for more than 800 years

the castle was the home of the Vavasour family who built it in the lovely white limestone from their quarry at Thevesdale – the same quarry that provided the stone for York Minster and King's College Chapel, Cambridge. The well-maintained gardens and nature trail are open to the public while guided tours of the castle, with its superb Great Hall and 13th century chapel, are by prior arrangement only.

Long Marston

6½ miles W of York off the B1224

Lying on the edge of the Vale of York and sheltered by a hill, this village is an ancient agricultural community but, in July 1644, the peace of this tranquil village was shattered by one of the most important encounters of the Civil War. The Battle of Marston Moor took place just to the north of the village and it was one that the Royalists lost and so sealed their fate. The night before the battle, Oliver Cromwell and his chief officers stayed at **Long Marston Hall** and the bedroom they used is still called The Cromwell Room. Each year the anniversary of the battle is commemorated by the members of the Sealed Knot and, it is said, that the ghosts of those who fell in battle still haunt the site. Certainly, local farmers even now, occasionally, unearth cannonballs from the battle when they are out ploughing the fields.

Less than 100 years later, Long Marston Hall saw the birth, in 1707, of the mother of General James Wolfe, the famous English soldier who scaled the Heights of Abraham to relieve the siege of Quebec.

Selby

In 1069 a young monk named Benedict, from Auxerre in France, had a vision and, although the exact nature of the vision is unknown, he was inspired to set sail for York and, as his ship was sailing up the River Ouse near Selby, three swans flew in formation across its bows. (Three swans, incidentally, still form part of the town's coat of arms). Interpreting this as a sign of the Holy Trinity, Benedict promptly went ashore and set up a preaching cross under a great oak called the Stirhac. The small religious community he established beside the river went from strength to strength, acquiring many grants of land and, in 1100, it was given permission to build a monastery. Over the course of the next 120 years, the great **Selby Abbey** slowly took shape, the massively heavy Norman style of the earlier building gradually modulating into the much more delicate Early English style, and all of the abbey was built using a lovely cream-coloured stone.

However, over the centuries this sublime church has suffered more than most. During the Civil War it was severely damaged by Cromwell's troops who destroyed many of its statues and smashed much of its stained glass. Then, in 1690, the central tower collapsed and, for years afterwards, the abbey was neglected and, by the middle of the 18th century, a wall had been built across the chancel so that the nave could be used as a warehouse. That wall was removed during a major restoration in the 19th century but, in 1906, there was another calamity when a disastrous fire swept through the abbey. Visiting this serene and peaceful church today it is difficult to believe that it has endured so many misfortunes and yet remains so beautiful. Throughout all the abbey's misfortunes one particular feature has, however, survived intact – the famous Washington Window that depicts the coat of arms of John de Washington, Prior of the Abbey around 1415 and a direct ancestor of George Washington. Prominently displayed in this heraldic device is the stars and stripes motif later adapted for the national flag of the United States.

Away from the abbey church that dominates the town, Selby is an important market centre for the rich agricultural plains of the Vale of York that surround the town. Watered by the four great Yorkshire rivers, the Ouse, Wharfe, Derwent and Aire, and by the Selby Canal, this countryside is ideal for walking and cycling or for exploring the waterways on which a wide variety of rivercraft are available for hire. Meanwhile, devotees of railway history will want to pay their respects to Selby's old railway station that was built at the incredibly early date of 1834 and is the oldest surviving station in Britain.

Around Selby

Riccall

4 miles N of Selby off the A19

This ancient village is listed in the *Domesday Book* although its church does not feature as it was built shortly after the great survey. The south doorway of the church dates back to about 1160 and its fine details have been well preserved by a porch added in the 15th century. However, the village's great moment in history came just prior to the Norman invasion when, in 1066, the King Harold Hardrada of Norway and Earl Tostig sailed this far up the River Ouse with some three hundred ships. They had come to claim Northumbria from Tostig's half-brother King Harold of England but they were comprehensively defeated at the Battle of Stamford Bridge.

Riccall is a popular place with walkers as from here there are footpaths, southwards, along the River Ouse to Selby and, northwards, towards Bishopthorpe along the trackbed of the now dismantled York to Selby railway. This latter path is part of the 150-mile long **Trans Pennine Trail** linking the west coast at Liverpool with Hull on the east coast.

Just to the east of the village, the Yorkshire Wildlife Trust maintains the **Skipwith Common Nature Reserve**, some 500 acres of lowland heath that is one of the last such areas remaining in the north of England. Regarded as of national importance, the principal

The Boot and Shoe Inn

Main Street, Ellerton, York,
North Yorkshire YO42 4PB
Tel: 01757 288346

A truly superb village inn located in the tiny hamlet of Ellerton, **The Boot and Shoe Inn** is owned and personally run by Andrea and Kevin Young, who have been here since October of 2001. This friendly and welcoming couple have put their hearts and souls into giving the village the inn they deserve. Dating back in parts to the 1600s, this superb inn boasts many original features such as the

exposed beamed ceilings and enormous brickbuilt fireplace. A charm all of its own pervades this welcoming and convivial place, where locals and visitors alike are treated to the warmest hospitality. The inn is noted particularly for its food. Meals are served Friday and Saturday evenings from 7 to 9 p.m., and Sundays from midday until 2. The menu boasts a range of tempting traditional favourites – Andrea's home-made pies are particularly sought after. The finest and freshest locally-produced ingredients go into creating the selection of delicious dishes.

And to drink – the inn is open for liquid refreshment Monday to Friday from 5.30 and all day Saturdays, Sundays and Bank Holiday Mondays – there are four real ales available. Most come from the Old Mill Brewery at Snaith. Together with these there is a good choice of lagers, cider, stout, wines, spirits and soft drinks.

Outside, to the rear, there's a former paddock that is now a comfortable and welcoming beer garden. To the front of the inn there are tables and umbrellas where guests can enjoy the peace and relaxed atmosphere on fine days. The inn is found off the A64, some six miles southeast of York, and makes a great place to stop and rest for an hour or two while touring the many sights and attractions of the region.

Children welcome.

interest here is the variety of insect and birdlife, but the reserve also contains a number of ancient burial sites.

Hemingbrough

4 miles SE of Selby off the A63

For many years the only access to this village from the west was across the River Ouse but this was resolved in 1792 with the construction of the Selby toll bridge. Hemingbrough is surrounded by flat, open farmland and the elegant and lofty spire of **St Mary's Church**, which rises some 190 feet, is a well known local landmark. Inside, the church contains what are thought to be the oldest misericords in the country – they date from around 1200. These hinged wooden seats for the choir were designed to be folded back when they stood to sing and the medieval woodcarvers delighted in adorning the undersides with intricate carvings.

Drax

5 miles SE of Selby off the A645

Situated close to the River Ouse, this village's original name was 'Ealdedrege', meaning a portage – a place where boats were pulled from the water or dragged overland – and it featured in the *Domesday Book*. Although little remains of the Augustinian priory that was founded here in the 1130s, the parish church, which dates from before the Domesday Survey, has a Saxon christening font. However, the village is most famous for providing Ian Fleming with a sinister-sounding name for one of the villains in his James Bond thrillers and also for providing the National Grid with 10 per cent of all the electricity used in England and Wales. The largest coal-fired **Power Station** in Europe, Drax's vast cooling towers dominate the low-lying ground between the rivers Ouse and Aire. Drax power station has also found an unusual way of harnessing its waste heat by channelling some of it to a huge complex of glasshouses covering 20 acres while the rest goes to specially constructed ponds in which young eels are bred for the export market. Guided tours of the power station are available by prior arrangement.

Camblesforth

4 miles S of Selby off the A1041

Just to the south of this village is **Carlton Towers**, a fascinating stately home. This extraordinary building, "something between the Houses of Parliament and St Pancras Station," was created in the 1870s by two young English eccentrics, Henry, 9th Lord Beaumont, and Edward Welby Pugin, son of the eminent Victorian architect, AG Pugin. Together, they transformed the original traditional Jacobean house into an exuberant mock medieval fantasy in stone, complete with turrets, towers, gargoyles and heraldic shields. The richly-decorated High Victorian interior, designed in the manner of medieval banqueting halls, contains a minstrels' gallery and a vast Venetian-style drawing room. Both Beaumont and Pugin died in their 40s and both, not

The Royal Oak Inn Hotel

Main Street, Hirst Courtney, Selby,
North Yorkshire YO8 9QT
Tel/Fax: 01757 270633
e-mail: TheRoyalOakInnHotel@hotmail.com
website: www.royaloakinn-hotel.co.uk

The Royal Oak Inn Hotel stands in the lovely village of Hirst Courtney, on the Trans-Pennine Way south of Selby and reached east off the A1041, west off the A19. This distinguished hotel was built in the first years of the 20th century, when part of the premises was a blacksmith's and another formed the stables. Tastefully and sensitively converted and refurbished, it now comprises a Free House, restaurant and 10-room hotel. Cheerful and welcoming inside and out, this hidden gem is well worth seeking out.

This excellent inn is owned and personally run by Steven and Suzanne Whitley, with able assistance from Steven's sister Julie. Steven is a professional chef and has been here for 21 years. His experience shows in the range and high quality of the menu and daily specials, served at lunch (12 – 2) and dinner (6 – 9) Monday to Saturday, and from midday until 9 p.m. on Sundays. The restaurant seats 40 and includes no-smoking areas. Among the many superb dishes, Steven's home-made chips are particularly popular. Home-cooking is the byword here, and throughout the week, from Tuesday to Friday, different ingredients are highlighted: Tuesday is Fish 'n' Chip Night, Wednesday is Steak Night and Thursday is Chicken Night.

To drink, there's a good selection of keg ales, the real ale Tetleys, and a wide selection of wines, spirits and soft drinks.

The 10 superior ensuite guest bedrooms are located upstairs. Of different sizes, including a family room, the tariff includes breakfast and prices are static throughout the year. Reduced rates are available for longer stays.

To the rear of the property lies a half-acre camping and caravan park. Open all year round, its scenic location ensures an enjoyable experience surrounded by all the beauties of nature. Water taps and toilet facilities are available; electric hook-ups have recently been installed.

Children are welcome.

The Black Dog Inn

Selby Road, Camblesforth, nr Selby,
North Yorkshire YO8 8HX
Tel: 01757 618247

Four miles south of Selby on the A1941 Snaith road, **The Black Dog Inn** is in the very capable hands of Gary and Tracy Dolman, who took over the reins in May 2002. A local Yorkshire couple, they have made a great success of this late-19th century roadside inn through hard work, enthusiasm and a recognition of the virtues of good service and value for money. Behind its neat, attractive frontage, the interior is equally well looked after, providing a very pleasant, comfortable and traditional setting in which to enjoy a drink and a meal. Three rotating real ales are available, along with a good range of lagers, wines, spirits and soft drinks. The inn has been awarded the Cask Marque Award for the past two years.

Tracy is a superb cook, and in the spacious restaurant and non-smoking conservatory food is served every session. The menu and the specials board offer plenty of choice, and among the favourite dishes are Tracy's home-made pies, lasagne, steaks, salads and vegetarian options, all expertly prepared and presented. There's also a great range of sandwiches, toasties and jacket potatoes. The Black Dog has good off-road parking, and a beer garden, and on an adjacent site is a caravan and campsite that is open all year round – electric hook-ups are available.

surprisingly, bankrupt. Carlton Towers is now the Yorkshire home of the Duke of Norfolk and is unfortunately closed to the general public.

South Milford

7½ miles W of Selby off the A162

Just to the west of the village is the imposing 14th century **Steeton Hall Gatehouse**, all that remains of a medieval castle that was once owned by the Fairfax family. A forebear of the famous Cromwellian general is said to have ridden out from here on his way to carry off one of the nuns at Nun Appleton Priory to make her his bride. He was Sir William Fairfax and she was Isabel Thwaites, a wealthy heiress.

Sherburn in Elmet

8 miles W of Selby on the B1222

A small town, which was once the capital of the Celtic Kingdom of Elmete, Sherburn in Elmet is dominated by All Saints' Church that stands on a hill to the west. Dating from around 1120, the church's great glory is the nave, with its mighty Norman pillars and arcades, while a curiosity here is the 15th century Janus cross that was discovered in the churchyard during the 18th century. The vicar and churchwarden of the time both claimed the cross as their own and, unable to resolve their dispute, they had the cross sawn in half: the two beautifully carved segments are displayed on opposite sides of the south aisle.

PLACES TO STAY, EAT AND DRINK

Goodmanham Arms, Goodmanham, East Yorkshire	101	Pub with Food	p201
The Star At Sancton, Sancton, East Yorkshire	102	Pub and Restaurant	p202
The White Hart Inn, North Cave, East Yorkshire	103	Pub and Restaurant	p203
The Bear Inn, South Cave, East Yorkshire	104	Pub and Restaurant	p204
The Royal Oak, Portington, East Yorkshire	105	Pub with Food	p206
The Tiger Inn, Cottingham, East Yorkshire	106	Pub with Food	p209
Hornsea Folk Museum, Hornsea, East Yorkshire	107	Museum	p210
The Wrygarth Inn, Great Hatfield, East Yorkshire	108	Pub, Food and Accommodation	p210
The Lighthouse, Withernsea, East Yorkshire	109	Museum	p212
The Crooked Billet, Ryehill, East Yorkshire	110	Pub with Food	p212
The Crown & Anchor, Kilnsea, East Yorkshire	111	Pub, Food and Accommodation	p213
Ferguson Fawsitt Arms, Walkington, East Yorkshire	112	Pub, Restaurant and Accommodation	p215
The Star Inn, Nafferton, East Yorkshire	113	Pub, Restaurant and Accommodation	p216
Life Hill Farm, Sledmere, East Yorkshire	114	B&B and Self Catering	p218
The Old Mill Hotel, Langtoft, East Yorkshire	115	Hotel and Restaurant	p219
RSPB's Reserve, Bempton Cliffs, East Yorkshire	116	Visitor Attraction	p223

● Denotes entries in other chapters

5 East Yorkshire

The East Riding of Yorkshire tends to be overlooked by many visitors: it has none of the spectacular moorland and dale scenery of the North York Moors or the Yorkshire Dales, appears to lack the sophistication of Harrogate, Leeds and the county's other major towns and cities and, perhaps, more importantly, it is not on route to anywhere else. However, those who overlook East Yorkshire will find that they are missing out on discovering charming agricultural villages, a rich history and architectural gems such as Beverley Minster. One of Yorkshire's most beguiling towns, not only is it dominated by the soaring twin towers of the Minster, but Beverley is also home to the charming 12th-century St Mary's church that was built with the backing of the town's musical guilds and it is believed that one of its many wonderful carvings inspired Lewis Carroll to create the character of the March Hare.

To the south and east of Beverley lies the old Land of Holderness whose name comes from Viking times: a 'hold' was a man of high rank in the Danelaw and 'ness' has stayed in the language and means promontory. This area is quite different from any other in Yorkshire and its flat, wide plain has been fighting an incessant, and losing battle, with the North Sea that forms its eastern border. Gradually, the coastline is being eroded away and the southern tip, Spurn Head, is constantly being rearranged by the winter storms. However, this promontory

Humber Bridge at Sunset

protects the entrance to the River Humber that has, for centuries, been a major route inland. Here, on the northern banks lies the great port of Hull, more formally known as Kingston-upon-Hull, which first realised its potential when Edward I purchased land here from the monasteries to create a supply depot during his journey north to hammer the Scots. Still a major port, today, Hull is best known for the impressive Humber Bridge that lies just upstream although it was also the birthplace of the slavery abolitionist William Wilberforce.

Pocklington

Set amidst rich agricultural land, Pocklington is a lively market town with an unusual layout of twisting alleys running off the market place. Its splendid, mainly 15th-century church certainly justifies its title as the Cathedral of the Wolds (although strictly speaking Pocklington is just outside the Wolds). William Wilberforce, the famous slave law reformer, went to the old grammar school here and, a more dubious claim to fame, is that the last burning of a witch in England took place in Pocklington.

Founded in Saxon times by 'Pocela's people', Pocklington was mentioned in the *Domesday Book* as one of only two boroughs in Yorkshire's East Riding. Although the market has been in existence since the 13th century, it was the building in 1815 of a canal linking the town to the River Ouse, and later the arrival of the railway, which set the seal on the town's prosperity.

The people of Pocklington have good reason to be grateful to Major Percy Marlborough Stewart who, on his death in 1962, bequeathed **Burnby Hall and Gardens** to the town. A godson of the Duke of Marlborough and an expert huntsman, Stewart travelled the world no fewer than seven times before settling at the hall and, along with enjoying the glorious gardens that had been created under his direction, he also put his energies into amassing what is now the National Collection of Hardy Water Lilies. The gardens, which are open daily from March to September, provide a glorious haven of beauty and tranquillity and, along with the two lakes, there is a secret garden, a walled Victorian garden and natural woodland. Meanwhile, the Stewart Collection Museum, housed here, provides a fascinating insight into this interesting character and the times in which he lived.

Around Pocklington

Nunburnholme

3 miles SE of Pocklington off the A1079

Named after the Benedictine nuns who first settled here, the village church is well worth a visit as, just inside, is a 1,000 year old Saxon cross that is elaborately carved with arches, animals and representations of the Madonna. It was also here that the famous ornithologist, Rev Francis Orpen Morris, was born. Heavily influenced by the 18th-century naturalist Gilbert White, Morris wrote the multi-volumed *History of British Birds*.

Goodmanham

6½ miles SE of Pocklington off the A1079

During Saxon times, according to the Venerable Bede, there was a pagan temple at Goodmanham but, in AD 627 its priest, Coifu, was converted to the Christian faith and with his own hands destroyed the heathen shrine. Coifu's conversion so impressed Edwin, King of Northumbria that he also was baptised and made Christianity the official religion of his kingdom. However, other versions of the story attribute King Edwin's conversion to his being hopelessly enamoured with the beautiful Princess Aethelburh, daughter of the King of Kent. Aethelburh was a Christian and she refused to marry Edwin until he, too, had adopted her faith.

Just to the east of the village lies **Kiplingcotes Racecourse**, the site of the oldest horse race in England that was begun in 1519 and is run once every three years in March.

The Goodmanham Arms

Goodmanham, York YO43 3JA
Tel: 01430 873849
website: www.thegoodmanhamarms.org.uk

Located on the Wolds Way in the village that gives the pub its name, **The Goodmanham Arms** is a charming rural retreat where guests can savour great drink and hospitality. Open all day Saturday, Sunday and Bank Holidays, and from 4 p.m. Monday to Friday (except by appointment – please ring or visit the inn's website for details), this cracking inn has great style and a warm and convivial atmosphere.

Owner Peter Southcott is a local man who bought the pub in July of 2003 and has made it a great success. There are usually five real ales to be supped – Choirboys Dread, Randy Monk, Monks Revenge and Filthy Habit plus a guest ale – along with a good range of lagers, wines, cider, stout, spirits and soft drinks. The four regulars are brewed right here in the micro-brewery; Peter is more than happy to satisfy guests' curiosity as to the origins of their names. Complimentary sandwiches are served on Saturdays and Sundays to accompany drinks. Children welcome.

The Star @ Sancton

King Street, Sancton, nr Market Weighton,
North Yorkshire YO43 4QP
Tel: 01430 827269

The Star is a fine-looking old building situated on the main road (A1034) through the village of Sancton, a few miles southeast of Market Weighton. The premises date back at least 700 years and it is thought that it was originally a farmhouse that gave hospitality to cattlemen on their way to market. It has been licensed since 1710 and has been given a new lease of life by Ben and Lindsey Cox, who carried out a full internal refurbishment and re-opened for business in

December 2003. Ben is a talented chef who has worked in some of Yorkshire's best hotels, and the combination of the good food and the excellent hospitality has begun to attract not only a loyal band of locals but also visitors from much further afield. Behind the smart cream-painted exterior, the Star has a splendidly traditional appeal, and the bar features lots of wood – the floor, the furniture, the beams and the panelled walls and bar counter.

Bar food is served at lunchtime Tuesday to Saturday, while the main menu is available in the 20-cover non-smoking restaurant lunchtime and evening – booking is recommended at all times. Ben takes his inspiration from near and far in his dishes, which are all prepared and cooked on the premises.

Starters might include Toulouse sausage with herb polenta and red pesto dressing or a superb duck combination of pink breast, confit leg and pâté. Main courses include steaks served plain or with a choice of sauces – peppercorn & brandy, port & stilton, whisky & honey; seared swordfish steak niçoise; a classic steak & Black Sheep ale pie; and a pimento casserole with chickpeas, coriander and cumin. Sunday lunch sees traditional roasts with a fish and vegetarian alternative, and Ben's good work continues right to the end with luscious desserts such as bitter chocolate and hazelnut tart with cool mint ice

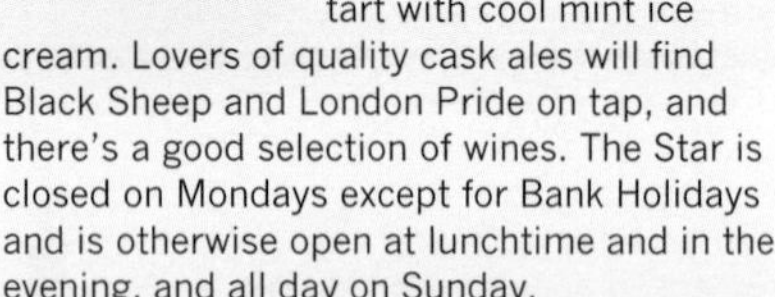

cream. Lovers of quality cask ales will find Black Sheep and London Pride on tap, and there's a good selection of wines. The Star is closed on Mondays except for Bank Holidays and is otherwise open at lunchtime and in the evening, and all day on Sunday.

Market Weighton

6½ miles SE of Pocklington on the A1079

Market Weighton is a busy little town with mellow 18th century houses clustered around an early Norman church. Buried somewhere in the churchyard is William Bradley, who was born at Market Weighton in 1787 and grew up to become the tallest man in England – he stood 7 feet 8 inches high and weighed 27 stones! William made a fortune by travelling the country and placing himself on display and he was even received at court by George III who, taking a fancy to the giant, gave him a huge gold watch to wear across his chest.

A couple of miles to the north lies **Londesborough Park,** a 400-acre estate that was once owned by the legendary railway entrepreneur, George Hudson. He had the York to Market Weighton railway diverted here so that he could build himself a comfortable private station and, although the railway has now disappeared, part of its route is included in the popular long distance footpath, the **Wolds Way**.

South Cave

13½ miles SE of Pocklington on the A1034

Officially a town with its very own Town Hall standing in the market place, the name is said to be a corruption of South

The Bear Inn

Market Place, South Cave,
East Yorkshire HU15 2AS
Tel: 01430 422461

The Bear Inn is a distinguished and elegant, spacious inn located in South Cave, found just off the main A63 and north on the A1034, not far from the River Humber and near the sights and attractions of Hull and Beverley. Classic inside and out, with a happy blend of traditional and modern features, the inn dates back in parts to the late 1500s and has been in its time a coaching inn and posting house. Each area of the pub is handsome and comfortable, tastefully

decorated and furnished and with a warm and welcoming ambience. Open every session Monday to Friday and all day at weekends, the inn boasts an impressive and huge below-ground cellar, and stocks three real ales – John Smiths, Black Sheep and Marstons Pedigree – together with a superb range of lagers, cider, stout, wines, spirits and soft drinks.

Excellent food is available Monday to Friday at lunch (12 – 2.30) and dinner (5 – 9.30), and Saturdays and Sundays from midday to 9.30 p.m. Booking is advised at weekends for this justly popular place, where the full and comprehensive menu and daily specials board of choice dishes that includes dishes from the grill, from the sea, home-made dishes and lots more. Local produce is used wherever possible, and meals are home-cooked to order. The impressive no-smoking restaurant seats 40 comfortably, and the bar and lounge are adorned with bygone memorabilia and other attractive ornaments.

Tenants Brian and Sharon and their friendly, capable staff offer all their guests a warm welcome, great service and genuine hospitality. This fine inn is well worth seeking out as it is a convivial yet relaxed place to enjoy a hearty meal or quiet drink.

Cove as the southern part of the village is set around a backwater of the River Humber. The village is separated into two by the grounds of the Cave Castle Golf Hotel, a building that dates back to Elizabethan times and was once the home of George Washington's great grandfather.

Welton

16½ miles SE of Pocklington on the A63

This pretty village, where a stream flows beside the village green and into a tree-encircled duck pond, has a Norman church with Pre-Raphaelite windows made by William Morris's company of craftsmen. The notorious highwayman Dick Turpin was not a local but his villainous, if romantic, career came to an end at Welton village when he was apprehended inside the Green Dragon inn. Local legend has it that this establishment gave him hospitality before he was taken off to the magistrates at Beverley, who committed him to the Assizes at York where he was found guilty and hanged in 1739.

North Ferriby

18 miles SE of Pocklington on the B1231

It was here, in 1946, that some late Bronze Age boats, dating from 890 BC to about 590 BC, were found on the shore. Made from planks held together with strips of yew, they indicate that travel on the River Humber had begun much earlier than had been previously thought. A model of the boats can be seen in Hull's Transport and Archaeology Museum.

Howden

13½ miles SW of Pocklington on the A63

Although not as grand as Yorkshire's other minsters, **Howden Minster**, which was built between the late 13th and the early 14th centuries, is a beautiful building despite the chancel and the chapter house having fallen into ruin after the Dissolution. Still one of the largest parish churches in East Yorkshire, from the top of its soaring 135 feet tower there are wonderful views of the surrounding countryside. When the medieval Prince Bishops of Durham held sway over most of northern England, they built a palace at Howden that they used as a pied-à-terre during their semi-royal progresses around their domain and also as a summer residence. The hall, known as the Bishop's Manor, of that 14th century palace still stands, although it is now much altered.

The town itself is a pleasing jumble of narrow, flagged and setted streets with a picturesque stone and brick Market Hall in the market place. The celebrated aircraft designer Barnes Wallis knew Howden well: he lived here while working on the R100 airship that was built at Hedon airfield nearby. It made its maiden flight in 1929 and successfully crossed the Atlantic. Another famous Howden resident was Neville Shute, an aeronautical engineer

The Royal Oak

Holme Road, A614, Portington, Howden,
East Yorkshire DN14 7NA
Tel: 01430 430563 Fax: 01430 430420
e-mail: theroyaloakfoggs@aol.com

The Royal Oak stands adjacent to the A614 between Howden and Market Weighton. It's an impressive place, friendly and family-run by Douglas and Elaine Smith with able assistance from their sons Darren and Timothy and daughter Katy (the family have been in the pub trade for 12 years). This Free House serves up great food, drink and lashings of hospitality, with real ales, an excellent menu and a convivial and welcoming ambience. Visitors come from miles around just for the food – and it's a journey well worth making!

who also worked on the R100, although he is, perhaps, best known as the author of such stirring novels as *A Town Like Alice*. At the nearby Breighton Aerodrome is the **Real Aeroplane Museum**, which illustrates the history of flight through the work of Yorkshire aviation pioneers.

About four miles northwest of Howden are the striking remains of **Wressle Castle** that was built in 1380 for Sir Henry Percy and is the only surviving example of a medieval fortified house in East Yorkshire. At the end of the Civil War, three of the castle's sides were pulled down and much of the rest was destroyed by fire in 1796 but two massive towers, the hall and the kitchens remain. The castle is not open to the public but there are excellent views from the village road while a fine old windmill nearby, provides, an extra visual bonus.

Goole

16 miles SW of Pocklington on the A614

Despite being some 50 miles from the sea, Goole lies at the hub of a waterways network that includes the River Ouse, the River Don (known here as the Dutch River), the River Aire and the Aire and Calder Navigation and it is England's most inland port. Life here is still centred on the docks, locks and canal basins that were built in the early 19th century and, now filled with hundreds of private leisure craft, the docks are still dominated by the distinctive 'Salt and Pepper' water towers.

The **Waterways Museum and Adventure Centre,** located on the dockside, tells the story of Goole's development as a canal terminus and port through a series of interactive exhibits and walk-in displays. Meanwhile, in the town centre the **Goole Museum and Art Gallery** provides more information on the port and the town.

Further down the River Humber is the **Blacktoft Sands RSPB Reserve** where the lagoons and reedbeds are home to many rare breeding birds including marsh harriers and avocets.

Stamford Bridge

7 miles NW of Pocklington on the A166

Hull Marina at Sunset

Everyone knows that 1066 was the year of the Battle of Hastings but, just a few days before that battle, King Harold had clashed at Stamford Bridge with his half-brother Tostig and Hardrada, King of Norway who, between them, had mustered some 60,000 men. On a rise near the corn mill is a stone commemorating the event with an inscription in English and Danish. Up until 1878, a Sunday in September was designated 'Spear Day Feast' in commemoration of the battle and, on this day, boat-shaped pies were made bearing the impression of the fatal spear, in memory of the Saxon soldier in his boat who slew the single Norseman defending the wooden bridge. Harold's troops were triumphant but immediately after this victory they marched southwards to Hastings and a much more famous defeat.

Hull

Hull's history as an important port goes back to 1293 when Edward I, travelling north on his way to hammer the Scots, stopped off here and immediately recognized the potential of the muddy junction where the River Hull flows into the Humber. The king bought the land from the monks of Meaux Abbey (at the usual royal discount) and the settlement, henceforth, was known as "Kinges town upon Hull". The port grew steadily through the centuries and, at one time, had the largest fishing fleet of any port in the country with more than 300 trawlers on its register. The primitive facilities were greatly improved by the construction of a state-of-the-art dock in 1778 but, now superseded, that dock has been converted into the handsome **Queen's Gardens**, one of the many attractive open spaces created by this flower-conscious city. The addition to waymarked walks, such as the Maritime Heritage Trail and the **Fish Pavement Trail**, help visitors to make the most of the city's dramatic waterfront.

During the Second World War Hull was mercilessly battered by the Luftwaffe: 7,000 people were killed and 92 per cent of its houses suffered bomb damage. However, Hull has risen phoenix-like from those ashes and is, today, the fastest growing port in England and the port area extends for seven miles along the River Humber with several miles of quays servicing a constant flow of commercial traffic arriving from, or departing for, every quarter of the globe. Every day, a succession of vehicle ferries link the city to the European gateways of Zeebrugge and Rotterdam.

A visit to Hull is an exhilarating experience at any time of the year but especially so in October. Back in the late 1200s the city was granted a charter to hold an autumn fair and, though this began as a fairly modest cattle and sheep market, over the centuries it burgeoned into the largest gathering of its kind in Europe. There are other annual events that take place here including an Easter Festival, an International Festival in mid summer, a Jazz on the Waterfront celebration in August, an International Sea Shanty Festival and a Literature Festival.

However, there is much to see here at anytime of year and, among the remarkable collection of historic houses, art galleries and museum, perhaps the most evocative is the **Wilberforce House Museum** in the old High Street. It was in this building, in 1759, that William Wilberforce was born and, later, it was from here that he and his father lavished thousands of pounds in bribes to get William elected as Hull's Member of Parliament. There was nothing unusual about that kind of corruption at the time, but William then redeemed himself by his resolute opposition to slavery. His campaign took more than 30 years and William was already on his deathbed before a reluctant Parliament finally outlawed the despicable trade. The museum presents a shaming history of the slave trade along with the more uplifting story of Wilberforce's efforts to eliminate it forever.

As a boy, Wilberforce attended the Old Grammar School, which was built in 1583, and this lovely building is now home to **Hands on History**, a museum of Victorian social history that also tells the story of Hull and its citizens. Also concerned with displaying images of life in Hull is **Streetlife, Hull's Museum of Transport**, which looks at 200 years of transport from penny farthing bicycles and carriages to the motor car and trams. However, the town's most unusual museum has to be the **Spurn Lighthouse**, which was once stationed on active duty off Spurn Point but that is now moored in the town's marina. Visitors can explore the 75 year old vessel with the help of its knowledgeable crew. More of Hull's maritime history is explained at the Maritime Museum that is housed in the impressive former Town Docks Office while, in the former corn exchange, is the **Hull and East Riding Museum**. Meanwhile, anyone looking for more cultural pursuits should visit the **Ferens Art Gallery** that houses a sumptuous collection of paintings and sculpture that ranges from European Old Masters to challenging contemporary art and includes works by Canelletto and Hockney.

Elsewhere in the town there is **Beverley Gate**, surrounded by an amphitheatre, where, in 1642, Charles I was turned back from the town and its arsenal and the 13th-century Holy Trinity Church is believed to be the largest parish church in England. However, while Hull is certainly famous as a port it is the **Humber Bridge**, five miles to the west, which people associate most with this ancient port. The longest single-span suspension bridge in the world, the bridge was opened in 1981 and it is so long that, due to the curvature of the Earth, the two towers appear to lean away from each other although they are perfectly vertical.

Before leaving Hull there are a couple of unusual features that are worth a mention – if not an explanation. Firstly, visitors to Hull will soon become aware of its unique pubic telephones. They are still the traditional, curvy-topped heavily, barred boxes but with the distinctive difference that they are all painted gleaming white. What is not apparent is that by some bureaucratic quirk, Hull remained the only municipally owned telephone company in Britain until it was floated on the Stock Exchange early in 2000. The second unusual feature in Hull can be found in Nelson Street where there are award winning public toilets. These spotless conveniences, complete with hanging baskets, have become a tourist attraction in their own right.

Around Hull

Hornsea

13 miles NE of Hull on the B1242

There was a settlement of sorts here before the Norman invasion but, today, it is best known as a seaside town with an excellent sandy beach, a promenade and plenty of amusements and attractions for all the family. The excellent **Hornsea Folk Museum** (see panel on page 210) occupies a Grade II listed former farmhouse and is well worth a visit.

The Tiger Inn

105 King Street, Cottingham,
East Yorkshire HU16 5QE
Tel: 01482 622970 Fax: 01482 845753

Draught cask Bass is the regular real ale at **The Tiger Inn**, a welcoming place found in Cottingham off the A164, north of Hull and south of Beverley. Experienced hosts Eric and Sarah Barker have been in the trade some 22 years, and provide excellent food, drink and hospitality every day. There's a good selection of draught keg ales, lagers, cider, stout, wines, spirits and soft drinks, together with a fine range of outstanding meals including hearty favourites such as rump steak, fish dishes and vegetarian choices served in hearty portions at very reasonable prices.

Hornsea Folk Museum

11 Newbegin, Hornsea,
East Yorkshire HU18 1AB
Tel: 01964 533443

Established in 1978, the excellent **Hornsea Folk Museum** occupies a Grade II listed former farmhouse where successive generations of the Burn family lived for 300 years up until 1952. Their way of life, the personalities and characters who influenced the development of the town or found fame in other ways, are explored in meticulously restored rooms brimming with furniture, decorations, utensils and tools of the Victorian period.

The kitchen, parlour, bedroom, have

fascinating displays of authentic contemporary artefacts, and the museum complex also includes a laundry, workshop, blacksmith's shop and a barn stocked with vintage agricultural implements.

Another popular attraction here is **Hornsea Freeport**, an extensive complex of shops where customers are invited to 'shop till they drop'. There are numerous retail outlets here selling all manner of items from designer wear to kitchenware.

Those looking for peace and tranquillity among all the bustle of this busy seaside town should make for **Hornsea Mere**, where there is an RSPB reserve centred on this large freshwater lake.

Sproatley

7 miles NE of Hull on the B1238

Just to the north of the village lies **Burton Constable Hall,** which is named after Sir John Constable who, in 1570, built this stately mansion that incorporates parts of an even older house dating back to the reign of King Stephen in the 1100s. The hall was again remodelled, on Jacobean lines, in the 18th century and contains some fine work by Chippendale, Adam and James Wyatt. In the famous Long Gallery

The Wrygarth Inn

Station Road, Great Hatfield,
East Yorkshire HU11 4UY
Tel: 01964 536994

Surrounded by beautiful open countryside in the hamlet of Great Hatfield, reached via unmarked roads between the A1242 and the B1243 or A165,south of Hornsea, **The Wrygarth Inn** is well worth seeking out. Taking its name from a one-time Lord of the Manor, this 18th century inn is open from midday every day, Tetleys is the real ale here and the menu boasts a range of hearty

favourites. Accommodation is also provided in three charming ensuite guest bedrooms.

hangs a remarkable collection of paintings, amongst them Holbein's portraits of *Sir Thomas Cranmer* and *Sir Thomas More* and Zucchero's *Mary, Queen of Scots*. Meanwhile, outside, there are extensive parklands designed by Capability Brown that were, apparently, inspired by the gardens at Versailles. Perhaps it was this connection that motivated the Constable family to suggest loaning the hall to Louis XVIII of France during his years of exile after the French Revolution. Also in the grounds of the hall are collections of agricultural machinery, horse-drawn carriages and 18th century scientific apparatus.

The descendants of the Constable family still bear the title Lords of Holderness and along with it the rights to any flotsam and jetsam washed ashore on the Holderness peninsula. Many years ago, when the late Brigadier Chichester Constable was congratulated on enjoying such a privilege, he retorted, *"I also have to pay for burying, or otherwise disposing of, any whale grounded on the Holderness shore – and it costs me about £20 a time!"* The huge bones of one such whale are still on show in the grounds of the hall.

Hedon

5½ miles E of Hull on the B1240

This delightful market town is dominated by its glorious Church of St Augustine that has become known as the King of Holderness because of its cathedral-like proportions. Work on the church was begun in 1190 to grand designs that reflected the prosperity of the town at the time but, when it was completed, in around 1435, the building was less opulent than originally foreseen as both the silting up of the local river and the Plague had taken its toll on the population. This, as the first port on the Humber, and its history can be discovered at the **Hedon Museum**.

To the southwest of Hedon lies **Fort Paull** that was originally constructed in 1542 as part of Henry VIII's great system of coastal defences. The fortress has a long and distinguished history as a fortress and it served right up until the end of the Second World War; however, today, it is a fascinating attraction that combines the history of British warfare with entertainment and leisure for all the family.

Halsham

11 miles E of Hull off the B1362

Halsham was once the seat of the Constable family, Lords of Holderness, before they moved to their stately new mansion at Burton Constable. On the edge of Halsham village, they left behind their imposing, domed mausoleum built in the late 1700s to house ancestors going back to the 12th century. Though not open to the public, the mausoleum is clearly visible from the Hull to Withernsea road.

Withernsea

15 miles E of Hull on the A1033

This small and traditional resort has a

The Lighthouse

Hull Road, Withernsea,
East Yorkshire HU19 2DY
Tel: 01964 614834

Withernsea Lighthouse uniquely towers 127 feet above the town. The base of the lighthouse features many exhibits, R.N.L.I., H.M. Coastguard, Ships Bells, models and old photography recording the history of ship wrecks and the Withernsea lifeboats and heroic crews who saved 87 lives between 1862 and 1913 and the history of the Spurn lifeboats.

The local history section shows photographs of the Victorian and Edwardian Withernsea town, including details of the pier, promenades past and present and the railway.

Views from the lamproom are breathtaking, especially after climbing 144 steps. A good mounted telescope improves the views and a certificate is the reward on descent. Non climbers see the town and coastline with a visual aid camera and monitor in the Base.

The cafe provides a welcome cup of tea and light refreshments. Souvenirs are on sale.

long, sandy beach as well as plenty of entertainment for all the family and also a busy market that is open several days a week. The most striking feature of the town is its old lighthouse and, from the 127 feet tower, there are some marvellous views from the lamp-room. Decommissioned in 1976, the building is now the **Lighthouse Museum**, covering two distinct areas: the history of the Royal National Lifeboat Institution and the actress Kay Kendall. Born in Withernsea and later achieving fame on the London stage as a sophisticated comedienne, Kay Kendall is best remembered for her role in *Genevieve*.

The Crooked Billet

Pitt Lane, Ryehill, East Yorkshire HU12 9NN
Tel: 01964 622303

The tiny village of Ryehill is set back from the main Hull-to-Withernsea Road, and it is here that **The Crooked Billet** serves up great food, drink and hospitality. This traditional country inn has been tending weary travellers since the late 1600s, and continues this tradition today with real ales, a range of homemade meals and friendly staff.

Convivial and relaxed, the inn's ancient beams, flagstone floors, real fires and the wealth of local memorabilia add to its inviting and comfortable ambience.

The Crown & Anchor

Main Road, Kilnsea,
East Yorkshire HU12 0UB
Tel: 01964 650276

Blessed by an unbeatable scenic location at Kilnsea looking towards Spurn Head and over the River Humber and the estuary to Lincolnshire, the superb **Crown & Anchor** is reached via unnumbered roads off the B1445.

Owner Jean, ably assisted by her sister Mary and brother-in-law Geoff, has been at this excellent Free House since April 2000. The décor and furnishings contribute to the inns wonderful character and paintings by local artists are displayed on the walls for you to admire and purchase if you wish.

Open every session October to Easter and all day every day from Easter to the end of September, the inn serves two real ales – Tetleys with Timothy Taylor Landlord – along with a range of lagers, cider, stout, wines, spirits and soft drinks.

The inn is justly famed for its food, available daily at lunch (12 – 2) and dinner (6 – 8.30 Sunday to Wednesday, 6 –9 Thursday to Saturday). Booking advised for Saturday evening and Sunday lunch. Guests choose from the menu and specials board from a selection of tempting dishes – specialities include fresh fish dishes and home-made steak-and-ale pie.

This fine inn also boasts four wonderful ensuite guest bedrooms, available all year round.

Her grandfather helped to build the lighthouse in 1892 and he was the last coxswain of the deep-sea lifeboat.

To the south of the resort stretches a desolate spit of flat windswept dunes, Spurn Point, which lead to Spurn Head, the narrow hook of ever-shifting sands that curls around the mouth of the Humber estuary. One of the oldest places in Britain, during the First World War there was a fort at the Head with a railway supply line but now all that can be seen is the lighthouse on the very tip of the point although around it are underground fortifications. Much of this fascinating land formation is now the **Spurn National Nature Reserve** and it is a fascinating place that is home to thousands of migrating birds.

Hessle

4 miles W of Hull off the A63

From the **Humber Bridge Country Park** there are not only superb views of the massive bridge, but also across the Humber Estuary. A haven for birds, this park is one of their most important feeding grounds on the east coast. Meanwhile, the Humber Bridge lies at the southern end of the 79-mile Wolds Way National Trail, a long distance footpath that follows the crescent of the Yorkshire Wolds.

It is here that the River Humber narrows and where the Romans maintained a ferry, the Transitus Maximus, a vital link in the route between Lincoln and York. The ferry remained in operation for almost 2,000 years until it was replaced, in 1981, by the Humber Bridge whose mighty pylons soar more than 800 feet above the village. The great bridge dwarfs Cliff Mill, built in 1810 to mill the local chalk and, although it remained wind-driven, a gas engine was installed in 1925.

Beverley Minster

Beverley

8 miles NW of Hull on the A1035

An attractive market town, Beverley was once the capital of Yorkshire's East Riding and it still retains its strong trading links with busy general and cattle markets. With a long history that dates back to before the Norman invasion, the town was, in the Middle Ages, one of the country's most prosperous and, today, it is a delightful architectural blend of past and present. However, the town's horizon is dominated by two key buildings: the medieval St Mary's Church and its majestic Minster whose twin towers soar over the old town. Founded in around AD 705, the **Beverley Minster** of today dates from 1220, as the previous building was destroyed by a great fire in 1188, and it took over 200 years to complete. As a result, the Minster provides a textbook demonstration of the evolving architectural styles of those decades. Amongst its many treasures are the superb, fine wood carvings from the Ripon school and a 1,000 year old fridstool, or sanctuary seat. Carved from a single block of stone, the fridstool is a relic from the earlier Saxon church that stood on this site. Under Saxon law, the fridstool provided refuge for any offender who managed to reach it and the canons would then try to resolve the dispute between the fugitive and his pursuer. If, after 30 days no solution had been found, the seeker of sanctuary was then given safe escort to the county boundary or the nearest port. The custom survived right up until Henry VIII's closure of the monasteries. Unlike the plain-cut fridstool, the stone canopy of the 14th-century Percy Shrine is elaborately decorated with carvings while there is also a wealth of wood carvings to be found, including those representing Stomach Ache, Toothache, Sciatica and Lumbago – four afflictions probably almost as fearsome to medieval people as the Four Riders of the Apocalypse.

Built with the backing of the town's musical guilds, **St Mary's Church**, which was established in the early 12th century, is also richly endowed with fine carvings, many of them brightly coloured, and striking sculptures. A series of ceiling panels depicts all the Kings of England from Sigebert (AD 623-37) to Henry VI. Originally, four legendary kings were also included, but one of them was replaced in recent times by a portrait of George VI. Lewis Carroll visited St Mary's when he stayed with friends in the town and was very taken with a stone carving of a rabbit – the inspiration, it is believed, for the March Hare in *Alice in Wonderland.*

Unlike many towns in the Middle Ages, Beverley did not have an encircling wall but, instead, the town fathers had a deep ditch excavated around it so that all goods had to pass through one of the gates and pay a toll. **North Bar**, one of the town's five medieval gatehouses, was built in 1409 and, with headroom of little more than 10 feet, is something of a traffic hazard, albeit a very attractive one. Adjacent to the Bar is Bar House, in which Charles I and his sons stayed in the 1630s. Another visitor to the town, famous for very different reasons, was the highwayman Dick Turpin who, in 1739, was brought before a magistrates' hearing conducted at one of the town's inns.

The wide market square in the heart of the town is graced by an elegant Market Cross, a circular pillared building that bears the arms of Queen Anne in whose reign it was built at the expense of the town's two Members of

The Star Inn

5 North Street, Nafferton, Driffield,
East Yorkshire YO25 4JW
Tel: 01377 254396
e-mail: naffertonstar@btconnect.com

Set in the picture-postcard village of Nafferton, found a couple of miles northeast of Driffield off the A166, **The Star Inn** is a quality establishment ideally situated for visiting the coasts, local harbours and the Yorkshire Wolds.

A privately-owned premises since November of 2003, the interior of this convivial inn has been totally and tastefully refurbished. Visitors come again and again to

sample the great food, drink and hospitality.

Open all day, every day for ale, John Smiths is the real ale here, together with a great range of keg draught ales, lagers, wines, spirits and soft drinks.

Home-cooked, home-prepared food is available daily from midday until about 8 p.m. The delicious steaks are very popular, as is the all-day breakfast, but the menu also boasts pork Valentine, Barnsley chops, pork sausages and other hearty country favourites. Wednesday night features a selection of curries at a special price that includes a free glass of wine. The wine list is select and features two superior whites and three reds. The mouth-

watering puddings are well worth saving room for. The restaurant area also doubles as an internet café.

A history of this distinguished pub, which dates back to the 19th century, is displayed in the main bar and in each of the guest chalets.

In 2003, five purpose-built chalets were added to the rear of the premises to provide excellent accommodation – plenty of space, good facilities, pleasant, clean and warm. The rooms are available all year round – guests can stay on room-only or bed-and-breakfast rates. All guests are guaranteed a warm welcome and a very comfortable stay.

Parliament. At that time, of course, parliamentary elections were flagrantly corrupt but at Beverley the tradition continued longer than in most places and, in 1868, the author Anthony Trollope stood as a candidate here, but was defeated in what was widely acknowledged as a breathtakingly fraudulent election.

The **Guildhall**, nearby, was built in 1762 and is still used as a courtroom and this impressive room has an ornate plasterwork ceiling on which there is an imposing Royal Coat of Arms and also the familiar figure of Justice holding a pair of scales although, unusually, she is not wearing a blindfold. When an 18th-century town clerk was asked the reason for this departure from tradition, he replied, '*In Beverley, Justice is not blind.*'

Beverley can boast three separate museums and galleries: the Beverley Art Gallery contains an impressive collection of local works including those by Frederick Elwell RA; the **East Yorkshire Regimental Museum** has six rooms of exhibits chronicling the area's long association with the regiment; and the **Museum of Army Transport** offers visitors a fascinating insight into the history of military transport from the days of the Boer War to the staff car that Field Marshal Montgomery used in France and Germany during the Second World War.

On the edge of the town is open pasture, Beverley Westwood, which provides a wonderful green belt of land and here, too, can be found **Beverley Racecourse**, where meetings have been taking place since the late 17th century. Meanwhile, serious walkers might care to follow some or all of the 15-mile **Hudson Way**, a level route that follows the track of the old railway from Beverley to Market Weighton. The Hudson Way wanders through the Wolds, sometimes deep in a cutting, sometimes high on an embankment, past an old windmill near Etton and through eerily abandoned stations.

Great Driffield

Located on the edge of the Wolds, Great Driffield is a busy little market town at the heart of an important corn growing area and, along with its weekly cattle market and general markets, plays host to the largest annual Agricultural Show in the country. Known as the 'Capital of the Wolds', the town prospered in the 19th century with the opening of the Driffield Canal that linked Driffield with the Rivers Hull and Humber and, although this is no longer open, there are plans to reconnect the town with the main canal network.

This town was once the capital of the Saxon Kingdom of Dear, a vast domain that extended over the whole of Northumbria and Yorkshire. It was a King of Dear who, for administrative convenience, divided the southern part of his realm into three parts, 'thriddings', and a word that gradually evolved into the famous 'Ridings' of Yorkshire. Later, after the Normans had subdued the Northern Rebellion of

1080, a castle was built here, Alfred's Castle, of which little remains today.

Driffield has expanded westwards to meet up with its smaller neighbour, **Little Driffield** and a tablet in the church here claims that, in the Saxon monastery that stood on this site, Aldred, King of Northumbria was buried in AD 705 after being wounded in a battle against the Danes.

Around Great Driffield

Huggate

9 miles W of Great Driffield off the A166

The village clusters around a pond that dates back to Saxon times and a large green with a well that claims to be the deepest in England. Tucked away in the heart of the Wolds, two long distance walks, the **Minster Way** and the Wolds Way, run to the north and south of Huggate.

Sledmere

7 miles NW of Driffield on the B1252

This village is home to **Sledmere House**, a noble Georgian mansion built by the Sykes family in the 1750s although there had been a house here since medieval times. Inside, there is fine furniture by Chippendale and Sheraton and superb decorated plasterwork by Joseph Rose, while the Turkish Room – inspired by the Sultan's salon in Istanbul's Valideh Mosque – is a dazzling example of oriental opulence.

The Sykes family set a shining example to other landowners in the Wolds by employing agricultural improvements that transformed this barren track of land into one of the most productive and best cultivated districts in the county. They also founded the famous Sledmere Stud and the 2nd Sir Tatton Sykes spent nearly two million pounds on building and restoring churches in the area. In 1911,

Sledmere House itself was ravaged by fire and, when a servant rushed in to tell Sir Tatton, then 85 years old, the news, he insisted on finishing his lunch. An armchair was set out on the lawn for him so that he could complete his meal in safety while his servants laboured to rescue the house's many treasures. After the fire, Sledmere was quickly restored and the Sykes family is still in residence. Along with the splendid interiors, another great feature of the house is its glorious Capability Brown landscaped parkland that contains a beautiful 18th-century rose garden and a much more recently laid-out knot garden. The house is open from Easter to September, but not on Saturdays or on Bank Holiday Mondays. The house's famous pipe organ is played for visitors on Wednesdays, Fridays and Sundays.

Across the road from Sledmere House are two remarkable, elaborately detailed, monuments: the **Eleanor Cross,** modelled on those set up by Edward I in memory of his Queen, was erected by Sir Tatton Sykes in 1900 while the **Waggoners Memorial**, designed by Sir Mark Sykes, commemorates the 1,000-strong company of men he raised from the Wolds during the First World War. Their knowledge of horses was invaluable in their role as members of the Army Service Corps and the finely-carved monument is made up of panels depicting the Waggoners' varied duties during the war.

The Old Mill Hotel & Restaurant

Mill Lane, Langtoft, Driffield,
East Yorkshire YO25 0BQ
Tel: 01377 267284 Fax: 01377 267383
email: enquiries@the-oldmill.com
website: www.the-oldmill.com

The Old Mill Hotel & Restaurant is a gracious and distinctive premises offering great food, drink and accommodation. Set in grounds surrounded by mature trees, this fine establishment is the place to enjoy a delicious meal, quiet drink and genuine hospitality.

After running a successful hotel in Scarborough for a number of years, John and Josie Perry became owners here in May of 2004. Their enthusiasm and hard work has enhanced this fine hotel's reputation for service and quality.

Open all year round, the hotel boasts nine comfortable and attractive ensuite guest bedrooms, all twins or doubles, available on a bed-and-breakfast basis.

Wold Gold is the locally-brewed ale on tap here, together with a range of other liquid refreshment: lager, cider, stout, wines, spirits and soft drinks.

The restaurant has long been renowned for its excellent food, served at lunch Thursday to Sunday (12 – 2) and every evening between 6 and 9.30 p.m. The à la carte menu, specials board and bar meals offer a full range of delicious choices for every diner. Booking required Thursday to Sunday. Children welcome.

Harpham

4½ miles NE of Great Driffield off the A614

To the south of the village, where the manor once stood, lies **Drummers Well**, which gained its interesting name during the 14th century. Then, the Lord of the Manor, while holding an archery day, accidentally pushed his drummer boy into the well where he subsequently drowned. The boy's mother, the local wise woman, on hearing the news, proclaimed that from then on the sound of drumming from the well would precede the death of any member of the lord's family.

Burton Agnes

6 miles NE of Great Driffield on the A614

The overwhelming attraction in this unspoilt village is the sublime Elizabethan mansion, Burton Agnes Hall, but visitors should not ignore **Burton Agnes Manor House** (English Heritage) that is a rare example of a Norman house: a building of great historical importance but burdened with a grimly functional architecture.

Built between 1598 and 1610, **Burton Agnes Hall** is much more appealing and it is particularly famous for its splendid Jacobean gatehouse, wondrously decorated ceilings and overmantels carved in oak, plaster and alabaster. Still lived in by the descendants of Sir Henry Griffith, who had the hall built, it is also home to a valuable collection of paintings and furniture dating from between the 17th and 19th centuries that includes a portrait of Oliver Cromwell as well as a large collection of Impressionist paintings. The gardens are equally impressive and, along with the yew topiary, there is an old walled garden filled with roses, clematis, herbs and other unusual plants. Open from April to October, other attractions here include a maze, a colours garden with giant board games and a café.

Rudston

8 miles NE of Great Driffield on the B1253

This village takes its name from the giant **Monolith** or 'rood-stone', which stands in the village churchyard. At some 26 feet high it is reputed to be the tallest in Britain and, local legends say that the monolith was a huge gritstone spear thrown by the Devil who was angered when a church was built on what was a sacred pagan site. However, it is far more likely that the giant stone was dragged from Cayton Bay, some 10 miles away, or is a relic from the Ice Age.

Carnaby

9 miles NE of Great Driffield on the A614

As this village lies close to one of East Yorkshire's foremost resorts it seems fitting that Carnaby is home to the **John Bull World of Rock**, where young and old can discover the history and delights of rock, toffee and chocolate making.

There is a tour of the factory with its tantalizing smells, while visitors can personalize their own stick of rock and then visit the shop and café. This popular attraction is open from Easter to October daily and during the week in the winter.

Bridlington

11½ miles NE of Great Driffield on the A165

Situated at the northern tip of the crescent of hills that form the Wolds, Bridlington, with its 10-mile stretch of sandy beach, award-winning promenades and historic harbour, is certainly one of the country's best loved seaside resorts. Here, there is a mixture of traditional entertainment, such as the funfair, amusement arcades and donkey rides and more modern family attractions like **Leisure World**, an indoor waterpark with wave pool, water slides and tropical rain storm. However, the old town, originally known as Burlington, lies a mile inland from the bustling seaside resort and here is **Bridlington Priory**, which was once one of the wealthiest houses in England but it was ruthlessly pillaged during the Reformation. Externally it is somewhat unprepossessing but, inside, the majestic 13th-century nave is unforgettably impressive. A corner of the Priory churchyard recalls one of the most tragic days in the town's history when, during a fearsome gale in January 1871, a whole fleet of ships foundered along the coast. Bridlington's lifeboat was launched but within minutes it was smashed to pieces and most of its crew perished. Twenty bodies were washed ashore and later buried in the priory churchyard: it was estimated that ten times as many souls found only a watery grave. This awesome tragedy is still recalled each year with a solemn service of remembrance when the lifeboat is drawn through the town.

Little remains of the priory today except for Bayle Gate, the gatehouse, which survived Henry VIII's dissolution and still stands proudly in the heart of Bridlington's old town. Today, it is home to the **Bayle Museum**, where the long history of the town and its people is brought vividly to life with the help of evocative old paintings, photographs and artefacts.

Bridlington Beach

It was here, in 1643, that Queen Henrietta Maria landed from a Dutch ship that was laden with arms and aid for her beleaguered husband, Charles I. Parliamentary naval vessels were in hot pursuit and having failed to capture their quarry, bombarded the town. Their cannon balls actually hit the Queen's lodging and Henrietta was forced to take cover in a ditch where, as she reported in a letter to her husband, "*the balls sang merrily over our heads, and a sergeant was killed not 20 paces from me.*" At this point Her Majesty deemed it prudent to retreat to the safety of Boynton Hall, three miles inland and well beyond the range of the Parliamentary cannons.

The seaside resort area of Bridlington was once known as Bridlington Quay and the harbour here is, undoubtedly, the centre of attraction for the town. Pleasure boats steam in and out of the difficult harbour mouth taking visitors to see the splendour of Flamborough Head during the summer while, to the south, are the town's best sandy beaches. To the north the sands give way, after a mile or so, and become pebbly with large numbers of rock pools under the high cliffs.

Situated in a dramatic cliff top position, on the northern outskirts of Bridlington, is **Sewerby Hall**, a monumental mansion that was built between 1714 and 1720. Set in 50 acres of garden and parkland, (where there is also a small zoo), the house was first opened to the public in 1936 by Amy Johnson, the dashing, Yorkshire-born pilot who had captured the public imagination by her daring solo flights to South Africa and Australia. The hall is now home to various collections including some fascinating memorabilia of Amy's pioneering feats along with displays of motor vehicles, archaeological finds and some remarkable paintings amongst which is perhaps the most famous portrait of Queen Henrietta Maria, wife of Charles I. Queen Henrietta loved this romantic image of herself as a young, carefree woman, but during the dark days of the Civil War she felt compelled to sell it to raise funds for the doomed Royalist cause that ended with her husband's execution. After passing through several hands, this haunting portrait of a queen touched by tragedy found its last resting place at Sewerby Hall. The hall is also the home of the **Museum of East Yorkshire**, which features a photographic gallery and a display of regional history along with a varied programme of regional contemporary arts and crafts.

Close by is **Bondville Miniature Village**, one of the finest model villages in the country and where there are more than 1000 hand-made and painted characters, over 200 individual and unique villages, and carefully crafted scenes of everyday life, all set in a beautifully landscaped 1-acre site. The village is naturally popular with children who are fascinated by features such as the steam train crossing the tiny river and passing the harbour with its fishing boats and cruisers.

Bempton

14 miles NE of Great Driffield on the B1229

At 400 feet high, **Bempton Cliffs** (see panel below) mark the northernmost tip of the great belt of chalk that runs diagonally across England from the Isle of Wight to Flamborough Head. The sheer cliffs at Bempton provide an ideal nesting place for huge colonies of fulmars, guillemots, kittiwakes, razorbills, puffins and Britain's largest seabird, the gannet. In Victorian times, a popular holiday sport was to shoot the birds from boats while, above them, crowds gathered to watch gangs of

RSPB's Bempton Cliffs Nature Reserve

RSPB North of England Office, 4 Benton Terrace, Sandyford Road, Newcastle upon Tyne NE2 1QU
Tel: 01912 813366

The chalk cliffs at Bempton form part of England's largest seabird colony between Flamborough Head and Bempton. Over 200,000 seabirds breed on the reserve alone. As well as managing reserves such as this the RSPB also works for the better protection of the marine environment.

For much of the year, the cliffs at Bempton are relatively quiet, but during the breeding season, between April and August, they are crammed with birds. The spectacle, noise, activity and smell all contribute to an overwhelming and memorable experience. As many seabird colonies are on remote islands Bempton offers a rare opportunity to watch breeding seabirds at close quarters.

Both puffins and gannets breed at Bempton. About 2,000 pairs of puffins return to the cliffs to breed. Each pair lays a single egg in a crevice in the rock face. The best time to see the puffins is between May and the end of July when they regularly visit their young with small fish. By August, the young puffins have left the cliffs to spend the winter on the North Sea.

Bempton has the largest mainland gannet colony (gannetry) in Britain. Over 2,500 pairs nest on the cliffs. Gannets can be seen here from January to November, but they are most active between April and August when they are breeding. They will travel up to 60 miles (100 kilometres) from the colony to find food. When fishing, gannets can dive from heights of up to 130 feet (40 metres), entering the water at up to 60 mph (95 kph).

Six other species of seabirds nest at Bempton Cliffs. Kittiwakes are the most numerous, with 45,000 pairs packed onto the cliffs. This member of the gull family can be most easily identified by its 'kittiwaak-kittiwaak' call. Guillemots and razorbills also nest on the narrow cliff ledges. Guillemots are browner than razorbills and have long, dark dagger like bills. Razorbills have broader, flattened bills, with a vertical white line near the tip.

Look out for the distinctive gliding flight of fulmars around the cliffs. They may look like a gull but are members of the petrel family. About 1,200 pairs nest on the ledges. Herring gulls and a few shags also nest on the cliffs.

'climmers' make a hair-raising descent by rope down the cliffs to gather the birds' eggs. The climmers also massacred kittiwakes in their thousands as kittiwake feathers were highly prized as accessories for hats and for stuffing mattresses. The first Bird Protection Act of 1869 was specifically designed to protect the kittiwakes at Bempton: although a ban on collecting eggs here did not come into force until 1954. Bempton Cliffs are now an RSPB bird sanctuary, a refuge during the April to August breeding season for more than 200,000 seabirds making this the largest colony in Britain.

Flamborough Head

15 miles NE of Great Driffield on the B1259

Flamborough Head

Here sea and land are locked in an unremitting battle as the huge waves of the North Sea roll in and slowly but remorselessly wash away the chalk cliffs and the shoreline. Paradoxically, the outcome of this elemental conflict is to produce one of the most picturesque locations on the Yorkshire coast and one that is much visited and much photographed. Victorian travel writers loved Flamborough and not just because of its dramatic scenery but also because of the people who believed in many strange superstitions: no boat would ever set sail on a Sunday, wool could not be wound in lamplight, anyone who mentioned a hare or pig while baiting the fishing lines was inviting doom and no fisherman would leave harbour unless he was wearing a navy-blue jersey, knitted by his wife in a cable, diamond mesh peculiar to the village and one that is still worn today. This fishing connection is renewed here every year, on the second Sunday in October, by a service dedicated to the Harvest of the Sea, when the area's seafarers gather together in a church decorated with crab pots and fishing nets.

Flamborough Head's first, and England's oldest surviving **Lighthouse** was built in 1674 and its beacon was a basket of burning coal. An octagonal chalk tower, it stands on the landward side of the present lighthouse that was constructed in 1806 and originally signalled with four white flashes. Developments over the years have included a fog horn, in 1859, and in more recent years, a signal of radio bleeps. Until it was automated in 1995, Flamborough Head was the last manned lighthouse on the east coast.

Just to the north of Flamborough is **Danes Dyke**, a huge rampart four miles long designed to cut off the headland from hostile invaders. However, its name is deceptive as the Danes had nothing to do with its construction and the dyke was in place long before they arrived. It is probable that sometime during the Iron Age, early Britons excavated this extraordinary defensive ditch and there are signs that it was strengthened and improved in the Dark Ages.

Skipsea

9½ miles SE of Great Driffield on the B1242

This is, perhaps, the best known town on the Holderness plain and, along with being a popular holiday resort, it has a long history that goes back 1,000 years. When William the Conqueror granted Drogo de Bevrere the Lordship of Holderness, Drogo, a Flemish adventurer, decided to build his castle on an island in the shallow lake that was known as Skipsea Mere. Constructed mostly of timber, the castle had not long been completed when Drogo made the foolish mistake of murdering his wife. In the normal course of events, a Norman lord could murder whomever he wished but Drogo's action was foolish because his wife was a niece of William I. Drogo was banished and his lands granted to a succession of other royal relatives, most of whom also came to a sticky end after becoming involved in rebellions and treasonable acts. The castle was finally abandoned in the mid-13th century and all that remains now is the great motte, or mound, on which it was built and the earth ramparts surrounding it.

Atwick

11½ miles SE of Great Driffield on the B1242

Like Hornsea and Skipsea, its two neighbours along the coast, the pretty village of Atwick once had its own mere. Some years ago, excavations in its dried-up bed revealed the fossilised remains of a huge Irish elk and the tusk of an ancient elephant, which provided clear proof of the tropical climate East Yorkshire enjoyed in those far-off days.

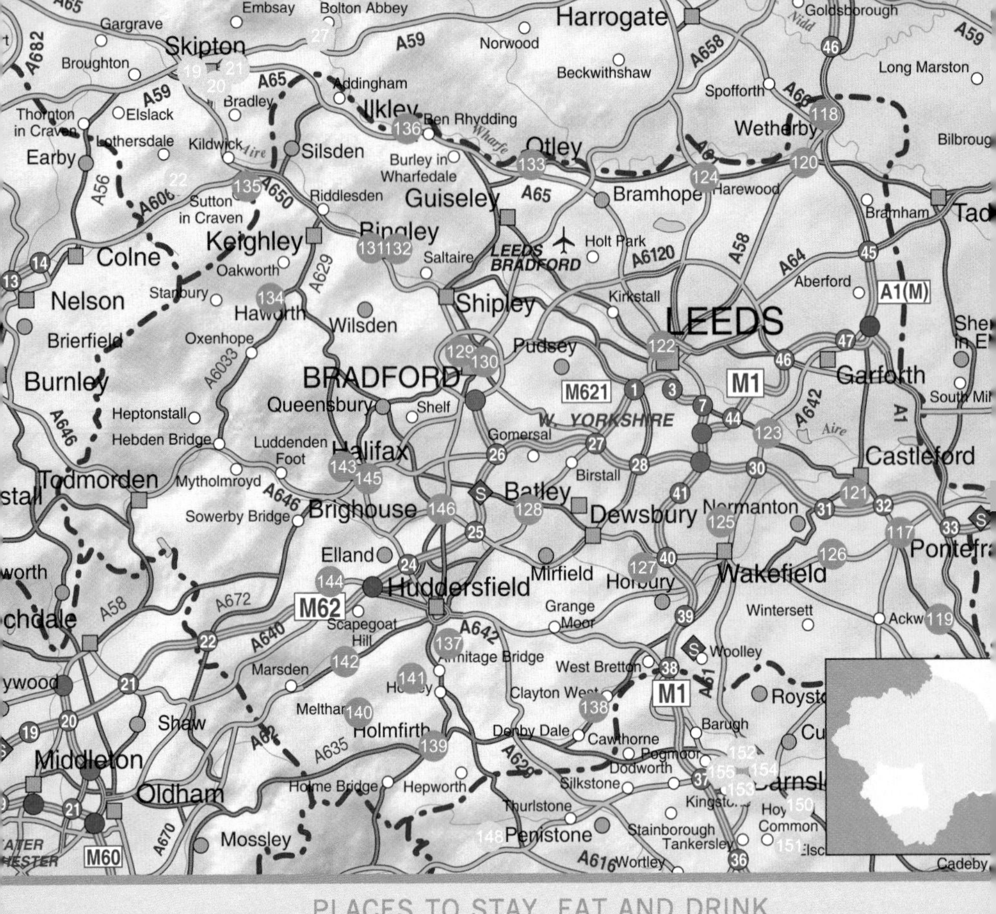

PLACES TO STAY, EAT AND DRINK

Denotes entries in other chapters

6 West Yorkshire

The county of West Yorkshire, while having the scenery of the Pennines, is still dominated by the effects of the Industrial Revolution that turned this region into one of the world's great wool manufacturing areas. The land had been farmed, mainly with sheep, since the Middle Ages and, in order to supplement their wages, the cottagers took to hand loom weaving in a room of their home. However, the advances in technology, beginning in the 18th century, replaced the single man powered

Brontë Falls, Haworth Moor

PLACES TO STAY, EAT AND DRINK

● Denotes entries in other chapters

looms with water powered machinery that was housed in the large mill buildings in the valley bottom and close to the source of power – the fast flowing streams and rivers coming down from the surroundings hills and moors.

Armley Mill, Leeds

During the 19th century there was an explosion of building and the quiet riverside villages grew into towns and the South Pennine textile boom was in full flow. At first the conditions in the mills were grim as, indeed, were the living conditions for the mill workers but, with the reduction in the hours of the working day, people were able to take the opportunity to discover, and in some cases rediscover, the beauty of the surrounding moorland. Not all the villages were completely taken over by the mills and, in many, the old stone-built weavers cottages, with their deep windows to let in light for the worker within, survive.

Although the Yorkshire woollen textile industry is now almost a thing of the past the heritage of those prosperous days can be seen in almost any town or village of the region. The wealthy mill owners built grand villas for themselves and also contributed to the construction of the marvellous array of opulent civic buildings that are such a feature of West Yorkshire towns. Today, however, many of the mills, which have remained redundant for decades are now being put to other use while places such as Bradford, Leeds, Huddersfield and Wakefield are finding new industries to take the place of the old. Naturally, too there is a wealth of interesting museums here that concentrate on the wool industry but there are also others such as the National Museum of Photograph, Film and Television, in Bradford, that look towards the future. Coal mining, too, was a feature of West Yorkshire and the National Coal Mining Museum, near Wakefield, provides visitors with the opportunity to go down a real mine shaft.

However, despite there being several grand stately homes in the area, such as Temple Newsam near Leeds, East Riddlesden Hall near Bradford and Harewood House, the foremost residence that most people make a pilgrimage too in West Yorkshire is The Parsonage at Howarth. It was here that the Brontë family moved to in 1820 and, surrounded by the wild Pennine landscape, the three sisters, Charlotte, Anne and Emily, became inspired by their surroundings and wrote some of the most moving novels in the English language. Now a museum dedicated to the tragic sisters, this fine Georgian house is a starting point for a 40-mile footpath that takes in many of the places that feature in the Brontë novels.

Pontefract

Shakespeare alluded to this town as 'Bloody Pomfret' (the original name of this settlement) in his play *Richard II* and it featured as a place of influence and power that was often visited by kings and their retinues and, indeed, in medieval England, the town was home to one of the greatest fortresses in Yorkshire. On a crag to the east of the town stand the great shattered towers of the once formidable **Pontefract Castle** that was built by Ilbert de Lacy in the 11th century. In medieval times the castle passed to the hands of the House of Lancaster and became a Royal Castle – Richard II was imprisoned here and tragically murdered in its dungeons on the orders of Henry Bolingbroke, who then assumed the crown as Henry IV. The castle was a major Royalist stronghold during the Civil War, after which it was destroyed by Cromwell's troops and, today, it remains as a gaunt ruin with only sections of the inner bailey and the lower part of the keep

surviving intact. There is an underground chamber, which was part of the dungeons, where prisoners carved their names so that they might not be utterly forgotten.

Another ancient site worth visiting is the **Pontefract Hermitage**, a little known monument that comprises two chambers and a well and it is reached by a spiral staircase that has been cut from the solid rockface. The first hermit recorded in the town was Peter of Pomfret who was executed in 1213 by King John for foretelling of his downfall. Many of the streets of Pontefract evoke memories of its medieval past with names such as Micklegate, Beast Fair, Shoe Market, Salter Row and Ropergate. Modern development has masked much of old Pontefract but there are still many old Georgian buildings and winding streets to be discovered. For an insight into the history of this old town, the **Pontefract Museum** has displays covering the ages from the time of the Normans to the present day. The museum is open all year round but is closed on Sundays.

The town's most famous products, of course, are Pontefract Cakes and liquorice root has been grown here since monastic times and there is even a small planting of liquorice in the local park. The town celebrates this unique heritage with the 5-day **Pontefract Liquorice Fayre** in mid-August that includes two days of jousting, archery and battle re-enactments at Pontefract Castle. Although liquorice roots were probably brought into this country by the Romans, 2,000 years ago, local legend suggests that their introduction was down to a schoolmaster. While strolling the beach, the teacher came across a bundle of liquorice branches and, thinking them an ideal weapon with which to administer discipline to his boys, he took the branches home. As the naughty boys were being 'caned' with the liquorice, they also bit into a piece to stifle their cries and so they discovered the plant's flavour and liquorice has been grown in the area ever since. Meanwhile, horseracing enthusiasts will know Pontefract as it has the longest, flat, circular **Racecourse** in Europe.

Around Pontefract

Aberford

10 miles N of Pontefract off the B1217

To the southeast of this village lies **Lotherton Estate and Gardens**, the home of the Gascoigne family, who owned several local coal mines and who created this charming house in the Edwardian era just before the horrors of the First World War. Colonel Gascoigne was an avid collector and the house is filled with furniture, paintings, porcelain and silver and, in particular, there is the Oriental Gallery that has a marvellous display of artefacts dating from the Neolithic period right through to the 19th century. The surrounding parkland is home to a herd of red deer and also a formal Edwardian Garden and a Bird Garden that houses over 200 species including Andean Condors. The estate and gardens are open throughout the year except for January, February and non Bank Holiday Mondays.

Bramham

13 miles N of Pontefract off the A1

Bramham Park, to the southwest of the village, is one of Yorkshire's most exquisite country houses and it has several features that make it particularly special. The house itself dates from the Queen Anne era and was built by Robert Benson, Lord Bingley, between 1698 and 1710, in the superbly proportioned elegant and restrained classical style that is typical of that era. However, the final effect is more French than English as the gardens were modelled on Louis XIV's Versailles, with ornamental canals and ponds, beech groves, statues, long avenues and a superb arboretum with a collection of rare and unusual trees. The interior contains elegant furniture and paintings by artists such as Kneller and Sir Joshua Reynolds while, in the grounds, there are formal gardens, follies and nature trails to explore.

Wetherby

17½ miles N of Pontefract on the A1

Due to its position on the Great North Road, this historic market town has also been a staging post and it lies halfway between London and Edinburgh. A bridge here across the River Wharfe was first mentioned in 1233 and, over the

The Gourmet Licensed Café & Tea Room

9 The Shambles, Wetherby, West Yorkshire LS22 6NE
Tel: 01937 586031

Business partners Alison and Tracy and their splendid staff make a great team at **The Gourmet Licensed Café & Tea Room**, which is located in The Shambles, the most historic part of Wetherby. Spread over two floors behind a striking modern stone frontage and open six days a week plus the occasional Sunday, The Gourmet, a non-smoking establishment, welcomes visitors for anything from a cup of speciality tea or coffee (they grind their own beans) to a full meal. The choice runs from toasts and teacakes to open sandwiches with delicious fillings like prawn and avocado or pork with cider chutney, salads, jacket potatoes, brunch specialities (bacon and scrambled egg on toasted muffin) and daily specials such as cheese and ham quiche or smoked salmon pâté. Afternoon tea with a ham sandwich and fruit scone with strawberry preserve and cream is served all day.

Tracy is in charge of the cooking and baking, while Alison looks after front of house and the office side of the business. They welcome bookings for private parties or functions, and they have a variety of preserves for sale; they also make excellent rich fruit cakes for special celebrations such as weddings or anniversaries.

The Fox & Hounds

Doncaster Road, Thorpe Audlin, Pontefract, West Yorkshire WF8 3EL
Tel: 01977 620082 Fax: 01977 621481

The Fox & Hounds is an impressive and welcoming inn located in Thorpe Audlin, on the A639 south of Pontefract and north of Adwick le Street.

Experienced licensees Geoff and Norma took over at this large and pristine pub in September of 2002. Along with the inn's manager, Paul, who has long experience as a chef, they and their friendly, conscientious staff offer all their guests great food, drink and genuine hospitality.

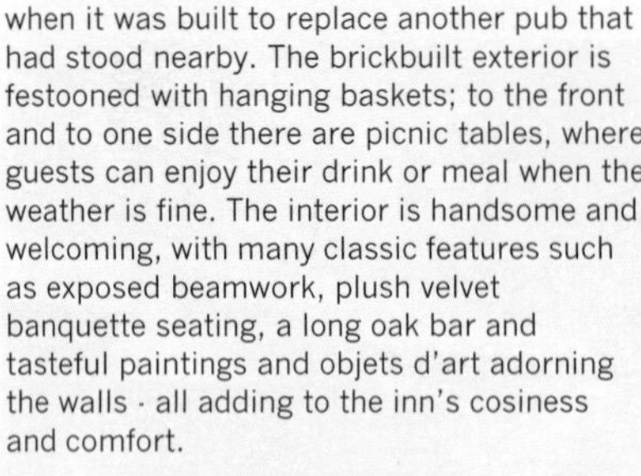

The premises date back to the 1950s, when it was built to replace another pub that had stood nearby. The brickbuilt exterior is festooned with hanging baskets; to the front and to one side there are picnic tables, where guests can enjoy their drink or meal when the weather is fine. The interior is handsome and welcoming, with many classic features such as exposed beamwork, plush velvet banquette seating, a long oak bar and tasteful paintings and objets d'art adorning the walls - all adding to the inn's cosiness and comfort.

Open from midday until 11 p.m. Monday to Saturday, and from midday to 10.30 p.m. on Sundays, the inn is well-stocked with lagers (John Smiths is the popular choice here), cider, stout, a good wine list, spirits and a range of soft drinks.

Quality food is available weekdays from midday until 9 p.m., and on weekends from midday to 10 p.m. Diners choose off the printed menu or the specials board from a selection of expertly prepared dishes such as garlic chicken, Hungarian goulash, mixed grills, rogan josh, surf and turf and ocean delights specials. Weekday lunchtimes there's a Carvery; on Sundays the Carvery is open all day, though guests can still choose dishes from the menu or specials board instead. The tempting puddings are also well worth leaving room for, with tempting morsels such as Knickerbocker Glory or home-made rhubarb crumble.

Eighty per cent of the premises is no-smoking. Children welcome.

The Half Moon

Harewood Road, Collingham, Wetherby, West Yorkshire LS22 5BL
Tel: 01937 572641 Fax: 01937 579578

Standing in the village of Collingham (at the junction of the A58 and A659) near Harewood House, **The Half Moon** is an impressive and gracious inn that has recently been tastefully and lovingly refurbished, in keeping with its early 19th-century origins.

The superior menu offers expertly prepared old favourites given a new twist, such as pork chop with caramelised apple and grain-mustard mash, pan-fried salmon with basil mash and sun-dried tomato pesto, minced lamb, vegetable and herb pie, and penne pasta in a wild mushroom and spring onion sauce. These tempting main courses are matched by equally mouth-watering desserts. There is also a separate children's menu, a range of baguettes filled with meat, seafood or cheeses, and a snack menu available from midday until 10 p.m. every day and featuring spring rolls, samosas, onion rings and other light bites. All dishes using fresh produce, much of it sourced locally and all home-cooked and prepared to order. The real ales here are John Smiths and two guest ales, together with a full complement of lagers, cider, stout, wines, spirits and soft drinks.

years, this has been widened considerably. From the footpath that passes under the bridge, walkers can see evidence of the building work that was undertaken in both the 18th and the 19th centuries.

Ackworth

3 miles S of Pontefract off the A628

The village is home to the famous Ackworth School that was founded by the Quakers in 1779 and that stands opposite a row of early 19th century cottages. Outside the village a Plague Stone can still be seen beside the road where villagers left money in exchange for food that was brought here when Ackworth was cut off during an outbreak of the Plague.

South Elmsal

7 miles S of Pontefract on the B6474

Now a lively market and shopping area, South Elmsal has maintained its mining heritage as it remains the home of the Frickley Colliery Brass Band. Early in the 17th century it was the birthplace of Colonel John Morris who took Pontefract Castle for the Royalists in 1648 and held on to it for 10 months despite almost overwhelming attacks by Cromwell's troops.

Castleford

3 miles NW of Pontefract on the A656

It was here that the Romans crossed the

The Rising Sun

Whitwood Common Lane, Whitwood,
Castleford, West Yorkshire WF10 5PT
Tel: 01977 554766 Fax: 01977 554271
e-mail: rising-sun@btconnect.com
website: www.risingsun-castleford.co.uk

The Rising Sun, one of the most popular inns in the region, is a handsome whitewashed inn that began life as the Miners' Welfare Institute back in 1908, designed by the esteemed architect C F A Voysey and retaining his original stone mullions and leaded glass. Impressively long, with a distinctive tower at one end, and filled with light from the numerous casement windows, this charming inn stands in the village of Whitwood, recorded in the

Domesday Book as Witewood. Great attention has been paid to the decor and furnishings, and it has built up a reputation as one of the best inns in the region for hospitality and fine food. Tasteful, airy and spacious throughout, the inn boasts a restaurant, conservatory and lounge bar and the splendid Palm Court, which stands to the rear. This was formerly the Old Memorial Hall, now impressively and elegantly refurbished and available for morning coffee, afternoon tea, functions and conferences, with seating for up to 100, it also holds a Civil Ceremony license for Weddings.

Food is served at The Rising Sun every day – booking is advised for Saturday evenings and Sunday lunch – and visitors can choose from the printed menu and a daily changing specials board. All the dishes are freshly prepared and home-cooked, and the range of dishes offers something for every palate. The lunchtime menu, served from noon to 4.30, offers hot and cold sandwiches and baguettes, burgers, jacket potatoes and omelettes, and the kitchen really comes into its own with the main menu. Typical dishes on the wide-ranging menu run from the Rising Sun's famous marinated chicken salad with sun-blushed tomatoes, olives, toasted cashew nuts, roasted red onions and buffalo mozzarella to hearty beef stew, pork fillet with a whisky and grain mustard sauce, haddock with mash and a lobster sauce, Thai green vegetable curry, grills, lots of ways with pasta in the Italian corner and classic desserts such as apple pie, cheesecake, jam roly poly or spotted dick. The two real ales served in the bar are Tetleys and Timothy Taylor Landlord, together with a full selection of draught keg bitters, cider, stout, lagers, wines, spirits and soft drinks. Local woman Maureen Madeley has been the licensee here for eight years and with her cheerful, helpful staff she ensures that all their guests have a pleasant time at the inn. The Rising Sun has a function room, a Marquee and a Mediterranean-style patio with garden furniture under parasols and plenty of off-road parking.

River Aire and then built a fort to protect this important crossing but, sadly, little remains of the settlement that they called 'Legioleum' although archaeological finds from that period can be seen in the town's excellent **Castleford Museum Room** at the town Library. Here, not only are these remains exhibited but there are also displays on the lives of ordinary people in Victorian Castleford.

Civic Hall, Leeds

The home of Allison's flour, which is still stone ground on the banks of the river, Castleford was also, in 1898, the birthplace of the internationally renowned sculptor Henry Moore. One of the most influential artists of the 20th century, the town has honoured its famous son with **Moore Square**, a fine area of York stone paving with a series of large stone archways, that stands close to where the family's home once stood – it was demolished in the 1970s.

Leeds

In recent years, the city of Leeds has seen something of a renaissance – its waterfront, neglected and derelict for so long, is now buzzing with new developments and abandoned warehouses have been imaginatively transformed into fashionable bars, restaurants and tourist attractions – and this is taking place less than 15 minutes walk from the shopping centre. Perhaps the most talked about store in Leeds is Harvey Nichols whose Knightsbridge emporium enjoyed a heightened reputation in the 1990s thanks to the BBC series *Absolutely Fabulous*. In parallel with these developments the Aire and Calder Navigation, which is set to celebrate its 300th birthday, is also being transformed to enable leisure traffic to use the waterway as well as freight. Leeds is a major European cultural centre too with its own opera and ballet companies, Northern Ballet Theatre and Opera North, while the West Yorkshire Playhouse, regarded as the 'National Theatre of the North', is a showcase for classic British and European drama as well as work by new Yorkshire writers.

Henry Moore Institute

74 The Headrow, Leeds,
West Yorkshire LS1 3AH
General Enquiries: 0113 246 7467
Library & Archive: 0113 246 9469
Information Line: 0113 234 3158
Fax: 0113 246 1481
e-mail: hmi@henry moore.ac.uk

The Henry Moore Institute in Leeds is a unique resource devoted exclusively to sculpture, with a programme comprising exhibitions, collections and research. The centre was established by the Henry Moore foundation as a partnership with Leeds city council in 1982. In 1993 it moved from Leeds city art gallery to the newly converted Henry Moore institute next door.

Whereas the Henry Moore foundation at Moore's home in Perry Green in Hertfordshire devotes its activities exclusively to the work of Henry Moore himself, in Leeds they are concerned with the subject of sculpture in general; both historic and contemporary, and of any nationality.

Exhibitions, collections and research make important links with each other and help to define the programme. Though some exhibitions may travel from elsewhere, most are generated from within and draw on research activity or collection development. The content of the collections is substantially British and is designed to represent a cross section of material which all, in different ways, represents and documents sculptural activity.

Meanwhile, situated adjacent to the monumental City Hall, the **Leeds City Art Gallery** boasts an exceptional collection of Victorian and Pre-Raphaelite paintings, French Post-Impressionist paintings along with major works by Courbet, Lowry, Sickert, Stanley Spencer and Bridget Riley. Linked to the gallery is the **Henry Moore Institute** (see panel above), the first centre in Europe devoted to the display and study of sculpture of all periods. Housed in an award-winning conversion of a Victorian merchant's townhouse, the institute is also concerned with developing interest, knowledge and appreciation of sculpture. There is also the Craft Centre and Design Gallery where ceramics, jewellery and small pieces of furniture, by both local and national craftspeople, are for sale.

Leeds, like much of West Yorkshire, owes much of its prosperity to wool and, found in what was the largest woollen mill in the world, Armley Mills, is the **Leeds Industrial Museum**. Situated on the banks of the River Aire, visitors can explore the city's rich industrial past through displays and exhibits that include textile and clothing industries, printing, engineering and photography. Meanwhile, at the **Thackray Medical Museum**, one of the largest museums of its kind in Europe, visitors get the chance to look at the development of medicine through the eyes of ordinary people. There are more than 25,000 extraordinary objects in its collection and they range from a surgical chain saw and Prince Albert's medical chest through to a 17th century correction frame. There are several themed exhibitions here, including one that illustrates how surgery was performed in the days before anaesthetics, while another allows visitors to walk into a giant gut and explore the human body with the help of Sherlock Bones.

Royal Armouries Museum

However, one of the city's most fascinating places must be the **Royal Armouries**, which was opened by the Queen in 1998, and that traces the development of arms and armour from the 5th century BC to modern times. The museum utilises interactive computer displays, videos, films, music and poetry to tell the story of arms and armour in battle, self-defence, sport and fashion while, outside, the Tiltyard features jousting and hunting tournaments daily from April to September and a bustling Menagerie Court includes displays of falcons, hunting dogs and horses. This world renowned collection includes the only surviving elephant armour in a public collection and Henry VIII's elaborate tournament armour.

Lovers of real ale may well want to take advantage of a joint ticket that gives admission to both the Royal Armouries and **Tetley's Brewery Wharf**, where visitors can learn how Joshua Tetley founded his great empire and also learn the secret of his famous brew. Costumed actors depict how the English pub has played an important part in British life throughout the centuries and the centre also includes traditional pub games, working Shire horses, a shop and café.

To the southeast of the city centre, between the River Aire and the canal, lies **Thwaite Mills Watermill**, an early 19th century mill, with two giant waterwheels, which once sustained a small, self-sufficient community. Meanwhile, to the southwest of the city is **Temple Newsam House**, a wonderful Tudor-Jacobean mansion that is known as the Hampton Court of the North. Set in 1,200 acres of parkland landscaped by Capability Brown, the house boasts extensive collections of decorative arts displayed in their original room settings,

The Three Horseshoes

16 Leeds Road, Oulton, Leeds LS26 8JU
Tel/Fax: 0113 2822370

On a prominent corner site in a southeastern suburb of Leeds, **The Three Horseshoes** presents a really stunning face to the world. Its yellow-painted façade is almost literally covered in hanging baskets – even the pub 'sign' is a triangle of red wreaths in the shape of horseshoes. This outstanding inn, which is run by leaseholders Geoff and Norma Wilkinson and managers Patrick and Eileen

Boyes, is frequent winner of Leeds in Bloom competitions, and since the Wilkinsons arrived in 1992 has never been lower than second in the spring awards, nor lower than third in the summer awards. In 2003, it was runner-up in the Yorkshire in Bloom awards. The promise of the outside is more than fulfilled within, where the building's 17th century origins are evident: black beams, blackwood furniture, a black-panelled bar counter and a wealth of gleaming copper and brass create a wonderfully traditional atmosphere, and a rugged stone hearth is surmounted by a gnarled black mantle, copper pans, antique firearms and a splendid old Murphy's clock. At least three well-kept cask ales are always on tap, and excellent home-cooked food is served lunchtime and evening and all day on Sunday. The menu offers plenty of choice to suit all tastes and appetites, but many of the regulars return time and time again for the speciality haddock and chips. No bookings are taken, so it's best to arrive early to be sure of a table.

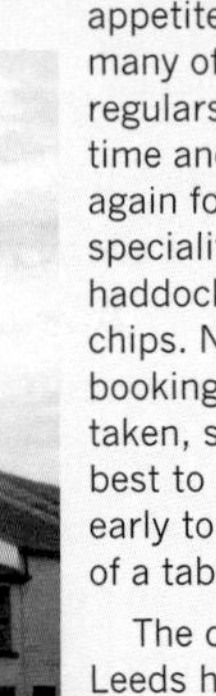

The city of Leeds has been transformed over the last few years, and offers a vast variety of attractions for the visitor, including numerous fine old buildings, museums, galleries, a revitalised waterfront, open spaces and fine shops. All these are within a short walk or drive of the Three Horseshoes, which deserves its own place on the itinerary of anyone visiting the great city.

which feature interior design styles from the 16th to the 20th centuries, and amongst the collections is one of the largest displays of Chippendale furniture in the country. Adjacent to Temple Newsam House is the country's largest approved Rare Breeds Centre – Home Farm. Visitors to this working farm will see pigs, goats, horses and poultry alongside interesting displays of vintage farm machinery and past farming methods.

Around Leeds

Harewood

7½ miles N of Leeds on the A61

One of the grandest stately homes in the country, **Harewood House** (see panel below) was built at a time when many of the most illustrious names in the history of English architecture, interior decoration, furniture making and landscape gardening were all at the peak of their powers. Therefore, in the mid-17th century, when Edwin Lascelles conceived the idea for Harewood, he was able to employ the dazzling talents of Robert Adam for the interiors, John Carr as the architect, Thomas Chippendale as his cabinet maker and Capability Brown, who landscaped the grounds. Edwin's son, Edward, was one of the first to patronise a young artist named JMW Turner and many of Turner's paintings are still here along with hundreds of others by numerous distinguished painters collected by later generations of the family. Many of the finest of them are displayed in a superb

Harewood House

Moor House, Harewood, Leeds,
West Yorkshire LS17 9LQ
Tel: 0113 2181023 Fax: 0113 2181002
e-mail: anita.o@harewood.org
website: www.harewood.org

Designed in 1759 by John Carr, **Harewood House** is the home of the Queen's cousin, the Earl of Harewood. His mother, HRH Princess Mary, Princess Royal lived at Harewood for 35 years and much of her Royal memorabilia is still displayed.

The House, renowned for its stunning architecture and exquisite Adam interiors, contains a rich collection of Chippendale furniture, fine porcelain and outstanding art collections from Italian Renaissance masterpieces and Turner watercolours to contemporary works. The Victorian kitchen, contains "the best collection of noble household copperware in the country" giving visitors a glimpse into an essential area of yesteryear's below-stairs life.

The inspiring Grounds, enfold Gardens which include a restored parterre Terrace, oriental Rock Garden, Walled Garden, lakeside and woodland walks, a Bird Garden and for youngsters, the thrills and excitement of the Adventure Playground!

Throughout the season Harewood hosts a number of special events including open air concerts, theatre performances, craft festivals, car rallies and much more! Harewood House is easily accessible and is just 20 minutes drive from Leeds City Centre or 45 minutes from York.

gallery that extends along the whole west end of the house and is some 76 feet long. Amongst the masterpieces on show are works by Bellini, Titian, Veronese, El Greco and Tintoretto, while family portraits by Reynolds, Hoppner and Gainsborough look down from the silk-covered walls of the opulent drawing rooms. Elsewhere in the house there is a display of Royal memorabilia that belonged to Lord Harewood's mother, HRH Princess Mary, the Princess Royal. Along with superb gardens, charming walks and a Bird Garden that is home to some 120 exotic species, the grounds also feature an Adventure Playground, boat trips on the lake and an extensive events and exhibitions programme throughout the season.

Wakefield

7½ miles SE of Leeds on the A642

One of the oldest towns in Yorkshire, Wakefield stands on a hill guarding an important crossing of the River Calder. Its defensive position has always been important and it was the Battle of Wakefield in 1460, when the Duke of York was defeated, which gave rise to the mocking song *The Grand Old Duke of York*. It is also claimed by many that Robin Hood had his origins in Wakefield and, indeed, in the Court Rolls a 'Robin Hode' is noted as living here in the 14th century with his wife Matilda before fleeing to the woods of Sherwood Forest. Also medieval in origin are the **Wakefield Miracle Plays** that explore Old and New Testament stories in vivid language. The 600-year-old cycle is performed in the cathedral precincts as part of the city's annual Festival.

There are four main streets in the city, Westgate, Northgate, Warrengate and Kirkgate, which still preserve the medieval city plan and one of the most striking buildings that survives from that time is the tiny Chantry Chapel of St Mary, on Wakefield Bridge, which dates from the mid-1300s and is the best of only four such examples of bridge chapels in England. It is believed to have been built by Edward IV to commemorate the brutal murder of his brother Edmund. In medieval times, it was not unusual to build a chapel on a bridge as it was convenient for the priest when ministering to travellers. The stone bridge on which it is built was of great economic importance to the town as it provided a vital river crossing for travellers who had to pay a toll when making the crossing. Grandest of all the city's buildings though is **Wakefield Cathedral** that was begun in Norman times, rebuilt in 1329 and refashioned in 1470 when its magnificent 247 feet high spire – the highest in Yorkshire – was added. The eastern extension to the cathedral is a 20th century addition and it was considered necessary after the church became a cathedral in 1888. Other interesting buildings in the town include the stately Town Hall, the huge County Hall, the recently restored Edwardian Theatre Royal and many fine

Georgian and Regency terraces and squares. A further cultural attraction is the **Wakefield Art Gallery**, housed in an attractive former Victorian vicarage just a short stroll from the town centre. Here, the exhibits include one of the most important collections of modern British Art, with works by Henry Moore and Barbara Hepworth along with works by many other major modern British artists.

Wakefield Museum, located in a 1820s building next to the Town Hall, was originally a music saloon and then a Mechanics' Institute but it now houses collections illustrating the history and archaeology of Wakefield and its people from prehistoric times to the present day. There is also a permanent display of exotic birds and animals that were collected by the noted 19th century traveller, naturalist and eccentric Charles Waterton, who lived at nearby Walton Hall where he created the world's first nature reserve. Meanwhile, the **Steven G. Beaumont Museum** houses an unusual exhibition of medical memorabilia and, in particular, it tells the story of the local lunatic asylum that was founded in 1818 and only closed in 1995. The museum, which has a scale model of the original early 19th century building, is only open on Wednesdays. Lastly, the birthplace of the 19th century novelist George Gissing, is now the Gissing Centre, which displays memorabilia associated with the man and also the literary life of the city. The centre is open on Saturdays from April to October.

Just south of the city centre, lies **Sandal Castle**, a 12th century motte-and-bailey fortress that was later replaced by a stone castle that overlooks the site of the Battle of Wakefield in 1460. Such was this castle's importance that Richard III was planning to make Sandal his permanent northern stronghold when he was killed at Bosworth Field. Today all that remains are ruins as the castle was destroyed by Cromwell's troops after a siege in 1645.

The Junction

Ackworth Road, Featherstone, Wakefield,
West Yorkshire WF7 5AR
Tel: 01977 792217

A large and impressive public house, once known as the Junction Hotel, **The Junction** – as its name tells us – is situated at a crossroads in the village of Featherstone that lead to Pontefract and Ackworth. Once home of Waller's Brewery, where ale was brewed on the premises, this fine inn is run by Fred Lavine, well known in the locality as he spent 33 years as steward, groundsman and kit man for the Featherstone Rugby League Club. Rugby League photos adorn the walls, complementing the handsome wood panelling, deep green paintwork and plush seating.

Open all day every day for ale, Tetleys is the cask ale here, along with a good choice of keg bitters, lagers, cider, stout, wines, spirits and soft drinks.

Great food is served Monday to Friday 12 – 7, Saturday 12 – 3 and Sunday 12 – 4. Guests choose off the printed menu and specials board from a range of delicious dishes such as steak and mushroom pie, roast beef, lamb, pork, vegetarian meals and more.

Children's meals available. This large inn can also play host to business meetings, parties and other functions.

From here there are magnificent views across the Calder Valley and the finds made during recent excavations of the site can be found in Wakefield's museum.

A few miles to the southeast from Wakefield lies **Nostell Priory** (National Trust), one of the most popular tourist venues in this area although the term 'priory' is misleading since the building seen today is, in fact, a large Palladian building erected on the site of an old Augustinian priory. It was in 1733 that the owner, Sir Rowland Winn, commissioned James Paine to build a grand mansion here even though the architect was only 19 years old at the time and this was his first major project. Thirty years later, only half the state rooms were constructed and Sir Rowland's son, also named Rowland, engaged an up and coming young designer to complete the decoration. The young man's name was Robert Adam and between 1766 and 1776 his dazzling designs produced an incomparable sequence of interiors.

There was a third man of genius involved in the story of Nostell Priory, the cabinet maker Thomas Chippendale, and what is believed to be his 'apprentice piece', made around 1735, is on display here – an extraordinary Doll's House complete with the most elaborate detail. Today, Nostell Priory can boast the most comprehensive collection in the world of Chippendale's work. The priory is open from March to October and at weekends during November and December.

Meanwhile, to the southwest of Wakefield, at Caphouse Colliery, in Overton, there is the **National Coal Mining Museum**. Along with guided underground tours led by local miners, visitors can see outdoor machinery, a working steam winder, and pit ponies; for the children there is an adventure playground and nature trails.

Wintersett

12½ miles SE of Leeds off the A638

Found on the historic estate of Walton Hall, once the home of the famous 19th century naturalist Charles Waterton, is the **Heronry and Waterton Countryside Discovery Centre** that provides information and exhibitions on the surrounding country park, which includes two reservoirs and woodland that was once part of the ancient Don Forest. The centre is open daily all year round except Saturdays and Mondays.

Batley

6 miles S of Leeds on the A653

This typical industrial town is home to the **Bagshaw Museum**, which is housed inside a strangely gothic residence in Wilton Park. The museum was founded by the Bagshaw family and much of the collections here were gathered by them on their travels including items brought back from Alaska by Violet Bagshaw in her 100th year! From ancient Egypt to Asia and the Americas, there are all manner of exhibits and they, along with the exotic interior of this Victorian house, make a visit here particularly memorable. Meanwhile, in the park itself there are nature trails and also the **Butterfly Conservation Centre**, which houses a rich assortment of butterflies, many of which are becoming close to extinction in the wild. The centre is open from April to September.

Elsewhere in the town there is the Batley Art Gallery, which plays host to a changing programme of exhibitions that, in particular, feature local artists, while, in the historic Alexandra Mill, there is the **Skopos Motor Museum**. The collection of cars on display here ranges from a Benz Motor Wagon of 1885 to the latest Ferrari F40 and the museum also boasts the only surviving Bramham – chassis number 128. The museum is open from Wednesday to Sunday.

Woolley

12½ miles S of Leeds off the A61

Despite being surrounded by industrial towns, Woolley has managed to retain its rural air and its old hall, now a course and conference centre, stands on land that was originally enclosed as a hunting park in the reign of Henry VII. Just to the northeast lies **Newmillerdam Country Park and Boathouse** that was, in the 19th century, part of the Chevet Estate and a playground for the local Pilkington family. The boathouse, built in the 1820s, has been restored as a visitor centre (open every Sunday and Bank Holiday Monday), while the rest

Heath House

Chancery Road, Ossett,
West Yorkshire WF5 9RZ
Tel/Fax: 01924 260654
Mobile: 07752 172703
e-mail: jo.holland@amserve.net
website: www.heath-house.co.uk

Quality accommodation is on hand at **Heath House**, an impressive guest house built in 1854 by Henry Greaves, a local mill owner, for his bride. It is located a mile and a half from the centre of Dewsbury on the A638.

Owner Jo Holland was born here, and has been providing excellent bed and breakfast accommodation since 1997. It is set in four and a half acres of well-tended grounds, with marvellous views in every direction. There's a real warmth to the house, with many repeat visitors who come back for Jo's unparalleled hospitality.

There are five lovely letting rooms, three of which are on the ground floor; some have ramp access. Each room is individually decorated and furnished; all are ensuite. Prices are static throughout the year and the tariff includes one of the finest breakfasts you'll find. There's a special offer of seven nights for the price of six, breakfast times are flexible, and children are welcome. Pets by arrangement. No smoking.

of the 240-acre country park offers ample opportunity for walking and nature spotting.

Just to the northwest lies **Woolley Edge**, from where there are wonderful views out across Emley Moor and, on a clear day, to Barnsley. The discovery of a flint axe, as well as flints and scrapers from the Iron Age, suggest that there have been settlements here since prehistoric times.

West Bretton

12½ miles S of Leeds on the A637

Set in the beautiful 18th century parkland of Bretton Hall, the **Yorkshire Sculpture Park** has a regularly changing programme of indoor and outdoor exhibitions, while more permanent features include a collection of works in many different styles, from 19th century bronzes by Rodin to contemporary sculptures. A display of monumental bronzes by Henry Moore has been sited within the adjacent 100-acre Bretton Country Park, which was designed in the style of Capability Brown in the 18th century and has a series of self-guided trails.

Birstall

6 miles SW of Leeds on the A643

This town is home to **Oakwell Hall**, an Elizabethan manor house that dates from 1583 and it is, arguably, one of England's most charming historic houses. Now set out as a 17th century home, the panelled rooms contain a fine collection of oak furniture, reproduction soft furnishings and items of domestic life. Meanwhile, the gardens contain period plants, including culinary and medicinal herbs, while the grounds are now Oakwell Hall Country Park. Charlotte Brontë visited the Hall in the 19th century and it appears as 'Fieldhead' in her novel Shirley.

Gomersal

8 miles SW of Leeds on the A643

This ancient village, which featured in the *Domesday Book*, is home to another house that featured in Charlotte Brontë's famous novel, *Shirley*. The **Red House**, which dates back to 1660, was the home of the woollen cloth merchants, the Taylor family, and the author often came here to see her close friend Mary Taylor in the 1830s and the house features as 'Briarmains' in her famous novel. Today, the house is just as the two young ladies would have remembered it as it now portrays, faithfully, middle class domestic life in the early Victorian era. There is an elegant parlour and a stone floored kitchen while, outside, in a restored barn, the Secret's Out Gallery explores the authors connections with the Spen Valley.

Dewsbury

9 miles SW of Leeds on the A62

This ancient town has its roots in the 7th century when, according to legend, St Paulinus baptised converts to Christianity in the River Calder. Now standing on this spot is 12th century **Dewsbury Minster** although the tower is a later addition and it was erected in 1767 to a design by the eminent York architect, John Carr. The interior has some interesting features, amongst them fragments of an Anglo-Saxon cross and coffin lids, but the Minster is perhaps best known for its custom of tolling the 'Devil's Knell' on Christmas Eve to ward off evil spirits with a bell known as Black Tom. Patrick Brontë was curate of Dewsbury between 1809-11, his daughter Charlotte taught at Wealds House School nearby and it was Miss Wooler, the school's headmistress, who later gave

her away when she was married.

Right from the beginning of the Industrial Revolution, Dewsbury became the heart of the West Riding's heavy woollen area and the invention, by a Yorkshire man, of the rag-grinding machine in the 1830s, which enabled woollen cloth to be reprocessed as 'shoddy and mungo', enabled the town to develop as a manufacturer of quality blankets, coats and military uniforms. The steam powered local mills, of which there were many, also used locally mined coal. Although the textile industry has declined and has given way to modern industrial processes, many of the grand Victorian buildings, built on the back of the wealth and pride that the woollen trade brought to Dewsbury remain and these are highlighted by the Town Hall of 1889.

The **Dewsbury Museum** is dedicated

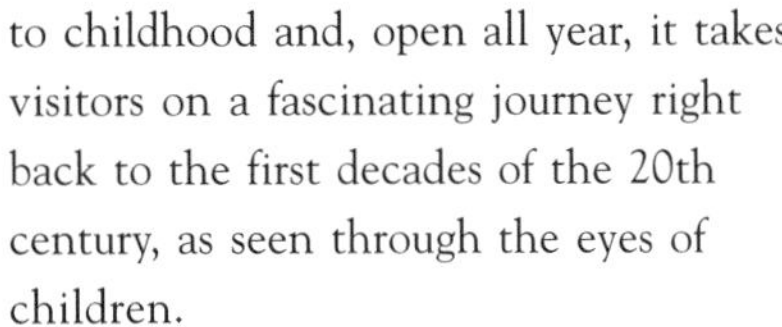

to childhood and, open all year, it takes visitors on a fascinating journey right back to the first decades of the 20th century, as seen through the eyes of children.

Kirkstall

2½ miles NW of Leeds on the A65

One of the most complete ruins in this part of Yorkshire, building work began on **Kirkstall Abbey** in 1152 by the Cistercians and was completed within a generation and it is regarded by many as representing Cistercian architecture at its most monumental. It was executed with the typical early Cistercian austerity, as can be seen in the simplicity of the outer domestic buildings, while the bell tower, a 16th century addition, was in contravention of the rule of the Order that there were to be no stone bell towers as they were considered an unnecessary vanity. Also in this area is the Abbey House Museum where visitors can wander through the re-created streets, shops and workplaces of 19th century Leeds and see how people lived and worked. After viewing the barbers, pawnbrokers, mourning warehouse and other shops, there are several other galleries to explore including one of the history of nearby Kirkstall

Kirkstall Abbey

Abbey. The museum is open all year but closed on Mondays.

Bradford City Hall

Bradford

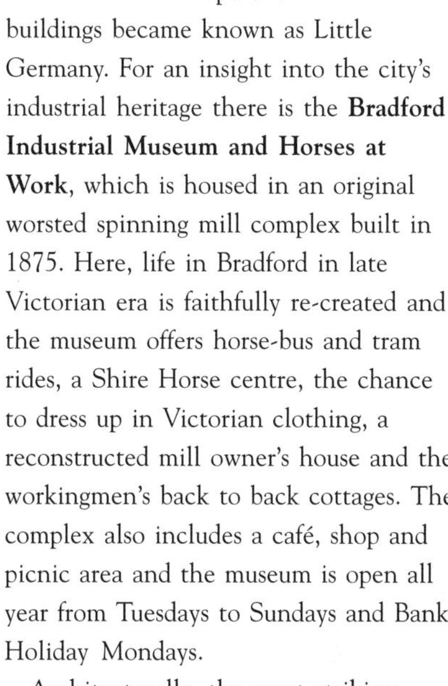

Ever since the 16th century, Bradford has been associated with the wool and textile industries and, in the 19th century, the area where the wealthy wool merchants' settled and erected their opulent buildings became known as Little Germany. For an insight into the city's industrial heritage there is the **Bradford Industrial Museum and Horses at Work**, which is housed in an original worsted spinning mill complex built in 1875. Here, life in Bradford in late Victorian era is faithfully re-created and the museum offers horse-bus and tram rides, a Shire Horse centre, the chance to dress up in Victorian clothing, a reconstructed mill owner's house and the workingmen's back to back cottages. The complex also includes a café, shop and picnic area and the museum is open all year from Tuesdays to Sundays and Bank Holiday Mondays.

Architecturally, the most striking building in Bradford must be **Lister's Mill**, whose huge ornate chimney dominates the city skyline and it is claimed that the chimney is wide enough at the top to drive a horse and cart around. The mill fell silent some years ago though its exterior has been cleared up and there are plans to use it to house a museum to the industry that brought the city its wealth – wool. A rather quirkier sign of the city's former riches is **Undercliffe Cemetery** where the wool barons were buried, each in a more opulent Gothic mausoleum than the last. It is easy to spend an hour here admiring the Victorian funereal art on show with the cityscape laid out below. The fact that the city has a **Cathedral** is an indication of its importance and the first evidence of Christian worship on this site is provided by the remains of a Saxon preaching cross. Today, the cathedral contains many items of interest, including beautiful stained glass windows, some of which were designed by William Morris, carvings and statuary. Bradford was awarded city status in 1897.

However, Bradford does not only look back to its past but also to the future and it is home to the very popular **National Museum of Photography, Film and Television** (see panel on page 248) that houses IMAX, one of the largest

National Museum of Photography, Film and Television

Bradford, West Yorkshire BD1 1NQ
Tel: 01274 202030 Fax: 01274 723155
website: www.nmpft.org.uk

The award-winning **National Museum of Photography, Film and Television** features five floors of highly interactive displays including galleries dedicated to digital technology, news, animation, television, light and photography. Other highlights are a Special Exhibitions Gallery with a regularly changing programme of major shows, Power Pod ride simulator and the spectacular giant screen 2D and 3D IMAX cinema. Recently opened is Insight: Collection and Research Centre where visitors can experience the delights of the museum's collection first hand. Open all year 1000-1800 Tuesday to Sunday and Bank and main school holiday Monday.

cinema screens in the world. This huge, wrap-around screen shows such heart-stopping scenes as roller-coaster rides and Alpine mountaineering and, such is its size, that those watching become completely enthralled in the action. There are five floors to explore and the many displays and exhibitions, many of them interactive, include such themes as virtual reality, news, animation and light. The museum is open from Tuesdays to Sundays and Bank Holiday and school holiday Mondays. Of related interest is the **Colour Museum**, Britain's only museum of colour, where the concept of colour, how it is perceived by both humans and animals and its importance are explored. Visitors have the opportunity to mix coloured lights and experience strange and fascinating colour illusions. Meanwhile, in the Colour and Textiles gallery, the interesting story of dyeing and textile printing, from the early days in Ancient Egypt through to the 21st century, is told. Modern, computerised technology also allows visitors to take charge of a dye making factory and to decorate a room. The museum is open from Tuesdays to Saturdays all year round.

Found in Lister Park, the collections at the **Cartwright Hall Art Gallery** reflect the diverse cultural mix that helps to make Bradford the unique city that it has become in the 21st century. From Victorian paintings and sumptuous Indian silks to the challenges of contemporary art, this gallery is as interesting and far reaching as the city itself.

Bradford, too, has been the birthplace of several notable people including the composer Frederick Delius, the Modernist painter David Hockney (whose work can be seen in Salts Mill, Saltaire) and the writer JB Priestley. Born in Mannheim Road in 1894, Priestley worked as a wool office clerk in the city before joining up to fight in the First World War. It was his novel, *The*

Good Companions, about a troupe of touring actors that was published in 1929, which made his name but he is, perhaps, remembered best for his play, the Yorkshire-based comedy, *When We Are Married*. When Priestley died in 1984, Bradford's City Hall's bell tolled every minute for an hour.

Around Bradford

Shipley

3½ miles N of Bradford on the A6037

Although Shipley is mainly industrial, **Shipley Glen** (see panel below) is a very popular area for tourists and, within the grounds, is a narrow gauge, cable hauled tramway, built in 1895, which carries passengers a quarter of a mile up the side of a steep hill and passes through Walker Wood, which is famous for its bluebells.

Saltaire

4 miles N of Bradford off the A657

This model village was created by Titus Salt for the workers at his mill and he proved to be a very benevolent employer and was determined to provide his workers with everything essential for a decent standard of living. Built between 1851 and 1876, the facilities in the village were designed to cater for all their needs – health, leisure and education – but there were no public houses. The spiritual needs of the work force were attended to by the elegant Congregational church that has been described as the most beautiful Free Church in the north of England. A statue of Titus Salt stands in nearby Robert's Park (where swearing and gambling were banned) above the figures of a llama and an alpaca whose wool he imported for spinning in his mills.

The **Victoria Boat House** was built in 1871 and has been beautifully restored, with an open fire, pianola and wind-up gramophone, all re-creating a traditional parlour atmosphere where visitors can enjoy cream teas and attend special Victorian Evenings in the dress of that time. Also in Saltaire is the **Museum of**

Shipley Glen Cable Tramway

95 Frizinghall Road, Bradford,
West Yorkshire BD9 4LU
Tel: 01274 492026
website: www.glentramway.co.uk

The Tramway, built in 1895, is situated near the World Heritage Site of Saltaire, and runs up the wooded hillside to enable visitors to reach the delights of Shipley Glen. The area is a popular visitor attraction, with pub, café, Children's Fun Fair, Countryside Centre and wooded valley studded with glacial rocks.

The trams trundle up and down the quarter mile long narrow gauge tracks on what is considered to be Britain's oldest working cable tramway. Open every weekend afternoon (Sundays only Nov, Jan & Feb.) plus weekday afternoons May to August inclusive.

Thimble, Bobbin and Shuttle Cottages at Gilstead Bingley

Owners address: March Cote Farm,
Cottingley, Bingley, West Yorkshire
BD16 1UB
Tel: 01274 487433 Fax: 01274 561074
Mobile: 07880 720 194
e-mail: jean.warin@nevisuk.net
website: www.yorkshirenet.co.uk/accgde/marchcote
or www.tuckedup.com/marchcotefarm.htm
Tourist Board Reg: 3/4 Stars

The **Thimble, Bobbin and Shuttle** self-catering cottages are as charming as their names suggest: three comfortable and cosy holiday spots situated in tranquil countryside just 20 minutes from Bradford and 30 minutes from Leeds. Dating back some 200 years, these homes-from-home are decorated and furnished to a high standard. Each has a spacious double bedroom and can accommodate an extra single bed or cot if required, Bobbin has an extra bedroom and bed settee. The kitchens are equipped with every amenity: electric cooker, microwave, fridge freezer, washer/dryer and in some a dishwasher. All boast pretty gardens.

Bed and breakfast accommodation is available at March Cote Farm, a beautiful 17th-century farmhouse set in a spacious mature garden amid 100 acres of a working livestock farm. Here can be found a double room and one family room, all with either ensuite or private facilities.

Owners George and Jean Warin are practiced hosts who ensure that all their guests receive the warmest welcome and excellent hospitality.

Oakwood Hall Hotel

Lady Lane, Bingley,
West Yorkshire BD16 4AW
Tel: 01274 564123/563569
Fax: 01274 561477
website: www.oakwoodhall.co.uk

The very impressive **Oakwood Hall Hotel** began life as the home of a wealthy Victorian wool baron and stands in two acres of grounds on the outskirts of Bingley, overlooking the Aire valley. This magnificent country house hotel is a listed building in the Gothic style and a happy marriage of outstanding original features such as the wealth of polished oak and stone-built fireplaces with every modern comfort and convenience.

Oakwood Hall has 20 ensuite guest bedrooms which combine luxury with comfort and all the modern facilities expected in a hotel of this standing, each is furnished and decorated to the highest standard. Four of the rooms are on the ground floor.

The restaurant is renowned for its superb food at both lunch (Sunday to Friday 12 – 2) and dinner (daily 7 – 10). The excellent menus feature a tempting range of traditional English and international dishes. Booking is advised at all times for this justly popular dining experience. A wide range of wines, spirits and traditional hand pulled beers are served in the comfortable bar, part of which overlooks the secluded landscaped gardens and terraces. Ample car parking is available to the front and side of the hotel.

Victorian Reed Organs that has a collection of more than 45 instruments, including harmonicas and an American organ, which are demonstrated from time to time, and some of which are available for visitors to try. However, this village is not completely locked into the past and the former Salt's Mill has been converted into the **1853 David Hockney Gallery** that displays the world's largest collection of paintings by the internationally acclaimed artist who was born in Bradford in 1937.

Saltaire Mill

Guiseley

6 miles N of Bradford off the A65

This village is home to the most famous fish and chip shop in the world, **Harry Ramsden's**. Harry's career as the world's most successful fish fryer began in Bradford where he was the first to offer a sit-down fish and chip meal. The moved to Guiseley came in 1928 and the original white-painted wooden hut, just 10 feet by 6 feet, in which he started business can still be seen on the site today. The present building holds its place in the *Guinness Book of Records* as the world's busiest fish and chip restaurant, serving nearly one million customers each year.

Guiseley also maintains an ancient ceremony in August that is known as 'Clipping the Church' when the parishioners move in a procession around the parish church to symbolise their love for the building. The word 'clipping' is Old English and means encircling.

Otley

8 miles N of Bradford on the A660

Despite now being part of the Leeds Metropolitan District, Otley has retained its distinctive character and still boasts a busy cobbled market place, with a maypole standing on the site of the old market cross, and many little alleyways and courtyards. Each May the Wharfedale Agricultural Show, founded in 1799 and the oldest show of its kind in England, is held in a nearby field. Even older is Prince Henry's Grammar School, founded in 1602 by James I and named after his eldest son. On the front of the building in Manor Square is a statue of Thomas Chippendale, the great furniture maker who was born in Otley in 1718. In 1754 Chippendale published *The Gentleman and Cabinet-Maker's*

The Spite Inn

Newall-with-Clifton, Otley,
West Yorkshire LS21 2EY

Tel: 01943 463063

The Spite Inn, a superb public house situated a mile outside of Otley towards Blubberhouses, is a spacious and welcoming Yorkshire stone building offering great food, drink and hospitality. Graham and Sue became managers here in 2000, then two years later became the leaseholders. Graham does all the cooking – meals are served Monday to Saturday at lunch (12 – 2), dinner (Tuesday to Thursday 6 – 8, Friday and Saturday 6 – 9) and Sundays from 12 – 5.

Among his specialities are steak and ale pie and fish pie but this is only a tiny sampling of the range of delights on the menu and specials board. Booking is advised Saturday evenings, and on Sundays when the carvery is complemented by the printed menu. Children are welcome and there is a non-smoking area. Meals however can be enjoyed anywhere in the pub or in the attractive beer garden, which commands spectacular views over Lower Wharfedale. Major credit cards welcome.

There are always three to four real ales on tap, together with Tetleys and a full selection of wines, spirits, cider, stout and soft drinks. The pub is open every session Monday to Wednesday, and all day Thursday to Saturday (11 – 11) and Sunday (12 – 10.30). The name? Well, the story goes that there were once two pubs in the village – this one, known as The Roebuck and another, The Travellers Rest – each with its own loyal following. One evening a curious local from The Travellers Rest decided to sample the ale at the Roebuck, but the landlord there, recognising him as an 'outlander', gave him the cold shoulder. Returning to The Travellers, he told the regulars that he'd 'been met by spite and malice'. Over subsequent years the Roebuck became known as The Spite, and the Travellers as The Malice. The latter is now a private house, but The Spite lives on to tell the tale.

Director, which was immensely influential in both Britain and the USA. His own workshop produced a comparatively small number of pieces but he gave his name to a style that dominated a generation and is still highly prized today.

Otley's parish church dates from Saxon times although the main body was constructed in the 11th century. Close by is an unusual memorial, a stone model of **Bramhope Railway Tunnel**, with its impressive crenellated entrance portals. The tunnel was built in the 1830s on the Leeds to Thirsk railway line and more than 30 labourers died during its construction and it is this tragic loss of life that the model commemorates. An attractive feature of the town is the **Chevin Forest Park**, a forested ridge above the town that can be reached by a delightful walk that starts alongside the River Wharfe.

Burley in Wharfedale

8 miles N of Bradford off the A65

Mentioned in the 10th century Saxon Chronicle as 'Burhleg' and in the *Domesday Book* as 'Burghelai', Burley in Wharfedale remained a small riverside settlement until the 1790s when the Industrial Revolution reached the village. Many of the terraces of stone-built cottages, designed for the village's mill workers, have survived and are now highly desirable residences. Burley's population has doubled since the 1920s but the Main Street is still lined with Yorkshire stone cottages and houses and the surrounding hills frame every view.

Thornton

4 miles W of Bradford on the B6145

This village is an essential stopping place on the Brontë trail for it was here that the three sisters were born, at 74 Market Street, which is now open to the public as the **Brontë Birthplace**. Their father was the vicar of Thornton at the time and one of the treasures of his parish church is the font, inscribed with the date 1687, in which Charlotte, Emily and Anne were all baptised. Charlotte was only 4 years old, her two sisters still toddlers, when the family moved a few miles northwest to Haworth after their father had been appointed rector of the parish.

Oxenhope

8½ miles W of Bradford on the A6033

An attractive village, Oxenhope has over 70 listed buildings and these include a Donkey Bridge, two milestones, a mounting block, a cowshed and pigsty! A particular feature of the early farmhouses here are their narrow mullioned windows that gave the maximum light for weaving and some had a door at the first-storey level so that the pieces could be taken out. The first mill here was built in 1792. During the 19th century there were up to 20 mills in Oxenhope producing worsted cloth.

Many scenes for classic 1970s film,

The Railway Children, were set here using local views, local people and the local station on the **Keighley and Worth Valley Railway** that serves the village. A terminus of this famous line, the station also has a train viewing area, a shop and a buffet car.

Haworth

8½ miles NW of Bradford off the A6033

It was this once bleak, moorland town, in its dramatic setting, which fired the romantic imaginations of the Brontë sisters but, today, Haworth has been transformed into a lively, attractive place, with wonderful tea houses, street theatre, and antique and craft shops, and it is very different to how it must have been in the Brontë's days. Then it was a thriving industrial town that was squalid with the smoke from its chimneys and filled with the noise of the clattering looms that were rarely still. It is, however, worth exploring the ginnels and back roads off the steeply rising high street, to get a feeling of what the place was like in the days of the Brontës.

The Parsonage, built in 1777, is the focus of most Brontë pilgrimages and it is now given over to the **Brontë Parsonage Museum** (see panel below) and the Brontë Society have restored the interior to be as close as possible to the house in which the sisters lived with their father and brother. There are exhibitions and displays of contemporary material, personal belongings, letters, and portraits, as well as a priceless collection of manuscripts, first editions and memorabilia in the newer extension. Here, too, visitors can see the

Brontë Parsonage Museum

Haworth, Keighley,
West Yorkshire BD22 8DR
Tel: 01535 642323
website: www.bronte.pig.uk

Charlotte, Emily and Anne Brontë, were the authors of some of the greatest books in the English language. Haworth Parsonage was their much loved home and *Jane Eyre, Wuthering Heights* and *The Tenant of Wildfell Hall* were all written here. Set between the unique village of Haworth and the wild moorland beyond, this homely Georgian house still retains the atmosphere of the Brontës time. The rooms they once used daily are filled with the Brontës furniture, clothes and personal possessions. Here you can marvel at the handwriting in their tiny manuscript books, admire Charlotte's wedding bonnet and imagine meeting Emily's pets from her wonderfully lifelike drawings.

Gain an insight into the place and objects that inspired their work.

world famous 'little books' the sisters wrote in their own minute handwriting that was made to look like printed text and there are also some of their drawings, from cartoons to copies of Thomas Bewick's engravings, on show. The Brontë family moved to this fine Georgian house in 1820 when Patrick Brontë, the sisters' father, became the local parson.

Main Street, Haworth

Taking their inspiration from the surrounding bleak and lonely Haworth Moor, and from the stories they made up as children, the three sisters, Anne, Charlotte, and Emily, under their male pen names, all became published authors while Branwell, their brother, though by all accounts a scholar, sought refuge in the beer at the local inn. Then the tuberculosis that had attacked the family earlier returned and, one by one, Patrick Brontë's surviving children finally succumbed to the terrible disease. The story of the Brontë family is one of tragedy but the circumstances of their deaths were all too common in the 19th century and graphically illustrate the harshness of life just 150 years ago.

Many visitors are drawn to the area by the story of the family and the Brontë Way, a 40 mile linear footpath with a series of four guided walks, links the places that provided inspiration to the sisters. The most exhilarating and popular excursion is that to **Top Withins**, a favourite place of Emily's and the inspiration for the 'Wuthering Heights' of her novel. It is said that the ghost of Emily Brontë has been seen walking, with her head bowed, between the Parsonage and Top Withins Farm. The route also takes into account a great variety of scenery, from the wild moorlands to pastoral countryside. Brontë enthusiasts can also sit in the Black Bull, where Branwell sent himself to an early grave on a mixture of strong Yorkshire ale, opium and despair (although the last two are not available here these days). The Post Office, from where the sisters sent their manuscripts to London publishers, is still as it was, as is the Sunday School at which they all taught. Sadly, the church that they all attended no longer exists, although Charlotte, Emily and Branwell all lie in a vault in the new church, which dates

Top Withens, Haworth Moor

from 1879: their sister Anne is buried in Scarborough.

As well as being a place of pilgrimage for Brontë enthusiasts, Haworth is popular with devotees of steam railways and the town is the headquarters of the Keighley & Worth Valley Railway, a thriving volunteer-run railway that serves six stations most of which are still gas-lit. The railway owns an extensive and varied collection of locomotives and everything combines to re-create the atmosphere of the days of steam. There are daily services during July and August and intermittent services throughout the rest of the year.

Stanbury

10 miles NW of Bradford off the A6033

Close to the village lies **Ponden Mill** that was, in the heyday of Yorkshire's textile industry, one of the largest working mills in the country and, at the height of its production, cloth from Ponden Mill was exported around the world. Though the vast majority of the mills have now closed and the Yorkshire textile industry is almost a thing of the past, Ponden Mill is still open, this time as a retail centre selling all manner of textiles from home furnishings and linens to country clothing. There is also the opportunity here to visit a clog shop where traditional methods of manufacture are still on show.

Oakworth

8½ miles NW of Bradford off the A629

Those visiting Oakworth may find its splendid and authentic Edwardian station, on the Keighley and Worth Valley Railway line, somewhat familiar as it not only featured in the classic children's film, *The Railway Children*, but also in episodes of the television series *Sherlock Holmes*. Further up the line lies Ingrow West station that is home to the **Museum of Rail Travel** and where fascinating collections of historic railway carriages, along with elderly steam locomotives, are on display. The museum concentrates on telling the story of rail travel from the point of view of the ordinary passenger. Further along the line again lies Damems Station – Britain's smallest.

Keighley

8 miles NW of Bradford on the A629

Lying at the junction of the Rivers Worth and Aire, this bustling textile and engineering town, despite its

Keighley and Worth Valley Railway

modern redevelopment, still retains a strangely nostalgic air of the Industrial Revolution of 18th and 19th centuries. It was that era of rapid growth that created the town seen today, beginning at Low Mill in 1780, when cotton spinning on a factory scale was first introduced. Reminders of hardships endured by the many factory workers of that time can be seen in the labyrinth of ginnels and terraces that lie amid the many elaborately decorated mills. There are delightful carvings and, on one early mill chimney, are three heads, one wearing a top hat while, in contrast, there is the classical French-styled **Dalton Mill** in Dalton Lane with its ornate viewing gallery.

The centre of Keighley is dominated by impressive Victorian civic buildings, built on the prosperity the textile industry brought to the town, and a beautifully set out covered shopping precinct, where the statue of legendary local giant, Rombald, stands. The parish church, also in the centre, is famous as the site where Patrick Brontë often officiated at marriages. The graveyard contains 15th century headstones as well as a crude cross, made from four carved heads, which is believed to be Saxon in origin. Above the town, the workers were able to escape from the industrial landscape to walk in Park Woods and it remains a pleasant place today that affords magnificent views of the

town below.

Outside the town centre is **Cliffe Castle** that, despite its deceptive name, is, in fact, a grand late 19th century mansion complete with a tower, battlements and parkland, which once belonged to local mill owners, the Butterfields. It now houses Keighley Museum, which concentrates on the fascinating local topography and geology of Airedale as well as the history of the town. Also housed in the museum is the hand loom, complete with unfinished cloth, that was used by Timmy Feather, the last hand loom weaver in England. Part of the building is still furnished and decorated in the lavish style of the 1880s.

From Keighley southwards runs the line of the Keighley and Worth Valley Railway to Haworth. This restored steam railway line passes through some attractive small villages and some notable stations that include Haworth, the Brontë village. An award-winning visitor attraction, steam trains run every weekend, and daily throughout the summer, and this is a wonderful way to explore this delightful part of West Yorkshire. Not only is Keighley station one of the termini of the line but it also has a turntable, picnic area and a souvenir kiosk.

From the heart of industrial Keighley, there is an interesting 5-mile walk, the **Worth Way**, which leads to the eastern edge of the Worth Valley at Oxenhope. This landscape has changed little since the time when Mrs Gaskell wrote about the area while visiting Charlotte Brontë in 1856.

Riddlesden

8 miles NW of Bradford off the A629

Although parts of **East Riddlesden Hall** (National Trust) date back to Saxon times, the main building was constructed in the 1630s by James Murgatroyd, a wealthy Halifax clothier and merchant. A fine example of a 17th century manor house, the gabled hall is built of dark stone with mullioned windows and it retains its original centre hall, superb period fireplaces, oak panelling and plaster ceilings. Meanwhile, the house is furnished in the Jacobean style, which is complemented by carved likenesses of Charles I and his Queen, Henrietta Maria, and an impressive collection of embroideries, textiles and Yorkshire oak furniture can also be seen within. The hall is said to be haunted by the ghost of a lady dressed in blue who wanders along the building's passageways and it is probably this ghost that sets rocking the child's cradle. East Riddlesden Hall also has one of the largest and most impressive timber framed barns in the north of England that now houses a collection of farm waggons and agricultural equipment. The house stands in glorious grounds, with mature beech trees, which also include lavender, herbs, mixed herbaceous borders and the Orchard Garden, home to old varieties of apple trees. East Riddlesden Hall is open from April to October.

Silsden

11½ miles NW of Bradford on the A6034

This well-contained stone built industrial town, which spreads uphill from the Leeds and Liverpool Canal, owes its development, like so many other towns and villages in the area, to the textile industry. Rows of terraced cottages and houses lie on the steep hillsides and there is newer housing on the outskirts of the town. Silsden was the birthplace of Augustus Spencer, Principal of the Royal College of Art (1900-20), whose memorial can be seen in the 18th century parish church.

Ilkley

9½ miles NW of Bradford on the A65

Originally an Iron Age settlement, Ilkley was eventually occupied by the Romans who built a camp here to protect their crossing of the River Wharfe. They named their settlement 'Olicana' and so gave rise to Ilkley's present name with the addition of the familiar ley that is Anglo-Saxon for pasture. Found behind the Manor House is the site of the Roman fort of **Olicana** although all that remains today is a small portion of the 1st-century fortification. Close to this site is the medieval **All Saints' Church** that was built on the site of a Saxon place of worship. Though the doorway dates from the 13th century and the tower from the 15th century, the most interesting feature here must be the 17th century box pew and the medieval font that is made from local stone. Meanwhile, now housed in the town's museum are the altars, carved in gritstone, which are dedicated to the Roman gods.

The spring at **White Wells** began to bring more visitors to the town in the 18th century and, in 1765, Squire

Middleton built walls around this moorland spring so that patients could both bathe in and drink the pure cold water. The roof was added at a later date and one bath is still open for the public to view. It was the early Victorian era that saw the development of the hydros, hydropathic treatment hotels, which provided hot and cold treatments based on the ideas of Dr Preissnitz of Austria who, in 1843, became the director of Britain's first Hydro at nearby Ben Rhydding. The coming of the railways from Leeds and Bradford in the 1860s and 70s, during a period of growth in the Yorkshire woollen industry, saw the town take on a new rôle as a fashionable commuter town. Wool manufacturers and their better-paid employees came to Ilkley not only to enjoy the superb amenities but to build handsome villas.

If it was in Bradford and Leeds that people made their brass, so it was said at the time, then it was usually at Ilkley that it was spent. Even today, Ilkley sports some remarkable and opulent Victorian architecture as proof of this and Ilkley's patrons and well-to-do citizens gave the town a splendid Town Hall, Library, Winter Gardens and King's Hall and this sense of elegance is still present along The Grove. It is a delight to have morning coffee in the famous Betty's Coffee House and discerning shoppers will find a wealth of choice, some in a perfectly preserved Victorian arcade complete with beautiful potted palms and balconies.

Between the remains of the Roman fort and the River Wharfe, lie the **Riverside Gardens**, a favourite place for a stroll that might lead over a 17th century packhorse bridge across the river. On the side of this bridge, beside the stone steps, the flood levels of the river have been marked, along with the dates. On the opposite side of the River Wharfe is **The Lido**, one of the few surviving outdoor swimming pools in Yorkshire. Its idyllic surroundings and extensive terraces make it a popular place in summer while, next to the Lido, is an indoor pool that is open all year round. From the Lido, a footpath leads up to Middleton Woods that, in May, are a sea of bluebells.

Housed in a building that dates from the 15th, 16th and 17th centuries, which is complete with mullioned windows, carved beams and an interesting wall privy, is the **Manor House Art Gallery and Museum**. The museum, on the ground floor, tells the history of Ilkley from its prehistoric routes through to its development as a Victorian spa town while, upstairs, the art gallery hosts a programme of temporary exhibitions throughout the year.

Addingham

12 miles NW of Bradford off the A65

Although Addingham dates back to Saxon times, it was named after a Saxon chieftain, Adda, the village enjoyed its greatest prosperity in the 18th century when no fewer than five water mills lined the banks of the Wharfe. Four of them were textile mills and no longer operate, but the fifth, a timber mill, is still working.

Ben Rhydding

9½ miles NW of Bradford off the A65

The original Ben Rhydding Hydropathic Hotel, opened in 1844 by a consortium of Leeds businessmen, was built in the Scottish baronial style that was so popular at the time. However, by 1908 interest in hydropathy had declined and the exuberant building became the Ben Rhydding Golf Hotel. Later it was turned into flats but finally demolished in 1955.

Although the name suggests some Scottish connection – and the surrounding scenery certainly has a Caledonian grandeur – Ben Rhydding is actually derived from nearby Bean Rhydding, or bean clearing.

Huddersfield

This town's earliest roots can be found on the 1,000-feet-high **Castle Hill** that has been occupied as a defence since the Stone Age and simple tools, flints, bone needles, combs and pottery dating back to 2000 BC have been unearthed here. The much later ramparts of an Iron Age fort, built here around 600 BC, can also still be seen although this fort was destroyed by a mysterious fire just 200 years after it was built. In 1147 the Normans repaired the earthworks and built a motte-and-bailey castle here, which gave the hill its name, which was apparently used as a base for hunting. The hill was also used as a beacon when England was threatened by the Spanish Armada, and again during the Napoleonic wars. The lofty **Jubilee Tower**, built in 1897 to celebrate Queen Victoria's Diamond Jubilee, is the most recent structure on the summit and it was funded by public subscription.

However, the Huddersfield of today dates, in essence, from the 18th and 19th centuries when the town developed rapidly, with the help of the then lords of the manor, the Ramsden family, as a woollen town and its worsted cloth was exported all over the world. This booming textile industry has left a wealth of grand Victorian buildings that include the stately railway station, which was designed by James Pigott of York and was built between 1846-50, and the Italianate Town Hall. The town's **Tolson Memorial Museum** paints a vivid and intriguing picture of Huddersfield and its people from prehistoric times through to the present day. One of the most popular exhibits is the collection of vintage vehicles and motoring memorabilia in the 'Going Places' collection while other displays trace the story of the Industrial Revolution, which was so important to the growth of the town, and the political protests it engendered. There is also a programme of special exhibitions and the museum is open daily all year round. Meanwhile, the **Huddersfield Art Gallery**, which holds the Kirklees

Collection of British Art covering the last 150 years, has a lively programme of exhibitions that showcases contemporary art from regional, national and international artists.

The town is also home to two canals that helped to link Huddersfield not only with the national canal network but also with other industrial towns. Completed in 1780 and paid for by the Ramsden family, the **Huddersfield Broad Canal** was constructed to link the town with the Calder and Hebble Navigation. The canal's Aspley Basin was, in the heyday of the waterway, a busy area of docks and warehouses and, today, it is home to a marina while the warehouses have been converted into offices and flats. Later, in 1794, work on the **Huddersfield Narrow Canal**, which links the town with Ashton-under-Lyne, began and its centrepiece, the Standedge Tunnel, took 17 years to complete. The longest, highest and deepest canal tunnel in the country, it, along with the rest of the canal, was abandoned but has now reopened with its own visitor centre. The **Standedge Visitor Centre**, at **Marsden**, houses an exciting and interactive exhibition telling the story of the canal and the tunnel's construction and, from here, visitors can travel through the famous tunnel. Originally opened in 1811, the tunnel, one of the great feats of canal engineering, was designed by Thomas Telford and is regarded as one of the Seven Wonders of the British Canal

The Barn House & Cruck Cottage

Ashes Common Farm, Ashes Lane,
Almondbury, Huddersfield,
West Yorkshire HD4 6TE
Tel: 01484 426507 Fax: 01484 426507
e-mail: enquiries@ashescommonfarm.co.uk
website: www.ashescommonfarm.co.uk

Ashes Farm Cottages offer top-of-the-range self-catering accommodation in quiet countryside surrounded by fields, with magnificent panoramic views. The outstanding **Barn House** is a classic early 17th-century pillar-and-aisle barn converted into beautiful holiday accommodation for six to eight people. The original pillars and roof timbers are exposed, and branch out above the living room, furnished with great taste and style with supremely comfortable sofas and chairs and Persian rugs over the polished wood floor. Stairs lead to the galleried sitting area, and up to one of the three double bedrooms.

Cruck Cottage, which sleeps four, dates back to the early 17th century. Exposed beams and timbers again add to the charm of the place, which has three bedrooms. Both properties feature fully-equipped kitchens including washing machine and dryer, and are available all year round, for weekly or longer stays. Children welcome. Pets by arrangement. For a truly relaxing break in splendid comfort amid magnificent surroundings, look no further.

Network. Meanwhile, the countryside surrounding the centre offers a wide range of activities, including walking, cycling and fishing, and this area of outstanding natural beauty is also a haven for wildlife.

Around Huddersfield

Clayton West

8 miles SE of Huddersfield on the A636

A popular attraction at Clayton West is the **Kirklees Light Railway**, a 15" gauge steam railway that runs along the old Lancashire and Yorkshire Clayton West branch line and through gently rolling farmland for about four miles with a quarter-mile long tunnel adding to the thrill. The large station and combined visitor centre at Clayton West provides passengers with comfortable, spacious surroundings in which to await for their train or take advantage of the light refreshment café and the souvenir shop. The railway operates daily during the season and every weekend throughout the year. There is also a programme of events and theme days that take place throughout the year.

Denby Dale

7½ miles SE of Huddersfield on the A636

This village has found fame as the 'Pie Village' as, over the years, it has become known for its production of gigantic meat pies. The first of these huge dishes was baked in 1788 to celebrate George III's return to sanity while later ones have been made to mark such important national events as the victory of Waterloo and Queen Victoria's Jubilee. Meanwhile, in 1928, a vast pie meal was organised to raise funds for the Huddersfield Royal Infirmary but the festivities were almost cancelled when the organisers discovered that a large part of the pie had gone bad and four barrowloads of stinking meat were secretly spirited away. Perhaps, because of that mishap, no more great pies were attempted until 1964 when it was decided to commemorate the four royal births of that year and, on this occasion, two walls of Hector Buckley's barn, in which the pie had been baked, had to be demolished to get it out. The most recent pie was made to celebrate the new millennium and it weighed in at 12 tonnes!

Armitage Bridge

2½ miles S of Huddersfield off the A616

This village is home to the **North Light Gallery** that concentrates on hosting major exhibitions of the very best in 20th century and contemporary art while, throughout the year, the North Light Studio holds classes and a programme of weekend workshops.

Honley

3½ miles S of Huddersfield off the A616

The centre of this delightful little Pennine village has been designated as a site of historic interest and, here, there are charming terraces of weavers' cottages and interesting alleyways while, in the churchyard of St Mary's, the old village stocks can still be seen. The Coach and Horses Inn has strong connections with the Luddite movement of the early 1800s and it was here, in 1812, that two Luddites, Benjamin Walker and Thomas Smith, spent the night drinking after murdering a mill owner at nearby Marsden. They were later arrested, convicted and executed at York. Not far from the inn is another interesting feature – an old well dated 1796 – whose date stone warns passers-by they will be fined 10 shillings for 'defouling' the water.

Holmfirth

6 miles S of Huddersfield on the A6024

As with many towns and villages in the West Riding of Yorkshire, Holmfirth's development came with the Industrial Revolution and the advent of the textile industry. The proximity to the moorland sheep and the convenience of the town's fast flowing streams and river saw, first weavers' cottages and then more and more impressive mills built here and, today, local firms still supply materials to some of the top names in the fashion industry. As a result, this is a town with numerous narrow alleyways, or 'ginnels' that climb steeply up from the valley bottom to weavers' hamlets with their cottages easily recognisable by their long mullioned windows that let in as much natural light as possible.

However, today, Holmfirth is familiar to television viewers around the world as it is the location for the long running BBC comedy *Last of the Summer Wine.* Visitors to this little Pennine town can enjoy an authentic bacon buttie in the real Sid's Café, gaze at Nora Batty's cottage and sit in the famous pub. Here, too, is the **Last of the Summer Wine Exhibition** that covers the nearly 30 years of this, the longest running television comedy series, through photographs, memorabilia and a display of some of the unusual inventions devised by the characters. The exhibition is open daily and is found in what was formerly, during filming, Compo's house.

Another popular attraction in the town is the **Bamfords Postcard Collection** that displays a comprehensive exhibition of the traditional saucy seaside postcards and the patriotic First World War postcards produced by Bamfords of Holmfirth in the first half of the 20th century. The company also produced hymn sheets and, rather surprisingly, many early silent movies.

As with so many of these Pennine villages, the moorland waters that were so vital for the textile industry also caused tragedy when they burst their banks and, at Holmfirth, there have

The Crossroads Inn

Penistone Road, New Mill, Holmfirth, West Yorkshire HD9 7JL
Tel: 01484 683567
e-mail: thecrossroadsinn@aol.com

Located just a short drive out of New Mill towards Denby Dale on the A635, a few miles from Holmfirth, **The Crossroads Inn** is a superb place enjoying a very scenic location. A former coaching inn that dates back to the late 1700s, this fine inn was once known as The Toss a Coin (the premises having been won on the toss of a coin).

Elegant inside and out, original features include the low-beamed ceilings and exposed brickwork. Open all day every day for ale, there are three real ales on offer: Marstons Pedigree, Riding Bitter and a changing guest ale.

Delicious food is served weekdays at lunch (12 – 2.30) and dinner (5.30 – 9.30), and weekends from midday until 9.30 p.m. inclusive. The no-smoking restaurant seats 74. A sample of the daily specials includes fresh fish dishes, spring lamb and fajitas, while the bar menu offers a range of sandwiches, potato wedges, burgers and more.

To the rear of this excellent inn there are extensive gardens overlooking lovely countryside. The gardens includes a large climbing frame and other diversions for children.

Durker Roods Hotel

Bishopsway, Meltham, nr Huddersfield,
West Yorkshire HD9 4JA
Tel: 01484 851413 Fax: 01484 851843
e-mail: spencer@durkerroodshotel.co.uk
web: www.durkerroodshotel.co.uk

'West Yorkshire's Warmest Welcome' is the promise made by Matthew and Spencer King, resident proprietors of the **Durker Roods Hotel**. An impressive mansion built in 1870 by a local businessman as his private residence, it was converted into a hotel in 1975 and has been very much part of local life ever since. It quickly established a fine reputation for hospitality, and the owning Kings Inn Company have totally transformed the hotel with major refurbishment of the bedrooms, restaurant, bar and banqueting suite. The 30 bedrooms are all very warm and comfortable, with en suite facilities, television and hospitality trays; they include singles, doubles, twins and family rooms, and a sumptuous, romantic bridal suite. Guests with mobility difficulties are catered for in ground-floor rooms, and there are access ramps and toilets for the disabled.

The hotel's bar, originally the music room, is a popular meeting place, and in the elegant non-smoking dining area visitors can look forward to a splendid meal expertly prepared from the finest and freshest ingredients sourced locally as far as possible. The choice is excellent, including all-time favourites such as lasagne, roasts and turkey curry; salads and omelettes; fish dishes – scampi, haddock, plaice, salmon supreme on a bed of dill mash with a lemon butter sauce; classic grills; and specialities like pork loin joint with all the trimmings, steak & mushroom pie and savoury pancakes with delicious fillings such as spinach and ricotta or mixed seafood. There's a separate menu of senior citizens lunchtime and early evening specials, and a bar menu for lighter meals. Booking is recommended at the weekend. The banqueting suite, named after Sir David Brown of Aston Martin fame who had his family home here, is an elegant setting for weddings, private parties and other special occasions; it has seats for up to 120, an integral bar and a dance floor.

Durker Roods Hotel is located just off the B6108 in the former mill town of Meltham, about five miles southwest of Huddersfield.

been three major floods. The worst occurred in 1852 when the nearby Bilbury Reservoir burst its banks, destroying mills, cottages and farms, and killing 81 people. A pillar near the church records the height the waters reached. Holmfirth has a lovely Georgian church, built in 1777-8 in neo-classical style to the designs of Joseph Jagger. The gable faces the street and the tower is constructed at the eastern end against a steep hillside.

Hepworth

7 miles S of Huddersfield on the A616

What does one make of a village that lies on the River Jordan, has a house that has always been known as Solomon's Temple (although no-one knows why) and a parcel of land called Paradise, the only place, it is said, where fruit trees will grow. There are some other curious names here including Meal Hill, where the Romans brought their hand-mill stones to grind corn, and **Barracks Fold**, the area where, during the Plague, the healthy barricaded themselves against the infected. There are still some triangular patches of land in the village that are believed to contain the common graves of the Plague victims.

Holmbridge

6½ miles SW of Huddersfield on the A6024

This charming village stands at the head of a steep-sided valley and enjoys picturesque views of the Pennines and the Holme valley. There are cottages here dating from the 1700s and the area is known for its unusual style of architecture: four-decker cottages dug into the hillside – the lower cottage is approached from the front, the upper cottage is reached by a steep flight of stone steps leading round the back.

One of the highlights of the village year is the **Sunday School Feast** when, with the Hinchcliffe Mill Brass Band leading the way, the Sunday school children, teachers, relatives, friends and members of the congregation proceed around the village, stopping at certain places to sing a few verses of the chosen feast hymns on their way to Dam Head. Here they hold a United Sing and a short open-air service. Everyone then repairs to the parish hall for tea, a feature of which is the School Cake, a fruity and spicy bread cake.

Meltham

6½ miles SW of Huddersfield on the B6107

A typical Pennine mill town, Meltham is mostly Victorian but it also has a handsome Georgian parish church dating from 1786 that is challenged in size by the spacious Baptist Chapel that was rebuilt in 1864. Only two textile mills have survived here but the Meltham Mills Band, founded in 1845, is still thriving and has won many competitions throughout the country, including the British Championships. Some customs of the past have also managed to survive: on Collap Monday

The Kings Arms

23/25 Midway, South Crosland,
Huddersfield, West Yorkshire HD4 7DA
Tel: 01484 661669 Fax: 01484 660427

The Kings Arms is a superb inn that is renowned for its cuisine. Set in the picturesque village of South Crosland, found a few miles from Meltham or east off the A62, the inn boasts a classic interior décor and furnishings – tasteful, comfortable and always welcoming.

Open all day Tuesday to Sunday and from 4 p.m. on Mondays, real ales here are Black Sheep and Tetleys, together with a good selection of lagers, wines, stout, cider, spirits and soft drinks.

Delicious meals are served at lunch (Tuesday to Friday and Sunday) and dinner (Tuesday to Saturday), with a changing seasonal menu of everything from hearty sandwiches and light bites to tempting dishes making use of the freshest seafood, pork, lamb, chicken, beef and vegetables, such as seared king scallops, rump of lamb Provençale, pave of halibut with dried herbs, slow-roasted pork cutlet with spring greens, and mozzarella and herb rice cake with young broad beans and poached egg.

The restaurant boasts superb views of the Yorkshire Moors, while the snug area overlooks Castle Hill and the surrounding valley.

(the day before Shrove Tuesday), the town's shopkeepers distribute free sweets to children; there is carol singing on Christmas Eve in the centre of the village; and, on Whit Monday, the different congregations of churches and chapels join in the Whitsuntide Walk around the town accompanied by the brass band.

Marsden

7 miles SW of Huddersfield on the A62

Situated at the head of the Colne valley, this village is an historic Trans-Pennine crossing point with the Standedge rail and canal tunnels and a packhorse route that leads out of the valley. It also has strong links with the Luddites who were opposed to the changes, particularly in mechanisation, that the Industrial Revolution brought. Situated above the village is the **Marsden Moor Estate** (National Trust), a tract of nearly 6,000 acres of Pennine moorland that is full of industrial architecture. Public footpaths criss-cross this land that, as well as providing grazing for sheep, is home to numerous moorland birds including golden plover, grouse, curlew, snipe and twite. Meanwhile, the moorland's deep peat provides a habitat for acid-loving plants and animals that can survive in this bleak and exposed environment.

Cookhouse Café

17 Station Road, Slaithwaite, Huddersfield, West Yorkshire HD7 5AW
Tel: 01484 842269

Delicious food is on the menu every day at the excellent **Cookhouse Café**, a charming and welcoming place with a simple Shaker-style décor, filled with light. Open Monday to Friday 7.30 a.m. – 3 p.m., Saturday 7.30 – 1.30 and Sunday 9.30 – 1, specialities here include the mouth-watering breakfasts, a wide selection of hot and cold sandwiches and expertly prepared main courses. On Sundays, traditional roasts are added to the menu. Chef and owner Michelle Powell enjoys a growing reputation among locals and visitors alike for the high standard of her cooking and hospitality.

Scapegoat Hill

3½ miles W of Huddersfield off the A640

About a mile south of the oddly-named Scapegoat Hill is the **Colne Valley Museum** that is housed in three 19th century weavers' cottages near to the parish church. Visitors can see a loom chamber with working hand looms and a Spinning Jenny; a weavers' living room of 1850 and a gas-lit clogger's shop of 1910. On two weekends a year, a craft weekend is held when many different skills and other traditional activities are demonstrated. Light refreshments are available and there is also a museum shop. Run entirely by its members, the museum has featured many times on television and is open at weekends and Bank Holidays throughout the year.

Sowerby Bridge

6½ miles NW of Huddersfield on the A6026

An important crossing of both the Rivers Ryburn and Calder in medieval times, and possibly as far back as the Roman occupation, Sowerby Bridge first had water powered mills as early as the 14th century. The mills, first used for grinding corn, moved into textile production and, by the 1850s, they were all steam driven and so a phenomenal 500 years of water powered textile production here ceased. Many of the mills have taken their own place in the history of the industry and, in particular, **Greenups Mill**, built in 1792, was the first integrated woollen mill in Yorkshire and here all the textile processes were brought under one roof. Alongside stood Longbottoms Mill, of 1770, which was a domestic 'factory' and used only manual power while, close by, was the steam driven Carlton Mill of 1850. Together, these three mills, all powered by a different source, formed a complex that was unique and two of them can still be seen today.

As the mills developed so, too, did the transport system and one of the first turnpike roads in Britain was built through Sowerby Bridge in 1735. Just a short time later the Calder and Hebble Navigation, surveyed by John Smeaton, the designer of the Eddystone Lighthouse, was opened in 1770 and the Rochdale Canal, of 1804, followed soon afterwards. A reminder of the busy days of the canal is the **Tuel Lane Lock and Tunnel** that joined the two man-made waterways and, reopened in 1996, it is a terrific sight to see the narrowboats going through what is the deepest lock in the country. Meanwhile, the **Wharf**, one of the country's greatest canal trans-shipping centres between the two canals, is still home to several interesting buildings including Calder House, built in 1779 for the first manager of the navigation and Salt Warehouse, of 1796.

However, one reminder of the town's pre Industrial past is **County Bridge**, an important river crossing in the 14th century, when the construction was made of wood, but this was followed by the present stone bridge in 1517. Added to over the centuries, most notably in 1632 and 1875, it was here that a watch was kept during both the Black Plague and the Civil War.

Halifax

6 miles NW of Huddersfield on the A629

Halifax boasts one of Yorkshire's most impressive examples of municipal architecture and one of Europe's finest and most complete 18th century buildings, the glorious **Piece Hall**. It possesses a large quadrangle, where regular markets are held on Fridays and Saturdays, which is surrounded by

Shears Inn

1 Paris Gates, Boys Lane, Halifax HX3 9EZ
Tel: 01422 362936
Fax: 01422 352936

Owners Kathryn and Dean are the welcoming hosts at **Shears Inn**, a real hidden gem that has been described as Halifax's Best Kept Secret. Long famous for its unique character, the inn has recently been given a top-to-toe refurbishment, with more furniture, more displays and many more pictures of old Halifax on the walls; a charming paved outside area with garden furniture and parasols is an added attraction. Open all day, every day, Shears is a great place for lovers of real ale – there's always an excellent choice of quality cask ales that typically includes Best, Golden Best, Landlord and Ram Tam from the Keighley brewer Timothy Taylor, Black Sheep from Masham and Copper Dragon 1816 brewed in nearby Skipton.

Food is served every lunchtime and Monday to Friday evenings, and because of its popularity it's always a good idea to book. The choice runs from hot and cold

sandwiches and filled king-size Yorkshire puddings to fish specials, grills and vegetarian options, and traditional roasts add to the choice on Sunday. Tucked away among some of the city's fine old heritage mill buildings, Shears Inn is a treasure that once found has for many become a lifelong friend.

Piece Hall, Halifax

the stocks for three days with the stolen goods on their back and then executed by guillotine. However, in 1650, the threat of an uprising, following the conviction of two men for stealing a pair of horses and some cloth, put an end to this drastic form of justice.

classically styled colonnades and balconies behind which are some 40 specialist shops. On Thursdays a flea market is held here and there is a lively and varied programme of events for all the family throughout the season. There's also an art gallery with a varied programme of contemporary exhibitions and workshops, a museum and tea room. The Town Hall, designed by Sir Charles Barry, architect of the Houses of Parliament, is another notable building, while there is the attractive Borough Market, constructed in cast iron and glass with an ornate central clock. In Gibbet Street stands a grisly reminder of the past, a replica of a guillotine, whose original blade is kept in the **Piece Hall Museum**. From the mid-14th century onwards, Halifax became notorious for its harsh treatment of petty criminals and anyone who stole goods worth more than a few pence (in today's money 13p), were imprisoned for a week, put in

Halifax also boasts the largest parish church in England that dates from the 12th and 13th centuries and is of almost cathedral like proportions. It has a lovely wooden ceiling, constructed in 1635, and visitors should look out for Old Tristram, a life-sized wooden effigy of a beggar, reputedly based on a local character, which served as the church poor box and still does.

Right next door to Piece Hall, lies the **Calderdale Industrial Museum** that houses still-working looms and mill machinery and holds hand textile demonstrations. From the Great Wheel to the Spinning Jenny, from mining to moquette, from steam engines to toffee, the museum provides a riveting insight into Halifax's industrial heritage. Also, amongst the many displays is one celebrating the town's greatest contribution to modern travel – the cats-eye! Meanwhile, situated next to

The Duke of York

Stainland Road, Stainland, Halifax,
West Yorkshire HX4 9EH
Tel: 01422 370217

The Duke of York is an outstanding inn set in the village of Stainland, reached east off the A58 and west of Huddersfield. Licensees James and Maria have been here since 2003, bringing their enthusiasm and warm hospitality to making this venture a great success. The food, drink and hospitality are all second to none.

Formerly three cottages dating back to the mid-18th century, in the early 19th the cottages were converted to create a large and impressive public house. The interior boasts a striking and comfortable décor and furnishings, with a mix of traditional and modern elements including the stone-built bar, exposed brickwork and walls painted a deep red. The dining area has polished wood floors, stylish seating and floor-to-ceiling windows looking out over the small and attractive beer garden and rolling countryside beyond.

Closed Mondays until 5 p.m. (except Bank Holidays), the inn is open every session Tuesday to Thursday and all day Friday to Sunday. Four real ales, all from the Thwaites Brewery range, are served alongside a good range of lagers, cider, stout, wines, spirits and soft drinks.

Food is available Tuesday to Saturday 12 – 2 and 6 – 9, Sundays 12 – 9, with a range of dishes to tempt every palate, including home-made pies, Cajun chicken, giant haddock and more. Maria does all the cooking, and she is an accomplished chef. Booking is recommended Friday to Sunday. The lunchtime 'lite bite' menu (available Tuesday to Friday) features hearty favourites such as gammon with egg and chips, haddock, scampi or liver and sausage casserole with mash. Monday evening's tea-time special (served 5 – 7 p.m.) offer a three-course menu with a choice of three starters, main courses and puddings. All dishes are created using the freshest ingredients.

Halifax railway station, **Eureka!** is Britain's first, and only, interactive museum designed especially for children between 3 and 12 years of age and, throughout, there are exhibits that can not only be seen but touched, listened to and smelt. With more than 400 larger-than-life exhibits and exciting activities available, Eureka! opens up a fascinating world of hands-on exploration. A team of 'Enablers' help children make the most of their visit and there are regular temporary exhibitions. The museum is open all year round and there is also a shop and a café.

View over Halifax

Now a vibrant complex of businesses, galleries, theatre, café and design and book shops, **Dean Clough** is housed in a magnificent Victorian carpet mill that is a reminder of Halifax's textile heritage. Built between 1840 and 1870 by the Crossley family, this mill was once home to one of the world's leading carpet factories but, in 1982, it ceased production.

On the eastern outskirts of the town lies **Shibden Hall and Park** (see panel below), the home of the Lister family for

Shibden Hall

Lister's Road, Halifax,
West Yorkshire HX3 6XG

For over 300 years this was the Lister's family home, but **Shibden Hall** itself is even older, built in 1420. Generations have lived and worked here and today the hall reflects this continual development. The rooms, ranging from the 17th century to the 20th century, are set out as if someone has just slipped out for a moment. There is the 17th century barn with its display of carriages and the Folk Museum that shows how craftsmen worked in the 19th century. Open from March to November, 1100-1700 Monday to Saturday, 1200 to 1700 Sunday. December to February, 1100-1600 Monday to Saturday, 1200 to 1600 Sunday.

over 300 years, although the hall predates them and was built in around 1420. A distinctive timber framed house, which has been carefully furnished to reflect the various periods of its history, the hall gives the impression that the family living here will return at any moment. The 17th century barn behind the hall is now a Folk Museum and here, with no electricity, craftsmen work in wood and iron.

Also on the outskirts of the town is the **Bankfield Museum**, the home, between 1837 and 1886, of Edward Akroyd, the largest wool manufacturer in Britain. He lavished money and attention on the building, transforming it from a modest town house into a magnificent Italianate mansion with elaborate ceilings, staircases and plasterwork. After his death, his sumptuous home became a museum and now houses an internationally important collection of textiles and costumes from around the world. Contemporary crafts are also featured and the museum hosts an interesting programme of temporary exhibitions, workshops, seminars, master classes and gallery demonstrations. Here, too, is a Toy Gallery, the **Duke of Wellington's Regimental Museum** and the Marble Gallery that sells contemporary crafts. Surrounding his house, Akroyd built a model village, called Akroydon, that, with its terraced houses, allotments, park and church, was the first 'urban' village. The museum is

Apricot Square

21 Bethel Street, Brighouse,
West Yorkshire HD6 1JR
Tel:01484 712006

Home-baking and home-cooking are the order of the day at the marvellous **Apricot Square**, set in the heart of Brighouse. Beverley, Cath and Vicky have created a warm and welcoming place with polished wood floors and modern seating and décor, an upstairs dining area (also available for functions) and a charming outdoor courtyard area.

There are several different menus offering up a range of delicious hot and cold snacks and meals including favourites such as home-baked scones and cakes, a choice of freshly-cooked and prepared breakfasts, sandwiches, salads, hot puddings, ice-creams, jacket potatoes and main meals that include a very good selection of vegetarian dishes. There's a special coffee menu and a variety of freshly-squeezed juices and other beverages. Children are made most welcome – there are toys and crayons available for their enjoyment.

Open: Monday to Saturday 8 a.m. – 4 p.m.

open all year from Tuesday to Sunday and on Bank Holiday Mondays.

Mytholmroyd

10 miles NW of Huddersfield on the A646

Prior to the 1600s, the valley bottom in what is now Mytholmroyd, was marshy and of little use as foundations for a village, though some of the outlying farms in the area date from the late 14th century. However, with the need to build more mills close to a supply of water, the land was improved and Mytholmroyd joined the age of the Industrial Revolution.

Each spring the town plays host to the **World Dock Pudding Championships**. Dock Pudding is unique to this corner of the county and is made from the weed *Polygonum Bistorta* or sweet dock (which should never be confused with the larger docks that are commonly used for easing nettle stings). In spring, the plant grows profusely and local people pick it by the bagful. The docks are then mixed with young nettles, and other essential ingredients, then cooked to produce a green and slimy delicacy the appearance of which is found by many to be rather off-putting. It is usually served with bacon after having been fried in bacon fat and is believed to cure acne and cleanse the blood.

Hebden Bridge

12 miles NW of Huddersfield on the A646

Originally a river crossing over the Calder for packhorses laden with cloth, salt and food, the stone bridge seen today dates from 1510 and this beautiful area was once known as 'Hep Dene' meaning Rose Valley. Today the town has lost none of its beauty as it nestles amongst the Pennine hillsides, and it is, therefore, hard to believe that this was one of the first purpose-built industrial towns in the world and Hebden Bridge grew rapidly as the demand for textiles boomed. Over the years, the town has seen many changes of fortune and, today, though textiles have now gone, it is a place of bookshops, antique shops, restaurants, and a market.

Found in St George's Square, in the heart of the town, is the historic **Hebden Bridge Mill** that, for almost 700 years, has been powered by the fast-flowing waters of the River Hebden. For over four centuries this was a manorial corn mill before it was converted into a textile mill that was finally abandoned in the 1950s. Now lovingly restored, the mill is home to various stylish shops, restaurants and craft workshops.

The **Rochdale Canal**, which flows through the town, was completed in 1798 and it was constructed to link the Calder and Hebble Navigation with the Bridgwater and Ashton canals from Lancashire. Used by commercial traffic until 1939, the canal has been repaired and sections of it, including that between Hebden Bridge and Todmorden, are now open to traffic though, now, it consists mainly of pleasure craft. Horse drawn or motor boat cruises are available from the marina.

To the northwest of Hebden Bridge lies the **Land Farm Sculpture Garden and Gallery**, a delightful woodland garden created over some 30 years from a barren Pennine hillside that faces north and lies some 1,000 feet above sea level. Attached to the house is an art gallery and both are open at weekends and Bank Holidays from May to the end of August.

Heptonstall

12½ miles NW of Huddersfield off the A646

This charming hilltop village, which was once home to many hand loom weavers, is one of the main tourist centres in Calderdale and it overlooks Hebden Bridge and **Hardcastle Crags** (National Trust), a popular beauty spot. A beautiful wooded valley, from the crags there are several interesting walks along the purpose built footpaths. Heptonstall is also one of only three places in Britain where two churches occupy the same churchyard. In this case, the original church, which dates from 1256, was struck by lightning in the 1830s and a new church was built next to the ruin. Every year, on Good Friday, the Paceggers Play takes place in Weavers Square. An ancient method of storytelling, the actors, dressed in elaborate costumes, tell the legend of St George.

Todmorden

14 miles NW of Huddersfield on the A646

This is another, typical mill town that grew with the expansion of the textile industry but, before the 19th century, Todmorden had been a spartan place with many of the villagers eking out frugal lives by hand loom weaving. Following the building of the first mill here Todmorden began to grow and the highly ornate and flamboyant public buildings were, in the main, built by the mill owners.

Firstly producing wool or worsted cloth, the mills soon turned to cotton spinning and weaving and the proximity to Manchester, both a source of raw material and a market place for the finished product, was an important factor in the change of direction. In 1798, the Rochdale Canal reached Todmorden and along this stretch, from Manchester to Sowerby Bridge, across the Pennines, the canal has some 92 locks, one of the most unusual of which is the Guillotine Lock.

Though many towns that owe their existence to industry also bear the scars, Todmorden has retained all its charm and character and is an excellent place to visit for those interested in architecture. It boasts a magnificent **Town Hall**, designed by John Gibson and opened in 1875, which is one of the finest municipal buildings of its size in the country. As the grand old building once stood half in Yorkshire and half in Lancashire, the ornate carving in the pediment represents the farming and iron trades of Yorkshire in the right panel and the cotton trade of Lancashire in the left.

However, some buildings here do predate the Industrial Revolution and, in particular, there is **Todmorden Hall**, which dates back to 1293. Occupied by the Radcliffe family, who built up the estate around it, in the early 17th century, the old timber-framed building was replaced by one built of stone and, inside, it has some wonderful panelling and a grand heraldic fireplace. Housed in an early 19th century listed building, the **Todmorden Toy and Model Museum** is ideal for all the family who will enjoy this nostalgic journey back to childhood. Open from Wednesday to Sunday, the museum also buys and sells toys and models.

PLACES TO STAY, EAT AND DRINK

The Old Vicarage Restaurant, Ridgeway Village, South Yorkshire	147	Restaurant	p282
The Stanhope, Dunford Bridge, South Yorkshire	148	Restaurant	p284
The Arundel, Ecclesfield, South Yorkshire	149	Pub and Restaurant	p285
The Drop Inn, Low Valley, South Yorkshire	150	Pub, Restaurant and Accommodation	p286
The Crown Inn, Elsecar, South Yorkshire	151	Pub with Food	p287
The Cooper Gallery, Barnsley, South Yorkshire	152	Art Gallery	p288
The Full House & Sangdao's Thai Restaurant, Monk Bretton, South Yorkshire	153	Pub and Restaurant	p288
Cannon Hall Museum, Cawthorne, South Yorkshire	154	Museum	p291
Cannon Hall Open Farm, Cawthorne, South Yorkshire	155	Visitor Attraction	p292
Doncaster Museum & Art Gallery, Doncaster, South Yorkshire	156	Museum	p293
Cusworth Hall (Museum of South Yorkshire Life), Doncaster, South Yorkshire	157	Museum	p294
The Duke of Leeds, Wales, South Yorkshire	158	Pub and Restaurant	p296
The Plough Inn, Wath-upon-Dearne, South Yorkshire	159	Pub with Food	p299

● Denotes entries in other chapters

7 South Yorkshire

South Yorkshire is a region of great antiquity and, in many places, the industries with which the county is associated go hand in hand with more agrarian pursuits such as farming and agriculture. Principally a coal-mining area, iron-founding and -smelting have also taken place here for centuries. The main centre here is Sheffield, which rightly claims to be England's greenest city; in addition to its own wealth of parks and green space, the wild open spaces of the Pennine moorlands of the Peak District National Park roll right up to its western boundaries.

Sheffield Cathedral

Sheffield's prosperity is founded on steel and, in particular, cutlery. Though there are few ancient buildings to explore in England's fourth-largest city there are many museums and galleries on offer to the visitor. To the north of Sheffield is Barnsley, the county town of South Yorkshire, whose prosperity comes from the rich seams of coal that have been exploited in the local area. Meanwhile, to the east lies Rotherham, where iron ore has been mined and smelted since the 12th century. While its wealth is certainly based upon the metal, Rotherham is also the home of Rockingham pottery that was once favoured by royalty.

Further east again is the charming riverside town of Doncaster, which was established by the Romans and certainly today has the air of a pleasant market town. However, this was once one of the country's most important centres of steam locomotive manufacture and it is famous for having created the *Mallard*, which still holds the record for the top speed attained by a steam train. Today, though, Doncaster is best known as the home of the St Leger, Britain's oldest classic horse race.

Elsewhere in the county visitors can discover the delights of Roche Abbey, a 12th century Cistercian house, Conisbrough Castle, which boasts the oldest stone keep in England, and the faded Victorian grandeur of Brodsworth Hall.

Sheffield Town Hall

Sheffield

The city takes its name from the River Sheaf, which is one of two rivers (the other being the Don) running through it. England's fourth-largest city, Sheffield is best known for its manufacture of stainless steel and cutlery though, today, many people will associate it with the successful film, *The Full Monty*, which was made in and around the city. However, despite its heavy industry, its location, beside the River Don, in the foothills of the Pennines, and surrounded by a landscape of valleys and woods, ensures that there is attractive countryside right on the city's doorstep. Sheffield is also the fastest-growing city in Yorkshire, having outstripped Leeds for this title within the last two years. Extensive city planning and regeneration work has helped this vibrant city go from strength to strength.

Sheffield's story is, of course, the story of steel. As early as the 17th century Sheffield was gaining a reputation for its knives and tools and, later that century, it began to make its own steel. During the Industrial Revolution, these industries expanded rapidly and, thanks to Benjamin Huntsman's invention, in 1742, the industry was transformed and, by the mid-19th century, Sheffield was producing 90 per cent of the country's steel. Harry Brearley's accidental discovery of stainless steel in 1913 saw the industry develop further and, today, though the workforces required in the industry are reduced, the output of steel, cutlery, surgical instruments and cutting edges has never been higher.

Despite its relatively long history, Sheffield has few ancient buildings and its only remaining medieval building is the **Cathedral of St Peter and St Paul**, whose notable architectural features include the chancel roofs and, in the Chapter House, there are stained glass windows that depict the city's history. Facing the cathedral is the **Cutlers'**

Hall, built in 1832, an imposing building that houses the Cutlers' Company's wonderful collection of silverware and cutlery. There are guided tours of the hall and the collection and, amongst the unusual artefacts on display is an ornate silver galleon and a huge penknife with almost 100 blades.

For an insight into Sheffield's industrial past there is the **City Museum**, which houses the city's collection of cutlery as well as displays of archaeological finds, decorative arts and both natural and social history. The museum, found in Weston park, is open Tuesday to Sunday and Bank Holiday Mondays all year round. Also in Weston Park is the **Mappin Art Gallery**, a leading centre for contemporary arts, which hosts a major programme of exhibitions while also displaying the city's collection of traditional paintings that includes superb portraits, landscapes and still life. However, it is the **Millennium Galleries** that have helped to establish the city as a cultural force in the north of England. A remarkable building of white columns and striking glass arches, it holds four unique galleries that not only showcase Sheffield's impressive metalware collection but also provide space to show the city's wonderful collection of paintings, drawings and natural history exhibits.

Sheffield, too, has several interesting museums and the premier one is the **Kelham Island Museum**, a living museum that tells the story of Sheffield. Visitors can see the mighty River Don Engine, the most powerful working steam engine in Europe, in steam; reconstructed workshops; the 'Little Mesters' working cutler; and craftspeople demonstrating traditional 'Made in Sheffield' skills. For children up to 9 years old, The Melting Shop provides an interactive experience where they can 'clock on' to become a piece of steel – including being rolled and hammered! The museum is open daily all year except Fridays and Saturdays.

Meanwhile, the **Traditional Heritage Museum**, offers a unique collection of displays on life and work in the city between the 1850s and the 1950s while, at the University, the **Turner Museum of Glass** contains over 300 items of contemporary and art glass from Europe and the United States along with

Mappin Art Gallery

THE OLD VICARAGE RESTAURANT

Ridgeway Village, Sheffield,
South Yorkshire S12 3XW
Tel: 0114 247 5814 Fax: 0114 247 7079
e-mail: eat@theoldvicarage.co.uk
website: www.theoldvicarage.co.uk

The Old Vicarage Restaurant is an historic and elegant place that is justly famed for its superb food. Although situated half a mile into Derbyshire, this excellent restaurant, which stands in two acres of grounds, is Sheffield's 'jewel in the crown' for fine dining. Ridgeway once formed the barrier between Mercia and Cumbria, and nearby High Lane once divided the areas run by the respective Sheriffs of Nottingham and Yorkshire. Building on the vicarage began in 1841 and was completed in 1846. The grounds are well tended and include many rare trees and plants from all over the world, including a very impressive cedar of Lebanon.

Owner Tessa Bramley created this wonderful restaurant as executive chef some 18 years ago, and was joined by co-chef Nathan Smith in 1994. Year by year the restaurant's reputation has grown with national awards being earned regularly, culminating in the honour of a Michelin star in 1999 - an award which has been retained ever since. Open Tuesday to Friday for lunch and Tuesday to Saturday for dinner, booking is required for Friday and Saturday. Open other times for parties by arrangement. Tessa has designed the menus, and in her spare time writes superb cookery books. The menus are seasonal and offer, as might be expected from a restaurant that has won kudos far and wide for its outstanding food, a range of the best of British cooking using the freshest ingredients. Many of the dishes Tessa learned from her grandmother, and include hearty and traditional meals that are

expertly prepared and presented. Baked fillet of wild Whitby sea bass and caramelised baby fennel with lavender roasted Jersey Royals and a balsamic reduction, Thyme roasted local english partridge with forcemeat, mulberry and crab apple jelly and winter greens with toasted almonds tossed in almond oil, or Gooseberry and elderflower sorbet in a basket of chocolate croquant with gooseberry fool and a selection of some of Yorkshire and Derbyshire's finest farmhouse cheese make up just a sampling of the fabulous cuisine served.

Elegance is the byword here, with the classic décor and furnishings adding to the refined and intimate ambience and to guests' enjoyment of the wonderful food.

a unique collection of over 100 drinking glasses. Housed in an original Georgian factory, built around a central courtyard, the Butcher Works, which is now occupied by small businesses, is regularly used as a film location and the **Cultural Industries Quarter** is home to many of South Yorkshire's finest skilled artists and craftspeople.

Although there are few ancient buildings remaining in Sheffield, the city's most picturesque museum is undoubtedly the **Bishop's House Museum** that dates from around 1500 and is the earliest timber-framed house still standing here. Many original features survive and the Bedchamber and Great Parlour are furnished in the style of the home of a prosperous 17th century yeoman. There are also displays on Sheffield in Tudor and Stuart times, and changing exhibitions on local history themes. A museum of a very different nature is the **Sheffield Bus Museum**, housed in the Tinsley Tram sheds on Sheffield Road. The collection includes many types of bus and other transport-related exhibits such as destination blinds, old timetables and models. The museum also houses the Tinsley Model Railway layout. Finally, the city's large Victorian Fire and Police Station is now home to the **Fire Police Museum** where not only is there a comprehensive display of fire appliances and equipment from the 18th century to the present day but it also houses an exhibition on the police force complete with some of their vehicles. The museum is open on Sundays and Bank Holiday Mondays.

However, Sheffield is not all hustle and bustle, buildings and industry and here, too, can be found numerous parks including its largest, Graves Park, that was given to the city by Alderman Graves before the Second World War. Perhaps, though, the city's most peaceful place must be the **Sheffield Botanical Gardens** where the collections of shrubs and trees are set within a historic landscape that was first opened in 1836. The gardens are open daily all year round until dusk. Even in the heart of the city the brand new Winter Gardens provide an oasis of greenery even in the depths of the coldest months of the year. It stands alongside the impressive Millennium Galleries.

Sheffield is also a popular place for students, with two first-class institutions – the University of Sheffield and Sheffield Hallam University – attracting students from around the country and all over the world. Many choose to stay on at graduation, leading to the creation of tens of thousands of new flats and living spaces and the regeneration of large swathes of the city.

The Showroom is the home of independent and alternative cinema, with an impressive programme of film showings, forums and guest speakers on the world of cinema.

The city's nightlife centres around West Street, but even here an oasis of calm can be found at Spa 1877. Housed in one of Sheffield's major Victorian landmark buildings - the former Glossop Road Baths – the spa recaptures the traditional Turkish Bath experience.

Abbeydale Road South has become a mecca for diners, with rows of distinguished eateries covering many nations of the globe. Within a short walk visitors can find restaurants specialising in the cuisines of Japan, the Mediterranean, Spain, Mexico and more.

Around Sheffield

Wentworth

7 miles N of Sheffield of the B6090

This historic village is home to the palatial 18th century mansion, **Wentworth Woodhouse**, which boasts the longest frontage in England, some 600 feet long. Although the house is not open to the public this wonderful façade can be seen from the surrounding deer park through which there are lovely walks that include a follies trail. The follies and monuments date from the 1700s and the most curious of these is the Needle's Eye that consists of a tower with a stone urn on top and it is pierced by a carriageway. Legend says it was built in response to a wager by the Marquis of Rockingham, owner of Wentworth Woodhouse, that he could drive through the eye of a needle. Another bizarre monument is the Hoober Stand, the most prominent of the follies, which stands at 518 feet above sea level and is a triangular tower some 100 feet high. There are fine views from the tower's viewing gallery that can be reached by climbing the 155 steps inside. One monument that is open to the public is the Wentworth Mausoleum that was built in 1788 in memory of the 2nd Marquis.

Tankersley

7½ miles N of Sheffield of the A6195

This parish is mentioned in the *Domesday Book* and the hall here was used in the now classic film of the 1970s, *Kes*. During the War of the Roses, between the houses of York and Lancaster, Tankersley Park was the site of a battle while, later, it again saw conflict during the Civil War when the Royalists gained victory over the troops of Cromwell. In the 14th century church of St Peter there are cannon balls and a bullet that were found after the latter conflict.

The Drop Inn

19 Providence Street, Low Valley, Wombwell, Barnsley, South Yorkshire S73 8AN
Tel: 01226 751092

Found off the main A635 between Darfield and the centre of Wombwell, **The Drop Inn** is a convivial and welcoming inn dating back to the late 19th century, when it began life as the Bricklayers Arms. With over 20 years' experience, leaseholders Anne and Mark arrived in 2004 and have brought their enthusiasm and expertise to bear on making this inn a success.

The excellent restaurant seats 100, and serves delicious food Monday to Saturday 12 – 2 and 5 – 8, Sundays 12 – 4. The menu offers hearty favourites such as hot sandwiches, giant Yorkshire puddings filled with beef, chilli con carne, chicken and mushroom, steak and kidney and other fillings, freshly made sandwiches and more. Booking is advised at all times.

There's a full range of draught keg ales together with lagers, cider, stout, wines, spirits and soft drinks.

The chalet-style accommodation adjacent to the inn features two bedrooms and bath per chalet. The tariff includes a hearty breakfast, and the rooms are available all year round. Children welcome.

Elsecar

8½ miles NE of Sheffield off the B6097

This is an excellent example of an early industrial village whose economy was based on coal mining and iron working that were developed by the Earls Fitzwilliam of Wentworth Woodhouse. Along with one of the area's prettiest small parks and its attractive stone cottages built for the miners and foundry workers, there is a reservoir here that is popular with both fishermen and bird watchers. The village is also home to **Elsecar Heritage Centre**, an imaginative science and history centre that is fun and educational for all the family. Housed in these restored workshops, which were once owned by the Earls Fitzwilliam, visitors can discover hands-on science in the Power House where the amount of energy it takes to hoover a carpet or mow the lawn is calculated. At Ches, a working metalsmith uses traditional techniques to fashion numerous tools and utensils while, at Coddswallop, the National Bottle Museum, there are all manner of bottles, pot lids, Wade and Doulton pottery and numerous other collectables to see. Finally, there is also the chance to take a nostalgic journey on the Elsecar Steam Railway. The centre is open daily throughout the year.

The Crown Inn

22 Hill Street, Elsecar, Barnsley,
South Yorkshire S74 8AE
Tel: 01226 743851

Just steps away from the Elsecar Heritage Centre, and some 8½ miles northeast of Sheffield, **The Crown Inn** is a welcoming and tasteful pub offering great food, drink and hospitality. The specialities here include Barnsley chops, home-made pies and a selection of home-made puddings. All are hearty and delicious. Manager John Dye is a professional chef who has worked all over the country. The atmosphere is always warm and welcoming.

Barnsley

12 miles N of Sheffield on the A61

The county town of South Yorkshire, Barnsley stands on the River Dearne and derived its Victorian prosperity from the rich seams of coal found in the local area. It has an appropriately imposing Town Hall although the building is comparatively recent and was completed in 1933 while, nearby, the **Cooper Gallery** (see panel on page 288) is a lively centre for the arts that hosts a varied programme of exhibitions throughout the year as well as housing a fine permanent collection.

To the south of the town is the **Worsbrough Mill Museum and Country Park**, a grade II listed mill that dates from around 1625 although it is known that there was a mill here since the time of the Domesday Survey. A steam mill was added in the 19th century and, now, both have been restored to full working order to form the centrepiece of an industrial museum. Wholemeal flour, ground at the mills, can be bought here. The mills are set within a beautiful 200-acre country park, whose reservoir attracts a great variety of birds including heron.

Oughtibridge

4½ miles NW of Sheffield on the A6102

This pleasing village is set on the west bank of the River Don and it looks out

Traditional Yorkshire Puddings, Barnsley

The Cooper Gallery

Church Street, Barnsley,
South Yorkshire S70 2AH
Tel: 01226 774467 Fax: 01226 773594
e-mail: grahamriding@barnsley.gov.uk

The Cooper Gallery situated close to Barnsley town centre, holds a regular programme of contemporary art exhibitions including the Craft Showcase featuring work by local and regional craft designers. It is also the home for the Cooper Trustees' collection of 17th to 20th century paintings, water colours and drawings.

There are four main areas to the Cooper Gallery: The Down to Earth cafe offers a range of home made soups and sandwiches, delicious cakes and freshly made coffee. The reception counter within the cafe area is also fitted with an induction loop system for visitors with hard of hearing: The 3 Galleries which are painted in white are used for visiting contemporary exhibitions such as the South Yorkshire Open Art and touring exhibitions: In the Fox Wing the mood changes to a more sedate style. The permanent collection is displayed at its best with the Cooper Trustees' collection of paintings and drawings by famous artists such as J.M.W. Turner, Henry Moore, Jacob Kromer, Edward Lear and Edward Wadsworth. Upstairs in the Sadler Room work by community groups, educational activities, meetings and seminars are all held. This room also hosts music events, poetry readings and arts workshops for all ages. The space is fully fitted with an induction loop system for visitors with hard of hearing.

The Cooper Gallery is a friendly, accessible venue for all visitors to enjoy themselves. It is fully accessible to people with disabilities. We want all visitors to enjoy their time at The Cooper Gallery so, please pass on any ideas, thoughts or comments about the Gallery to staff.

across to the tree-covered slopes of **Wharncliffe Wood**. The settlement dates back to Saxon times at least but surprisingly there is no church and no evidence of there ever having been one.

Wharncliffe Side

5½ miles NW of Sheffield on the A6102

Nestling in the valley below Wharncliffe

The Full House & Sangdao's Thai Restaurant

Rotherham Road, Monk Bretton, Barnsley,
South Yorkshire S71 2NW
Tel: 01226 284503 Fax: 01226 246928
Mobile: 07900 266616
e-mail: fullhousepub@fsmail.net

Business partners Karen and Sangdao bring a wealth of experience to making **The Full House** pub and **Sangdao's Thai Restaurant** a success – Sangdao runs two other Thai restaurants (in Newmarket and Saffron Walden) and Karen runs another inn (in

Cambridge). Recently refurbished, it is well worth a visit for the excellent ales, food and atmosphere.

Crags, Wharncliffe Side is a popular residential location for commuters to Sheffield and Stocksbridge. An old tradition in the village tells of the Dragon of Wantly that lurked in the recesses of the crags and terrorized the local people until a knight, by the name of More, fought the monster and killed it. A cave up on the crags is still called the Dragon's Den and local children experience an enjoyable frisson of terror by shouting into its depths. Another ancient tradition in the village is the Whitsuntide walk when Sunday school children process around Wharncliffe Side stopping at various points to sing hymns.

Wortley

8 miles NW of Sheffield on the A629

This village's name comes from the Saxon meaning 'clearing for growing vegetables' and archaeological investigations on Wharncliffe Chase have indicated that there was a small British settlement here during the time of the Roman occupation. Mentioned in the *Domesday Book*, although it had declined in importance since the reign of Edward the Confessor, in the late 12th century Cistercian monks began to lay the foundations of the iron industry and iron forging began here in the Middle Ages. In the 16th century, Sir Thomas Wortley built Wharncliffe Lodge as a hunting lodge and, just over a century later, during the Civil War, Sir Francis Wortley raised a private army of 900 to fight for the king's cause.

The ancestral home of the Wortley family, **Wortley Hall** was built in the late 16th century on the site of an older residence but, over the centuries it has been much altered and even left to decay. Restoration work was carried out in the late 18th and early 19th century and it was also around this time that the landscaping and ornamental planning of the grounds and gardens took place.

Back in the village there are the School and Schoolhouse, that were built in 1874 by the Wortley family and only closed in 1993, while the oldest house in the village, **Tividale Cottage**, was practically rebuilt and certainly modernised in 1983. Once the headmaster's house, in early 1700s, this was the home of headmaster, William Nevison, and the cottage is thought to have been the birthplace of his son, the highwayman, John Nevison.

Just outside the village are Top and Low Forge, which are said to have been in operation in the 12th century although the earliest documentation dates from 1567. However, by the 17th century these two forges were working ceaselessly, along with many others in the area, and, while Top Forge closed in 1912, Low Forge continued production until 1929.

Penistone

12 miles NW of Sheffield on the A628

Perched some 700 feet above sea level, Penistone is one of the highest market towns in England and it provides a gateway to the Peak District National

Park, which extends for some 30 miles to the south of the town. Penistone's oldest building is the 15th century tower of its parish church that overlooks a graveyard in which ancestors of the poet William Wordsworth are buried. Later centuries added an elegant Dissenters' Chapel (in the 1600s) and a graceful Cloth Hall in the 1700s to the town. Today, the town's links with farming continue to be strong and the annual Penistone Agricultural Society Show, founded over 100 years ago, continues to attract visitors from near and far.

Thurlstone

12½ miles NW of Sheffield off the A628

Thurlstone developed when the first settlers realised that the nearby moors provided extensive grazing for sheep and the lime-free waters of the River Don were ideal for the washing of wool. Today the village still has some fine examples of the weavers' cottages that sprang up during the early 19th century and the best of these can be seen on Tenter Hill. Here the finished cloth would have been dried and stretched on 'tenters' - large wooden frames placed outside on the street that gave the road its name.

The village's most famous son was Nicholas Saunderson, born in 1682, who was blinded by smallpox at the age of two. He taught himself to read by passing his fingers over the tombstones in Penistone churchyard, some 150 years before the introduction of Braille. Nicholas went on to attend grammar school and then climb the ladder of academia to become Professor of Mathematics at Cambridge University.

Silkstone

12 miles NW of Sheffield off the A628

The travel writer Arthur Mee dubbed Silkstone's parish church 'The Minster of the Moors' and it is indeed a striking building though the present church, parts of which date back to Norman times, probably stands on the site of an older Saxon building. Most of the present church dates from the golden age of English ecclesiastical architecture – the 15th century. Outside, there are graceful flying buttresses and wonderfully weird gargoyles while, inside, the ancient oak roofs sprout floral bosses on moulded beams and the old box-pews and lovely medieval screens all add to the charm. Meanwhile, in the churchyard is a memorial to 26 children who were drowned while they worked underground in Husker Pit in 1838.

To the southeast lie **Wentworth Castle Gardens**, a wonderful historic garden with an impressive collection of plants including the national collections of rhododendrons, magnolia and *X Williamsii camellias*. Also in the grounds are some magnificent follies including a Gothic castle and an obelisk dedicated to Lady Mary Wortley Montague.

Cawthorne

13½ miles NW of Sheffield on the A635

This picturesque village has many historical links with the nearby estate of Cannon Hall, the home of the Spencer family from the mid-17th century. Cawthorne's major industry at the time was a mix of farming, coal and iron and the Spencers had interests in the local iron industry and owned Barnby Furnace, just a mile to the east of the village.

Cannon Hall Museum (see panel below) is housed in a magnificent 18th century country house that is set in formal gardens and historic parkland. Designed by John Carr of York and the home, for 200 years, of the Spencer-Stanhope family, the rooms provide the perfect backdrop for the museum's fine collections of pottery, furniture, paintings, glass and Moorcroft. Meanwhile, the Charge Gallery documents the history of the 13th and 18th Royal Hussars. The museum is open everyday during the summer, except non Bank Holiday Mondays, and at the weekends in the winter.

Set in the grounds of Cannon Hall Country Park is the **Cannon Hall Open Farm** (see panel on page 292), a family-run farm that is home to hundreds of animals and where visitors can see a real farm at work, help feed the animals and catch up on the new animals being born. Also here is an adventure playground, a farm shop, a gift shop and a tea rooms.

Also in the village is the **Cawthorne Victoria Jubilee Museum**, which houses original collections of butterflies, moths, birds, eggs, fossils and domestic artefacts.

Cannon Hall Museum

Cawthorne, Barnsley,
South Yorkshire S75 4AT
Tel: 01226 790270
e-mail: cannonhall@barnsley.gov.uk

Set in 70 acres of historic parkland and gardens, **Cannon Hall Museum** provides an idyllic and tranquil setting for a day out. For two hundred years Cannon Hall was home to the Spencer-Stanhope family. From the 1760s the architect John Carr of York was commissioned to extend and alter the house while the designer Richard Woods was hired to landscape the park and gardens. Over forty varieties of pear trees still grow in the historic walled garden, as well as peaches and nectarines. The famed Cannon Hall vine grows in one of the greenhouses. The park provides an ideal setting for a picnic, outdoor activities and games. Cannon Hall was sold by the family in the early 1950s to Barnsley Council and was first opened as a museum in 1957. The Hall now contains collections of furniture, paintings, glassware and pottery, much of which is displayed in period settings. It also houses 'Charge', the Regimental Museum of the 13th/18th Hussars (QMO).

The Victorian Kitchen Café near the gardens is open each weekend and during the school holidays for home-made light refreshments in the traditional setting of the original kitchens and Servant's Hall. The Museum also has a shop stocking a range of greetings cards, local history books, confectionery and giftware. Off the A635 Barnsley to Huddersfield Road. Easy access from junctions 37 or 38 of the M1

Cannon Hall Open Farm

Cawthorne, Barnsley,
South Yorkshire S75 4AT
Tel: 01226 790427

The combination of animals, beautiful countryside and value for money make **Cannon Hall Open Farm** a place which appeals to the whole family. There are plenty of baby animals on show whatever time of the year you choose to visit this award winning venue. There's always something new to see on each trip and the playful piglets are popular all year round. Spring lambing is a favourite time for many and lambs are born from Christmas right through to Easter when pygmy goat kids arrive. These little fellows will be particularly keen to meet you if you pick up a bag of animal food at the farm entrance. Blossom the huge shire horse is often hungry too and, like the donkeys, hates to be left out when there is food around. Alongside those animals you might expect to find on a farm you'll also find unusual creatures like Llamas and Wallabies and, if you're really lucky you might see a baby Joey peeping out of it's mothers pouch.

There's an adventure playground providing fun for the children. A spacious tea room serving high quality fresh ground coffee, speciality teas and everything from a quick snack to a hot meal. In the farm shop you will find wonderful farm produce alongside a wide army of food, toys and gift items. There's plenty to interest the casual browser or the shopper in search of something a little different. Huge displays of pickles, jams and chutneys weigh down the shelves. It's hard not to find something you like!. The fresh meat section boasts a wide variety of superb sausages along with wonderful dry cured bacon and ham. You'll find perfectly matured traditional beef, fine lamb and tender pork. If you've forgotten just how good food can taste, you'll find plenty of reminders at the Good Life Farm Shop. Parking is available next to the farm and is free for coaches and disabled visitors who will find good facilities and easy access to the farm.

This quaint little museum provides interest for all the family and it is open from April to end of October at the weekends and Bank Holidays.

Doncaster

The Romans named their riverside settlement beside the River Don, 'Danum', and a well-preserved stretch of the road they built here can be seen just west of Adwick le Street. A lively shopping centre today, with a market that takes place every Tuesday, Friday and Saturday, the market has existed here since Roman times although the first charter was not granted to Doncaster until 1194 by Richard I. The large triangular market place today was laid down in medieval times and here can be found the Market Hall, built in 1849, and the stately Corn Exchange building of 1866. The modern town boasts some other impressive buildings, including the **Mansion House** built in 1748 and designed by James Paine and it remains one of only three civic mansion houses in England. The house is open by appointment only. Meanwhile, the parish church was rebuilt in 1858 by Sir Giles Gilbert Scott and it is an outstanding example of Gothic revival architecture with its lofty tower that rises some 170 feet high and is crowned by pinnacles.

Surprisingly, Doncaster was once one of the most important centres for the production of steam engines and, over the years, thousands were built here, including both the *Flying Scotsman* and the *Mallard*. The *Mallard* still holds the record as the fastest steam train in the world when it achieved a top speed of 125 mph in July 1938. For a further insight into the history of the town and surrounding area, there is the **Doncaster Museum** (see panel below) which contains several exciting and informative exhibitions on the various aspects of natural history, local history and archaeology. While the Art Gallery has a lively programme of temporary exhibitions as well as permanent displays of fine and decorative art. Housed in the same building is the **Regimental Museum of the King's Own Yorkshire Light Infantry**, which reflects the history of this famous local regiment.

There is no-one connected with racing who has not heard of the St Leger, the oldest of England's great classic races, which has been held at Doncaster since 1776. There has been horse racing here since at least the beginning of the 17th century and, today, in the Yorkshire tradition, **Doncaster Racecourse** remains a magnet for racing enthusiasts.

On the northwestern outskirts of the town lies **Cusworth Hall** (see panel on page 294), a splendid Georgian mansion built in the 1740s and surrounded by a landscaped park that is home to the Museum of South Yorkshire Life. The displays of local history here, which cover the last 250 years of the area, include agriculture, mining, the railways, crafts and costume, and they show the changes in the work, home and social lives of the people of South Yorkshire over that period.

A little further northwest of Doncaster, lies **Brodsworth Hall** (English Heritage), a remarkable example of a Victorian mansion that

Doncaster Museum & Art Gallery

Chequer Road, Doncaster,
South Yorkshire DN1 2AE
Tel: 01302 734293 Fax: 01302 735409
website: www.doncaster.gov.uk

Located near to the town centre the museum displays important collections of natural history, archaeology, local history and fine and decorative art. There is also a large and varied temporary exhiibition programme throughout the year; details are available on request. (During 2002 the ground floor gallery is being refurbished).

The Regimental Museum of the Kings' Own Yorkshire Light Infantry is housed in the same building and includes one of the most extensive medal collections to be exhibited in any museum in this country.

There are no steps to the museum from the car park. A lift provides access to all the upper galleries. Toilets have facilities for people with disabilities and baby change.

Cusworth Hall (Museum of South Yorkshire Life)

Cusworth Lane, Doncaster,
South Yorkshire DN5 7TU
Tel: 01302 782342
website: www.doncaster.gov.uk

Cusworth Hall is an imposing 18th century country house set in extensive landscaped parklands. It houses the Museum of South Yorkshire Life which illustrates the changing home, work and social life of people and communities across the region in the last 250 years.

There is access to the ground floor of the museum via a wheelchair lift. The public toilets in the East Wing contain facilities for people with disabilities.There is a regular programme of seasonal events as well as a series of temporary exhibitions.

has survived with much of its original furnishings and decorations intact. When Charles and Georgiana Thellusson, their six children and 15 servants moved into the new hall in 1863 the house must have seemed the last word in both grandeur and utility. A gasworks in the grounds supplied the lighting and no fewer than eight water-closets were distributed around the house although, rather surprisingly, only two bathrooms were installed. However, more immediately impressive to visitors are the opulent furnishings, paintings, statuary and decoration. The sumptuous reception rooms have now a rather faded grandeur and English Heritage has deliberately left it so, preserving the patina of time throughout the house to produce an interior that is both fascinating and evocative. A vanished way of life is also brought to life in the huge kitchen, complete with its original utensils, and the cluttered servants wing. The hall stands in 15 acres of beautifully restored Victorian gardens complete with a summer house in the form of a classical temple, a Target Range where the family practised its archery, and a Pets Cemetery where the family dogs and a prized parrot bearing the unimaginative name of 'Polly' were buried between 1894 and 1988. There is also a fascinating exhibition illustrating the family's obsession – yachting.

Around Doncaster

Norton

8 miles N of Doncaster off the A19

This sizeable village is located close to the border between North and West Yorkshire and was once a busy farming, mining and quarrying centre; however, nowadays, it is a peaceful place and a tranquil base for commuters to Doncaster and Pontefract. The most impressive building in the village is the ancient parish church of St Mary Magdalene whose splendid 14th century west tower is considered by many to be the finest in

Yorkshire. Once there was also a priory here, standing beside the River Went, but now only a fragment of wall remains but the old water mill has survived.

Stainforth

7½ miles NE of Doncaster off the A614

Once an important trading centre and inland port on the River Don, Stainforth also stands on the banks of the **Stainforth and Keadby Canal**, which still has a well-preserved dry dock and a 19th century blacksmith's shop. This area of low, marshy ground was drained by Dutch engineers in the 1600s to produce rich, peaty farmland that continues to be drained by slow moving dykes and canals and, today, it retains the air of a quiet backwater amongst the fields. The rich peat resources here are commercially exploited, in part, but also provide a congenial home for a great deal of natural wildlife.

Fishlake

8½ miles NE of Doncaster off the A614

Set along the banks of the River Don, which is known here as the Dutch River, Fishlake is virtually an island since it is surrounded by rivers and canals and can only be entered by crossing a bridge. A charming place, the village has a striking medieval church famous for its elaborately carved Norman doorway, an ancient windmill and a welcoming traditional inn.

Thorne

10 miles NE of Doncaster on the A614

This ancient market town on the River Don has been a port since at least 1500 and ships have sailed from here to York, Hull, London and Europe, while the waterfront was busy with boat builder's yards where vessels of up to 400 tons were built.

In 1802, Thorne gained a second waterfront, on the newly constructed Stainforth and Keadby Canal that attracted most of the water traffic away from the unpredictable River Don. As late as 1987 there were still boat building yards at work here but, in that year, they finally closed and the area is being carefully developed in a way that will commemorate the town's heritage.

Branton

4½ miles E of Doncaster off the B1396

Surrounded by agricultural land, Brockholes Farm has been a working farm since 1759 and one where the traditional farming skills have been passed down from one generation to the next.

Today, at **Brockhole Riding and Visitor Centre**, visitors can see demonstrations of those same skills, such as those carried out by the farrier and the shepherd, as well as seeing many animals associated with traditional free range farming.

There is also a riding centre here that

The Duke of Leeds

Church Street, Wales,
South Yorkshire S26 5LQ
Tel: 01909 770301

Standing in the charming village of Wales opposite the Church in the appropriately named Church Street, found off the B6060 and just a short drive from junction 31 of the M1, **The Duke of Leeds** is a distinguished and comfortable inn offering great food, drink and hospitality.

The inn dates back to 1730 and began life under the name The Cockerel. Much mystery surrounds its change of name, but records show that by the end of the 1700s it had taken on its present moniker.

Plush and with a cosy air while also being spacious, the inn is decorated and furnished to a high standard of comfort, with open brickbuilt fires and plenty of light streaming in through the casement windows.

The owners are Jill and Ghaf – Jill has nearly 30 years' experience in the trade, and makes all her guests feel most welcome. This is Ghaf's first venture into this type of business, and he brings a wealth of enthusiasm to the role.

This Free House is open every session and serves up four real ales – John Smiths, Directors and two changing guest ales – together with a range of lagers, cider, stout, wines, spirits and soft drinks.

Excellent food is served daily at lunch (12 – 2.30) and dinner (5 – 10 p.m.). Jill is a terrific cook, and she and the inn's chef create a tempting range of hearty favourites. Home-cooking is top of the agenda, with dishes cooked and prepared to order. The no-smoking dining area seats 40. Another quiet dining area has recently been christened 'Poets' Corner', and has poems displayed on the walls. Guests can also dine in the Smoke Room and small garden area. Children welcome. Upstairs there's a large function room that can accommodate 100 people and is eminently suitable for celebrations of any occasion. It is planned that the function room will also be the venue for regular themed evenings in future.

caters for complete beginners through to experienced riders and, along with professional instructors, they have a range of horses and ponies to suit all ages and abilities.

Finningley

6½ miles E of Doncaster on the A614

A unique feature of this pleasant village, which lies close to the Nottinghamshire border, is its five village greens, the main one having a duck pond complete with weeping willows.

Finningley has a beautiful Norman church with a rectors' list dating back to 1293 and a post office that has been in the same family for 5 generations. Just before the Second World War, Finningley RAF airfield was built to the west of the village and, although the airfield is no longer in regular use, it provides the venue for an annual **Air Show** that includes some spectacular flying displays.

Bawtry

8 miles SE of Doncaster on the A614

This pleasant little market town stands close to the Nottinghamshire border and, in medieval times, it was customary for the Sheriff of South Yorkshire to welcome visiting kings and queens here as they crossed into the county. In the mid-15th century the then Sheriff, Sir Robert Bowes, accompanied by 200 gentlemen dressed in velvet and 4,000 yeomen on horseback, greeted Henry VIII at Bawtry and, in the name of Yorkshire, presented him with a purse containing the huge sum of £900 in gold.

North Anston

12 miles S of Doncaster on the A57

This village, which is separated from its neighbour South Anston by the main road, is home to the **Tropical Butterfly House, Wildlife and Falconry Centre** where, not only can visitors see the exotic butterflies, birds, snakes and crocodiles in a tropical jungle setting but also enjoy outdoor falconry displays and, at the baby farm animal area, bottle feed the lambs (depending on the season). The centre, which is open all year, also has a nocturnal reptile room, a nature trail and a children's outdoor play area.

Wales

13½ miles S of Doncaster on the B6059

A mile or so to the west of Wales lies the **Rother Valley Country Park** that provides excellent facilities for water sports including sailing, windsurfing, canoeing and jet skiing, as well as a cable water ski tow. Visitors can hire equipment or use their own, and training courses from beginner to instructor level are available in various water sports. Other attractions at this 750-acres country park include a lakeside golf course, a Craft Centre with craftspeople at work, adventure playgrounds, a nature trail, cycle routes and cycle hire, bridleways, gift shop and a cafeteria.

Thorpe Salvin

14 miles S of Doncaster off the A57

This attractive village is home to the now ruined **Thorpe Salvin Hall**, which dates from 1570, and that is thought to have been the inspiration for Torquilstone in Sir Walter Scott's novel *Ivanhoe*.

Maltby

7 miles SW of Doncaster on the B6376

To the southeast of this village lies the dramatic ruins of **Roche Abbey** (English Heritage) that was founded in 1174 by Cistercian monks and takes it name from the rocky limestone outcrop on which it is situated. The majestic remains of this once great abbey stand in a landscape that was created by Capability Brown in the 1770s as part of the grounds of Sandbeck Park, the home of the Earls of Scarborough.

Renishaw

18 miles SW of Doncaster on the A616

This sizeable village gives its name to **Renishaw Hall**, the home of Sir Reresby and Lady Sitwell, which can be found just a mile or so to the west. The beautiful formal Italian gardens and 300 acres of wooded park are open to visitors, along with a nature trail and a Sitwell family Museum, the John Piper Art Gallery, a display of Fiori de Henriques sculptures in the Georgian stables, and a café. The grounds are open from April to September from Fridays to Sundays and on Bank Holiday Mondays (and also on Thursdays during July and August) while the hall itself is open to group and connoisseur tours by special arrangement only.

Cadeby

4 miles SW of Doncaster off the A630

Listed in the *Domesday Book* as 'Catebi', this pleasant little village is surrounded on all sides by prime agricultural land. For centuries Cadeby had no church of its own and its residents had to travel two miles to the parish church in Sprotbrough until, finally, in 1856, the owners of the huge Sprotbrough estate, the Copley family, paid for a church to be built in the village. Designed by Sir George Gilbert Scott, the architect of St Pancras Station in London, the church resembles a medieval estate barn with its steeply pitched roofs and lofty south porch. A century and a half later, Cadeby is again without a church since Sir George's attractive building has recently been declared redundant.

Conisbrough

5 miles SW of Doncaster on the A630

The town is best known for the 11th century **Conisbrough Castle** (English Heritage) that features prominently in one of the most dramatic scenes in Sir Walter Scott's novel *Ivanhoe*. The most impressive medieval building in South

Conisbrough Castle

Plantagenet, the 5th Earl, this wooden construction was deemed inadequate for a family of such wealth and status so Hamelin ordered the construction of a stone keep, to his own designs, in 1180. After the demise of the family, the castle was abandoned as a residence and it was saved from dereliction during the Civil War as it was indefensible as a fortress. After some 500 years of neglect, the castle's keep once again has a roof to protect it from the elements, along with

Yorkshire, Conisbrough Castle boasts the oldest circular keep in England, which rises some 90 feet and is more than 50 feet wide. The keep is situated on a man-made hill that dates back to Saxon times. Once the northern stronghold of the de Warenne family, Earls of Surrey, it was William, the 1st Earl, who built the original timber motte-and-bailey castle on this site just after the Norman Conquest but, by the times of Hamelin

two new floors, and it is now safe for generations to come. As well as a series of events being held here throughout the year, the castle has a visitor centre, a presentation detailing its history and a tea room. Conisbrough Castle is open daily throughout the year.

This town is also home to the **Earth Centre**, a place of the future, which lies close to Conisbrough Station. Through a series of compelling indoor and outdoor

exhibitions, the centre uses the latest technology to explain the wonders of this planet and also how they are best preserved. Set beside the River Don, visitors can tour the unusual garden, taste the delicious organic food, go pond-dipping and enjoy the sweet smell of the environmentally friendly sewage works!

Swinton

8½ miles SW of Doncaster on the B6090

This is the town that is home of the world famous Rockingham porcelain and the story of the amazing small country pottery, which grew to become the king's porcelain manufacturer before falling into bankruptcy, is told in a special gallery at Clifton Park Museum, Rotherham. However, here visitors can still see the secluded Swinton Pottery site where, in beautiful surroundings, the **Waterloo Kiln** built in 1815 and the Pottery Ponds are the only surviving landmarks of the renowned Rockinghan Porcelain work. Unfortunately, only the exterior of the building can be viewed.

Rotherham

11 miles SW of Doncaster on the A630

There has been a settlement here since prehistoric times but it was the Romans, who exploited the local iron ore, who made the first attempts at establishing a permanent town here. A market town for 900 years, Rotherham is steeped in history but throughout the last 2,000 years it seems unable to escape its iron roots. While the monks from Kirkstead Abbey, in nearby Lincolnshire, mined and smelted iron ore near here in the 12th century, it was not until the Industrial Revolution that Rotherham became, primarily, an industrial town. From the mid-18th century, the Walker Company of Rotherham was famous for its cannons and their products featured, to lethal effect, in the American War of Independence and at the Battle of Trafalgar. The company also built bridges, amongst them Southwark Bridge in London and the bridge at Sunderland and, when the Walkers' Rotherham works closed in the 1820s, several of their former employees set up their own works, a move that was to place the town in the forefront of the iron founding industry in the 19th century. Rotherham, today, is still a leading site of the country's steel industry, along with glass, mining and engineering.

This rich industrial heritage can be explored at the massive former steelworks at Templeborough that are now the **Magna Science Adventure Centre**. Divided into four hands-on explorative exhibitions – earth, air, fire and water – visitors can unearth the mysteries of the natural world. In the water challenge there are pumps and locks to investigate as well as salmon to catch, while the fire centre has a larger than life size lava lamp. The subterranean playground of Earth provides the opportunity to operate a real JCB and explode a rock face and, in

Air, visitors can spin in a gyroscope chair and also feel the sensations of flying. Naturally, Magna also provides an intimate insight into the lives of steelworkers and visitors can see a powerful arc furnace being brought back to life.

Though somewhat tamer than Magna, the fine collections at the **Clifton Park Museum** are no less interesting. Housed in the late 18th century mansion, whose interior has changed little since it was built in 1783 for the Rotherham ironmaster, Joshua Walker, the museum has displays of Yorkshire pottery, including an impressive collection of Rockingham made at nearby Swinton, English glass and silver, Victorian domestic items and local and natural history displays. Meanwhile, the grounds around the house now form the borough's largest urban park. The museum is open daily all year except Fridays. Another museum of interest is the **York and Lancaster Regimental Museum**, housed in the Central Library and Arts Centre. The regiment had strong ties with South Yorkshire and its recruits are drawn mainly from Barnsley, Sheffield and Rotherham. The displays include historic uniforms, campaign relics and over 1,000 medals, amongst them nine Victoria Cross. There are also sections on local militia, rifle volunteers and the territorials.

The town's most striking building, however, is undoubtedly the **Church of All Saints** and, with its soaring tower, pinnacled buttresses and battlements and imposing porch, it is one of the finest examples of Perpendicular architecture in Yorkshire. The church dates mainly from the 15th century although there is evidence of an earlier Saxon church, dating from AD 937, on the site. A church here was listed in the *Domesday Book* and in 1161 the monks of Rufford Abbey were granted the right to prospect for and to smelt iron, and to plant an orchard, and from that day industry has existed side by side with agriculture. Rotherham is also home to one of only four surviving medieval chantry chapels that are situated on a bridge in England and the **Chapel on the Bridge**, now superbly restored, features a beautiful new stained glass window that illustrates the story of the town.

Along with being able to claim to be the birthplace of both the screw down water tap and the Bailey Bridge, which was said by Sir Winston Churchill to have shortened the Second World War by at least two years, Rotherham is also associated with several notable figures throughout its long history. Thomas Rotherham, the Chancellor of England in the 15th century was born here as was Ebenezer Elliot, who was influential in repealing the Corn Laws in 1846, Sandy Powell, who coined the phrase, "*can you hear me mother*" and, finally, the England goalkeeper, David Seaman.

To the south of the town lies **Ulley Country Park** that incorporates a reservoir, with excellent coarse fishing, and a nature reserve in a park that nestles between the surrounding hills.

TOURIST INFORMATION CENTRES

AYSGARTH FALLS

Aysgarth Falls National Park Centre
Aysgarth Falls
Leyburn
North Yorkshire
DL8 3TH
Tel: 01969 663424 or 01969 663759
Fax: 01969 663105 or 01969 667165
e-mail: aysgarth@ytbtic.co.uk

BARNSLEY

46 Eldon Street
Barnsley
South Yorkshire
S70 2JL
Tel: 01226 206757
Fax: 01226 206757
e-mail: barnsley@ytbtic.co.uk

BATLEY

The Mill Discount Department Store
Bradford Road
Batley
Yorkshire
WF17 5LZ
Tel: 01924 426670
Fax: 01924 446096 or 01924 446096
e-mail: batley@ytbtic.co.uk

BEVERLEY

34 Butcher Row
Beverley
East Yorkshire
HU17 0AB
Tel: 01482 867430 or 01482 391672
Fax: 01482 391674
e-mail: beverley,tic@eastriding.gov.uk

BRADFORD

City Hall
Bradford
West Yorkshire
BD1 1HY
Tel: 01274 433678
Fax: 01274 739067
e-mail: tourist.information@bradford.gov.uk

BRIDLINGTON

25 Prince Street
Bridlington
East Riding of Yorkshire
YO15 2NP
Tel: 01262 673474
Fax: 01262 401797
e-mail: bridlington@ytbtic.co.uk

BRIGG

The Buttercross
Market Place
Brigg
North Lincolnshire
DN20 8ER
Tel: 01652 657053 or 01724 297353
Fax: 01652 657053
e-mail: brigg.tic@northlincs.gov.uk

CLEETHORPES

42-43 Alexandra Road
Cleethorpes
North East Lincolnshire
DN35 8LE
Tel: 01472 323111 or 01472 323222
Fax: 01472 323112
e-mail:
cleethorpes@ytbtic04.freeserve.co.uk

DANBY

The Moors Centre
Danby Lodge
Lodge Lane
Danby, Whitby
North Yorkshire
YO21 2NB
Tel: 01439 772737 or 01439 772738
Fax: 01287 660308
e-mail:
moorscentre@northyorkmoors-npa.gov.uk

DONCASTER

Central Library
Waterdale
Doncaster
South Yorkshire
DN1 3JE
Tel: 01302 734309
Fax: 01302 735385 or 01302 734302
e-mail: tourist.information@doncaster.gov.uk

FILEY

The Evron Centre
John Street
Filey
North Yorkshire
YO14 9DW
Tel: 01723 383637 or 01723 383637
Fax: 01723 518001 or 01723 363785
e-mail: fileytic@scarborough.gov.uk

GRASSINGTON

National Park Centre
Colvend, Hebden Road
Grassington
North Yorkshire
BD23 5LB
Tel: 01756 752774
Fax: 01756 753358
e-mail: grassington@ytbtic.co.uk

GUISBOROUGH

Priory Grounds
Church Street
Guisborough
TS14 6HG
Tel: 01287 633801
Fax: 01287 633801
e-mail:
guisborough_tic@redcar-cleveland.gov.uk

HALIFAX

Piece Hall
Halifax
West Yorkshire
HX1 1RE
Tel: 01422 368725 or 01422 843831
Fax: 01422 354264 or 01422 845266
e-mail: halifax@ytbtic.co.uk

HARROGATE

Royal Baths
Crescent Road
Harrogate
North Yorkshire
HG1 2RR
Tel: 01423 537300
Fax: 01423 537305
e-mail: tic@harrogate.gov.uk

HAWES

Dales Countryside Museum
Station Yard
Hawes
North Yorkshire
DL8 3NT
Tel: 01969 667450 or 01969 663494
Fax: 01969 667165
e-mail: hawes@ytbtic.co.uk

HAWORTH

2/4 West Lane
Haworth
Near Keighley
West Yorkshire
BD22 8EF
Tel: 01535 642329
Fax: 01535 647721
e-mail: haworth@ytbtic.co.uk

HEBDEN BRIDGE

Visitor and Canal Centre
New Road
Hebden Bridge
West Yorkshire
HX7 8AF
Tel: 01422 843831 or 01422 368725
Fax: 01422 845266 or 01422 354264
e-mail: hebdenbridge@ytbtic.co.uk

HELMSLEY

The Town Hall
Market Place
Helmsley
North Yorkshire
YO62 5BL
Tel: 01439 770173 or 01439 771116
Fax: 01439 771881
e-mail: helmsley@ytbtic.co.uk

HOLMFIRTH

49-51 Huddersfield Road
Holmfirth
West Yorkshire
HD9 3JP
Tel: 01484 222444 or 01484 223200
Fax: 01484 222445
e-mail: holmfirth.tic@kirklees.gov.uk

HORNSEA

120 Newbegin
Hornsea
HU18 1PB
Tel: 01964 536404
Fax: 01964 536404
e-mail: hornsea@ytbtic.co.uk

HORTON-IN-RIBBLESDALE

Pen-y-ghent Cafe
Horton-in-Ribblesdale
Settle
North Yorkshire
BD24 0HE
Tel: 01729 860333
Fax: 01729 860333
e-mail: horton@ytbtic.co.uk

HUDDERSFIELD

3 Albion Street
Huddersfield
West Yorkshire
HD1 2NW
Tel: 01484 223200
Fax: 01484 223202
e-mail: huddersfield.tic@kirklees.gov.uk

HULL (PARAGON STREET)

1 Paragon Street
Hull
East Yorkshire
HU1 3NA
Tel: 01482 223559
Fax: 01482 613959
e-mail: tourist.information@hullcc.gov.uk

HUMBER BRIDGE

North Bank Viewing Area
Ferriby Road
Hessle
East Yorkshire
HU13 0LN
Tel: 01482 640852
Fax: 01482 640852
e-mail: humberbridge@ytbtic.co.uk

ILKLEY

Station Rd
Ilkley
West Yorkshire
LS29 8HA
Tel: 01943 602319
Fax: 01943 436235
e-mail: ilkleytic@bradford.gov.uk

INGLETON

The Community Centre Car Park
Ingleton
North Yorkshire
LA6 3HG
Tel: 015242 41049 or 01524241647
Fax: 015242 41701
e-mail: ingleton@ytbtic.co.uk

KNARESBOROUGH

9 Castle Courtyard
Market Place
Knaresborough
North Yorkshire
HG5 8AE
Tel: 01423 866886 or 01423 537300
Fax: 01423 866886 or 01423 537305
e-mail: kntic@harrogate.gov.uk

LEEDS

Gateway Yorkshire
PO Box 244
The Arcade, City Station
Leeds
West Yorkshire
LS1 1PL
Tel: 0113 242 5242
Fax: 0113 246 8246
e-mail: tourinfo@leeds.gov.uk

LEEMING BAR

The Yorkshire Maid
The Great North Road
Leeming Bar
Bedale
North Yorkshire
DL8 1DT
Tel: 01677 424262
Fax: 01677 423069
e-mail: leeming@ytbtic.co.uk

LEYBURN

4 Central Chambers
Railway Street
Leyburn
North Yorkshire
DL8 5BB
Tel: 01969 623069
Fax: 01969 622833
e-mail: leyburn@ytbtic.co.uk

MALHAM

National Park Centre
Malham
Skipton
North Yorkshire
BD23 4DA
Tel: 01729 830363
Fax: 01729 830673
e-mail: malham@ytbtic.co.uk

MALTON

58 Market Place
Malton
North Yorkshire
YO17 7LW
Tel: 01653 600048
Fax: 01653 698374
e-mail: malton@ytbtic.co.uk

OTLEY

Otley Library & Tourist Information
4 Boroughgate
Otley
West Yorkshire
LS21 3AL
Tel: 0113 247 7707
Fax: 0113 224 3286
e-mail: otleytic@leedslearning.net

PATELEY BRIDGE

18 High Street
Pateley Bridge
North Yorkshire
HG3 5AW
Tel: 01423 711147 or 01423 537300
Fax: 01423 711147 or 01423 537305
e-mail: pbtic@harrogate.gov.uk

PICKERING

Ropery House
The Ropery
Pickering
North Yorkshire
YO18 8DY
Tel: 01751 473791 or 01751 476899
Fax: 01751 473487
e-mail: pickering@ytbtic.co.uk

REDCAR

West Terrace
Esplanade
Redcar
Cleveland
TS10 3AE
Tel: 01642 471921
Fax: 01642 471921
e-mail: redcar_tic@redcar-cleveland.gov.uk

REETH

Hudson House
The Green
Reeth
Richmond
North Yorkshire
DL11 6TB
Tel: 01748 884059 or 01748 880020
Fax: 01748 880012 or 01969 663105
e-mail: reeth@ytbtic.co.uk

RICHMOND

Friary Gardens
Victoria Road
Richmond
North Yorkshire
DL10 4AJ
Tel: 01748 850252 or 01748 825994
Fax: 01748 825994
e-mail: richmond@ytbtic.co.uk

RIPON

Minster Road
Ripon
North Yorkshire
HG4 1LT
Tel: 01765 604625 or 01423 537300
Fax: 01765 604625 or 01423 537305
e-mail: ripontic@harrogate.gov.uk

ROTHERHAM VISITOR CENTRE

40 Bridgegate
Rotherham
South Yorkshire
S60 1PQ
Tel: 01709 835904 or 01709 336887
Fax: 01709 336888
e-mail: tic@rotherham.gov.uk

SALTBURN

3 Station Buildings
Station Square
Saltburn-by-Sea
Cleveland
TS12 1AQ
Tel: 01287 622422
Fax: 01287 625074
e-mail: saltburn_tic@redcar-cleveland.gov.uk

SCARBOROUGH

Unit 3, Pavilion House
Valley Bridge Road
Scarborough
North Yorkshire
YO11 1UZ
Tel: 01723 383636
Fax: 01723 507302
e-mail: scarboroughtic@scarborough.gov.uk

SCARBOROUGH (HARBOURSIDE)

Harbourside TIC
Sandside
Scarborough
North Yorkshire
YO11 1PP
Tel: *Operated by: Scarborough TIC, Pavilion House*
Fax: 01723 507302
e-mail: harboursidetic@scarborough.gov.uk

SCUNTHORPE

Scunthorpe Central Library
Carlton Street
Scunthorpe
North Lincolnshire
DN15 6TX
Tel: 01724 297354 or 01724 860161
Fax: 01724 859737
e-mail: scunthorpe.tic@northlincs.gov.uk

SELBY

Visitor Information Centre
52 Micklegate
Selby
YO8 4EQ
Tel: 01757 212181 or 01757 702020
Fax: 01757 705396
e-mail: selby@ytbtic.co.uk

SETTLE

Town Hall
Cheapside
Settle
North Yorkshire
BD24 9EJ
Tel: 01729 825192
Fax: 01729 824381
e-mail: settle@ytbtic.co.uk

SHEFFIELD

Visitor Information Point
Winter Garden
Sheffield
Tel: 0114 2211900
e-mail: visitor@sheffield.gov.uk

SKIPTON

35 Coach Street
Skipton
North Yorkshire
BD23 1LQ
Tel: 01756 792809
Fax: 01756 700709
e-mail: skipton@ytbtic.co.uk

SUTTON BANK

Sutton Bank Visitor Centre
Sutton Bank
Thirsk
North Yorkshire
YO7 2EH
Tel: 01845 597426
Fax: 01845 597113
e-mail: suttonbank@ytbtic.co.uk

THIRSK

Thirsk Tourist Information Centre
49 Market Place
Thirsk
North Yorkshire
YO7 1HA
Tel: 01845 522755
Fax: 01845 526230
e-mail: thirsktic@hambleton.gov.uk

TODMORDEN

15 Burnley Road
Todmorden
West Yorkshire
OL14 7BU
Tel: 01706 818181 or 01422 843831
Fax: 01706 818181 or 01422 845266
e-mail: todmorden@ytbtic.co.uk

WAKEFIELD

9 The Bull Ring
Wakefield
West Yorkshire
WF1 1HB
Tel: 0845 601 8353 or 01924 305000/1
Fax: 01924 305775
e-mail: tic@wakefield.gov.uk

WETHERBY

Wetherby Library & Tourist Information Centre
17 Westgate
Wetherby
West Yorkshire
LS22 6LL
Tel: 01937 582151
Fax: 01937 586964
e-mail: wetherbytic@leedslearning.net

WHITBY

Langborne Road
Whitby
North Yorkshire
YO21 1YN
Tel: 01723 383637
Fax: 01947 606137
e-mail: whitbytic@scarborough.gov.uk

WITHERNSEA

131 Queen Street
Withernsea
HU19 2DJ
Tel: 01964 615683
Fax: 01964 615683

YORK (DE GREY ROOMS)

The De Grey Rooms
Exhibition Square
York
North Yorkshire
YO1 7HB
Tel: 01904 621756
Fax: 01904 639986
e-mail: tic@york-tourism.co.uk

YORK (RAILWAY STATION)

Outer Concourse
Railway Station
Station Road
York
North Yorkshire
YO24 1AY
Tel: 01904 621756
Fax: 01904 624173
e-mail: kg@ytbyork.swiftserve.net

LIST OF ADVERTISERS

N

O

P

Q

R

S

INDEX OF TOWNS, VILLAGES AND PLACES OF INTEREST

A

B

C

D

R

S

T

W

Y

Travel Publishing

The Hidden Places

Regional and National guides to the less well-known places of interest and places to eat, stay and drink

Hidden Inns

Regional guides to traditional pubs and inns throughout the United Kingdom

Golfers Guides

Regional and National guides to 18 hole golf courses and local places to stay, eat and drink

Regional and National guides to the traditional countryside of Britain and Ireland with easy to read facts on places to visit, stay, eat, drink and shop

For more information:

Phone: 0118 981 7777 **Fax:** 0118 982 0077
e-mail: adam@travelpublishing.co.uk **website:** www.travelpublishing.co.u

HIDDEN PLACES ORDER FORM

To order any of our publications just fill in the payment details below and complete the order form. For orders of less than 4 copies please add £1 per book for postage and packing. Orders over 4 copies are P & P free.

Please Complete Either:

I enclose a cheque for £ [ ] made payable to Travel Publishing Ltd

Or:

Card No: [ ] Expiry Date: [ ]

Signature: [ ]

Name: [ ]

Address: [ ]

Tel no: [ ]

Please either send, telephone, fax or e-mail your order to:

Travel Publishing Ltd, 7a Apollo House, Calleva Park, Aldermaston, Berkshire RG7 8TN

Tel: 0118 981 7777 Fax: 0118 982 0077 e-mail: karen@travelpublishing.co.uk

	Price	Quantity
Hidden Places Regional Titles		
Cambs & Lincolnshire	£8.99	....
Chilterns	£8.99	....
Cornwall	£8.99	....
Derbyshire	£8.99	....
Devon	£8.99	....
Dorset, Hants & Isle of Wight	£8.99	....
East Anglia	£8.99	....
Gloucs, Wiltshire & Somerset	£8.99	....
Heart of England	£8.99	....
Hereford, Worcs & Shropshire	£8.99	....
Highlands & Islands	£8.99	....
Lake District & Cumbria	£8.99	....
Lancashire & Cheshire	£8.99	....
Lincolnshire & Notts	£8.99	....
Northumberland & Durham	£8.99	....
Sussex	£8.99	....
Yorkshire	£8.99	....
Hidden Places National Titles		
England	£11.99	....
Ireland	£11.99	....
Scotland	£11.99	....
Wales	£11.99	....

	Price	Quantity
Hidden Inns Titles		
East Anglia	£7.99	....
Heart of England	£7.99	....
Lancashire & Cheshire	£7.99	....
North of England	£7.99	....
South	£7.99	....
South East	£7.99	....
South and Central Scotland	£7.99	....
Wales	£7.99	....
Welsh Borders	£7.99	....
West Country	£7.99	....
Yorkshire	£7.99	....
Country Living Rural Guides		
East Anglia	£10.99	....
Heart of England	£10.99	....
Ireland	£11.99	....
North East	£10.99	....
North West	£10.99	....
Scotland	£11.99	....
South of England	£10.99	....
South East of England	£10.99	....
Wales	£11.99	....
West Country	£10.99	....

Total Quantity [ ]

Post & Packing [ ] Total Value [ ]

HIDDEN PLACES ORDER FORM

To order any of our publications just fill in the payment details below and complete the order form. For orders of less than 4 copies please add £1 per book for postage and packing. Orders over 4 copies are P & P free.

Please Complete Either:

I enclose a cheque for £ [ ] made payable to Travel Publishing Ltd

Or:

Card No: [ ] Expiry Date: [ ]

Signature: [ ]

Name: [ ]

Address: [ ]

Tel no: [ ]

Please either send, telephone, fax or e-mail your order to:

Travel Publishing Ltd, 7a Apollo House, Calleva Park, Aldermaston, Berkshire RG7 8TN
Tel: 0118 981 7777 Fax: 0118 982 0077 e-mail: karen@travelpublishing.co.uk

	Price	Quantity
Hidden Places Regional Titles		
Cambs & Lincolnshire	£8.99	....
Chilterns	£8.99	....
Cornwall	£8.99	....
Derbyshire	£8.99	....
Devon	£8.99	....
Dorset, Hants & Isle of Wight	£8.99	....
East Anglia	£8.99	....
Gloucs, Wiltshire & Somerset	£8.99	....
Heart of England	£8.99	....
Hereford, Worcs & Shropshire	£8.99	....
Highlands & Islands	£8.99	....
Lake District & Cumbria	£8.99	....
Lancashire & Cheshire	£8.99	....
Lincolnshire & Notts	£8.99	....
Northumberland & Durham	£8.99	....
Sussex	£8.99	....
Yorkshire	£8.99	....
Hidden Places National Titles		
England	£11.99	....
Ireland	£11.99	....
Scotland	£11.99	....
Wales	£11.99	....

	Price	Quantity
Hidden Inns Titles		
East Anglia	£7.99	....
Heart of England	£7.99	....
Lancashire & Cheshire	£7.99	....
North of England	£7.99	....
South	£7.99	....
South East	£7.99	....
South and Central Scotland	£7.99	....
Wales	£7.99	....
Welsh Borders	£7.99	....
West Country	£7.99	....
Yorkshire	£7.99	....
Country Living Rural Guides		
East Anglia	£10.99	....
Heart of England	£10.99	....
Ireland	£11.99	....
North East	£10.99	....
North West	£10.99	....
Scotland	£11.99	....
South of England	£10.99	....
South East of England	£10.99	....
Wales	£11.99	....
West Country	£10.99	....

Total Quantity [ ]

Post & Packing [ ] Total Value [ ]

HIDDEN PLACES ORDER FORM

To order any of our publications just fill in the payment details below and complete the order form. For orders of less than 4 copies please add £1 per book for postage and packing. Orders over 4 copies are P & P free.

Please Complete Either:

I enclose a cheque for £ [ ] made payable to Travel Publishing Ltd

Or:

Card No: [ ] Expiry Date: [ ]

Signature: [ ]

Name: [ ]

Address: [ ]

Tel no: [ ]

Please either send, telephone, fax or e-mail your order to:

Travel Publishing Ltd, 7a Apollo House, Calleva Park, Aldermaston, Berkshire RG7 8TN
Tel: 0118 981 7777 Fax: 0118 982 0077 e-mail: karen@travelpublishing.co.uk

	Price	Quantity
Hidden Places Regional Titles		
Cambs & Lincolnshire	£8.99	....
Chilterns	£8.99	....
Cornwall	£8.99	....
Derbyshire	£8.99	....
Devon	£8.99	....
Dorset, Hants & Isle of Wight	£8.99	....
East Anglia	£8.99	....
Gloucs, Wiltshire & Somerset	£8.99	....
Heart of England	£8.99	....
Hereford, Worcs & Shropshire	£8.99	....
Highlands & Islands	£8.99	....
Lake District & Cumbria	£8.99	....
Lancashire & Cheshire	£8.99	....
Lincolnshire & Notts	£8.99	....
Northumberland & Durham	£8.99	....
Sussex	£8.99	....
Yorkshire	£8.99	....
Hidden Places National Titles		
England	£11.99	....
Ireland	£11.99	....
Scotland	£11.99	....
Wales	£11.99	....

	Price	Quantity
Hidden Inns Titles		
East Anglia	£7.99	....
Heart of England	£7.99	....
Lancashire & Cheshire	£7.99	....
North of England	£7.99	....
South	£7.99	....
South East	£7.99	....
South and Central Scotland	£7.99	....
Wales	£7.99	....
Welsh Borders	£7.99	....
West Country	£7.99	....
Yorkshire	£7.99	....
Country Living Rural Guides		
East Anglia	£10.99	....
Heart of England	£10.99	....
Ireland	£11.99	....
North East	£10.99	....
North West	£10.99	....
Scotland	£11.99	....
South of England	£10.99	....
South East of England	£10.99	....
Wales	£11.99	....
West Country	£10.99	....

Total Quantity [ ]

Post & Packing [ ] Total Value [ ]

READER REACTION FORM

The *Travel Publishing* research team would like to receive reader's comments on any visitor attractions or places reviewed in the book and also recommendations for suitable entries to be included in the next edition. This will help ensure that the *Hidden Places series of Guides* continues to provide its readers with useful information on the more interesting, unusual or unique features of each attraction or place ensuring that their visit to the local area is an enjoyable and stimulating experience. To provide your comments or recommendations would you please complete the forms below and overleaf as indicated and send to:

The Research Department, Travel Publishing Ltd,
7a Apollo House, Calleva Park, Aldermaston, Reading, RG7 8TN.

Your Name:

Your Address:

Your Telephone Number:

Please tick as appropriate:

Comments ☐ Recommendation ☐

Name of Establishment:

Address:

Telephone Number:

Name of Contact:

READER REACTION FORM

Comment or Reason for Recommendation:

READER REACTION FORM

The *Travel Publishing* research team would like to receive reader's comments on any visitor attractions or places reviewed in the book and also recommendations for suitable entries to be included in the next edition. This will help ensure that the *Hidden Places series of Guides* continues to provide its readers with useful information on the more interesting, unusual or unique features of each attraction or place ensuring that their visit to the local area is an enjoyable and stimulating experience. To provide your comments or recommendations would you please complete the forms below and overleaf as indicated and send to:

The Research Department, Travel Publishing Ltd,
7a Apollo House, Calleva Park, Aldermaston, Reading, RG7 8TN.

Your Name:

Your Address:

Your Telephone Number:

Please tick as appropriate:

Comments ☐ Recommendation ☐

Name of Establishment:

Address:

Telephone Number:

Name of Contact:

READER REACTION FORM

Comment or Reason for Recommendation:

....

....

....

....

....

....

....

....

....

....

....

....

READER REACTION FORM

The *Travel Publishing* research team would like to receive reader's comments on any visitor attractions or places reviewed in the book and also recommendations for suitable entries to be included in the next edition. This will help ensure that the *Hidden Places series of Guides* continues to provide its readers with useful information on the more interesting, unusual or unique features of each attraction or place ensuring that their visit to the local area is an enjoyable and stimulating experience. To provide your comments or recommendations would you please complete the forms below and overleaf as indicated and send to:

The Research Department, Travel Publishing Ltd,
7a Apollo House, Calleva Park, Aldermaston, Reading, RG7 8TN.

Your Name:

Your Address:

Your Telephone Number:

Please tick as appropriate:

Comments ☐ Recommendation ☐

Name of Establishment:

Address:

Telephone Number:

Name of Contact:

READER REACTION FORM

Comment or Reason for Recommendation: